I0013559

# NCO User Guide

A catalogue record for this book is available from the Hong Kong Public Libraries.

Published in Hong Kong by Samurai Media Limited.

Email: info@samuraimedia.org

ISBN 978-988-8407-02-6



Background Cover Image by https://www.flickr.com/people/webtreatsetc/

# Table of Contents

# Foreword

NCO is the result of software needs that arose while I worked on projects funded by NCAR, NASA, and ARM. Thinking they might prove useful as tools or templates to others, it is my pleasure to provide them freely to the scientific community. Many users (most of whom I have never met) have encouraged the development of NCO. Thanks espcially to Jan Polcher, Keith Lindsay, Arlindo da Silva, John Sheldon, and William Weibel for stimulating suggestions and correspondence. Your encouragment motivated me to complete the *NCO User Guide*. So if you like NCO, send me a note! I should mention that NCO is not connected to or officially endorsed by Unidata, ACD, ASP, CGD, or Nike.

Charlie Zender
May 1997
Boulder, Colorado

Major feature improvements entitle me to write another Foreword. In the last five years a lot of work has been done to refine NCO. NCO is now an open source project and appears to be much healthier for it. The list of illustrious institutions that do not endorse NCO continues to grow, and now includes UCI.

Charlie Zender
October 2000
Irvine, California

The most remarkable advances in NCO capabilities in the last few years are due to contributions from the Open Source community. Especially noteworthy are the contributions of Henry Butowsky and Rorik Peterson.

Charlie Zender
January 2003
Irvine, California

NCO was generously supported from 2004–2008 by US National Science Foundation (NSF) grant IIS-0431203 (`http://www.nsf.gov/awardsearch/showAward.do?AwardNumber=0431203`). This support allowed me to maintain and extend core NCO code, and others to advance NCO in new directions: Gayathri Venkitachalam helped implement MPI; Harry Mangalam improved regression testing and benchmarking; Daniel Wang developed the server-side capability, SWAMP; and Henry Butowsky, a long-time contributor, developed `ncap2`. This support also led NCO to debut in professional journals and meetings. The personal and professional contacts made during this evolution have been immensely rewarding.

Charlie Zender
March 2008
Grenoble, France

The end of the NSF SEI grant in August, 2008 curtailed NCO development. Fortunately we could justify supporting Henry Butowsky on other research grants until May, 2010 while he developed the key `ncap2` features used in our climate research. And recently the NASA ACCESS program commenced funding us to support netCDF4 group functionality. Thus NCO will grow and evade bit-rot for the foreseeable future.

I continue to receive with gratitude the thanks of NCO users at nearly every scientific meeting I attend. People introduce themselves, shake my hand and extol NCO, often effusively, while I grin in stupid embarassment. These exchanges lighten me like anti-gravity. Sometimes I daydream how many hours NCO has turned from grunt work to productive research for researchers world-wide, or from research into early happy-hours. It's a cool feeling.

Charlie Zender
April, 2012
Irvine, California

The NASA ACCESS 2011 program generously supported (Cooperative Agreement NNX12AF48A) NCO from 2012–2015. This allowed us to produce the first iteration of a Group-oriented Data Analysis and Distribution (GODAD) software ecosystem. Shifting more geoscience data analysis to GODAD is a long-term plan. Then the NASA ACCESS 2013 program agreed to support (Cooperative Agreement NNX14AH55A) NCO from 2014–2016. This support permits us to implement support for Swath-like Data (SLD). Most recently, the DOE has funded me to implement NCO re-gridding and parallelization in support of their ACME program. After many years of crafting NCO as an after-hours hobby, I finally have the cushion necessary to give it some real attention. And I'm looking forward to this next, and most intense yet, phase of NCO development.

Charlie Zender
June, 2015
Irvine, California

# Summary

This manual describes NCO, which stands for netCDF Operators. NCO is a suite of programs known as *operators*. Each operator is a standalone, command line program executed at the shell-level like, e.g., `ls` or `mkdir`. The operators take netCDF files (including HDF5 files constructed using the netCDF API) as input, perform an operation (e.g., averaging or hyperslabbing), and produce a netCDF file as output. The operators are primarily designed to aid manipulation and analysis of data. The examples in this documentation are typical applications of the operators for processing climate model output. This stems from their origin, though the operators are as general as netCDF itself.

# 1 Introduction

## 1.1 Availability

The complete NCO source distribution is currently distributed as a *compressed tarfile* from `http://sf.net/projects/nco` and from `http://dust.ess.uci.edu/nco/nco.tar.gz`. The compressed tarfile must be uncompressed and untarred before building NCO. Uncompress the file with '`gunzip nco.tar.gz`'. Extract the source files from the resulting tarfile with '`tar -xvf nco.tar`'. GNU `tar` lets you perform both operations in one step with '`tar -xvzf nco.tar.gz`'.

The documentation for NCO is called the *NCO User Guide*. The *User Guide* is available in PDF, Postscript, HTML, DVI, TEXinfo, and Info formats. These formats are included in the source distribution in the files `nco.pdf`, `nco.ps`, `nco.html`, `nco.dvi`, `nco.texi`, and `nco.info*`, respectively. All the documentation descends from a single source file, `nco.texi`[1]. Hence the documentation in every format is very similar. However, some of the complex mathematical expressions needed to describe `ncwa` can only be displayed in DVI, Postscript, and PDF formats.

A complete list of papers and publications on/about NCO is available on the NCO homepage. Most of these are freely available. The primary refereed publications are ZeM06 and Zen08. These contain copyright restrictions which limit their redistribution, but they are freely available in preprint form from the NCO.

If you want to quickly see what the latest improvements in NCO are (without downloading the entire source distribution), visit the NCO homepage at `http://nco.sf.net`. The HTML version of the *User Guide* is also available online through the World Wide Web at URL `http://nco.sf.net/nco.html`. To build and use NCO, you must have netCDF installed. The netCDF homepage is `http://www.unidata.ucar.edu/software/netcdf`.

New NCO releases are announced on the netCDF list and on the `nco-announce` mailing list `http://lists.sf.net/mailman/listinfo/nco-announce`.

## 1.2 How to Use This Guide

Detailed instructions about how to download the newest version (`http://nco.sf.net/#Source`), and how to complie source code (`http://nco.sf.net/#bld`), as well as a FAQ (`http://nco.sf.net/#FAQ`) and descriptions of Known Problems (`http://nco.sf.net/#bug`) etc. are on our homepage (`http://nco.sf.net/`).

There are twelve operators in the current version (4.6.4-beta01). The function of each is explained in Chapter 4 [Reference Manual], page 137. Many of the tasks that NCO can accomplish are described during the explanation of common NCO Features (see Chapter 3 [Shared features], page 29). More specific use examples for each operator can be seen by visiting the operator-specific examples in the Chapter 4 [Reference Manual], page 137.

[1] To produce these formats, `nco.texi` was simply run through the freely available programs `texi2dvi`, `dvips`, `texi2html`, and `makeinfo`. Due to a bug in TEX, the resulting Postscript file, `nco.ps`, contains the Table of Contents as the final pages. Thus if you print `nco.ps`, remember to insert the Table of Contents after the cover sheet before you staple the manual.

These can be found directly by prepending the operator name with the xmp_ tag, e.g., http://nco.sf.net/nco.html#xmp_ncks. Also, users can type the operator name on the shell command line to see all the available options, or type, e.g., 'man ncks' to see a help man-page.

NCO is a command-line language. You may either use an operator after the prompt (e.g., '$' here), like,

```
$ operator [options] input [output]
```

or write all commands lines into a shell script, as in the CMIP5 Example (see Chapter 7 [CMIP5 Example], page 295).

If you are new to NCO, the Quick Start (see Chapter 6 [Quick Start], page 293) shows simple examples about how to use NCO on different kinds of data files. More detailed "real-world" examples are in the Chapter 7 [CMIP5 Example], page 295. The [General Index], page 333, is presents multiple keyword entries for the same subject. If these resources do not help enough, please see Section 1.7 [Help Requests and Bug Reports], page 15.

## 1.3 Operating systems compatible with NCO

In its time on Earth, NCO has been successfully ported and tested on so many 32- and 64-bit platforms that if we did not write them down here we would forget their names: IBM AIX 4.x, 5.x, FreeBSD 4.x, GNU/Linux 2.x, LinuxPPC, LinuxAlpha, LinuxARM, LinuxSparc64, LinuxAMD64, SGI IRIX 5.x and 6.x, MacOS X 10.x, DEC OSF, NEC Super-UX 10.x, Sun SunOS 4.1.x, Solaris 2.x, Cray UNICOS 8.x–10.x, and Microsoft Windows (95, 98, NT, 2000, XP, Vista, 7, 8, 10). If you port the code to a new operating system, please send me a note and any patches you required.

The major prerequisite for installing NCO on a particular platform is the successful, prior installation of the netCDF library (and, as of 2003, the UDUnits library). Unidata has shown a commitment to maintaining netCDF and UDUnits on all popular UNIX platforms, and is moving towards full support for the Microsoft Windows operating system (OS). Given this, the only difficulty in implementing NCO on a particular platform is standardization of various C-language API system calls. NCO code is tested for ANSI compliance by compiling with C99 compilers including those from GNU ('gcc -std=c99 -pedantic -D_BSD_SOURCE -D_POSIX_SOURCE' -Wall)[2], Comeau Computing ('como --c99'), Cray ('cc'), HP/Compaq/DEC ('cc'), IBM ('xlc -c -qlanglvl=extc99'), Intel ('icc -std=c99'), LLVM ('clang'), NEC ('cc'), PathScale (QLogic) ('pathcc -std=c99'), PGI ('pgcc -c9x'), SGI ('cc -c99'), and Sun ('cc'). NCO (all commands and the libnco library) and the C++ interface to netCDF (called libnco_c++) comply with the ISO C++ standards as implemented by Comeau Computing ('como'), Cray ('CC'), GNU ('g++ -Wall'), HP/Compaq/DEC ('cxx'), IBM ('xlC'), Intel ('icc'), Microsoft ('MVS'), NEC ('c++'), PathScale (Qlogic) ('pathCC'), PGI ('pgCC'), SGI ('CC -LANG:std'), and Sun ('CC -LANG:std'). See nco/bld/Makefile and nco/src/nco_c++/Makefile.old for more details and exact settings.

---

[2] The '_BSD_SOURCE' token is required on some Linux platforms where gcc dislikes the network header files like netinet/in.h).

Until recently (and not even yet), ANSI-compliant has meant compliance with the 1989 ISO C-standard, usually called C89 (with minor revisions made in 1994 and 1995). C89 lacks variable-size arrays, restricted pointers, some useful `printf` formats, and many mathematical special functions. These are valuable features of C99, the 1999 ISO C-standard. NCO is C99-compliant where possible and C89-compliant where necessary. Certain branches in the code are required to satisfy the native SGI and SunOS C compilers, which are strictly ANSI C89 compliant, and cannot benefit from C99 features. However, C99 features are fully supported by modern AIX, GNU, Intel, NEC, Solaris, and UNICOS compilers. NCO requires a C99-compliant compiler as of NCO version 2.9.8, released in August, 2004.

The most time-intensive portion of NCO execution is spent in arithmetic operations, e.g., multiplication, averaging, subtraction. These operations were performed in Fortran by default until August, 1999. This was a design decision based on the relative speed of Fortran-based object code vs. C-based object code in late 1994. C compiler vectorization capabilities have dramatically improved since 1994. We have accordingly replaced all Fortran subroutines with C functions. This greatly simplifies the task of building NCO on nominally unsupported platforms. As of August 1999, NCO built entirely in C by default. This allowed NCO to compile on any machine with an ANSI C compiler. In August 2004, the first C99 feature, the `restrict` type qualifier, entered NCO in version 2.9.8. C compilers can obtain better performance with C99 restricted pointers since they inform the compiler when it may make Fortran-like assumptions regarding pointer contents alteration. Subsequently, NCO requires a C99 compiler to build correctly[3].

In January 2009, NCO version 3.9.6 was the first to link to the GNU Scientific Library (GSL). GSL must be version 1.4 or later. NCO, in particular `ncap2`, uses the GSL special function library to evaluate geoscience-relevant mathematics such as Bessel functions, Legendre polynomials, and incomplete gamma functions (see Section 4.1.22 [GSL special functions], page 178).

In June 2005, NCO version 3.0.1 began to take advantage of C99 mathematical special functions. These include the standarized gamma function (called `tgamma()` for "true gamma"). NCO automagically takes advantage of some GNU Compiler Collection (GCC) extensions to ANSI C.

As of July 2000 and NCO version 1.2, NCO no longer performs arithmetic operations in Fortran. We decided to sacrifice executable speed for code maintainability. Since no objective statistics were ever performed to quantify the difference in speed between the Fortran and C code, the performance penalty incurred by this decision is unknown. Supporting Fortran involves maintaining two sets of routines for every arithmetic operation. The `USE_FORTRAN_ARITHMETIC` flag is still retained in the `Makefile`. The file containing the Fortran code, `nco_fortran.F`, has been deprecated but a volunteer (Dr. Frankenstein?) could resurrect it. If you would like to volunteer to maintain `nco_fortran.F` please contact me.

---

[3] NCO may still build with an ANSI or ISO C89 or C94/95-compliant compiler if the C pre-processor undefines the `restrict` type qualifier, e.g., by invoking the compiler with '`-Drestrict=''`'.

### 1.3.1 Compiling NCO for Microsoft Windows OS

NCO has been successfully ported and tested on most Microsoft Windows operating systems including: XP SP2/Vista/7. Support is provided for compiling either native Windows executables, using the Microsoft Visual Studio 2010 Compiler, or with Cygwin, the UNIX-emulating compatibility layer with the GNU toolchain. The switches necessary to accomplish both are included in the standard distribution of NCO.

Using Microsoft Visual Studio (MVS), one must build NCO with the C++ compiler since MVS does not support C99. Qt, a convenient integrated development environment, was used to convert the project files to MVS format. The Qt files themselves are distributed in the `nco/qt` directory.

Using the freely available Cygwin (formerly gnu-win32) development environment[4], the compilation process is very similar to installing NCO on a UNIX system. Set the `PVM_ARCH` preprocessor token to `WIN32`. Note that defining `WIN32` has the side effect of disabling Internet features of NCO (see below). NCO should now build like it does on UNIX.

The least portable section of the code is the use of standard UNIX and Internet protocols (e.g., `ftp`, `rcp`, `scp`, `sftp`, `getuid`, `gethostname`, and header files `<arpa/nameser.h>` and `<resolv.h>`). Fortunately, these UNIX-y calls are only invoked by the single NCO subroutine which is responsible for retrieving files stored on remote systems (see Section 3.7 [Remote storage], page 36). In order to support NCO on the Microsoft Windows platforms, this single feature was disabled (on Windows OS only). This was required by Cygwin 18.x—newer versions of Cygwin may support these protocols (let me know if this is the case). The NCO operators should behave identically on Windows and UNIX platforms in all other respects.

## 1.4 Symbolic Links

NCO relies on a common set of underlying algorithms. To minimize duplication of source code, multiple operators sometimes share the same underlying source. This is accomplished by symbolic links from a single underlying executable program to one or more invoked executable names. For example, `nces` and `ncrcat` are symbolically linked to the `ncra` executable. The `ncra` executable behaves slightly differently based on its invocation name (i.e., '`argv[0]`'), which can be `nces`, `ncra`, or `ncrcat`. Logically, these are three different operators that happen to share the same executable.

For historical reasons, and to be more user friendly, multiple synonyms (or pseudonyms) may refer to the same operator invoked with different switches. For example, `ncdiff` is the same as `ncbo` and `ncpack` is the same as `ncpdq`. We implement the symbolic links and synonyms by the executing the following UNIX commands in the directory where the NCO executables are installed.

```
ln -s -f ncbo ncdiff    # ncbo --op_typ='-'
ln -s -f ncra nces      # ncra --pseudonym='nces'
```

[4] The Cygwin package is available from
`http://sourceware.redhat.com/cygwin`
Currently, Cygwin 20.x comes with the GNU C/C++ compilers (`gcc`, `g++`. These GNU compilers may be used to build the netCDF distribution itself.

```
ln -s -f ncra ncrcat    # ncra --pseudonym='ncrcat'
ln -s -f ncbo ncadd     # ncbo --op_typ='+'
ln -s -f ncbo ncsubtract # ncbo --op_typ='-'
ln -s -f ncbo ncmultiply # ncbo --op_typ='*'
ln -s -f ncbo ncdivide   # ncbo --op_typ='/'
ln -s -f ncpdq ncpack    # ncpdq
ln -s -f ncpdq ncunpack  # ncpdq --unpack
# NB: Windows/Cygwin executable/link names have '.exe' suffix, e.g.,
ln -s -f ncbo.exe ncdiff.exe
...
```

The imputed command called by the link is given after the comment. As can be seen, some these links impute the passing of a command line argument to further modify the behavior of the underlying executable. For example, `ncdivide` is a pseudonym for `ncbo --op_typ='/'`.

## 1.5 Libraries

Like all executables, the NCO operators can be built using dynamic linking. This reduces the size of the executable and can result in significant performance enhancements on multiuser systems. Unfortunately, if your library search path (usually the `LD_LIBRARY_PATH` environment variable) is not set correctly, or if the system libraries have been moved, renamed, or deleted since NCO was installed, it is possible NCO operators will fail with a message that they cannot find a dynamically loaded (aka *shared object* or '`.so`') library. This will produce a distinctive error message, such as '`ld.so.1: /usr/local/bin/nces: fatal: libsunmath.so.1: can't open file: errno=2`'. If you received an error message like this, ask your system administrator to diagnose whether the library is truly missing[5], or whether you simply need to alter your library search path. As a final remedy, you may re-compile and install NCO with all operators statically linked.

## 1.6 netCDF2/3/4 and HDF4/5 Support

netCDF version 2 was released in 1993. NCO (specifically `ncks`) began soon after this in 1994. netCDF 3.0 was released in 1996, and we were not exactly eager to convert all code to the newer, less tested netCDF implementation. One netCDF3 interface call (`nc_inq_libvers`) was added to NCO in January, 1998, to aid in maintainance and debugging. In March, 2001, the final NCO conversion to netCDF3 was completed (coincidentally on the same day netCDF 3.5 was released). NCO versions 2.0 and higher are built with the `-DNO_NETCDF_2` flag to ensure no netCDF2 interface calls are used.

However, the ability to compile NCO with only netCDF2 calls is worth maintaining because HDF version 4, aka HDF4 or simply HDF,[6] (available from HDF (`http://hdfgroup.org`)) supports only the netCDF2 library calls (see `http://hdfgroup.org/UG41r3_html/SDS_SD.fm12.html#47784`). There are two versions of HDF. Currently HDF version 4.x

[5] The `ldd` command, if it is available on your system, will tell you where the executable is looking for each dynamically loaded library. Use, e.g., `ldd `which nces``.

[6] The Hierarchical Data Format, or HDF, is another self-describing data format similar to, but more elaborate than, netCDF. HDF comes in two flavors, HDF4 and HDF5. Often people use the shorthand HDF to refer to the older format HDF4. People almost always use HDF5 to refer to HDF5.

supports the full netCDF2 API and thus NCO version 1.2.x. If NCO version 1.2.x (or earlier) is built with only netCDF2 calls then all NCO operators should work with HDF4 files as well as netCDF files[7]. The preprocessor token `NETCDF2_ONLY` exists in NCO version 1.2.x to eliminate all netCDF3 calls. Only versions of NCO numbered 1.2.x and earlier have this capability.

HDF version 5 became available in 1999, but did not support netCDF (or, for that matter, Fortran) as of December 1999. By early 2001, HDF5 did support Fortran90. Thanks to an NSF-funded "harmonization" partnership, HDF began to fully support the netCDF3 read interface (which is employed by NCO 2.x and later). In 2004, Unidata and THG began a project to implement the HDF5 features necessary to support the netCDF API. NCO version 3.0.3 added support for reading/writing netCDF4-formatted HDF5 files in October, 2005. See Section 3.9 [File Formats and Conversion], page 41, for more details.

HDF support for netCDF was completed with HDF5 version version 1.8 in 2007. The netCDF front-end that uses this HDF5 back-end was completed and released soon after as netCDF version 4. Download it from the netCDF4 (`http://my.unidata.ucar.edu/content/software/netcdf/netcdf-4`) website.

NCO version 3.9.0, released in May, 2007, added support for all netCDF4 atomic data types except `NC_STRING`. Support for `NC_STRING`, including ragged arrays of strings, was finally added in version 3.9.9, released in June, 2009. Support for additional netCDF4 features has been incremental. We add one netCDF4 feature at a time. You must build NCO with netCDF4 to obtain this support.

NCO supports many netCDF4 features including atomic data types, Lempel-Ziv compression (deflation), chunking, and groups. The new atomic data types are `NC_UBYTE`, `NC_USHORT`, `NC_UINT`, `NC_INT64`, and `NC_UINT64`. Eight-byte integer support is an especially useful improvement from netCDF3. All NCO operators support these types, e.g., `ncks` copies and prints them, `ncra` averages them, and `ncap2` processes algebraic scripts with them. `ncks` prints compression information, if any, to screen.

NCO version 3.9.1 (June, 2007) added support for netCDF4 Lempel-Ziv deflation. Lempel-Ziv deflation is a lossless compression technique. See Section 3.30 [Deflation], page 107, for more details.

NCO version 3.9.9 (June, 2009) added support for netCDF4 chunking in `ncks` and `ncecat`. NCO version 4.0.4 (September, 2010) completed support for netCDF4 chunking in the remaining operators. See Section 3.28 [Chunking], page 91, for more details.

NCO version 4.2.2 (October, 2012) added support for netCDF4 groups in `ncks` and `ncecat`. Group support for these operators was complete (e.g., regular expressions to select groups and Group Path Editing) as of NCO version 4.2.6 (March, 2013). See Section 3.13 [Group Path Editing], page 52, for more details. Group support for all other operators was finished in the NCO version 4.3.x series completed in December, 2013.

---

[7] One must link the NCO code to the HDF4 MFHDF library instead of the usual netCDF library. Apparently '`MF`' stands for Multi-file not for Mike Folk. In any case, until about 2007 the MFHDF library only supported netCDF2 calls. Most people will never again install NCO 1.2.x and so will never use NCO to write HDF4 files. It is simply too much trouble.

Support for netCDF4 in the first arithmetic operator, `ncbo`, was introduced in NCO version 4.3.0 (March, 2013). NCO version 4.3.1 (May, 2013) completed this support and introduced the first example of automatic group broadcasting. See Section 4.3 [ncbo netCDF Binary Operator], page 207, for more details.

netCDF4-enabled NCO handles netCDF3 files without change. In addition, it automagically handles netCDF4 (HDF5) files: If you feed NCO netCDF3 files, it produces netCDF3 output. If you feed NCO netCDF4 files, it produces netCDF4 output. Use the handy-dandy '`-4`' switch to request netCDF4 output from netCDF3 input, i.e., to convert netCDF3 to netCDF4. See Section 3.9 [File Formats and Conversion], page 41, for more details.

When linked to a netCDF library that was built with HDF4 support[8], NCO automatically supports reading HDF4 files and writing them as netCDF3/netCDF4/HDF5 files. NCO can only write through the netCDF API, which can only write netCDF3/netCDF4/HDF5 files. So NCO can *read* HDF4 files, perform manipulations and calculations, and then it must *write* the results in netCDF format.

NCO support for HDF4 has been quite functional since December, 2013. For best results install NCO versions 4.4.0 or later on top of netCDF versions 4.3.1 or later. Getting to this point has been an iterative effort where Unidata improved netCDF library capabilities in response to our requests. NCO versions 4.3.6 and earlier do not explicitly support HDF4, yet should work with HDF4 if compiled with a version of netCDF (4.3.2 or later?) that does not unexpectedly die when probing HDF4 files with standard netCDF calls. NCO versions 4.3.7–4.3.9 (October–December, 2013) use a special flag to workaround netCDF HDF4 issues. The user must tell these versions of NCO that an input file is HDF4 format by using the '`--hdf4`' switch.

When compiled with netCDF version 4.3.1 (20140116) or later, NCO versions 4.4.0 (January, 2014) and later more gracefully handle HDF4 files. In particular, the '`--hdf4`' switch is obsolete. Current versions of NCO use netCDF to determine automatically whether the underlying file is HDF4, and then take appropriate precautions to avoid netCDF4 API calls that fail when applied to HDF4 files (e.g., `nc_inq_var_chunking()`, `nc_inq_var_deflate()`). When compiled with netCDF version 4.3.2 (20140423) or earlier, NCO will report that chunking and deflation properties of HDF4 files as `HDF4_UNKNOWN`, because determining those properties was impossible. When compiled with netCDF version 4.3.3-rc2 (20140925) or later, NCO versions 4.4.6 (October, 2014) and later fully support chunking and deflation features of HDF4 files. The '`--hdf4`' switch is supported (for backwards compatibility) yet redundant (i.e., does no harm) with current versions of NCO and netCDF.

Converting HDF4 files to netCDF: Since NCO reads HDF4 files natively, it is now easy to convert HDF4 files to netCDF files directly, e.g.,

```
ncks        fl.hdf fl.nc # Convert HDF4->netCDF4 (NCO 4.4.0+, netCDF 4.3.1+)
ncks --hdf4 fl.hdf fl.nc # Convert HDF4->netCDF4 (NCO 4.3.7-4.3.9)
```

The most efficient and accurate way to convert HDF4 data to netCDF format is to convert to netCDF4 using NCO as above. Many HDF4 producers (NASA!) love to use netCDF4 types, e.g., unsigned bytes, so this procedure is the most typical. Conversion of

[8] The procedure for doing this is documented at `http://www.unidata.ucar.edu/software/netcdf/docs/build_hdf4.html`.

HDF4 to netCDF4 as above suffices when the data will only be processed by NCO and other netCDF4-aware tools.

However, many tools are not fully netCDF4-aware, and so conversion to netCDF3 may be desirable. Obtaining any netCDF file from an HDF4 is easy:

```
ncks -3 fl.hdf fl.nc       # HDF4->netCDF3 (NCO 4.4.0+, netCDF 4.3.1+)
ncks -4 fl.hdf fl.nc       # HDF4->netCDF4 (NCO 4.4.0+, netCDF 4.3.1+)
ncks -6 fl.hdf fl.nc       # HDF4->netCDF3 64-bit  (NCO 4.4.0+, ...)
ncks -7 -L 1 fl.hdf fl.nc # HDF4->netCDF4 classic (NCO 4.4.0+, ...)
ncks --hdf4 -3 fl.hdf fl.nc # HDF4->netCDF3 (netCDF 4.3.0-)
ncks --hdf4 -4 fl.hdf fl.nc # HDF4->netCDF4 (netCDF 4.3.0-)
ncks --hdf4 -6 fl.hdf fl.nc # HDF4->netCDF3 64-bit  (netCDF 4.3.0-)
ncks --hdf4 -7 fl.hdf fl.nc # HDF4->netCDF4 classic (netCDF 4.3.0-)
```

As of NCO version 4.4.0 (January, 2014), these commands work even when the HDF4 file contains netCDF4 atomic types (e.g., unsigned bytes, 64-bit integers) because NCO can autoconvert everything to atomic types supported by netCDF3[9].

As of NCO version 4.4.4 (May, 2014) both `ncl_convert2nc` and NCO have built-in, automatic workarounds to handle element names that contain characters that are legal in HDF though are illegal in netCDF. For example, slashes and leading special characters are are legal in HDF and illegal in netCDF element (i.e., group, variable, dimension, and attribute) names. NCO converts these forbidden characters to underscores, and retains the original names of variables in automatically produced attributes named `hdf_name`[10].

Finally, in February 2014, we learned that the HDF group has a project called H4CF (described here (`http://hdfeos.org/software/h4cflib.php`)) whose goal is to make HDF4 files accessible to CF tools and conventions. Their project includes a tool named `h4tonccf` that converts HDF4 files to netCDF3 or netCDF4 files. We are not yet sure what advantages or features `h4tonccf` has that are not in NCO, though we suspect both methods have their own advantages. Corrections welcome.

As of 2012, netCDF4 is relatively stable software. Problems with netCDF4 and HDF libraries have mainly been fixed. Binary NCO distributions shipped as RPMs and as debs have used the netCDF4 library since 2010 and 2011, respectively.

---

[9] Prior to NCO version 4.4.0 (January, 2014), we recommended the `ncl_convert2nc` tool to convert HDF to netCDF3 when both these are true: 1. You must have netCDF3 and 2. the HDF file contains netCDF4 atomic types. More recent versions of NCO handle this problem fine, and include other advantages so we no longer recommend `ncl_convert2nc` because `ncks` is faster and more space-efficient. Both automatically convert netCDF4 types to netCDF3 types, yet `ncl_convert2nc` cannot produce full netCDF4 files. In contrast, `ncks` will happily convert HDF straight to netCDF4 files with netCDF4 types. Hence `ncks` can and does preserve the variable types. Unsigned bytes stay unsigned bytes. 64-bit integers stay 64-bit integers. Strings stay strings. Hence, `ncks` conversions often result in smaller files than `ncl_convert2nc` conversions. Another tool useful for converting netCDF3 to netCDF4 files, and whose functionality is, we think, also matched or exceeded by `ncks`, is the Python script `nc3tonc4` by Jeff Whitaker.

[10] Two real-world examples: NCO translates the NASA CERES dimension `(FOV) Footprints` to `_FOV_Footprints`, and `Cloud & Aerosol, Cloud Only, Clear Sky w/Aerosol, and Clear Sky` (yes, the dimension name includes whitespace and special characters) to `Cloud & Aerosol, Cloud Only, Clear Sky w_Aerosol, and Clear Sky` `ncl_convert2nc` makes the element name netCDF-safe in a slightly different manner, and also stores the original name in the `hdf_name` attribute.

One must often build NCO from source to obtain netCDF4 support. Typically, one specifies the root of the netCDF4 installation directory. Do this with the `NETCDF4_ROOT` variable. Then use your preferred NCO build mechanism, e.g.,

```
export NETCDF4_ROOT=/usr/local/netcdf4 # Set netCDF4 location
cd ~/nco;./configure --enable-netcdf4  # Configure mechanism -or-
cd ~/nco/bld;./make NETCDF4=Y allinone # Old Makefile mechanism
```

We carefully track the netCDF4 releases, and keep the netCDF4 atomic type support and other features working. Our long term goal is to utilize more of the extensive new netCDF4 feature set. The next major netCDF4 feature we are likely to utilize is parallel I/O. We will enable this in the MPI netCDF operators.

## 1.7 Help Requests and Bug Reports

We generally receive three categories of mail from users: help requests, bug reports, and feature requests. Notes saying the equivalent of "Hey, NCO continues to work great and it saves me more time everyday than it took to write this note" are a distant fourth.

There is a different protocol for each type of request. The preferred etiquette for all communications is via NCO Project Forums. Do not contact project members via personal e-mail unless your request comes with money or you have damaging information about our personal lives. *Please use the Forums*—they preserve a record of the questions and answers so that others can learn from our exchange. Also, since NCO is government-funded, this record helps us provide program officers with information they need to evaluate our project.

Before posting to the NCO forums described below, you might first register (`https://sf.net/account/register.php`) your name and email address with SourceForge.net or else all of your postings will be attributed to *nobody*. Once registered you may choose to *monitor* any forum and to receive (or not) email when there are any postings including responses to your questions. We usually reply to the forum message, not to the original poster.

If you want us to include a new feature in NCO, check first to see if that feature is already on the TODO (`file:./TODO`) list. If it is, why not implement that feature yourself and send us the patch? If the feature is not yet on the list, then send a note to the NCO Discussion forum (`http://sf.net/p/nco/discussion/9829`).

Read the manual before reporting a bug or posting a help request. Sending questions whose answers are not in the manual is the best way to motivate us to write more documentation. We would also like to accentuate the contrapositive of this statement. If you think you have found a real bug *the most helpful thing you can do is simplify the problem to a manageable size and then report it.* The first thing to do is to make sure you are running the latest publicly released version of NCO.

Once you have read the manual, if you are still unable to get NCO to perform a documented function, submit a help request. Follow the same procedure as described below for reporting bugs (after all, it might be a bug). That is, describe what you are trying to do, and include the complete commands (run with '`-D 5`'), error messages, and version of NCO (with '`-r`'). Post your help request to the NCO Help forum (`http://sf.net/p/nco/discussion/9830`).

If you think you used the right command when NCO misbehaves, then you might have found a bug. Incorrect numerical answers are the highest priority. We usually fix those within one or two days. Core dumps and sementation violations receive lower priority. They are always fixed, eventually.

How do you simplify a problem that reveal a bug? Cut out extraneous variables, dimensions, and metadata from the offending files and re-run the command until it no longer breaks. Then back up one step and report the problem. Usually the file(s) will be very small, i.e., one variable with one or two small dimensions ought to suffice. Run the operator with '`-r`' and then run the command with '`-D 5`' to increase the verbosity of the debugging output. It is very important that your report contain the exact error messages and compile-time environment. Include a copy of your sample input file, or place one on a publicly accessible location, of the file(s). If you are sure it is a bug, post the full report to the NCO Project buglist (`http://sf.net/p/nco/bugs`). Otherwise post all the information to NCO Help forum (`http://sf.net/p/nco/discussion/9830`).

Build failures count as bugs. Our limited machine access means we cannot fix all build failures. The information we need to diagnose, and often fix, build failures are the three files output by GNU build tools, `nco.config.log.${GNU_TRP}.foo`, `nco.configure.${GNU_TRP}.foo`, and `nco.make.${GNU_TRP}.foo`. The file `configure.eg` shows how to produce these files. Here `${GNU_TRP}` is the "GNU architecture triplet", the *chip-vendor-OS* string returned by `config.guess`. Please send us your improvements to the examples supplied in `configure.eg`. The regressions archive at `http://dust.ess.uci.edu/nco/rgr` contains the build output from our standard test systems. You may find you can solve the build problem yourself by examining the differences between these files and your own.

# 2 Operator Strategies

## 2.1 Philosophy

The main design goal is command line operators which perform useful, scriptable operations on netCDF files. Many scientists work with models and observations which produce too much data to analyze in tabular format. Thus, it is often natural to reduce and massage this raw or primary level data into summary, or second level data, e.g., temporal or spatial averages. These second level data may become the inputs to graphical and statistical packages, and are often more suitable for archival and dissemination to the scientific community. NCO performs a suite of operations useful in manipulating data from the primary to the second level state. Higher level interpretive languages (e.g., IDL, Yorick, Matlab, NCL, Perl, Python), and lower level compiled languages (e.g., C, Fortran) can always perform any task performed by NCO, but often with more overhead. NCO, on the other hand, is limited to a much smaller set of arithmetic and metadata operations than these full blown languages.

Another goal has been to implement enough command line switches so that frequently used sequences of these operators can be executed from a shell script or batch file. Finally, NCO was written to consume the absolute minimum amount of system memory required to perform a given job. The arithmetic operators are extremely efficient; their exact memory usage is detailed in Section 2.9 [Memory Requirements], page 24.

## 2.2 Climate Model Paradigm

NCO was developed at NCAR to aid analysis and manipulation of datasets produced by General Circulation Models (GCMs). GCM datasets share many features with other gridded scientific datasets and so provide a useful paradigm for the explication of the NCO operator set. Examples in this manual use a GCM paradigm because latitude, longitude, time, temperature and other fields related to our natural environment are as easy to visualize for the layman as the expert.

## 2.3 Temporary Output Files

NCO operators are designed to be reasonably fault tolerant, so that a system failure or user-abort of the operation (e.g., with `C-c`) does not cause loss of data. The user-specified *output-file* is only created upon successful completion of the operation[1]. This is accomplished by performing all operations in a temporary copy of *output-file*. The name of the temporary output file is constructed by appending `.pid<process ID>.<operator name>.tmp` to the user-specified *output-file* name. When the operator completes its task with no fatal errors, the temporary output file is moved to the user-specified *output-file*. This imbues the process with fault-tolerance since fatal error (e.g., disk space fills up) affect only the temporary output file, leaving the final output file not created if it did not already exist. Note the construction of a temporary output file uses more disk space than just overwriting existing files "in place" (because there may be two copies of the same file on disk until the NCO operation successfully concludes and the temporary output file overwrites the existing *output-file*).

---

[1] The `ncrename` and `ncatted` operators are exceptions to this rule. See Section 4.13 [ncrename netCDF Renamer], page 278.

Also, note this feature increases the execution time of the operator by approximately the time it takes to copy the *output-file*[2]. Finally, note this fault-tolerant feature allows the *output-file* to be the same as the *input-file* without any danger of "overlap".

Over time many "power users" have requested a way to turn-off the fault-tolerance safety feature of automatically creating a temporary file. Often these users build and execute production data analysis scripts that are repeated frequently on large datasets. Obviating an extra file write can then conserve significant disk space and time. For this purpose NCO has, since version 4.2.1 in August, 2012, made configurable the controls over temporary file creation. The '`--wrt_tmp_fl`' and equivalent '`--write_tmp_fl`' switches ensure NCO writes output to an intermediate temporary file. This is and has always been the default behavior so there is currently no need to specify these switches. However, the default may change some day, especially since writing to RAM disks (see Section 3.33 [RAM disks], page 110) may some day become the default. The '`--no_tmp_fl`' switch causes NCO to write directly to the final output file instead of to an intermediate temporary file. "Power users" may wish to invoke this switch to increase performance (i.e., reduce wallclock time) when manipulating large files. When eschewing temporary files, users may forsake the ability to have the same name for both *output-file* and *input-file* since, as described above, the temporary file prevented overlap issues. However, if the user creates the output file in RAM (see Section 3.33 [RAM disks], page 110) then it is still possible to have the same name for both *output-file* and *input-file*.

```
ncks in.nc out.nc # Default: create out.pid.tmp.nc then move to out.nc
ncks --wrt_tmp_fl in.nc out.nc # Same as default
ncks --no_tmp_fl in.nc out.nc # Create out.nc directly on disk
ncks --no_tmp_fl in.nc in.nc # ERROR-prone! Overwrite in.nc with itself
ncks --create_ram --no_tmp_fl in.nc in.nc # Create in RAM, write to disk
ncks --open_ram --no_tmp_fl in.nc in.nc # Read into RAM, write to disk
```

There is no reason to expect the fourth example to work. The behavior of overwriting a file while reading from the same file is undefined, much as is the shell command '`cat foo > foo`'. Although it may "work" in some cases, it is unreliable. One way around this is to use '`--create_ram`' so that the output file is not written to disk until the input file is closed, See Section 3.33 [RAM disks], page 110. However, as of 20130328, the behavior of the '`--create_ram`' and '`--open_ram`' examples has not been thoroughly tested.

The NCO authors have seen compelling use cases for utilizing the RAM switches, though not (yet) for combining them with '`--no_tmp_fl`'. NCO implements both options because they are largely independent of eachother. It is up to "power users" to discover which best fit their needs. We welcome accounts of your experiences posted to the forums.

Other safeguards exist to protect the user from inadvertently overwriting data. If the *output-file* specified for a command is a pre-existing file, then the operator will prompt the user whether to overwrite (erase) the existing *output-file*, attempt to append to it, or abort the operation. However, in processing large amounts of data, too many interactive questions slows productivity. Therefore NCO also implements two ways to override its own safety features, the '`-O`' and '`-A`' switches. Specifying '`-O`' tells the operator to overwrite any existing *output-file* without prompting the user interactively. Specifying '`-A`' tells the

[2] The OS-specific system move command is used. This is `mv` for UNIX, and `move` for Windows.

operator to attempt to append to any existing *output-file* without prompting the user interactively. These switches are useful in batch environments because they suppress interactive keyboard input.

## 2.4 Appending Variables

Adding variables from one file to another is often desirable. This is referred to as *appending*, although some prefer the terminology *merging*[3] or *pasting*. Appending is often confused with what NCO calls *concatenation*. In NCO, concatenation refers to splicing a variable along the record dimension. The length along the record dimension of the output is the sum of the lengths of the input files. Appending, on the other hand, refers to copying a variable from one file to another file which may or may not already contain the variable[4]. NCO can append or concatenate just one variable, or all the variables in a file at the same time.

In this sense, `ncks` can append variables from one file to another file. This capability is invoked by naming two files on the command line, *input-file* and *output-file*. When *output-file* already exists, the user is prompted whether to *overwrite*, *append/replace*, or *exit* from the command. Selecting *overwrite* tells the operator to erase the existing *output-file* and replace it with the results of the operation. Selecting *exit* causes the operator to exit—the *output-file* will not be touched in this case. Selecting *append/replace* causes the operator to attempt to place the results of the operation in the existing *output-file*, See Section 4.8 [ncks netCDF Kitchen Sink], page 237.

The simplest way to create the union of two files is

```
ncks -A fl_1.nc fl_2.nc
```

This puts the contents of `fl_1.nc` into `fl_2.nc`. The '`-A`' is optional. On output, `fl_2.nc` is the union of the input files, regardless of whether they share dimensions and variables, or are completely disjoint. The append fails if the input files have differently named record dimensions (since netCDF supports only one), or have dimensions of the same name but different sizes.

## 2.5 Simple Arithmetic and Interpolation

Users comfortable with NCO semantics may find it easier to perform some simple mathematical operations in NCO rather than higher level languages. `ncbo` (see Section 4.3 [ncbo netCDF Binary Operator], page 207) does file addition, subtraction, multiplication, division, and broadcasting. It even does group broadcasting. `ncflint` (see Section 4.7 [ncflint netCDF File Interpolator], page 234) does file addition, subtraction, multiplication and interpolation. Sequences of these commands can accomplish simple yet powerful operations from the command line.

---

[3] The terminology *merging* is reserved for an (unwritten) operator which replaces hyperslabs of a variable in one file with hyperslabs of the same variable from another file

[4] Yes, the terminology is confusing. By all means mail me if you think of a better nomenclature. Should NCO use *paste* instead of *append*?

## 2.6 Statistics vs. Concatenation

The most frequently used operators of NCO are probably the *statisticians* (i.e., tools that do statistics) and concatenators. Because there are so many types of statistics like averaging (e.g., across files, within a file, over the record dimension, over other dimensions, with or without weights and masks) and of concatenating (across files, along the record dimension, along other dimensions), there are currently no fewer than five operators which tackle these two purposes: `ncra`, `nces`, `ncwa`, `ncrcat`, and `ncecat`. These operators do share many capabilities[5], though each has its unique specialty. Two of these operators, `ncrcat` and `ncecat`, concatenate hyperslabs across files. The other two operators, `ncra` and `nces`, compute statistics across (and/or within) files[6]. First, let's describe the concatenators, then the statistics tools.

### 2.6.1 Concatenators `ncrcat` and `ncecat`

Joining together independent files along a common record dimension is called *concatenation*. `ncrcat` is designed for concatenating record variables, while `ncecat` is designed for concatenating fixed length variables. Consider five files, `85.nc`, `86.nc`, ... `89.nc` each containing a year's worth of data. Say you wish to create from them a single file, `8589.nc` containing all the data, i.e., spanning all five years. If the annual files make use of the same record variable, then `ncrcat` will do the job nicely with, e.g., `ncrcat 8?.nc 8589.nc`. The number of records in the input files is arbitrary and can vary from file to file. See Section 4.11 [ncrcat netCDF Record Concatenator], page 265, for a complete description of `ncrcat`.

However, suppose the annual files have no record variable, and thus their data are all fixed length. For example, the files may not be conceptually sequential, but rather members of the same group, or *ensemble*. Members of an ensemble may have no reason to contain a record dimension. `ncecat` will create a new record dimension (named *record* by default) with which to glue together the individual files into the single ensemble file. If `ncecat` is used on files which contain an existing record dimension, that record dimension is converted to a fixed-length dimension of the same name and a new record dimension (named `record`) is created. Consider five realizations, `85a.nc`, `85b.nc`, ... `85e.nc` of 1985 predictions from the same climate model. Then `ncecat 85?.nc 85_ens.nc` glues together the individual realizations into the single file, `85_ens.nc`. If an input variable was dimensioned [`lat`,`lon`], it will have dimensions [`record`,`lat`,`lon`] in the output file. A restriction of `ncecat` is that the hyperslabs of the processed variables must be the same from file to file. Normally this means all the input files are the same size, and contain data on different realizations of the same variables. See Section 4.5 [ncecat netCDF Ensemble Concatenator], page 228, for a complete description of `ncecat`.

`ncpdq` makes it possible to concatenate files along any dimension, not just the record dimension. First, use `ncpdq` to convert the dimension to be concatenated (i.e., extended

---

[5] Currently `nces` and `ncrcat` are symbolically linked to the `ncra` executable, which behaves slightly differently based on its invocation name (i.e., '`argv[0]`'). These three operators share the same source code, and merely have different inner loops.

[6] The third averaging operator, `ncwa`, is the most sophisticated averager in NCO. However, `ncwa` is in a different class than `ncra` and `nces` because it operates on a single file per invocation (as opposed to multiple files). On that single file, however, `ncwa` provides a richer set of averaging options—including weighting, masking, and broadcasting.

with data from other files) into the record dimension. Second, use `ncrcat` to concatenate these files. Finally, if desirable, use `ncpdq` to revert to the original dimensionality. As a concrete example, say that files `x_01.nc`, `x_02.nc`, ... `x_10.nc` contain time-evolving datasets from spatially adjacent regions. The time and spatial coordinates are `time` and `x`, respectively. Initially the record dimension is `time`. Our goal is to create a single file that contains joins all the spatially adjacent regions into one single time-evolving dataset.

```
for idx in 01 02 03 04 05 06 07 08 09 10; do # Bourne Shell
  ncpdq -a x,time x_${idx}.nc foo_${idx}.nc  # Make x record dimension
done
ncrcat foo_??.nc out.nc       # Concatenate along x
ncpdq -a time,x out.nc out.nc # Revert to time as record dimension
```

Note that `ncrcat` will not concatenate fixed-length variables, whereas `ncecat` concatenates both fixed-length and record variables along a new record variable. To conserve system memory, use `ncrcat` where possible.

### 2.6.2 Averagers `nces`, `ncra`, and `ncwa`

The differences between the averagers `ncra` and `nces` are analogous to the differences between the concatenators. `ncra` is designed for averaging record variables from at least one file, while `nces` is designed for averaging fixed length variables from multiple files. `ncra` performs a simple arithmetic average over the record dimension of all the input files, with each record having an equal weight in the average. `nces` performs a simple arithmetic average of all the input files, with each file having an equal weight in the average. Note that `ncra` cannot average fixed-length variables, but `nces` can average both fixed-length and record variables. To conserve system memory, use `ncra` rather than `nces` where possible (e.g., if each *input-file* is one record long). The file output from `nces` will have the same dimensions (meaning dimension names as well as sizes) as the input hyperslabs (see Section 4.6 [nces netCDF Ensemble Statistics], page 231, for a complete description of `nces`). The file output from `ncra` will have the same dimensions as the input hyperslabs except for the record dimension, which will have a size of 1 (see Section 4.10 [ncra netCDF Record Averager], page 262, for a complete description of `ncra`).

### 2.6.3 Interpolator `ncflint`

`ncflint` can interpolate data between or two files. Since no other operators have this ability, the description of interpolation is given fully on the `ncflint` reference page (see Section 4.7 [ncflint netCDF File Interpolator], page 234). Note that this capability also allows `ncflint` to linearly rescale any data in a netCDF file, e.g., to convert between differing units.

## 2.7 Large Numbers of Files

Occasionally one desires to digest (i.e., concatenate or average) hundreds or thousands of input files. Unfortunately, data archives (e.g., NASA EOSDIS) may not name netCDF files in a format understood by the '`-n` *loop*' switch (see Section 3.5 [Specifying Input Files], page 33) that automagically generates arbitrary numbers of input filenames. The '`-n` *loop*' switch has the virtue of being concise, and of minimizing the command line. This helps keeps output file small since the command line is stored as metadata in the `history` attribute (see Section 3.39 [History Attribute], page 129). However, the '`-n` *loop*' switch is useless when there is no simple, arithmetic pattern to the input filenames (e.g., h00001.nc, h00002.nc, ... h90210.nc). Moreover, filename globbing does not work when the input files are too numerous or their names are too lengthy (when strung together as a single argument) to be passed by the calling shell to the NCO operator[7]. When this occurs, the ANSI C-standard argc-argv method of passing arguments from the calling shell to a C-program (i.e., an NCO operator) breaks down. There are (at least) three alternative methods of specifying the input filenames to NCO in environment-limited situations.

The recommended method for sending very large numbers (hundreds or more, typically) of input filenames to the multi-file operators is to pass the filenames with the UNIX *standard input* feature, aka stdin:

```
# Pipe large numbers of filenames to stdin
/bin/ls | grep ${CASEID}_'......'.nc | ncecat -o foo.nc
```

This method avoids all constraints on command line size imposed by the operating system. A drawback to this method is that the history attribute (see Section 3.39 [History Attribute], page 129) does not record the name of any input files since the names were not passed on the command line. This makes determining the data provenance at a later date difficult. To remedy this situation, multi-file operators store the number of input files in the nco_input_file_number global attribute and the input file list itself in the nco_input_file_list global attribute (see Section 3.40 [File List Attributes], page 130). Although this does not preserve the exact command used to generate the file, it does retains all the information required to reconstruct the command and determine the data provenance.

A second option is to use the UNIX xargs command. This simple example selects as input to xargs all the filenames in the current directory that match a given pattern. For illustration, consider a user trying to average millions of files which each have a six character filename. If the shell buffer cannot hold the results of the corresponding globbing operator, ??????.nc, then the filename globbing technique will fail. Instead we express the filename pattern as an extended regular expression, ......\.nc (see Section 3.11 [Subsetting Files], page 46). We use grep to filter the directory listing for this pattern and to pipe the results to xargs which, in turn, passes the matching filenames to an NCO multi-file operator, e.g., ncecat.

```
# Use xargs to transfer filenames on the command line
/bin/ls | grep ${CASEID}_'......'.nc | xargs -x ncecat -o foo.nc
```

The single quotes protect the only sensitive parts of the extended regular expression (the grep argument), and allow shell interpolation (the ${CASEID} variable substitution) to proceed unhindered on the rest of the command. xargs uses the UNIX pipe feature to append the suitably filtered input file list to the end of the ncecat command options. The -o foo.nc switch ensures that the input files supplied by xargs are not confused with the output file name. xargs does, unfortunately, have its own limit (usually about 20,000 characters) on the size of command lines it can pass. Give xargs the '-x' switch to ensure it

[7] The exact length which exceeds the operating system internal limit for command line lengths varies from OS to OS and from shell to shell. GNU bash may not have any arbitrary fixed limits to the size of command line arguments. Many OSs cannot handle command line arguments (including results of file globbing) exceeding 4096 characters.

dies if it reaches this internal limit. When this occurs, use either the `stdin` method above, or the symbolic link presented next.

Even when its internal limits have not been reached, the `xargs` technique may not be sophisticated enough to handle all situations. A full scripting language like Perl can handle any level of complexity of filtering input filenames, and any number of filenames. The technique of last resort is to write a script that creates symbolic links between the irregular input filenames and a set of regular, arithmetic filenames that the '`-n loop`' switch understands. For example, the following Perl script creates a monotonically enumerated symbolic link to up to one million `.nc` files in a directory. If there are 999,999 netCDF files present, the links are named `000001.nc` to `999999.nc`:

```
# Create enumerated symbolic links
/bin/ls | grep \.nc | perl -e \
'$idx=1;while(<STDIN>){chop;symlink $_,sprintf("%06d.nc",$idx++);}'
ncecat -n 999999,6,1 000001.nc foo.nc
# Remove symbolic links when finished
/bin/rm ??????.nc
```

The '`-n loop`' option tells the NCO operator to automatically generate the filnames of the symbolic links. This circumvents any OS and shell limits on command line size. The symbolic links are easily removed once NCO is finished. One drawback to this method is that the `history` attribute (see Section 3.39 [History Attribute], page 129) retains the filename list of the symbolic links, rather than the data files themselves. This makes it difficult to determine the data provenance at a later date.

## 2.8 Large Datasets

*Large datasets* are those files that are comparable in size to the amount of random access memory (RAM) in your computer. Many users of NCO work with files larger than 100 MB. Files this large not only push the current edge of storage technology, they present special problems for programs which attempt to access the entire file at once, such as `nces` and `ncecat`. If you work with a 300 MB files on a machine with only 32 MB of memory then you will need large amounts of swap space (virtual memory on disk) and NCO will work slowly, or even fail. There is no easy solution for this. The best strategy is to work on a machine with sufficient amounts of memory and swap space. Since about 2004, many users have begun to produce or analyze files exceeding 2 GB in size. These users should familiarize themselves with NCO's Large File Support (LFS) capabilities (see Section 3.10 [Large File Support], page 46). The next section will increase your familiarity with NCO's memory requirements. With this knowledge you may re-design your data reduction approach to divide the problem into pieces solvable in memory-limited situations.

If your local machine has problems working with large files, try running NCO from a more powerful machine, such as a network server. If you get a memory-related core dump (e.g., '`Error exit (core dumped)`') on a GNU/Linux system, or the operation ends before the entire output file is written, try increasing the process-available memory with `ulimit`:

```
ulimit -f unlimited
```

This may solve constraints on clusters where sufficient hardware resources exist yet where system administrators felt it wise to prevent any individual user from consuming too much of resource. Certain machine architectures, e.g., Cray UNICOS, have special commands which allow one to increase the amount of interactive memory. On Cray systems, try to increase the available memory with the `ilimit` command.

The speed of the NCO operators also depends on file size. When processing large files the operators may appear to hang, or do nothing, for large periods of time. In order to see what the operator is actually doing, it is useful to activate a more verbose output mode. This is accomplished by supplying a number greater than 0 to the '`-D` *`debug-level`*' (or '`--debug-level`', or '`--dbg_lvl`') switch. When the *debug-level* is nonzero, the operators report their current status to the terminal through the *stderr* facility. Using '`-D`' does not slow the operators down. Choose a *debug-level* between 1 and 3 for most situations, e.g., `nces -D 2 85.nc 86.nc 8586.nc`. A full description of how to estimate the actual amount of memory the multi-file NCO operators consume is given in Section 2.9 [Memory Requirements], page 24.

## 2.9 Memory Requirements

Many people use NCO on gargantuan files which dwarf the memory available (free RAM plus swap space) even on today's powerful machines. These users want NCO to consume the least memory possible so that their scripts do not have to tediously cut files into smaller pieces that fit into memory. We commend these greedy users for pushing NCO to its limits!

This section describes the memory NCO requires during operation. The required memory is based on the underlying algorithms. The description below is the memory usage per thread. Users with shared memory machines may use the threaded NCO operators (see Section 3.3 [OpenMP Threading], page 29). The peak and sustained memory usage will scale accordingly, i.e., by the number of threads. Memory consumption patterns of all operators are similar, with the exception of `ncap2`.

### 2.9.1 Single and Multi-file Operators

The multi-file operators currently comprise the record operators, `ncra` and `ncrcat`, and the ensemble operators, `nces` and `ncecat`. The record operators require *much less* memory than the ensemble operators. This is because the record operators operate on one single record (i.e., time-slice) at a time, whereas the ensemble operators retrieve the entire variable into memory. Let $MS$ be the peak sustained memory demand of an operator, $FT$ be the memory required to store the entire contents of all the variables to be processed in an input file, $FR$ be the memory required to store the entire contents of a single record of each of the variables to be processed in an input file, $VR$ be the memory required to store a single record of the largest record variable to be processed in an input file, $VT$ be the memory required to store the largest variable to be processed in an input file, $VI$ be the memory required to store the largest variable which is not processed, but is copied from the initial file to the output file. All operators require $MI = VI$ during the initial copying of variables from the first input file to the output file. This is the *initial* (and transient) memory demand. The *sustained* memory demand is that memory required by the operators during the processing (i.e., averaging, concatenation) phase which lasts until all the input files have been processed. The operators have the following memory requirements: `ncrcat` requires $MS <= VR$. `ncecat` requires $MS <= VT$. `ncra` requires $MS = 2FR+VR$. `nces` requires $MS = 2FT+VT$. `ncbo` requires $MS <= 3VT$ (both input variables and the output variable). `ncflint` requires $MS <= 3VT$ (both input variables and the output variable). `ncpdq` requires $MS <= 2VT$ (one input variable and the output variable). `ncwa` requires $MS <= 8VT$ (see below). Note that only variables that are processed, e.g., averaged, concatenated, or differenced, contribute to $MS$. Variables that do not appear in the output file (see Section 3.11 [Subsetting Files], page 46) are never read and contribute nothing to the memory requirements.

Further note that some operators perform internal type-promotion on some variables prior to arithmetic (see Section 3.36 [Type Conversion], page 119). For example, `ncra`, `nces`, and `ncwa` all promote integer types to double-precision floating-point prior to arithmetic, then perform the arithmetic, then demote back to the original integer type after arithmetic. This preserves the on-disk storage type while obtaining the accuracy advantages of floating-point arithmetic. Since version 4.3.6 (released in September, 2013), NCO also by default converts single-precision floating-point to double-precision prior to arithmetic, which incurs the same RAM penalty. Hence, the sustained memory required for integer variables and single-precision floats are two or four-times their on-disk, uncompressed, unpacked sizes if they meet the rules for automatic internal promotion. Put another way, disabling auto-promotion of single-precision variables (with '`--flt`') considerably reduces the RAM footprint of arithmetic operators.

The '`--open_ram`' switch (and switches that invoke it like '`--ram_all`' and '`--diskless_all`') incurs a RAM penalty. These switches cause each input file to be copied to RAM upon opening. Hence any operator invoking these switches utilizes an additional $FT$ of RAM (i.e., $MS+ = FT$). See Section 3.33 [RAM disks], page 110, for further details.

`ncwa` consumes between two and eight times the memory of an `NC_DOUBLE` variable in order to process it. Peak consumption occurs when storing simultaneously in memory one input variable, one tally array, one input weight, one conformed/working weight, one weight tally, one input mask, one conformed/working mask, and one output variable. NCO's tally arrays are of type C-type `long`, whose size is 8-bytes on all modern computers, the same as `NC_DOUBLE`. When invoked, the weighting and masking features contribute up to three-eighths and two-eighths of these requirements apiece. If weights and masks are *not* specified (i.e., no '`-w`' or '`-a`' options) then `ncwa` requirements drop to $MS <= 3VT$ (one input variable, one tally array, and the output variable). The output variable is the same size as the input variable when averaging over a degenerate dimension. However, normally the output variable is much smaller than the input, and is often a simple scalar, in which case the memory requirements drop by $1VT$ since the output array requires essentially no memory.

All of this is subject to the type promotion rules mentioned above. For example, `ncwa` averaging a variable of type `NC_FLOAT` requires $MS <= 16VT$ (rather than $MS <= 8VT$) since all arrays are (at least temporarily) composed of eight-byte elements. Without mask or weights, the requirements for `NC_FLOAT` are $MS <= 6VT$ (rather than $MS <= 3VT$ as for `NC_DOUBLE`) due to temporary internal promotion of both the input variable and the output variable to type `NC_DOUBLE`. The '`--flt`' option that suppresses promotion reduces this to $MS <= 4VT$ (the tally elements do not change size), and to $MS <= 3VT$ when the output array is a scalar.

The above memory requirements must be multiplied by the number of threads *thr_nbr* (see Section 3.3 [OpenMP Threading], page 29). If this causes problems then reduce (with '`-t` *thr_nbr*') the number of threads.

### 2.9.2 Memory for `ncap2`

`ncap2` has unique memory requirements due its ability to process arbitrarily long scripts of any complexity. All scripts acceptable to `ncap2` are ultimately processed as a sequence of binary or unary operations. `ncap2` requires $MS <= 2VT$ under most conditions. An exception to this is when left hand casting (see Section 4.1.4 [Left hand casting], page 144) is used to stretch the size of derived variables beyond the size of any input variables. Let $VC$ be the memory required to store the largest variable defined by left hand casting. In this case, $MS <= 2VC$.

`ncap2` scripts are complete dynamic and may be of arbitrary length. A script that contains many thousands of operations, may uncover a slow memory leak even though each single operation consumes little additional memory. Memory leaks are usually identifiable by their memory usage signature. Leaks cause peak memory usage to increase monotonically with time regardless of script complexity. Slow leaks are very difficult to find. Sometimes a `malloc()` (or `new[]`) failure is the only noticeable clue to their existence. If you have good reasons to believe that a memory allocation failure is ultimately due to an NCO memory leak (rather than inadequate RAM on your system), then we would be very interested in receiving a detailed bug report.

## 2.10 Performance

An overview of NCO capabilities as of about 2006 is in Zender, C. S. (2008), "Analysis of Self-describing Gridded Geoscience Data with netCDF Operators (NCO)", Environ. Modell. Softw., doi:10.1016/j.envsoft.2008.03.004. This paper is also available at `http://dust.ess.uci.edu/ppr/ppr_Zen08.pdf`.

NCO performance and scaling for arithmetic operations is described in Zender, C. S., and H. J. Mangalam (2007), "Scaling Properties of Common Statistical Operators for Gridded Datasets", Int. J. High Perform. Comput. Appl., 21(4), 485-498, doi:10.1177/1094342007083802. This paper is also available at `http://dust.ess.uci.edu/ppr/ppr_ZeM07.pdf`.

It is helpful to be aware of the aspects of NCO design that can limit its performance:

1. No data buffering is performed during `nc_get_var` and `nc_put_var` operations. Hyperslabs too large to hold in core memory will suffer substantial performance penalties because of this.
2. Since coordinate variables are assumed to be monotonic, the search for bracketing the user-specified limits should employ a quicker algorithm, like bisection, than the two-sided incremental search currently implemented.
3. *C_format*, *FORTRAN_format*, *signedness*, *scale_format* and *add_offset* attributes are ignored by `ncks` when printing variables to screen.
4. In the late 1990s it was discovered that some random access operations on large files on certain architectures (e.g., UNICOS) were much slower with NCO than with similar operations performed using languages that bypass the netCDF interface (e.g., Yorick).

This may have been a penalty of unnecessary byte-swapping in the netCDF interface. It is unclear whether such problems exist in present day (2007) netCDF/NCO environments, where unnecessary byte-swapping has been reduced or eliminated.

# 3 Shared Features

Many features have been implemented in more than one operator and are described here for brevity. The description of each feature is preceded by a box listing the operators for which the feature is implemented. Command line switches for a given feature are consistent across all operators wherever possible. If no "key switches" are listed for a feature, then that particular feature is automatic and cannot be controlled by the user.

## 3.1 Internationalization

Availability: All operators

NCO support for *internationalization* of textual input and output (e.g., Warning messages) is nascent. We introduced the first foreign language string catalogues (French and Spanish) in 2004, yet did not activate these in distributions because the catalogues were nearly empty. We seek volunteers to populate our templates with translations for their favorite languages.

## 3.2 Metadata Optimization

Availability: All operators
Short options: None
Long options: '`--hdr_pad`', '`--header_pad`'

NCO supports padding headers to improve the speed of future metadata operations. Use the '`--hdr_pad`' and '`--header_pad`' switches to request that *hdr_pad* bytes be inserted into the metadata section of the output file. Future metadata expansions will not incur the netCDF3 performance penalty of copying the entire output file unless the expansion exceeds the amount of header padding exceeded. This can be beneficial when it is known that some metadata will be added at a future date. The operators which benefit most from judicious use of header padding are `ncatted` and `ncrename`, since they only alter metadata.

This optimization exploits the netCDF library `nc__enddef()` function, which behaves differently with different versions of netCDF. It will improve speed of future metadata expansion with `CLASSIC` and `64bit` netCDF files, though not necessarily with `NETCDF4` files, i.e., those created by the netCDF interface to the HDF5 library (see Section 3.9 [File Formats and Conversion], page 41).

## 3.3 OpenMP Threading

Availability: `ncap2`, `ncbo`, `nces`, `ncecat`, `ncflint`, `ncpdq`, `ncra`, `ncrcat`, `ncwa`
Short options: '`-t`'
Long options: '`--thr_nbr`', '`--threads`', '`--omp_num_threads`'

NCO supports shared memory parallelism (SMP) when compiled with an OpenMP-enabled compiler. Threads requests and allocations occur in two stages. First, users may request a specific number of threads *thr_nbr* with the '`-t`' switch (or its long option equivalents, '`--thr_nbr`', '`--threads`', and '`--omp_num_threads`'). If not user-specified, OpenMP obtains *thr_nbr* from the `OMP_NUM_THREADS` environment variable, if present, or from the OS, if not.

Caveat: Unfortunately, threading does not improve NCO throughput (i.e., wallclock time) because nearly all NCO operations are I/O-bound. This means that NCO spends negligible time doing anything compared to reading and writing. We have seen some and can imagine other use cases where `ncwa`, `ncpdq`, and `ncap2` (with long scripts) will complete faster due to threading. The main benefits of threading so far have been to isolate the serial from parallel portions of code. This parallelism is now exploited by OpenMP but then runs into the I/O bottleneck during output. The bottleneck will be ameliorated for large files by the use of MPI-enabled calls in the netCDF4 library when the underlying filesystem is parallel (e.g., PVFS or JFS). Implementation of the parallel output calls in NCO is not a goal of our current funding and would require new volunteers or funding.

NCO may modify *thr_nbr* according to its own internal settings before it requests any threads from the system. Certain operators contain hard-code limits to the number of threads they request. We base these limits on our experience and common sense, and to reduce potentially wasteful system usage by inexperienced users. For example, `ncrcat` is extremely I/O-intensive so we restrict *thr_nbr* <= 2 for `ncrcat`. This is based on the notion that the best performance that can be expected from an operator which does no arithmetic is to have one thread reading and one thread writing simultaneously. In the future (perhaps with netCDF4), we hope to demonstrate significant threading improvements with operators like `ncrcat` by performing multiple simultaneous writes.

Compute-intensive operators (`ncap2`, `ncwa` and `ncpdq`) benefit most from threading. The greatest increases in throughput due to threading occur on large datasets where each thread performs millions, at least, of floating-point operations. Otherwise, the system overhead of setting up threads probably outweighs the speed enhancements due to SMP parallelism. However, we have not yet demonstrated that the SMP parallelism scales beyond four threads for these operators. Hence we restrict *thr_nbr* <= 4 for all operators. We encourage users to play with these limits (edit file `nco_omp.c`) and send us their feedback.

Once the initial *thr_nbr* has been modified for any operator-specific limits, NCO requests the system to allocate a team of *thr_nbr* threads for the body of the code. The operating system then decides how many threads to allocate based on this request. Users may keep track of this information by running the operator with *dbg_lvl* > 0.

By default, threaded operators attach one global attribute, `nco_openmp_thread_number`, to any file they create or modify. This attribute contains the number of threads the operator used to process the input files. This information helps to verify that the answers with threaded and non-threaded operators are equal to within machine precision. This information is also useful for benchmarking.

## 3.4 Command Line Options

Availability: All operators

NCO achieves flexibility by using *command line options*. These options are implemented in all traditional UNIX commands as single letter *switches*, e.g., '`ls -l`'. For many years NCO used only single letter option names. In late 2002, we implemented GNU/POSIX extended or long option names for all options. This was done in a backward compatible way such that the full functionality of NCO is still available through the familiar single letter options. Many features of NCO introduced since 2002 now require the use of long options, simply because we have nearly run out of single letter options. More importantly, mnemonics for single letter options are often non-intuitive so that long options provide a more natural way of expressing intent.

Extended options, also called long options, are implemented using the system-supplied `getopt.h` header file, if possible. This provides the `getopt_long` function to NCO[1].

The syntax of *short options* (single letter options) is `-key value` (dash-key-space-value). Here, *key* is the single letter option name, e.g., '`-D 2`'.

The syntax of *long options* (multi-letter options) is `--long_name value` (dash-dash-key-space-value), e.g., '`--dbg_lvl 2`' or `--long_name=value` (dash-dash-key-equal-value), e.g., '`--dbg_lvl=2`'. Thus the following are all valid for the '`-D`' (short version) or '`--dbg_lvl`' (long version) command line option.

```
ncks -D 3 in.nc        # Short option, preferred form
ncks -D3 in.nc         # Short option, alternate form
ncks --dbg_lvl=3 in.nc # Long option, preferred form
ncks --dbg_lvl 3 in.nc # Long option, alternate form
```

The third example is preferred for two reasons. First, '`--dbg_lvl`' is more specific and less ambiguous than '`-D`'. The long option format makes scripts more self documenting and less error-prone. Often long options are named after the source code variable whose value they carry. Second, the equals sign `=` joins the key (i.e., *long_name*) to the value in an uninterruptible text block. Experience shows that users are less likely to mis-parse commands when restricted to this form.

### 3.4.1 Truncating Long Options

GNU implements a superset of the POSIX standard. Their superset accepts any unambiguous truncation of a valid option:

---

[1] If a `getopt_long` function cannot be found on the system, NCO will use the `getopt_long` from the `my_getopt` package by Benjamin Sittler `bsittler@iname.com`. This is BSD-licensed software available from `http://www.geocities.com/ResearchTriangle/Node/9405/#my_getopt`.

```
ncks -D 3 in.nc          # Short option
ncks --dbg_lvl=3 in.nc # Long option, full form
ncks --dbg=3 in.nc       # Long option, OK unambiguous truncation
ncks --db=3 in.nc        # Long option, OK unambiguous truncation
ncks --d=3 in.nc         # Long option, ERROR ambiguous truncation
```

The first four examples are equivalent and will work as expected. The final example will exit with an error since `ncks` cannot disambiguate whether '`--d`' is intended as a truncation of '`--dbg_lvl`', of '`--dimension`', or of some other long option.

NCO provides many long options for common switches. For example, the debugging level may be set in all operators with any of the switches '`-D`', '`--debug-level`', or '`--dbg_lvl`'. This flexibility allows users to choose their favorite mnemonic. For some, it will be '`--debug`' (an unambiguous truncation of '`--debug-level`', and other will prefer '`--dbg`'. Interactive users usually prefer the minimal amount of typing, i.e., '`-D`'. We recommend that re-usable scripts employ long options to facilitate self-documentation and maintainability.

This manual generally uses the short option syntax in examples. This is for historical reasons and to conserve space in printed output. Users are expected to pick the unambiguous truncation of each option name that most suits their taste.

### 3.4.2 Multi-arguments

As of NCO version 4.6.2 (November, 2016), NCO accepts multiple key-value pair options for a single feature to be joined together into a single extended argument called a *multi-argument*. Only four NCO features accept multiple key-value pairs that can be aggregated into multi-arguments. These features are: Global Attribute Addition options indicated via '`--gaa`' (see Section 3.38 [Global Attribute Addition], page 128); Image Manipulation indicated via '`--trr`'[2], Precision-Preserving Compression options indicated via '`--ppc`' (see Section 3.29.2 [Precision-Preserving Compression], page 98); and Regridding options are indicated via '`--rgr`' (see Section 3.23 [Regridding], page 78). Arguments to these four indicator options take the form of key-value pairs, e.g., '`--rgr` *key=val*'. These four features have so many options that making each key its own command line option would pollute the namespace of NCO's global options. Yet supplying multiple options to each indicator option one-at-a-time can result in command lines overpopulated with indicator switches (e.g., '`--rgr`'):

```
ncks --rgr grd_ttl='Title' --rgr grid=grd.nc --rgr latlon=129,256 \
     --rgr lat_typ=fv --rgr lon_typ=grn_ctr ...
```

Multi-arguments combine all the indicator options into one option that receives a single argument that comprises all the original arguments glued together by a delimiter, which is, by default, '`#`'. Thus the multi-argument version of the above example is

```
ncks --rgr grd_ttl='Title'#grid=grd.nc#latlon=129,256#lat_typ=fv#lon_typ=grn_ctr
```

Note the aggregation of all *key=val* pairs into a single argument. NCO simply splits this argument at each delimiter, and processes the sub-arguments as if they had been passed

---

2 NCO supports decoding ENVI images in support of the DOE Terraref project. These options are indicated via the `ncks` '`--trr`' switch, and are otherwise undocumented.

with their own indicator option. Multi-arguments produce the same results, and may be mixed with, traditional indicator options supplied one-by-one.

As mentioned previously, the multi-argument delimiter string is, by default, the hash-sign '#'. When any *key=val* pair contains the default delimiter, the user must specify a custom delimiter string so that options are parsed correctly. The options to change the multi-argument delimiter string are '--mta_dlm=*delim_string*' or '--dlm_mta=*delim_string*', where *delim_string* can be any single or multi-character string that (1) is not contained in any *key* or *val* string; and (2) will not confuse the shell. For example, to use multi-arguments to pass a string that includes the hash symbol (the default delimiter is '#'), one must also change the delimiter so something besides hash, e.g., a colon ':':

```
ncks --dlm=":" --gaa foo=bar:foo2=bar2:foo3,foo4="hash # is in value"
ncks --dlm=":" --gaa foo=bar:foo2=bar2:foo3,foo4="Thu Sep 15 13\:03\:18 PDT 2016"
ncks --dlm="csz" --gaa foo=barcszfoo2=bar2cszfoo3,foo4="Long text"
```

In the second example, the colons that are escaped with the backslash become literal characters. Many characters have special shell meanings and so must be escaped by a single or double backslash or enclosed in single quotes to prevent interpolation. These special characters include ':', '$', '%', '*', '@', and '&'. If *val* is a long text string that could contain the default delimiter, then delimit with a unique multi-character string such as 'csz' in the third example.

## 3.5 Specifying Input Files

Availability (-n): nces, ncecat, ncra, ncrcat
Availability (-p): All operators
Short options: '-n', '-p'
Long options: '--nintap', '--pth', '--path'

It is important that users be able to specify multiple input files without typing every filename in full, often a tedious task even by graduate student standards. There are four different ways of specifying input files to NCO: explicitly typing each, using UNIX shell wildcards, and using the NCO '-n' and '-p' switches (or their long option equivalents, '--nintap' or '--pth' and '--path', respectively). Techniques to augment these methods to specify arbitrary numbers (e.g., thousands) and patterns of filenames are discussed separately (see Section 2.7 [Large Numbers of Files], page 21).

To illustrate these methods, consider the simple problem of using ncra to average five input files, 85.nc, 86.nc, ... 89.nc, and store the results in 8589.nc. Here are the four methods in order. They produce identical answers.

```
ncra 85.nc 86.nc 87.nc 88.nc 89.nc 8589.nc
ncra 8[56789].nc 8589.nc
ncra 8?.nc 8589.nc
ncra -p input-path 85.nc 86.nc 87.nc 88.nc 89.nc 8589.nc
ncra -n 5,2,1 85.nc 8589.nc
```

The first method (explicitly specifying all filenames) works by brute force. The second method relies on the operating system shell to *glob* (expand) the *regular expression* `8[56789].nc`. The shell then passes the valid filenames (those which match the regular expansion) to `ncra`. In this case `ncra` never knows that a regular expression was used, because the shell intercepts and expands and matches the regular expression before `ncra` is actually invoked. The third method is uses globbing with a different regular expression that is less safe (it will also match unwanted files such as `81.nc` and `8Z.nc` if present). The fourth method uses the '`-p input-path`' argument to specify the directory where all the input files reside. NCO prepends *input-path* (e.g., `/data/username/model`) to all *input-files* (though not to *output-file*). Thus, using '`-p`', the path to any number of input files need only be specified once. Note *input-path* need not end with '`/`'; the '`/`' is automatically generated if necessary.

The last method passes (with '`-n`') syntax concisely describing the entire set of filenames[3]. This option is only available with the *multi-file operators*: `ncra`, `ncrcat`, `nces`, and `ncecat`. By definition, multi-file operators are able to process an arbitrary number of *input-files*. This option is very useful for abbreviating lists of filenames representable as *alphanumeric_prefix*+*numeric_suffix*+`.`+*filetype* where *alphanumeric_prefix* is a string of arbitrary length and composition, *numeric_suffix* is a fixed width field of digits, and *filetype* is a standard filetype indicator. For example, in the file `ccm3_h0001.nc`, we have *alphanumeric_prefix* = `ccm3_h`, *numeric_suffix* = `0001`, and *filetype* = `nc`.

NCO decodes lists of such filenames encoded using the '`-n`' syntax. The simpler (three-argument) '`-n`' usage takes the form `-n file_number,digit_number,numeric_increment` where *file_number* is the number of files, *digit_number* is the fixed number of numeric digits comprising the *numeric_suffix*, and *numeric_increment* is the constant, integer-valued difference between the *numeric_suffix* of any two consecutive files. The value of *alphanumeric_prefix* is taken from the input file, which serves as a template for decoding the filenames. In the example above, the encoding `-n 5,2,1` along with the input file name `85.nc` tells NCO to construct five (5) filenames identical to the template `85.nc` except that the final two (2) digits are a numeric suffix to be incremented by one (1) for each successive file. Currently *filetype* may be either be empty, `nc`, `h5`, `cdf`, `hdf`, `hd5`, or `he5`. If present, these *filetype* suffixes (and the preceding `.`) are ignored by NCO as it uses the '`-n`' arguments to locate, evaluate, and compute the *numeric_suffix* component of filenames.

Recently the '`-n`' option has been extended to allow convenient specification of filenames with "circular" characteristics. This means it is now possible for NCO to automatically generate filenames which increment regularly until a specified maximum value, and then wrap back to begin again at a specified minimum value. The corresponding '`-n`' usage becomes more complex, taking one or two additional arguments for a total of four or five, respectively: `-n file_number,digit_number,numeric_increment[,numeric_max[,numeric_min]]` where *numeric_max*, if present, is the maximum integer-value of *numeric_suffix* and *numeric_min*, if present, is the minimum integer-value of *numeric_suffix*. Consider, for example, the problem of specifying non-consecutive input files where the

[3] The '`-n`' option is a backward-compatible superset of the `NINTAP` option from the NCAR CCM Processor. The CCM Processor was custom-written Fortran code maintained for many years by Lawrence Buja at NCAR, and phased-out in the late 1990s. NCO stole some ideas, like `NINTAP`-functionality, from CCM Processor capabilities.

filename suffixes end with the month index. In climate modeling it is common to create summertime and wintertime averages which contain the averages of the months June–July–August, and December–January–February, respectively:

```
ncra -n 3,2,1 85_06.nc 85_0608.nc
ncra -n 3,2,1,12 85_12.nc 85_1202.nc
ncra -n 3,2,1,12,1 85_12.nc 85_1202.nc
```

The first example shows that three arguments to the '-n' option suffice to specify consecutive months (06, 07, 08) which do not "wrap" back to a minimum value. The second example shows how to use the optional fourth and fifth elements of the '-n' option to specify a wrap value. The fourth argument to '-n', when present, specifies the maximum integer value of *numeric_suffix*. In the example the maximum value is 12, and will be formatted as 12 in the filename string. The fifth argument to '-n', when present, specifies the minimum integer value of *numeric_suffix*. The default minimum filename suffix is 1, which is formatted as 01 in this case. Thus the second and third examples have the same effect, that is, they automatically generate, in order, the filenames 85_12.nc, 85_01.nc, and 85_02.nc as input to NCO.

As of NCO version 4.5.2 (September, 2015), NCO supports an optional sixth argument to '-n', the month-indicator. The month-indicator affirms to NCO that the right-most digits being manipulated in the generated filenames correspond to month numbers (with January formatted as 01 and December as 12). Moreover, it assumes digits to the left of the month are the year. The full (six-argument) '-n' usage takes the form -n *file_number,digit_number,month_increment,max_month,min_month,*'yyyymm'. The 'yyyymm' string is a clunky way (can you think of a clearer way?) to tell NCO to enumerate files in year-month mode. When present, 'yyyymm' string causes NCO to automatically generate series of filenames whose right-most two digits increment from *min_month* by *month_increment* up to *max_month* and then the leftmost digits (i.e., the year) increment by one, and the whole process is reapeated until the *file_number* filenames are generated.

```
ncrcat -n 3,6,1,12,1          198512.nc 198512_198502.nc
ncrcat -n 3,6,1,12,1,yyyymm   198512.nc 198512_198602.nc
ncrcat -n 3,6,1,12,12,yyyymm  198512.nc 198512_198712.nc
```

The first command concatenates three files (198512.nc, 198501.nc, 198502.nc) into the output file. The second command concatenates three files (198512.nc, 198601.nc, 198602.nc). The 'yyyymm'-indicator causes the left-most digits to increment each time the right-most two digits reach their maximum and then wrap. The first command does not have the indicator so it is always 1985. The third command concatenates three files (198512.nc, 198612.nc, 198712.nc).

## 3.6 Specifying Output Files

Availability: All operators
Short options: '-o'
Long options: '--fl_out', '--output'

NCO commands produce no more than one output file, *fl_out*. Traditionally, users specify *fl_out* as the final argument to the operator, following all input file names. This is the *positional argument* method of specifying input and ouput file names. The positional argument method works well in most applications. NCO also supports specifying *fl_out* using the command line switch argument method, '`-o fl_out`'.

Specifying *fl_out* with a switch, rather than as a positional argument, allows *fl_out* to precede input files in the argument list. This is particularly useful with multi-file operators for three reasons. Multi-file operators may be invoked with hundreds (or more) filenames. Visual or automatic location of *fl_out* in such a list is difficult when the only syntactic distinction between input and output files is their position. Second, specification of a long list of input files may be difficult (see Section 2.7 [Large Numbers of Files], page 21). Making the input file list the final argument to an operator facilitates using `xargs` for this purpose. Some alternatives to `xargs` are heinous and undesirable. Finally, many users are more comfortable specifying output files with '`-o fl_out`' near the beginning of an argument list. Compilers and linkers are usually invoked this way.

Users should specify *fl_out* using either (not both) method. If *fl_out* is specified twice (once with the switch and once as the last positional argument), then the positional argument takes precedence.

## 3.7 Accessing Remote Files

Availability: All operators
Short options: '`-p`', '`-l`'
Long options: '`--pth`', '`--path`', '`--lcl`', '`--local`'

All NCO operators can retrieve files from remote sites as well as from the local file system. A remote site can be an anonymous FTP server, a machine on which the user has `rcp`, `scp`, or `sftp` privileges, NCAR's Mass Storage System (MSS), or an OPeNDAP server. Examples of each are given below, following a brief description of the particular access protocol.

To access a file via an anonymous FTP server, simply supply the remote file's URL. Anonymous FTP usually requires no further credentials, e.g., no `.netrc` file is necessary. FTP is an intrinsically insecure protocol because it transfers passwords in plain text format. Users should access sites using anonymous FTP, or better yet, secure FTP (SFTP, see below) when possible. Some FTP servers require a login/password combination for a valid user account. NCO allows transactions that require additional credentials so long as the required information is stored in the `.netrc` file. Usually this information is the remote machine name, login, and password, in plain text, separated by those very keywords, e.g.,

```
machine dust.ess.uci.edu login zender password bushlied
```

Eschew using valuable passwords for FTP transactions, since `.netrc` passwords are potentially exposed to eavesdropping software[4].

SFTP, i.e., secure FTP, uses SSH-based security protocols that solve the security issues associated with plain FTP. NCO supports SFTP protocol access to files specified with a homebrew syntax of the form

```
sftp://machine.domain.tld:/path/to/filename
```

Note the second colon following the top-level-domain, `tld`. This syntax is a hybrid between an FTP URL and standard remote file syntax.

To access a file using `rcp` or `scp`, specify the Internet address of the remote file. Of course in this case you must have `rcp` or `scp` privileges which allow transparent (no password entry required) access to the remote machine. This means that `~/.rhosts` or `~/ssh/authorized_keys` must be set accordingly on both local and remote machines.

To access a file on a High Performance Storage System (HPSS) (such as that at NCAR, ECMWF, LANL, DKRZ, LLNL) specify the full HPSS pathname of the remote file. NCO will attempt to detect whether the local machine has direct (synchronous) HPSS access. In this case, NCO attempts to use the Hierarchical Storage Interface (HSI) command `hsi get`[5].

The following examples show how one might analyze files stored on remote systems.

```
ncks -l . ftp://dust.ess.uci.edu/pub/zender/nco/in.nc
ncks -l . sftp://dust.ess.uci.edu:/home/ftp/pub/zender/nco/in.nc
ncks -l . dust.ess.uci.edu:/home/zender/nco/data/in.nc
ncks -l . /ZENDER/nco/in.nc
ncks -l . /home/zender/nco/in.nc
ncks -l . http://thredds-test.ucar.edu/thredds/dodsC/testdods/in.nc
```

The first example works verbatim if your system is connected to the Internet and is not behind a firewall. The second example works if you have `sftp` access to the machine `dust.ess.uci.edu`. The third example works if you have `rcp` or `scp` access to the machine `dust.ess.uci.edu`. The fourth and fifth examples work on NCAR computers with local access to the HPSS `hsi get` command[6]. The sixth command works if your local version of NCO is OPeNDAP-enabled (this is fully described in Section 3.7.1 [OPeNDAP], page 38), or if the remote file is accessible via `wget`. The above commands can be rewritten using the '`-p` *`input-path`*' option as follows:

```
ncks -p ftp://dust.ess.uci.edu/pub/zender/nco -l . in.nc
```

---

[4] NCO does not implement command line options to specify FTP logins and passwords because copying those data into the `history` global attribute in the output file (done by default) poses an unacceptable security risk.

[5] The `hsi` command must be in the user's path in one of the following directories: `/usr/local/bin`, `/opt/hpss/bin`, or `/ncar/opt/hpss/hsi`. Tell us if the HPSS installation at your site places the `hsi` command in a different location, and we will add that location to the list of acceptable paths to search for `hsi`.

[6] NCO supported the old NCAR Mass Storage System (MSS) until version 4.0.7 in April, 2011. NCO supported MSS-retrievals via a variety of mechanisms including the `msread`, `msrcp`, and `nrnet` commands invoked either automatically or with sentinels like `ncks -p mss:/ZENDER/nco -l . in.nc`. Once the MSS was decommissioned in March, 2011, support for these retrieval mechanisms was replaced by support for HPSS in NCO.

```
ncks -p sftp://dust.ess.uci.edu:/home/ftp/pub/zender/nco -l . in.nc
ncks -p dust.ess.uci.edu:/home/zender/nco -l . in.nc
ncks -p /ZENDER/nco -l . in.nc
ncks -p /home/zender/nco -l . in.nc # HPSS
ncks -p http://thredds-test.ucar.edu/thredds/dodsC/testdods \
     -l . in.nc
```

Using '`-p`' is recommended because it clearly separates the *input-path* from the filename itself, sometimes called the *stub*. When *input-path* is not explicitly specified using '`-p`', NCO internally generates an *input-path* from the first input filename. The automatically generated *input-path* is constructed by stripping the input filename of everything following the final '`/`' character (i.e., removing the stub). The '`-l output-path`' option tells NCO where to store the remotely retrieved file. It has no effect on locally-retrieved files, or on the output file. Often the path to a remotely retrieved file is quite different than the path on the local machine where you would like to store the file. If '`-l`' is not specified then NCO internally generates an *output-path* by simply setting *output-path* equal to *input-path* stripped of any machine names. If '`-l`' is not specified and the remote file resides on the NCAR HPSS system, then the leading character of *input-path*, '`/`', is also stripped from *output-path*. Specifying *output-path* as '`-l ./`' tells NCO to store the remotely retrieved file and the output file in the current directory. Note that '`-l .`' is equivalent to '`-l ./`' though the latter is syntactically more clear.

### 3.7.1 OPeNDAP

The Distributed Oceanographic Data System (DODS) provides useful replacements for common data interface libraries like netCDF. The DODS versions of these libraries implement network transparent access to data via a client-server data access protocol that uses the HTTP protocol for communication. Although DODS-technology originated with oceanography data, it applyies to virtually all scientific data. In recognition of this, the data access protocol underlying DODS (which is what NCO cares about) has been renamed the Open-source Project for a Network Data Access Protocol, OPeNDAP. We use the terms DODS and OPeNDAP interchangeably, and often write OPeNDAP/DODS for now. In the future we will deprecate DODS in favor of DAP or OPeNDAP, as appropriate[7].

NCO may be DAP-enabled by linking NCO to the OPeNDAP libraries. This is described in the OPeNDAP documentation and automagically implemented in NCO build mechanisms[8]. The `./configure` mechanism automatically enables NCO as OPeNDAP clients if it can find

[7] DODS is being deprecated because it is ambiguous, referring both to a protocol and to a collection of (oceanography) data. It is superceded by two terms. DAP is the discipline-neutral Data Access Protocol at the heart of DODS. The National Virtual Ocean Data System (NVODS) refers to the collection of oceanography data and oceanographic extensions to DAP. In other words, NVODS is implemented with OPeNDAP. OPeNDAP is *also* the open source project which maintains, develops, and promulgates the DAP standard. OPeNDAP and DAP really are interchangeable. Got it yet?

[8] Automagic support for DODS version 3.2.x was deprecated in December, 2003 after NCO version 2.8.4. NCO support for OPeNDAP versions 3.4.x commenced in December, 2003, with NCO version 2.8.5. NCO support for OPeNDAP versions 3.5.x commenced in June, 2005, with NCO version 3.0.1. NCO support for OPeNDAP versions 3.6.x commenced in June, 2006, with NCO version 3.1.3. NCO support for OPeNDAP versions 3.7.x commenced in January, 2007, with NCO version 3.1.9.

the required OPeNDAP libraries[9]. in the usual locations. The `$DODS_ROOT` environment variable may be used to override the default OPeNDAP library location at NCO compile-time. Building NCO with `bld/Makefile` and the command `make DODS=Y` adds the (non-intuitive) commands to link to the OPeNDAP libraries installed in the `$DODS_ROOT` directory. The file `doc/opendap.sh` contains a generic script intended to help users install OPeNDAP before building NCO. The documentation at the OPeNDAP Homepage (`http://www.opendap.org`) is voluminous. Check there and on the DODS mail lists (`http://www.unidata.ucar.edu/software/dods/home/mailLists/`). to learn more about the extensive capabilities of OPeNDAP[10].

Once NCO is DAP-enabled the operators are OPeNDAP clients. All OPeNDAP clients have network transparent access to any files controlled by a OPeNDAP server. Simply specify the input file path(s) in URL notation and all NCO operations may be performed on remote files made accessible by a OPeNDAP server. This command tests the basic functionality of OPeNDAP-enabled NCO clients:

```
% ncks -O -o ~/foo.nc -C -H -v one -l /tmp \
  -p http://thredds-test.ucar.edu/thredds/dodsC/testdods in.nc
% ncks -H -v one ~/foo.nc
one = 1
```

The `one = 1` outputs confirm (first) that `ncks` correctly retrieved data via the OPeNDAP protocol and (second) that `ncks` created a valid local copy of the subsetted remote file. With minor changes to the above command, netCDF4 can be used as both the input and output file format:

```
% ncks -4 -O -o ~/foo.nc -C -H -v one -l /tmp \
  -p http://thredds-test.ucar.edu/thredds/dodsC/testdods in_4.nc
% ncks -H -v one ~/foo.nc
one = 1
```

And, of course, OPeNDAP-enabled NCO clients continue to support orthogonal features such as UDUnits (see Section 3.24 [UDUnits Support], page 84):

```
% ncks -u -C -H -v wvl -d wvl,'0.4 micron','0.7 micron' \
  -p http://thredds-test.ucar.edu/thredds/dodsC/testdods in_4.nc
% wvl[0]=5e-07 meter
```

The next command is a more advanced example which demonstrates the real power of OPeNDAP-enabled NCO clients. The `ncwa` client requests an equatorial hyperslab from remotely stored NCEP reanalyses data of the year 1969. The NOAA OPeNDAP server (hopefully!) serves these data. The local `ncwa` client then computes and stores (locally) the regional mean surface pressure (in Pa).

---

[9] The minimal set of libraries required to build NCO as OPeNDAP clients, where OPeNDAP is supplied as a separate library apart from `libnetcdf.a`, are, in link order, `libnc-dap.a`, `libdap.a`, and `libxml2` and `libcurl.a`.

[10] We are most familiar with the OPeNDAP ability to enable network-transparent data access. OPeNDAP has many other features, including sophisticated hyperslabbing and server-side processing via *constraint expressions*. If you know more about this, please consider writing a section on "OPeNDAP Capabilities of Interest to NCO Users" for incorporation in the *NCO User Guide*.

```
ncwa -C -a lat,lon,time -d lon,-10.,10. -d lat,-10.,10. -l /tmp -p \
http://www.esrl.noaa.gov/psd/thredds/dodsC/Datasets/ncep.reanalysis.dailyavgs/sur
  pres.sfc.1969.nc ~/foo.nc
```

All with one command! The data in this particular input file also happen to be packed (see Section 4.1.12 [Methods and functions], page 158), although this complication is transparent to the user since NCO automatically unpacks data before attempting arithmetic.

NCO obtains remote files from the OPeNDAP server (e.g., `www.cdc.noaa.gov`) rather than the local machine. Input files are first copied to the local machine, then processed. The OPeNDAP server performs data access, hyperslabbing, and transfer to the local machine. This allows the I/O to appear to NCO as if the input files were local. The local machine performs all arithmetic operations. Only the hyperslabbed output data are transferred over the network (to the local machine) for the number-crunching to begin. The advantages of this are obvious if you are examining small parts of large files stored at remote locations.

Natually there are many versions of OPeNDAP servers supplying data and bugs in the server can appear to be bugs in NCO. However, with very few exceptions[11] an NCO command that works on a local file must work across an OPeNDAP connection or else there is a bug in the server. This is because NCO does nothing special to handle files served by OPeNDAP, the whole process is (supposed to be) completely transparent to the client NCO software. Therefore it is often useful to try NCO commands on various OPeNDAP servers in order to isolate whether a problem may be due to a bug in the OPeNDAP server on a particular machine. For this purpose, one might try variations of the following commands that access files on public OPeNDAP servers:

```
# Strided access to HDF5 file
ncks -v Time -d Time,0,10,2 http://eosdap.hdfgroup.uiuc.edu:8080/opendap/data/NAS
# Strided access to netCDF3 file
ncks -O -D 1 -d time,1 -d lev,0 -d lat,0,100,10 -d lon,0,100,10 -v u_velocity htt
```

These servers were operational at the time of writing, March 2014. Unfortunately, administrators often move or rename path directories. Recommendations for additional public OPeNDAP servers on which to test NCO are welcome.

## 3.8 Retaining Retrieved Files

Availability: All operators
Short options: '`-R`'
Long options: '`--rtn`', '`--retain`'

In order to conserve local file system space, files retrieved from remote locations are automatically deleted from the local file system once they have been processed. Many NCO operators were constructed to work with numerous large (e.g., 200 MB) files. Retrieval of

[11] For example, DAP servers do not like variables with periods (".") in their names even though this is perfectly legal with netCDF. Such names may cause the DAP service to fail because DAP interprets the period as structure delimiter in an HTTP query string.

multiple files from remote locations is done serially. Each file is retrieved, processed, then deleted before the cycle repeats. In cases where it is useful to keep the remotely-retrieved files on the local file system after processing, the automatic removal feature may be disabled by specifying '-R' on the command line.

Invoking -R disables the default printing behavior of ncks. This allows ncks to retrieve remote files without automatically trying to print them. See Section 4.8 [ncks netCDF Kitchen Sink], page 237, for more details.

Note that the remote retrieval features of NCO can always be used to retrieve *any* file, including non-netCDF files, via SSH, anonymous FTP, or msrcp. Often this method is quicker than using a browser, or running an FTP session from a shell window yourself. For example, say you want to obtain a JPEG file from a weather server.

```
ncks -R -p ftp://weather.edu/pub/pix/jpeg -l . storm.jpg
```

In this example, ncks automatically performs an anonymous FTP login to the remote machine and retrieves the specified file. When ncks attempts to read the local copy of storm.jpg as a netCDF file, it fails and exits, leaving storm.jpg in the current directory.

If your NCO is DAP-enabled (see Section 3.7.1 [OPeNDAP], page 38), then you may use NCO to retrieve any files (including netCDF, HDF, etc.) served by an OPeNDAP server to your local machine. For example,

```
ncks -R -l . -p \
http://www.esrl.noaa.gov/psd/thredds/dodsC/Datasets/ncep.reanalysis.dailyavgs/surface
  pres.sfc.1969.nc
```

It may occasionally be useful to use NCO to transfer files when your other preferred methods are not available locally.

## 3.9 File Formats and Conversion

Availability: ncap2, nces, ncecat, ncflint, ncks, ncpdq, ncra, ncrcat, ncwa
Short options: '-3', '-4', '-5', '-6', '-7'
Long options: '--3', '--4', '--5', '--6', '--64bit_offset', '--7', '--fl_fmt', '--netcdf4'

All NCO operators support (read and write) all three (or four, depending on how one counts) file formats supported by netCDF4. The default output file format for all operators is the input file format. The operators listed under "Availability" above allow the user to specify the output file format independent of the input file format. These operators allow the user to convert between the various file formats. (The operators ncatted and ncrename do not support these switches so they always write the output netCDF file in the same format as the input netCDF file.)

### 3.9.1 File Formats

netCDF supports five types of files: CLASSIC, 64BIT_OFFSET, 64BIT_DATA, NETCDF4, and NETCDF4_CLASSIC. The CLASSIC format is the traditional 32-bit offset written by netCDF2 and netCDF3. As of 2005, nearly all netCDF datasets were in CLASSIC format. The

64BIT_OFFSET (originally called plain old 64BIT) format was added in Fall, 2004. As of 2010, many netCDF datasets were in 64BIT_OFFSET format. As of 2013, an increasing number of netCDF datasets were in NETCDF4_CLASSIC format. The 64BIT_DATA (aka CDF5 or PNETCDF) format was added in January, 2016.

The NETCDF4 format uses HDF5 as the file storage layer. The files are (usually) created, accessed, and manipulated using the traditional netCDF3 API (with numerous extensions). The NETCDF4_CLASSIC format refers to netCDF4 files created with the NC_CLASSIC_MODEL mask. Such files use HDF5 as the back-end storage format (unlike netCDF3), though they incorporate only netCDF3 features. Hence NETCDF4_CLASSIC files are entirely readable by applications that use only the netCDF3 API (though the applications must be linked with the netCDF4 library). NCO must be built with netCDF4 to write files in the new NETCDF4 and NETCDF4_CLASSIC formats, and to read files in these formats. Datasets in the default CLASSIC or the newer 64BIT_OFFSET formats have maximum backwards-compatibility with older applications. NCO has deep support for NETCDF4 formats. If performance or disk-space as important as backwards compatibility, then use NETCDF4_CLASSIC instead of CLASSIC format files. As of 2014, NCO support for the NETCDF4 format is nearly complete and the most powerful and disk/RAM efficient workflows will utilize this format.

As mentioned above, all operators write use the input file format for output files unless told otherwise. Toggling the short option '-6' or the long option '--6' or '--64bit_offset' (or their *key-value* equivalent '--fl_fmt=64bit_offset') produces the netCDF3 64-bit offset format named 64BIT_OFFSET. NCO must be built with netCDF 3.6 or higher to produce a 64BIT_OFFSET file. Using the '-4' switch (or its long option equivalents '--4' or '--netcdf4'), or setting its *key-value* equivalent '--fl_fmt=netcdf4' produces a NETCDF4 file (i.e., with all supported HDF5 features). Using the '-7' switch (or its long option equivalent '--7'[12], or setting its *key-value* equivalent '--fl_fmt=netcdf4_classic' produces a NETCDF4_CLASSIC file (i.e., with all supported HDF5 features like compression and chunking but without groups or new atomic types). Operators given the '-3' (or '--3') switch without arguments will (attempt to) produce netCDF3 CLASSIC output, even from netCDF4 input files.

Note that NETCDF4 and NETCDF4_CLASSIC are the same binary format. The latter simply causes a writing application to fail if it attempts to write a NETCDF4 file that cannot be completely read by the netCDF3 library. Conversely, NETCDF4_CLASSIC indicates to a reading application that all of the file contents are readable with the netCDF3 library. NCO has supported reading/writing basic NETCDF4 and NETCDF4_CLASSIC files since October, 2005.

### 3.9.2 Determining File Format

Input files often end with the generic .nc suffix that leaves (perhaps by intention) the internal file format ambiguous. There are at least three ways to discover the internal format of a netCDF-supported file. These methods determine whether it is a classic (32-bit offset) or newer 64-bit offset netCDF3 format, or is a netCDF4 format. Each method returns the information using slightly different terminology that becomes easier to understand with practice.

---

[12] The reason (and mnemonic) for '-7' is that NETCDF4_CLASSIC files include great features of both netCDF3 (compatibility) and netCDF4 (compression, chunking) and, well, $3 + 4 = 7$.

First, examine the first line of global metadata output by 'ncks -M':

```
% ncks -M foo_3.nc
Summary of foo_3.nc: filetype = NC_FORMAT_CLASSIC, 0 groups ...
% ncks -M foo_6.nc
Summary of foo_6.nc: filetype = NC_FORMAT_64BIT_OFFSET, 0 groups ...
% ncks -M foo_5.nc
Summary of foo_5.nc: filetype = NC_FORMAT_CDF5, 0 groups ...
% ncks -M foo_7.nc
Summary of foo_7.nc: filetype = NC_FORMAT_NETCDF4_CLASSIC, 0 groups ...
% ncks -M foo_4.nc
Summary of foo_4.nc: filetype = NC_FORMAT_NETCDF4, 0 groups ...
```

This method requires a netCDF4-enabled NCO version 3.9.0+ (i.e., from 2007 or later). As of NCO version 4.4.0 (January, 2014), ncks will also print the extended or underlying format of the input file. The extended filetype will be one of the six underlying formats that are accessible through the netCDF API. These formats are NC_FORMATX_NC3 (classic and 64-bit versions of netCDF3 formats), NC_FORMATX_NC_HDF5 (classic and extended versions of netCDF4, and "pure" HDF5 format), NC_FORMATX_NC_HDF4 (HDF4 format), NC_FORMATX_PNETCDF (PnetCDF format), NC_FORMATX_DAP2 (accessed via DAP2 protocol), and NC_FORMATX_DAP4 (accessed via DAP4 protocol). For example,

```
% ncks -D 2 -M hdf.hdf
Summary of hdf.hdf: filetype = NC_FORMAT_NETCDF4 (representation of \
  extended/underlying filetype NC_FORMAT_HDF4), 0 groups ...
% ncks -D 2 -M http://thredds-test.ucar.edu/thredds/dodsC/testdods/in.nc
Summary of http://thredds-test.ucar.edu/thredds/dodsC/testdods/in.nc: \
  filetype = NC_FORMAT_CLASSIC (representation of extended/underlying \
  filetype NC_FORMATX_DAP2), 0 groups
% ncks -D 2 -M foo_4.nc
Summary of foo_4.nc: filetype = NC_FORMAT_NETCDF4 (representation of \
  extended/underlying filetype NC_FORMAT_HDF5), 0 groups
```

The extended filetype determines some of the capabilities that netCDF has to alter the file.

Second, query the file with 'ncdump -k':

```
% ncdump -k foo_3.nc
classic
% ncdump -k foo_6.nc
64-bit offset
% ncdump -k foo_5.nc
cdf5
% ncdump -k foo_7.nc
netCDF-4 classic model
% ncdump -k foo_4.nc
netCDF-4
```

This method requires a netCDF4-enabled netCDF 3.6.2+ (i.e., from 2007 or later).

The third option uses the POSIX-standard od (octal dump) command:

```
% od -An -c -N4 foo_3.nc
   C   D   F 001
% od -An -c -N4 foo_6.nc
   C   D   F 002
% od -An -c -N4 foo_5.nc
   C   D   F 005
% od -An -c -N4 foo_7.nc
 211   H   D   F
% od -An -c -N4 foo_4.nc
 211   H   D   F
```

This option works without NCO and ncdump. Values of 'C D F 001' and 'C D F 002' indicate 32-bit (classic) and 64-bit netCDF3 formats, respectively, while values of '211 H D F' indicate either of the newer netCDF4 file formats.

### 3.9.3 File Conversion

Let us demonstrate converting a file from any netCDF-supported input format into any netCDF output format (subject to limits of the output format). Here the input file in.nc may be in any of these formats: netCDF3 (classic, 64bit_offset, 64bit_data), netCDF4 (classic and extended), HDF4, HDF5, HDF-EOS (version 2 or 5), and DAP. The switch determines the output format written in the comment:[13]

```
ncks --fl_fmt=classic in.nc foo_3.nc # netCDF3 classic
ncks --fl_fmt=64bit_offset in.nc foo_6.nc # netCDF3 64bit-offset
ncks --fl_fmt=64bit_data in.nc foo_5.nc # netCDF3 64bit-data
ncks --fl_fmt=cdf5 in.nc foo_5.nc # netCDF3 64bit-data
ncks --fl_fmt=netcdf4_classic in.nc foo_7.nc # netCDF4 classic
ncks --fl_fmt=netcdf4 in.nc foo_4.nc # netCDF4
ncks -3 in.nc foo_3.nc # netCDF3 classic
ncks --3 in.nc foo_3.nc # netCDF3 classic
ncks -6 in.nc foo_6.nc # netCDF3 64bit-offset
ncks --64 in.nc foo_6.nc # netCDF3 64bit-offset
ncks -5 in.nc foo_5.nc # netCDF3 64bit-data
ncks --5 in.nc foo_5.nc # netCDF3 64bit-data
ncks -4 in.nc foo_4.nc # netCDF4
ncks --4 in.nc foo_4.nc # netCDF4
ncks -7 in.nc foo_7.nc # netCDF4 classic
ncks --7 in.nc foo_7.nc # netCDF4 classic
```

Of course since most operators support these switches, the "conversions" can be done at the output stage of arithmetic or metadata processing rather than requiring a separate step. Producing (netCDF3) CLASSIC or 64BIT_OFFSET or 64BIT_DATA files from NETCDF4_CLASSIC files always works.

[13] The switches '-5', '--5', and 'pnetcdf' are reserved for PnetCDF files, i.e., NC_FORMAT_CDF5. Such files are similar to netCDF3 classic files, yet also support 64-bit offsets and the additional netCDF4 atomic types.

### 3.9.4 Autoconversion

Because of the dearth of support for netCDF4 amongst tools and user communities (including the CF conventions), it is often useful to convert netCDF4 to netCDF3 for certain applications. Until NCO version 4.4.0 (January, 2014), producing netCDF3 files from netCDF4 files only worked if the input files contained no netCDF4-specific features (e.g., atomic types, multiple record dimensions, or groups). As of NCO version 4.4.0, `ncks` supports *autoconversion* of many netCDF4 features to their closest netCDF3-compatible representations. Since converting netCDF4 to netCDF3 results in loss of features, "automatic down-conversion" may be a more precise description of what we term autoconversion.

NCO employs three algorithms to downconvert netCDF4 to netCDF3:

1. Autoconversion of atomic types: Autoconversion automatically promotes `NC_UBYTE` to `NC_SHORT`, and `NC_USHORT` to `NC_INT`. It automatically demotes the three types `NC_UINT`, `NC_UINT64`, and `NC_INT64` to `NC_INT`. And it converts `NC_STRING` to `NC_CHAR`. All numeric conversions work for attributes and variables of any rank. Two numeric types (`NC_UBYTE` and `NC_USHORT`) are *promoted* to types with greater range (and greater storage). This extra range is often not used so promotion perhaps conveys the wrong impression. However, promotion never truncates values or loses data (this perhaps justifies the extra storage). Three numeric types (`NC_UINT`, `NC_UINT64` and `NC_INT64`) are *demoted*. Since the input range is larger than the output range, demotion can result in numeric truncation and thus loss of data. In such cases, it would possible to convert the data to floating-point values instead. If this feature interests you, please be the squeaky wheel and let us know.

   String conversions (to `NC_CHAR`) work for all attributes, but not for variables. This is because attributes are at most one-dimensional and may be of any size whereas variables require gridded dimensions that usually do not fit the ragged sizes of text strings. Hence scalar `NC_STRING` attributes are correctly converted to and stored as `NC_CHAR` attributes in the netCDF3 output file, but `NC_STRING` variables are not correctly converted. If this limitation annoys or enrages you, please let us know by being the squeaky wheel.
2. Convert multiple record dimensions to fixed-size dimensions. Many netCDF4 and HDF5 datasets have multiple unlimited dimensions. Since a netCDF3 file may have at most one unlimited dimension, all but possibly one unlimited dimension from the input file must be converted to fixed-length dimensions prior to storing netCDF4 input as netCDF3 output. By invoking `--fix_rec_dmn all` the user ensures the output file will adhere to netCDF3 conventions and the user need not know the names of the specific record dimensions to fix. See Section 4.8 [ncks netCDF Kitchen Sink], page 237, for a description of the '`--fix_rec_dmn`' option.
3. Flattening (removal) of groups. Many netCDF4 and HDF5 datasets have group hierarchies. Since a netCDF3 file may not have any groups, groups in the input file must be removed. This is also called "flattening" the hierarchical file. See Section 3.13 [Group Path Editing], page 52, for a description of the GPE option '`-G :`' to flatten files.

Putting the three algorithms together, one sees that the recipe to convert netCDF4 to netCDF4 becomes increasingly complex as the netCDF4 features in the input file become more elaborate:

```
# Convert file with netCDF4 atomic types
```

```
ncks -3 in.nc4 out.nc3
# Convert file with multiple record dimensions + netCDF4 atomic types
ncks -3 --fix_rec_dmn=all in.nc4 out.nc3
# Convert file with groups, multiple record dimensions + netCDF4 atomic types
ncks -3 -G : --fix_rec_dmn=all in.nc4 out.nc3
```

Future versions of NCO may automatically invoke the record dimension fixation and group flattening when converting to netCDF3 (rather than requiring it be specified manually). If this feature would interest you, please let us know.

## 3.10 Large File Support

Availability: All operators
Short options: none
Long options: none

NCO has Large File Support (LFS), meaning that NCO can write files larger than 2 GB on some 32-bit operating systems with netCDF libraries earlier than version 3.6. If desired, LFS support must be configured when both netCDF and NCO are installed. netCDF versions 3.6 and higher support 64-bit file addresses as part of the netCDF standard. We recommend that users ignore LFS support which is difficult to configure and is implemented in NCO only to support netCDF versions prior to 3.6. This obviates the need for configuring explicit LFS support in applications (such as NCO) that now support 64-bit files directly through the netCDF interface. See Section 3.9 [File Formats and Conversion], page 41, for instructions on accessing the different file formats, including 64-bit files, supported by the modern netCDF interface.

If you are still interested in explicit LFS support for netCDF versions prior to 3.6, know that LFS support depends on a complex, interlocking set of operating system[14] and netCDF support issues. The netCDF LFS FAQ (`http://my.unidata.ucar.edu/content/software/netcdf/faq-lfs.html`) describes the various file size limitations imposed by different versions of the netCDF standard. NCO and netCDF automatically attempt to configure LFS at build time.

## 3.11 Subsetting Files

[14] Linux and AIX do support LFS.

Options `-g` *grp*
Availability: `ncbo`, `nces`, `ncecat`, `ncflint`, `ncks`, `ncpdq`, `ncra`, `ncrcat`, `ncwa`
Short options: '`-g`'
Long options: '`--grp`' and '`--group`'
Options `-v` *var* and `-x`
Availability: (`ncap2`), `ncbo`, `nces`, `ncecat`, `ncflint`, `ncks`, `ncpdq`, `ncra`, `ncrcat`, `ncwa`
Short options: '`-v`', '`-x`'
Long options: '`--variable`', '`--exclude`' or '`--xcl`'
Options `--unn`
Availability: `ncbo`, `nces`, `ncecat`, `ncflint`, `ncks`, `ncpdq`, `ncra`, `ncrcat`, `ncwa`
Short options:
Long options: '`--unn`' and '`--union`'
Options `--grp_xtr_var_xcl`
Availability: `ncks`
Short options:
Long options: '`--gxvx`' and '`--grp_xtr_var_xcl`'

Subsetting variables refers to explicitly specifying variables and groups to be included or excluded from operator actions. Subsetting is controlled by the '`-v` *var*`[,...]`' and '`-x`' options for directly specifying variables. Specifying groups, whether in addition to or instead of variables, is quite similar and is controlled by the '`-g` *grp*`[,...]`' and '`-x`' options. A list of variables or groups to extract is specified following the '`-v`' and '`-g`' options, e.g., '`-v time,lat,lon`' or '`-g grp1,grp2`'. Both options may be specified simultaneously and NCO will extract the intersection of the lists, i.e., only variables of the specified names found in groups of the specified names. The '`--unn`' option causes NCO to extract the union, rather than the intersection, of the specified groups and variables. Not using the '`-v`' or '`-g`' option is equivalent to specifying all variables or groupp, respectively. The '`-x`' option causes the list of variables specified with '`-v`' to be *excluded* rather than *extracted*. Thus '`-x`' saves typing when you only want to extract fewer than half of the variables in a file.

Variables or groups explicitly specified for extraction with '`-v` *var*`[,...]`' or '`-g` *grp*`[,...]`' *must* be present in the input file or an error will result. Variables explicitly specified for *exclusion* with '`-x -v` *var*`[,...]`' need not be present in the input file. To accord with the sophistication of the underlying hierarchy, group subsetting is controlled by a few powerful yet subtle syntactical distinctions. When learning this syntax it is helpful to keep in mind the similarity between group hierarchies and directory structures.

As of NCO 4.4.4 (June, 2014), `ncks` (alone) supports an option to include specified groups yet exclude specified variables. The '`--grp_xtr_var_xcl`' switch (with long option equivalent '`--gxvx`') extracts all contents of groups given as arguments to '`-g` *grp*`[,...]`', except for variables given as arguments to '`-v` *var*`[,...]`'. Use this when one or a few variables in hierarchical files are not to be extracted, and all other variables are. This is useful when coercing netCDF4 files into netCDF3 files such as with converting, flattening, or dismembering files (see Section 3.13.1 [Flattening Groups], page 52).

```
ncks --grp_xtr_var_xcl -g g1 -v v1 # Extract all of group g1 except v1
```

Two properties of subsetting, recursion and anchoring, are best illustrated by reminding the user of their UNIX equivalents. The UNIX command `mv src dst` moves `src` *and all its subdirectories* (and all their subdirectories etc.) to `dst`. In other words `mv` is, by default, *recursive*. In contrast, the UNIX command `cp src dst` moves `src`, and only `src`, to `dst`, If `src` is a directory, not a file, then that command fails. One must explicitly request to copy directories recursively, i.e., with `cp -r src dst`. In NCO recursive extraction (and copying) of groups is the default (like with `mv`, not with `cp`). Recursion is turned off by appending a trailing slash to the path.

These UNIX commands also illustrate a property we call *anchoring*. The command `mv src dst` moves (recursively) the source directory `src` to the destination directory `dst`. If `src` begins with the slash character then the specified path is relative to the root directory, otherwise the path is relative to the current working directory. In other words, an initial slash character anchors the subsequent path to the root directory. In NCO an initial slash anchors the path at the root group. Paths that begin and end with slash characters (e.g., `//`, `/g1/`, and `/g1/g2/`) are both anchored and non-recursive.

Consider the following commands, all of which may be assumed to end with '`in.nc out.nc`':

```
ncks -g  g1  # Extract, recursively, all groups with a g1 component
ncks -g  g1/ # Extract, non-recursively, all groups terminating in g1
ncks -g /g1  # Extract, recursively, root group g1
ncks -g /g1/ # Extract, non-recursively root group g1
ncks -g //   # Extract, non-recursively the root group
```

The first command is probably the most useful and common. It would extract these groups, if present, and all their direct ancestors and children: `/g1`, `/g2/g1`, and `/g3/g1/g2`. In other words, the simplest form of '`-g grp`' grabs all groups that (and their direct ancestors and children, recursively) that have `grp` as a complete component of their path. A simple string match is insufficient, *grp* must be a complete component (i.e., group name) in the path. The option '`-g g1`' would not extract these groups because `g1` is not a complete component of the path: `/g12`, `/fg1`, and `/g1g1`. The second command above shows how a terminating slash character `/` cancels the recursive copying of groups. An argument to '`-g`' which terminates with a slash character extracts the group and its direct ancestors, but none of its children. The third command above shows how an initial slash character `/` anchors the argument to the root group. The third command would not extract the group `/g2/g1` because the `g1` group is not at the root level, but it would extract, any group `/g1` at the root level and all its children, recursively. The fourth command is the non-recursive version of the third command. The fifth command is a special case of the fourth command.

As mentioned above, both '`-v`' and '`-g`' options may be specified simultaneously and NCO will, by default, extract the intersection of the lists, i.e., the specified variables found in the specified groups[15]. The '`--unn`' option causes NCO to extract the union, rather than the intersection, of the specified groups and variables. Consider the following commands (which may be assumed to end with '`in.nc out.nc`'):

---

[15] Intersection-mode can also be explicitly invoked with the '`--nsx`' or '`--intersection`' switches. These switches are supplied for clarity and consistency and do absolutely nothing since intersection-mode is the default.

```
# Intersection-mode subsetting (default)
ncks -g  g1  -v v1 # Yes: /g1/v1, /g2/g1/v1. No: /v1, /g2/v1
ncks -g /g1  -v v1 # Yes: /g1/v1, /g1/g2/v1. No: /v1, /g2/v1, /g2/g1/v1
ncks -g  g1/ -v v1 # Yes: /g1/v1, /g2/g1/v1. No: /v1, /g2/v1, /g1/g2/v1
ncks -v  g1/v1     # Yes: /g1/v1, /g2/g1/v1. No: /v1, /g2/v1, /g1/g2/v1
ncks -g /g1/ -v v1 # Yes: /g1/v1. No: /g2/g1/v1, /v1, /g2/v1 ...
ncks -v /g1/v1     # Yes: /g1/v1. No: /g2/g1/v1, /v1, /g2/v1 ...

# Union-mode subsetting (invoke with --unn or --union)
ncks -g  g1  -v v1 --unn # All variables in  g1 or progeny, or named v1
ncks -g /g1  -v v1 --unn # All variables in /g1 or progeny, or named v1
ncks -g  g1/ -v v1 --unn # All variables in  g1 or named v1
ncks -g /g1/ -v v1 --unn # All variables in /g1 or named v1
```

The first command ('-g g1 -v v1') extracts the variable v1 from any group named g1 or descendent g1. The second command extracts v1 from any root group named g1 and any descendent groups as well. The third and fourth commands are equivalent ways of extracting v1 only from the root group named g1 (not its descendents). The fifth and sixth commands are equivalent ways of extracting the variable v1 only from the root group named g1. Subsetting in union-mode (with '--unn') causes all variables to be extracted which meet either one or both of the specifications of the variable and group specifications. Union-mode subsetting is simply the logical "OR" of intersection-mode subsetting. As discussed below, the group and variable specifications may be comma separated lists of regular expressions for added control over subsetting.

Remember, if averaging or concatenating large files stresses your systems memory or disk resources, then the easiest solution is often to subset (with '-g' and/or '-v') to retain only the most important variables (see Section 2.9 [Memory Requirements], page 24).

```
ncks          in.nc out.nc # Extract all groups and variables
ncks -v scl   # Extract variable scl from all groups
ncks -g g1    # Extract group g1 and descendents
ncks -x -g g1 # Extract all groups except g1 and descendents
ncks -g g2,g3 -v scl # Extract scl from groups g2 and g3
```

Overwriting and appending work as expected:

```
# Replace scl in group g2 in out.nc with scl from group g2 from in.nc
ncks -A -g g2 -v scl in.nc out.nc
```

Due to its special capabilities, ncap2 interprets the '-v' switch differently (see Section 4.1 [ncap2 netCDF Arithmetic Processor], page 138). For ncap2, the '-v' switch takes no arguments and indicates that *only* user-defined variables should be output. ncap2 neither accepts nor understands the -x and -g switches.

Regular expressions the syntax that NCO use pattern-match object names in netCDF file against user requests. The user can select all variables beginning with the string 'DST' from an input file by supplying the regular expression '^DST' to the '-v' switch, i.e., '-v '^DST''. The meta-characters used to express pattern matching operations are '^$+?.*[]{}|'. If the regular expression pattern matches *any* part of a variable name then that variable is selected. This capability is also called *wildcarding*, and is very useful for sub-setting large data files.

Extended regular expressions are defined by the POSIX `grep -E` (aka `egrep`) command. As of NCO 2.8.1 (August, 2003), variable name arguments to the '`-v`' switch may contain *extended regular expressions*. As of NCO 3.9.6 (January, 2009), variable names arguments to `ncatted` may contain *extended regular expressions*. As of NCO 4.2.4 (November, 2012), group name arguments to the '`-g`' switch may contain *extended regular expressions*.

Because of its wide availability, NCO uses the POSIX regular expression library `regex`. Regular expressions of arbitary complexity may be used. Since netCDF variable names are relatively simple constructs, only a few varieties of variable wildcards are likely to be useful. For convenience, we define the most useful pattern matching operators here:

'^' Matches the beginning of a string

'$' Matches the end of a string

'.' Matches any single character

The most useful repetition and combination operators are

'?' The preceding regular expression is optional and matched at most once

'*' The preceding regular expression will be matched zero or more times

'+' The preceding regular expression will be matched one or more times

'|' The preceding regular expression will be joined to the following regular expression. The resulting regular expression matches any string matching either subexpression.

To illustrate the use of these operators in extracting variables and groups, consider file `in_grp.nc` with groups `g0`–`g9`, and subgroups `s0`–`s9`, in each of those groups, and file `in.nc` with variables `Q`, `Q01`–`Q99`, `Q100`, `QAA`–`QZZ`, `Q_H2O`, `X_H2O`, `Q_CO2`, `X_CO2`.

```
ncks -v '.+' in.nc                 # All variables (default)
ncks -v 'Q.?' in.nc                # Variables that contain Q
ncks -v '^Q.?' in.nc               # Variables that start with Q
ncks -v '^Q+.?.' in.nc             # Q, Q0--Q9, Q01--Q99, QAA--QZZ, etc.
ncks -v '^Q..' in.nc               # Q01--Q99, QAA--QZZ, etc.
ncks -v '^Q[0-9][0-9]' in.nc       # Q01--Q99, Q100
ncks -v '^Q[[:digit:]]{2}' in.nc # Q01--Q99
ncks -v 'H2O$' in.nc               # Q_H2O, X_H2O
ncks -v 'H2O$|CO2$' in.nc          # Q_H2O, X_H2O, Q_CO2, X_CO2
ncks -v '^Q[0-9][0-9]$' in.nc      # Q01--Q99
ncks -v '^Q[0-6][0-9]|7[0-3]' in.nc # Q01--Q73, Q100
ncks -v '(Q[0-6][0-9]|7[0-3])$' in.nc # Q01--Q73
ncks -v '^[a-z]_[a-z]{3}$' in.nc # Q_H2O, X_H2O, Q_CO2, X_CO2
ncks -g 'g.' in_grp.nc             # 10 Groups g0-g9
ncks -g 's.' in_grp.nc        # 100 sub-groups g0/s0, g0/s1, ... g9/s9
ncks -g 'g.' -v 'v.' in_grp.nc     # All variables 'v.' in groups 'g.'
```

Beware—two of the most frequently used repetition pattern matching operators, '*' and '?', are also valid pattern matching operators for filename expansion (globbing) at the shell-level. Confusingly, their meanings in extended regular expressions and in shell-level filename expansion are significantly different. In an extended regular expression, '*' matches zero or more occurences of the preceding regular expression. Thus 'Q*' selects all variables, and 'Q+.*' selects all variables containing 'Q' (the '+' ensures the preceding item matches at least once). To match zero or one occurence of the preceding regular expression, use '?'. Documentation for the UNIX `egrep` command details the extended regular expressions which NCO supports.

One must be careful to protect any special characters in the regular expression specification from being interpreted (globbed) by the shell. This is accomplish by enclosing special characters within single or double quotes

```
ncra -v Q?? in.nc out.nc    # Error: Shell attempts to glob wildcards
ncra -v '^Q+..' in.nc out.nc # Correct: NCO interprets wildcards
ncra -v '^Q+..' in*.nc out.nc # Correct: NCO interprets, Shell globs
```

The final example shows that commands may use a combination of variable wildcarding and shell filename expansion (globbing). For globbing, '*' and '?' *have nothing to do* with the preceding regular expression! In shell-level filename expansion, '*' matches any string, including the null string and '?' matches any single character. Documentation for `bash` and `csh` describe the rules of filename expansion (globbing).

## 3.12 Subsetting Coordinate Variables

Availability: `ncap2`, `ncbo`, `nces`, `ncecat`, `ncflint`, `ncks`, `ncpdq`, `ncra`, `ncrcat`, `ncwa`
Short options: '`-C`', '`-c`'
Long options: '`--no-coords`', '`--no-crd`', '`--crd`', '`--coords`'

By default, coordinates variables associated with any variable appearing in the *input-file* will be placed in the *output-file*, even if they are not explicitly specified, e.g., with the '`-v`' switch. Thus variables with a latitude coordinate `lat` always carry the values of `lat` with them into the *output-file*. This feature can be disabled with '`-C`', which causes NCO to not automatically add coordinates to the variables appearing in the *output-file*. However, using '`-C`' does not preclude the user from including some coordinates in the output files simply by explicitly selecting the coordinates with the -v option. The '`-c`' option, on the other hand, is a shorthand way of automatically specifying that *all* coordinate variables in the *input-files* should appear in the *output-file*. Thus '`-c`' allows the user to select all the coordinate variables without having to know their names. As of NCO version 4.4.5 (July, 2014) both '`-c`' and '`-C`' honor the CF `ancillary_variables` convention described in Section 3.41 [CF Conventions], page 131. As of NCO version 4.0.8 (April, 2011) both '`-c`' and '`-C`' honor the CF `bounds` convention described in Section 3.41 [CF Conventions], page 131. As of NCO version 4.6.4 (January, 2017) both '`-c`' and '`-C`' honor the CF `cell_measures` convention described in Section 3.41 [CF Conventions], page 131. As of NCO version 4.4.9 (May, 2015) both '`-c`' and '`-C`' honor the CF `climatology` convention described in Section 3.41 [CF Conventions], page 131. As of NCO version 3.9.6 (January, 2009) both '-c' and '-C' honor the CF `coordinates` convention described in Section 3.41 [CF Conventions], page 131. As of NCO version 4.6.4 (January, 2017) both '-c' and '-C' honor the CF `formula_terms` convention described in Section 3.41 [CF Conventions], page 131. As of NCO version 4.6.0 (May, 2016) both '-c' and '-C' honor the CF `grid_mapping` convention described in Section 3.41 [CF Conventions], page 131.

## 3.13 Group Path Editing

Options `-G` *`gpe_dsc`*
Availability: `ncbo`, `ncecat`, `nces`, `ncflint`, `ncks`, `ncpdq`, `ncra`, `ncrcat`, `ncwa`
Short options: '`-G`'
Long options: '`--gpe`'

*Group Path Editing*, or GPE, allows the user to restructure (i.e., add, remove, and rename groups) in the output file relative to the input file based on the instructions they provide. As of NCO 4.2.3 (November, 2012), all operators that accept netCDF4 files with groups accept the '-G' switch, or its long-option equivalent '--gpe'. To master GPE one must understand the meaning of the required *gpe_dsc* structure/argument that specifies the transformation of input-to-output group paths.

Each *gpe_dsc* contains up to three elements (two are optional) in the following order:
*gpe_dsc = grp_pth:lvl_nbr* or *grp_pth@lvl_nbr*

*grp_pth* Group Path. This (optional) component specifies the output group path that should be appended after any editing (i.e., deletion or truncation) of the input path is performed.

*lvl_nbr* The number of levels to delete (from the head) or truncate (from the tail) of the input path.

If both components of the argument are present, then a single character, either the colon or at-sign (`:` or `@`), must separate them. If only *grp_pth* is specifed, the separator character may be omitted, e.g., '`-G g1`'. If only *lvl_nbr* is specifed, the separator character is still required to indicate it is a *lvl_nbr* arugment and not a *grp_pth*, e.g., '`-G :-1`' or '`-G @1`'.

If the at-sign separator character `@` is used instead of the colon separator character `:`, then the following *lvl_nbr* arugment must be positive and it will be assumed to refer to Truncation-Mode. Hence, '`-G :-1`' is the same as '`-G @1`'. This is simply a way of making the *lvl_nbr* argument positive-definite.

### 3.13.1 Deletion, Truncation, and Flattening of Groups

GPE has three editing modes: Delete, Truncate, and Flatten. Select one of GPE's three editing modes by supplying a *lvl_nbr* that is positive, negative, or zero for Delete-, Truncate- and Flatten-mode, respectively.

In Delete-mode, *lvl_nbr* is a positive integer which specifies the maximum number of group path components (i.e., groups) that GPE will try to delete from the head of *grp_pth*.

For example *lvl_nbr* = 3 changes the input path `/g1/g2/g3/g4/g5` to the output path `/g4/g5`. Input paths with *lvl_nbr* or fewer components (groups) are completely erased and the output path commences from the root level.

In other words, GPE is tolerant of specifying too many group components to delete. It deletes as many as possible, without complaint, and then begins to flatten the file (which fails if namespace conflicts arise).

In Truncate-mode, *lvl_nbr* is a negative integer which specifies the maximum number of group path components (i.e., groups) that GPE will try to truncate from the tail of *grp_pth*. For example *lvl_nbr* = −3 changes the input path `/g1/g2/g3/g4/g5` to the output path `/g1/g2`. Input paths with *lvl_nbr* or fewer components (groups) are completely erased and the output path commences from the root level.

In Flatten-mode, indicated by the separator character alone or with *lvl_nbr* = 0, GPE removes the entire group path from the input file and constructs the output path beginning at the root level. For example `-G :0` and `-G :` are identical and change the input path `/g1/g2/g3/g4/g5` to the output path `/` whereas `-G g1:0` and `-G g1:` are identical and result in the output path `/g1` for all variables.

Subsequent to the alteration of the input path by the specified editing mode, if any, GPE prepends (in Delete Mode) or Appends (in Truncate-mode) any specifed *grp_pth* to the output path. For example `-G g2` changes the input paths `/` and `/g1` to `/g2` and `/g1/g2`, respectively. Likewise, `-G g2/g3` changes the input paths `/` and `/g1` to `/g2/g3` and `/g1/g2/g3`, respectively. When *grp_pth* and *lvl_nbr* are both specified, the editing actions are taken in sequence so that, e.g., `-G g1/g2:2` changes the input paths `/` and `/h1/h2/h3/h4` to `/g1/g2` and `/g1/g2/h3/h4`, respectively. Likewise, `-G g1/g2:-2` changes the input paths `/` and `/h1/h2/h3/h4` to `/g1/g2` and `/h1/h2/g1/g2`, respectively.

Combining GPE with subsetting (see Section 3.11 [Subsetting Files], page 46) yields powerful control over the extracted (or excluded) variables and groups and their placement in the output file as shown by the following commands. All commands below may be assumed to end with '`in.nc out.nc`'.

```
# Prepending paths without editing:
ncks                     # /g?/v? -> /g?/v?
ncks               -v v1 # /g?/v1 -> /g?/v1
ncks        -g g1        # /g1/v? -> /g1/v?
ncks -G o1               # /g?/v? -> /o1/g?/v?
ncks -G o1 -g g1         # /g1/v? -> /o1/g1/v?
ncks        -g g1 -v v1 # /g1/v1 -> /g1/v1
ncks -G o1         -v v1 # /g?/v1 -> /o1/g?/v1
ncks -G o1 -g g1 -v v1 # /g1/v1 -> /o1/g1/v1
ncks -G g1 -g /  -v v1 # /v1    -> /g1/v1
ncks -G g1/g2      -v v1 # /g?/v1 -> /g1/g2/g?/v1
# Delete-mode: Delete from and Prepend to path head
# Syntax: -G [ppn]:lvl_nbr = # of levels to delete
ncks -G :1    -g g1    -v v1 # /g1/v1    -> /v1
ncks -G :1    -g g1/g1 -v v1 # /g1/g1/v1 -> /g1/v1
ncks -G :2    -g g1/g1 -v v1 # /g1/g1/v1 -> /v1
```

```
ncks -G :2    -g g1    -v v1 # /g1/v1    -> /v1
ncks -G g2:1  -g g1    -v v1 # /g1/v1    -> /g2/v1
ncks -G g2:2  -g g1/g1 -v v1 # /g1/g1/v1 -> /g2/v1
ncks -G g2:1  -g /     -v v1 # /v1       -> /g2/v1
ncks -G g2:1           -v v1 # /v1       -> /g2/v1
ncks -G g2:1  -g g1/g1 -v v1 # /g1/g1/v1 -> /g2/g1/v1
# Flatten-mode: Remove all input path components
# Syntax: -G [apn]: colon without numerical argument
ncks -G :            -v v1 # /g?/v1    -> /v1
ncks -G :   -g g1    -v v1 # /g1/v1    -> /v1
ncks -G :   -g g1/g1 -v v1 # /g1/g1/v1 -> /v1
ncks -G g2:          -v v1 # /g?/v1    -> /g2/v1
ncks -G g2:                # /g?/v?    -> /g2/v?
ncks -G g2: -g g1/g1 -v v1 # /g1/g1/v1 -> /g2/v1
# Truncate-mode: Truncate from and Append to path tail
# Syntax: -G [apn]:-lvl_nbr = # of levels to truncate
# NB: -G [apn]:-lvl_nbr is equivalent to -G [apn]@lvl_nbr
ncks -G :-1   -g g1    -v v1 # /g1/v1    -> /v1
ncks -G :-1   -g g1/g2 -v v1 # /g1/g2/v1 -> /g1/v1
ncks -G :-2   -g g1/g2 -v v1 # /g1/g2/v1 -> /v1
ncks -G :-2   -g g1    -v v1 # /g1/v1    -> /v1
ncks -G g2:-1          -v v1 # /g?/v1    -> /g2/v1
ncks -G g2:-1 -g g1    -v v1 # /g1/v1    -> /g2/v1
ncks -G g1:-1 -g g1/g2 -v v1 # /g1/g2/v1 -> /g1/g1/v1
```

### 3.13.2 Moving Groups

Until fall 2013 (netCDF version 4.3.1-pre1), netCDF contained no library function for renaming groups, and therefore `ncrename` cannot rename groups. However, NCO built on earlier versions of netCDF than 4.3.1 can use a GPE-based workaround mechanism to "rename" groups. The GPE mechanism actually *moves* (i.e., copies to a new location) groups, a more arduous procedure than simply renaming them. GPE applies to all selected groups, so, in the general case, one must move only the desired group to a new file, and then merge that new file with the original to obtain a file where the desired group has been "renamed" and all else is unchanged. Here is how to "rename" group `/g4` to group `/f4` with GPE instead of `ncrename`

```
ncks -O -G f4:1 -g g4 ~/nco/data/in_grp.nc ~/tmp.nc # Move /g4 to /f4
ncks -O -x -g g4 ~/nco/data/in_grp.nc ~/out.nc # Excise /g4
ncks -A ~/tmp.nc ~/out.nc # Add /f4 to new file
```

If the original group `g4` is not excised from `out.nc` (step two above), then the final output file would contain both `g4` and a copy named `f4`. Thus GPE can be used to both "rename" and copy groups. The recommended way to rename groups when when netCDF version 4.3.1 is availale is to use `ncrename` (see Section 4.13 [ncrename netCDF Renamer], page 278).

One may wish to flatten hierarchical group files for many reasons. These include 1. Obtaining flat netCDF3 files for use with tools that do not work with netCDF4 files,

2. Splitting apart hierarchies to re-assemble into different hierarchies, and 3. Providing a subset of a hierarchical file with the simplest possible storage structure.

```
ncks -O -G : -g cesm -3 ~/nco/data/cmip5.nc ~/cesm.nc # Extract /cesm to /
```

The `-3` switch[16] specifies the output dataset should be in netCDF3 format, the `-G :` option flattens all extracted groups, and the `-g cesm` option extracts only the `cesm` group and leaves all other groups (e.g., `ecmwf`, `giss`).

### 3.13.3 Dismembering Files

Let us show how to completely disaggregate (or, more memorably) *dismember* a hierarchical dataset. For now we take this to mean: store each group as a standalone flat dataset in netCDF3 format. This can be accomplished by looping the previous example over all groups. This script `ncdismember` dismembers the input file *fl_in* specified in the first argument and places the resulting files in the directory *drc_out* specified by the second argument:

```
cat > ~/ncdismember << 'EOF'
#!/bin/sh

# Purpose: Dismember netCDF4/HDF5 hierarchical files. CF-check them.
# Place each input file group in separate netCDF3 output file
# Described in NCO User Guide at http://nco.sf.net/nco.html#dismember
# Requirements: NCO 4.3.x+, UNIX shell utilities awk, grep, sed
# Optional: Decker CFchecker https://bitbucket.org/mde_/cfchecker

# Usage:
# ncdismember <fl_in> <drc_out> [cf_chk] [cf_vrs] [opt]
# where fl_in is input file/URL to dismember, drc_out is output directory
# CF-compliance check is performed when optional third argument is not '0'
# Default checker is Decker's cfchecker installed locally
# Specify cf_chk=nerc for smallified uploads to NERC checker
# Optional fourth argument cf_vrs is CF version to check
# Optional fifth argument opt passes straight-through to ncks
# Arguments must not use shell expansion/globbing
# NB: ncdismember does not clean-up output directory, so user must
# chmod a+x ~/sh/ncdismember
# Examples:
# ncdismember ~/nco/data/mdl_1.nc /data/zender/tmp
# ncdismember http://dust.ess.uci.edu/nco/mdl_1.nc /tmp
# ncdismember http://thredds-test.ucar.edu/thredds/dodsC/testdods/foo.nc /tmp
# ncdismember ~/nco/data/mdl_1.nc /data/zender/nco/tmp cf
# ncdismember ~/nco/data/mdl_1.nc /data/zender/nco/tmp nerc
# ncdismember ~/nco/data/mdl_1.nc /data/zender/nco/tmp cf 1.3
# ncdismember ~/nco/data/mdl_1.nc /data/zender/nco/tmp cf 1.5 --fix_rec_dmn=all

# Command-line argument defaults
```

[16] Note that the `-3` switch should appear *after* the `-G` and `-g` switches. This is due to an artifact of the GPE implementation which we wish to remove in the future.

```
fl_in="${HOME}/nco/data/mdl_1.nc" # [sng] Input file to dismember/check
drc_out="${DATA}/nco/tmp" # [sng] Output directory
cf_chk='0' # [flg] Perform CF-compliance check? Which checker?
cf_vrs='1.5' # [sng] Compliance-check this CF version (e.g., '1.5')
opt='' # [flg] Additional ncks options (e.g., '--fix_rec_dmn=all')
# Use single quotes to pass multiple arguments to opt=${5}
# Otherwise arguments would be seen as ${5}, ${6}, ${7} ...

# Command-line argument option parsing
if [ -n "${1}" ]; then fl_in=${1}; fi
if [ -n "${2}" ]; then drc_out=${2}; fi
if [ -n "${3}" ]; then cf_chk=${3}; fi
if [ -n "${4}" ]; then cf_vrs=${4}; fi
if [ -n "${5}" ]; then opt=${5}; fi

# Prepare output directory
echo "NCO dismembering file ${fl_in}"
fl_stb=$(basename ${fl_in})
drc_out=${drc_out}/${fl_stb}
mkdir -p ${drc_out}
cd ${drc_out}
chk_dck='n'
chk_nrc='n'
if [ ${cf_chk} = 'nerc' ]; then
    chk_nrc='y'
fi # chk_nrc
if [ ${cf_chk} != '0' ] && [ ${cf_chk} != 'nerc' ]; then
    chk_dck='y'
    hash cfchecker 2>/dev/null || { echo >&2 "Local cfchecker command not found, w
fi # !cf_chk
# Obtain group list
grp_lst=`ncks --cdl -m ${fl_in} | grep '// group' | awk '{$1=$2=$3="";sub(/^  */,"
IFS=$'\n' # Change Internal-Field-Separator from <Space><Tab><Newline> to <Newline
for grp_in in ${grp_lst} ; do
    # Replace slashes by dots for output group filenames
    grp_out=`echo ${grp_in} | sed 's/\///' | sed 's/\//./g'`
    if [ "${grp_out}" = '' ]; then grp_out='root' ; fi
    # Tell older NCO/netCDF if HDF4 with --hdf4 switch (signified by .hdf/.HDF suf
    hdf4=`echo ${fl_in} | awk '{if(match(tolower($1),".hdf$")) hdf4="--hdf4"; prin
    # Flatten to netCDF3, anchor, no history, no temporary file, padding, HDF4 fla
    cmd="ncks -O -3 -G : -g ${grp_in}/ -h --no_tmp_fl --hdr_pad=40 ${hdf4} ${opt}
    # Use eval in case ${opt} contains multiple arguments separated by whitespace
    eval ${cmd}
    if [ ${chk_dck} = 'y' ]; then
       # Decker checker needs Conventions <= 1.6
       no_bck_sls=`echo ${drc_out}/${grp_out} | sed 's/\\\ / /g'`
       ncatted -h -a Conventions,global,o,c,CF-${cf_vrs} ${no_bck_sls}.nc
```

```
    else # !chk_dck
       echo ${drc_out}/${grp_out}.nc
    fi # !chk_dck
done
if [ ${chk_dck} = 'y' ]; then
    echo 'Decker CFchecker reports CF-compliance of each group in flat netCDF3 format'
    cfchecker -c ${cf_vrs} *.nc
fi
if [ ${chk_nrc} = 'y' ]; then
    # Smallification and NERC upload from qdcf script by Phil Rasch (PJR)
    echo 'Using remote CFchecker http://puma.nerc.ac.uk/cgi-bin/cf-checker.pl'
    cf_lcn='http://puma.nerc.ac.uk/cgi-bin/cf-checker.pl'
    for fl in ${drc_out}/*.nc ; do
        fl_sml=${fl}
        cf_out=${fl%.nc}.html
        dmns=`ncdump -h ${fl_in} | sed -n -e '/dimensions/,/variables/p' | grep = | se
        hyp_sml=''
        for dmn in ${dmns}; do
            dmn_lc=`echo ${dmn} | tr "[:upper:]" "[:lower:]"`
            if [ ${dmn_lc} = 'lat' ] || [ ${dmn_lc} = 'latitude' ] || [ ${dmn_lc} = 'l
                hyp_sml=`echo ${hyp_sml}" -d ${dmn},0"`
            fi # !dmn_lc
        done
        # Create small version of input file by sampling only first element of lat, lo
        ncks -O ${hyp_sml} ${fl} ${fl_sml}
        # Send small file to NERC checker
        curl --form cfversion=1.6 --form upload=@${fl_sml} --form press="Check%20file"
        # Strip most HTML to improve readability
        cat ${cf_out} | sed -e "s/<[^>]*>//g" -e "/DOCTYPE/,/\]\]/d" -e "s/CF-Conventi
        echo "Full NERC compliance-check log for ${fl} in ${cf_out}"
    done
fi # !nerc
EOF
chmod 755 ~/ncdismember # Make command executable
/bin/mv -f ~/ncdismember ~/sh # Store in location on $PATH, e.g., /usr/local/bin

zender@roulee:~$ ncdismember ~/nco/data/mdl_1.nc ${DATA}/nco/tmp
NCO dismembering file /home/zender/nco/data/mdl_1.nc
/data/zender/nco/tmp/mdl_1.nc/cesm.cesm_01.nc
/data/zender/nco/tmp/mdl_1.nc/cesm.cesm_02.nc
/data/zender/nco/tmp/mdl_1.nc/cesm.nc
/data/zender/nco/tmp/mdl_1.nc/ecmwf.ecmwf_01.nc
/data/zender/nco/tmp/mdl_1.nc/ecmwf.ecmwf_02.nc
/data/zender/nco/tmp/mdl_1.nc/ecmwf.nc
/data/zender/nco/tmp/mdl_1.nc/root.nc
```

A (potentially more portable) binary executable could be written to dismember all groups with a single invocation, yet dismembering without loss of information is possible now with this simple script on all platforms with UNIXy utilities. Note that all dimensions inherited by groups in the input file are correctly placed by `ncdismember` into the flat files. Moreover, each output file preserves the group metadata of all ancestor groups, including the global metadata from the input file. As written, the script could fail on groups that contain advanced netCDF4 features because the user requests (with the '`-3`' switch) that output be netCDF3 classic format. However, `ncks` detects many format incompatibilities in advance and works around them. For example, `ncks` autoconverts netCDF4-only atomic-types (such as `NC_STRING` and `NC_UBYTE`) to corresponding netCDF3 atomic types (`NC_CHAR` and `NC_SHORT`) when the output format is netCDF3.

### 3.13.4 Checking CF-compliance

One application of dismembering is to check the CF-compliance of each group in a file. When invoked with the optional third argumnt '`cf`', `ncdismember` passes each file it generates to freely available compliance checkers, such as `cfchecker`[17].

```
zender@roulee:~$ ncdismember ~/nco/data/mdl_1.nc /data/zender/nco/tmp cf
NCO dismembering file /home/zender/nco/data/mdl_1.nc
CFchecker reports CF-compliance of each group in flat netCDF3 format
WARNING: Using the default (non-CF) Udunits database
cesm.cesm_01.nc:
INFO: INIT:      running CFchecker version 1.5.15
INFO: INIT:      checking compliance with convention CF-1.5
INFO: INIT:      using standard name table version: 25, last modified: 2013-07-05T
INFO: INIT:      using area type table version: 2, date: 10 July 2013
INFO: 2.4:       no axis information found in dimension variables, not checking di
WARNING: 3:      variable "tas1" contains neither long_name nor standard_name attr
WARNING: 3:      variable "tas2" contains neither long_name nor standard_name attr
INFO: 3.1:       variable "tas1" does not contain units attribute
INFO: 3.1:       variable "tas2" does not contain units attribute
--------------------------------------------------
cesm.cesm_02.nc:
...
```

By default the CF version checked is determined automatically by `cfchecker`. The user can override this default by supplying a supported CF version, e.g., '`1.3`', as an optional fourth argument to `ncdismember`. Current valid CF options are '`1.0`', '`1.1`', '`1.2`', '`1.3`', '`1.4`', and '`1.5`'.

Our development and testing of `ncdismember` is funded by our involvement in NASA's Dataset Interoperability Working Group (DIWG (`https://wiki.earthdata.nasa.gov/display/ESDSWG/Dataset+Interoperability+Working+Group`)), though our interest extends beyond NASA datasets. Taken together, NCO's features (autoconversion to netCDF3 atomic types, fixing multiple record dimensions, autosensing HDF4 input, scoping rules for CF conventions) make `ncdismember` reliable and friendly for both dismembering hierarchi-

[17] CFchecker is developed by Michael Decker and Martin Schultz at Forschungszentrum Jülich and distributed at `https://bitbucket.org/mde_/cfchecker`.

cal files and for CF-compliance checks. Most HDF4 and HDF5 datasets can be checked for CF-compliance with a one-line command. Example compliance checks of common NASA datasets are at `http://dust.ess.uci.edu/diwg`. Our long-term goal is to enrich the hierarchical data model with the expressivity and syntactic power of CF conventions.

NASA asked the DIWG to prepare a one-page summary of the procedure necessary to check HDF files for CF-compliance:

```
cat > ~/ncdismember.txt << 'EOF'
    Preparing an RPM-based OS to Test HDF & netCDF Files for CF-Compliance

By Charlie Zender, UCI & NASA Dataset Interoperability Working Group (DIWG)

Installation Summary:
1. HDF4 [with internal netCDF support _disabled_]
2. HDF5
3. netCDF [with external HDF4 support _enabled_]
4. NCO
5. numpy
6. netcdf4-python
7. python-lxml
8. CFunits-python
9. CFChecker
10. ncdismember

All 10 packages can use default installs _except_ HDF4 and netCDF.
Following instructions for Fedora Core 20 (FC20), an RPM-based Linux OS
Feedback and changes for other Linux-based OS's welcome to zender at uci.edu
${H4DIR}, ${H5DIR}, ${NETCDFDIR}, ${NCODIR}, may all be different
For simplicity CZ sets them all to /usr/local

# 1. HDF4. Build in non-default manner. Turn-off its own netCDF support.
# Per http://www.unidata.ucar.edu/software/netcdf/docs/build_hdf4.html
# HDF4 support not necessary though it makes ncdismember more comprehensive
wget -c http://www.hdfgroup.org/ftp/HDF/HDF_Current/src/hdf-4.2.9.tar.gz
tar xvzf hdf-4.2.9.tar.gz
cd hdf-4.2.9
./configure --enable-shared --disable-netcdf --disable-fortran --prefix=${H4DIR}
make && make check && make install

# 2. HDF5. Build normally. RPM may work too. Please let me know if so.
# HDF5 is a necessary pre-requisite for netCDF4
wget -c ftp://ftp.unidata.ucar.edu/pub/netcdf/netcdf-4/hdf5-1.8.11.tar.gz
tar xvzf hdf5-1.8.11.tar.gz
cd hdf5-1.8.11
./configure --enable-shared --prefix=${H5DIR}
make && make check && make install
```

```
# 3. netCDF version 4.3.1 or later. Build in non-default manner with HDF4.
# Per http://www.unidata.ucar.edu/software/netcdf/docs/build_hdf4.html
# Earlier versions of netCDF may fail checking some HDF4 files
wget -c ftp://ftp.unidata.ucar.edu/pub/netcdf/netcdf-4.3.2.tar.gz
tar xvzf netcdf-4.3.2.tar.gz
cd netcdf-4.3.2
CPPFLAGS="-I${H5DIR}/include -I${H4DIR}/include" \
LDFLAGS="-L${H5DIR}/lib -L${H4DIR}/lib" \
./configure --enable-hdf4 --enable-hdf4-file-tests
make && make check && make install

# 4. NCO version 4.4.0 or later. Some RPMs available. Or install by hand.
# Later versions of NCO have much better support for ncdismember
wget http://nco.sourceforge.net/src/nco-4.4.4.tar.gz .
tar xvzf nco-4.4.4.tar.gz
cd nco-4.4.4
./configure --prefix=${NCODIR}
make && make install

# 5. numpy
sudo yum install numpy -y

# 6. netcdf4-python
sudo yum install netcdf4-python -y

# 7. python-lxml
sudo yum install python-lxml -y

# 8. CFunits-python. No RPM available. Must install by hand.
# http://code.google.com/p/cfunits-python/
wget http://cfunits-python.googlecode.com/files/cfunits-0.9.6.tar.gz .
tar xvzf cfunits-0.9.6.tar.gz
cd cfunits-0.9.6
sudo python setup.py install

# 9. CFChecker. No RPM available. Must install by hand.
# https://bitbucket.org/mde_/cfchecker
wget https://bitbucket.org/mde_/cfchecker/downloads/CFchecker-1.5.15.tar.bz2 .
tar xvjf CFchecker-1.5.15.tar.bz2
cd CFchecker
sudo python setup.py install

# 10. ncdismember. Copy script from http://nco.sf.net/nco.html#ncdismember
# Store dismembered files somewhere, e.g., ${DATA}/nco/tmp/hdf
mkdir -p ${DATA}/nco/tmp/hdf
# Many datasets work with a simpler command...
ncdismember ~/nco/data/in.nc ${DATA}/nco/tmp/hdf cf 1.5
```

```
ncdismember ~/nco/data/mdl_1.nc ${DATA}/nco/tmp/hdf cf 1.5
ncdismember ${DATA}/hdf/AMSR_E_L2_Rain_V10_200905312326_A.hdf \
            ${DATA}/nco/tmp/hdf cf 1.5
ncdismember ${DATA}/hdf/BUV-Nimbus04_L3zm_v01-00-2012m0203t144121.h5 \
            ${DATA}/nco/tmp/hdf cf 1.5
ncdismember ${DATA}/hdf/HIRDLS-Aura_L3ZAD_v06-00-00-c02_2005d022-2008d077.he5 ${DATA}/:
# Some datasets, typically .h5, require the --fix_rec_dmn=all argument
ncdismember_${DATA}/hdf/GATMO_npp_d20100906_t1935191_e1935505_b00012_c2011070715593206
ncdismember ${DATA}/hdf/mabel_l2_20130927t201800_008_1.h5 \
            ${DATA}/nco/tmp/hdf cf 1.5 --fix_rec_dmn=all
EOF
```

A PDF version of these instructions is available here (`http://dust.ess.uci.edu/diwg/ncdismember.pdf`).

## 3.14 C and Fortran Index conventions

Availability: `ncbo`, `nces`, `ncecat`, `ncflint`, `ncks`, `ncpdq`, `ncra`, `ncrcat`, `ncwa`
Short options: '`-F`'
Long options: '`--fortran`'

The '`-F`' switch changes NCO to read and write with the Fortran index convention. By default, NCO uses C-style (0-based) indices for all I/O. In C, indices count from 0 (rather than 1), and dimensions are ordered from slowest (inner-most) to fastest (outer-most) varying. In Fortran, indices count from 1 (rather than 0), and dimensions are ordered from fastest (inner-most) to slowest (outer-most) varying. Hence C and Fortran data storage conventions represent mathematical transposes of eachother. Note that record variables contain the record dimension as the most slowly varying dimension. See Section 4.9 [ncpdq netCDF Permute Dimensions Quickly], page 254, for techniques to re-order (including transpose) dimensions and to reverse data storage order.

Consider a file `85.nc` containing 12 months of data in the record dimension `time`. The following hyperslab operations produce identical results, a June-July-August average of the data:

```
ncra -d time,5,7 85.nc 85_JJA.nc
ncra -F -d time,6,8 85.nc 85_JJA.nc
```

Printing variable *three_dmn_var* in file `in.nc` first with the C indexing convention, then with Fortran indexing convention results in the following output formats:

```
% ncks -v three_dmn_var in.nc
lat[0]=-90 lev[0]=1000 lon[0]=-180 three_dmn_var[0]=0
...
% ncks -F -v three_dmn_var in.nc
lon(1)=0 lev(1)=100 lat(1)=-90 three_dmn_var(1)=0
...
```

## 3.15 Hyperslabs

Availability: `ncbo`, `nces`, `ncecat`, `ncflint`, `ncks`, `ncpdq`, `ncra`, `ncrcat`, `ncwa`
Short options: '`-d` *dim*,[*min*][,[*max*][,[*stride*]]]'
Long options: '`--dimension` *dim*,[*min*][,[*max*][,[*stride*]]]',
'`--dmn` *dim*,[*min*][,[*max*][,[*stride*]]]'

A *hyperslab* is a subset of a variable's data. The coordinates of a hyperslab are specified with the `-d` *dim*,[*min*][,[*max*][,[*stride*]]] short option (or with the same arguments to the '`--dimension`' or '`--dmn`' long options). At least one hyperslab argument (*min*, *max*, or *stride*) must be present. The bounds of the hyperslab to be extracted are specified by the associated *min* and *max* values. A half-open range is specified by omitting either the *min* or *max* parameter. The separating comma must be present to indicate the omission of one of these arguments. The unspecified limit is interpreted as the maximum or minimum value in the unspecified direction. A cross-section at a specific coordinate is extracted by specifying only the *min* limit and omitting a trailing comma. Dimensions not mentioned are passed with no reduction in range. The dimensionality of variables is not reduced (in the case of a cross-section, the size of the constant dimension will be one).

```
# First and second longitudes
ncks -F -d lon,1,2 in.nc out.nc
# Second and third longitudes
ncks -d lon,1,2 in.nc out.nc
```

As of version 4.2.1 (August, 2012), NCO allows one to extract the last $N$ elements of a hyperslab. Negative integers as *min* or *max* elements of a hyperslab specification indicate offsets from the end (Python also uses this convention). Consistent with this convention, the value '`-1`' (negative one) indicates the last element of a dimension, and negative zero is algebraically equivalent to zero and so indicates the first element of a dimension. Previously, for example, '`-d time,-2,-1`' caused a domain error. Now it means select the penultimate and last timesteps, independent of the size of the `time` dimension. Select only the first and last timesteps, respectively, with '`-d time,0`' and '`-d time,-1`'. Negative integers work for *min* and *max* indices, though not for *stride*.

```
# Second through penultimate longitudes
ncks -d lon,1,-2 in.nc out.nc
# Second through last longitude
ncks -d lon,1,-1 in.nc out.nc
# Second-to-last to last longitude
ncks -d lon,-3,-1 in.nc out.nc
# Second-to-last to last longitude
ncks -d lon,-3, in.nc out.nc
```

The '`-F`' argument, if any, applies the Fortran index convention only to indices specified as positive integers:

```
# First through penultimate longitudes
ncks -F -d lon,1,-2 in.nc out.nc (-F affects only start index)
```

```
# First through last longitude
ncks -F -d lon,1,-1 in.nc out.nc
# Second-to-last to penultimate longitude (-F has no effect)
ncks -F -d lon,-3,-1 in.nc out.nc
# Second-to-last to last longitude (-F has no effect)
ncks -F -d lon,-3, in.nc out.nc
```

Coordinate values should be specified using real notation with a decimal point required in the value, whereas dimension indices are specified using integer notation without a decimal point. This convention serves only to differentiate coordinate values from dimension indices. It is independent of the type of any netCDF coordinate variables. For a given dimension, the specified limits must both be coordinate values (with decimal points) or dimension indices (no decimal points).

If values of a coordinate-variable are used to specify a range or cross-section, then the coordinate variable must be monotonic (values either increasing or decreasing). In this case, command-line values need not exactly match coordinate values for the specified dimension. Ranges are determined by seeking the first coordinate value to occur in the closed range [*min*,*max*] and including all subsequent values until one falls outside the range. The coordinate value for a cross-section is the coordinate-variable value closest to the specified value and must lie within the range or coordinate-variable values. The *stride* argument, if any, must be a dimension index, not a coordinate value. See Section 3.16 [Stride], page 64, for more information on the *stride* option.

```
# All longitude values between 1 and 2 degrees
ncks -d lon,1.0,2.0 in.nc out.nc
# All longitude values between 1 and 2 degrees
ncks -F -d lon,1.0,2.0 in.nc out.nc
# Every other longitude value between 0 and 90 degrees
ncks -F -d lon,0.0,90.0,2 in.nc out.nc
```

As shown, we recommend using a full floating-point suffix of `.0` instead of simply `.` in order to make obvious the selection of hyperslab elements based on coordinate value rather than index.

User-specified coordinate limits are promoted to double-precision values while searching for the indices which bracket the range. Thus, hyperslabs on coordinates of type `NC_CHAR` are computed numerically rather than lexically, so the results are unpredictable.

The relative magnitude of *min* and *max* indicate to the operator whether to expect a *wrapped coordinate* (see Section 3.20 [Wrapped Coordinates], page 70), such as longitude. If *min* > *max*, the NCO expects the coordinate to be wrapped, and a warning message will be printed. When this occurs, NCO selects all values outside the domain [*max* < *min*], i.e., all the values exclusive of the values which would have been selected if *min* and *max* were swapped. If this seems confusing, test your command on just the coordinate variables with `ncks`, and then examine the output to ensure NCO selected the hyperslab you expected (coordinate wrapping is currently only supported by `ncks`).

Because of the way wrapped coordinates are interpreted, it is very important to make sure you always specify hyperslabs in the monotonically increasing sense, i.e., *min* < *max* (even if the underlying coordinate variable is monotonically decreasing). The only exception to this is when you are indeed specifying a wrapped coordinate. The distinction is crucial to understand because the points selected by, e.g., `-d longitude,50.,340.`, are exactly the complement of the points selected by `-d longitude,340.,50.`.

Not specifying any hyperslab option is equivalent to specifying full ranges of all dimensions. This option may be specified more than once in a single command (each hyperslabbed dimension requires its own `-d` option).

## 3.16 Stride

Availability: `ncbo`, `nces`, `ncecat`, `ncflint`, `ncks`, `ncpdq`, `ncra`, `ncrcat`, `ncwa`
Short options: '`-d` *dim*`,`[*min*][`,`[*max*][`,`[*stride*]]]'
Long options: '`--dimension` *dim*`,`[*min*][`,`[*max*][`,`[*stride*]]]',
'`--dmn` *dim*`,`[*min*][`,`[*max*][`,`[*stride*]]]'

All data operators support specifying a *stride* for any and all dimensions at the same time. The *stride* is the spacing between consecutive points in a hyperslab. A *stride* of 1 picks all the elements of the hyperslab, and a *stride* of 2 skips every other element, etc.. `ncks` multislabs support strides, and are more powerful than the regular hyperslabs supported by the other operators (see Section 3.19 [Multislabs], page 67). Using the *stride* option for the record dimension with `ncra` and `ncrcat` makes it possible, for instance, to average or concatenate regular intervals across multi-file input data sets.

The *stride* is specified as the optional fourth argument to the '`-d`' hyperslab specification: `-d` *dim*`,`[*min*][`,`[*max*][`,`[*stride*]]]. Specify *stride* as an integer (i.e., no decimal point) following the third comma in the '`-d`' argument. There is no default value for *stride*. Thus using '`-d time,,,2`' is valid but '`-d time,,,2.0`' and '`-d time,,,`' are not. When *stride* is specified but *min* is not, there is an ambiguity as to whether the extracted hyperslab should begin with (using C-style, 0-based indexes) element 0 or element '`stride-1`'. NCO must resolve this ambiguity and it chooses element 0 as the first element of the hyperslab when *min* is not specified. Thus '`-d time,,,`*stride*' is syntactically equivalent to '`-d time,0,,`*stride*'. This means, for example, that specifying the operation '`-d time,,,2`' on the array '`1,2,3,4,5`' selects the hyperslab '`1,3,5`'. To obtain the hyperslab '`2,4`' instead, simply explicitly specify the starting index as 1, i.e., '`-d time,1,,2`'.

For example, consider a file `8501_8912.nc` which contains 60 consecutive months of data. Say you wish to obtain just the March data from this file. Using 0-based subscripts (see Section 3.14 [C and Fortran Index Conventions], page 61) these data are stored in records 2, 14, ... 50 so the desired *stride* is 12. Without the *stride* option, the procedure is very awkward. One could use `ncks` five times and then use `ncrcat` to concatenate the resulting files together:

```
for idx in 02 14 26 38 50; do # Bourne Shell
  ncks -d time,${idx} 8501_8912.nc foo.${idx}
done
foreach idx (02 14 26 38 50) # C Shell
```

```
  ncks -d time,${idx} 8501_8912.nc foo.${idx}
end
ncrcat foo.?? 8589_03.nc
rm foo.??
```

With the *stride* option, ncks performs this hyperslab extraction in one operation:

```
ncks -d time,2,,12 8501_8912.nc 8589_03.nc
```

See Section 4.8 [ncks netCDF Kitchen Sink], page 237, for more information on ncks.

Applying the *stride* option to the record dimension in ncra and ncrcat makes it possible, for instance, to average or concatenate regular intervals across multi-file input data sets.

```
ncra -F -d time,3,,12 85.nc 86.nc 87.nc 88.nc 89.nc 8589_03.nc
ncrcat -F -d time,3,,12 85.nc 86.nc 87.nc 88.nc 89.nc 8503_8903.nc
```

## 3.17 Record Appending

Availability: ncra, ncrcat
Short options: None
Long options: '--rec_apn', '--record_append'

As of version 4.2.6 (March, 2013), NCO allows both Multi-File, Multi-Record operators (ncra and ncrcat) to append their output directly to the end of an existing file. This feature may be used to augment a target file, rather than construct it from scratch. This helps, for example, when a timeseries is concatenated from input data that becomes available in stages rather than all at once. In such cases this switch significantly speeds writing.

Consider the use case where one wishes to preserve the contents of fl_1.nc, and add to them new records contained in fl_2.nc. Previously the output had to be placed in a third file, fl_3.nc (which could also safely be named fl_2.nc), via

```
ncrcat -O fl_1.nc fl_2.nc fl_3.nc
```

Under the hood this operation copies all information in fl_1.nc and fl_2.nc not once but twice. The first copy is performed through the netCDF interface, as all data from fl_1.nc and fl_2.nc are extracted and placed in the output file. The second copy occurs (usually much) more quickly as the (by default) temporary output file is copied (sometimes a quick re-link suffices) to the final output file (see Section 2.3 [Temporary Output Files], page 17). All this copying is expensive for large files.

The '--record_append' switch appends all records in fl_2.nc to the end (after the last record) of fl_1.nc:

```
ncrcat --rec_apn fl_2.nc fl_1.nc
```

The ordering of the filename arguments may seem non-intuitive. If the record variable represents time in these files, then the values in fl_1.nc precede those in fl_2.nc, so why do the files appear in the reverse order on the command line? fl_1.nc is the last file named because it is the pre-existing output file to which we will append all the other input files listed (in this case only fl_2.nc). The contents of fl_1.nc are completely preserved, and only values in fl_2.nc (and any other input files) are copied. This switch avoids the necessity of copying all of fl_1.nc through the netCDF interface to a new output file. The '--rec_apn' switch automatically puts NCO into append mode (see Section 2.4 [Appending Variables], page 19), so specifying '-A' is redundant, and simultaneously specifying overwrite mode with '-O' causes an error. By default, NCO works in an intermediate temporary file. Power users may combine '--rec_apn' with the '--no_tmp_fl' switch (see Section 2.3 [Temporary Output Files], page 17):

```
ncrcat --rec_apn --no_tmp_fl fl_2.nc fl_1.nc
```

This avoids creating an intermediate file, and copies only the minimal amount of data (i.e., all of fl_2.nc). Hence, it is fast. We recommend users try to understand the safety trade-offs involved.

## 3.18 Subcycle

Availability: ncra, ncrcat
Short options: '-d *dim*,[*min*][,[*max*][,[*stride*][,[*subcycle*]]]]'
Long options: '--mro' '--dimension *dim*,[*min*][,[*max*][,[*stride*][,[*subcycle*]]]]'
'--dmn *dim*,[*min*][,[*max*][,[*stride*][,[*subcycle*]]]]'

As of version 4.2.1 (August, 2012), NCO allows both Multi-File, Multi-Record operators, ncra and ncrcat, to extract and operate on multiple groups of records. These groups may be connected to physical *sub-cycles* of a periodic nature, e.g., months of a year, or hours of a day. Or they may be thought of as groups of a specifed duration. The feature and the terminology to describe it are new. For now, we call this the *subcycle feature*, sometimes abbreviated SSC[18].

The subcycle feature allows processing of groups of records separated by regular intervals of records. It is perhaps best illustrated by an extended example which describes how to solve the same problem both with and without the SSC feature.

The first task in climate data processing is often creating seasonal cycles. Suppose a 150-year climate simulation produces 150 output files, each comprising 12 records, each record a monthly mean: 1850.nc, 1851.nc, ... 1999.nc. Our goal is to create a single file containing the summertime (June, July, and August, aka JJA) mean. Traditionally, we would first compute the climatological monthly mean for each month of summer. Each of these is a 150-year mean, i.e.,

```
# Step 1: Create climatological monthly files clm06.nc..clm08.nc
for mth in {6..8}; do
  mm=`printf "%02d" $mth`
  ncra -O -F -d time,${mm},,12 -n 150,4,1 1850.nc clm${mm}.nc
done
# Step 2: Average climatological monthly files into summertime mean
```

[18] When originally released in 2012 this was called the *duration feature*, and was abbreviated DRN.

```
ncra -O clm06 clm07.nc clm08.nc clm_JJA.nc
```

So far, nothing is unusual and this task can be performed by any NCO version. The SSC feature makes obsolete the need for the shell loop used in Step 1 above.

The new SSC option aggregates more than one input record at a time before performing arithmetic operations, and, with an additional switch, allows us to archive those results in multiple-record output (MRO) files. This reduces the task of producing the climatological summertime mean to one step:

```
# Step 1: Compute climatological summertime mean
ncra -O -F -d time,6,,12,3 -n 150,4,1 1850.nc clm_JJA.nc
```

The SSC option instructs `ncra` (or `ncrcat`) to process files in groups of three records. To better understand the meaning of each argument to the '`-d`' hyperslab option, read it this way: "for the time dimension start with the sixth record, continue without end, repeat the process every twelfth record, and define a sub-cycle as three consecutive records".

A separate option, '`--mro`', instructs `ncra` to output its results from each sub-group, and to produce a *Multi-Record Output* (MRO) file rather than a *Single-Record Output* (SRO) file. Unless '`--mro`' is specified, `ncra` collects together all the sub-groups, operates on their ensemble, and produces a single output record. The addition of '`--mro`' to the above example causes `ncra` to archive all (150) annual summertime means to one file:

```
# Step 1: Archive all 150 summertime means in one file
ncra --mro -O -F -d time,6,,12,3 -n 150,4,1 1850.nc 1850_2009_JJA.nc
# ...or all (150) annual means...
ncra --mro -O -d time,,,12,12 -n 150,4,1 1850.nc 1850_2009.nc
```

These operations generate and require no intermediate files. This contrasts to previous NCO methods, which require generating, averaging, then catenating 150 files. The '`--mro`' option only works on `ncra` and has no effect on (or rather is redundant for) `ncrcat`, since `ncrcat` always outputs all selected records.

## 3.19 Multislabs

Availability: `ncbo`, `nces`, `ncecat`, `ncflint`, `ncks`, `ncpdq`, `ncra`, `ncrcat`
Short options: '`-d` *dim*`,`[*min*][`,`[*max*][`,`[*stride*]]]'
Long options: '`--dimension` *dim*`,`[*min*][`,`[*max*][`,`[*stride*]]]',
'`--dmn` *dim*`,`[*min*][`,`[*max*][`,`[*stride*]]]'
'`--msa_usr_rdr`', '`--msa_user_order`'

A multislab is a union of one or more hyperslabs. One defines multislabs by chaining together hyperslab commands, i.e., *-d* options (see Section 3.15 [Hyperslabs], page 62). Support for specifying a *multi-hyperslab* or *multislab* for any variable was first added to `ncks` in late 2002. The other operators received these capabilities in April 2008. Multi-slabbing is often referred to by the acronym MSA, which stands for "Multi-Slabbing Algorithm". As explained below, the user may additionally request that the multislabs be returned in the user-specified order, rather than the on-disk storage order. Although MSA user-ordering has been available in all operators since 2008, most users were unaware of it since the documentation (below, and in the man pages) was not written until July 2013.

Multislabs overcome many restraints that limit simple hyperslabs. A single *-d* option can only specify a contiguous and/or a regularly spaced multi-dimensional data array. Multislabs are constructed from multiple *-d* options and may therefore have non-regularly spaced arrays. For example, suppose it is desired to operate on all longitudes from 10.0 to 20.0 and from 80.0 to 90.0 degrees. The combined range of longitudes is not selectable in a single hyperslab specfication of the form '-d *dimension,min,max*' or '-d *dimension,min,max,stride*' because its elements are irregularly spaced in coordinate space (and presumably in index space too). The multislab specification for obtaining these values is simply the union of the hyperslabs specifications that comprise the multislab, i.e.,

```
ncks -d lon,10.,20. -d lon,80.,90. in.nc out.nc
ncks -d lon,10.,15. -d lon,15.,20. -d lon,80.,90. in.nc out.nc
```

Any number of hyperslabs specifications may be chained together to specify the multislab. MSA creates an output dimension equal in size to the sum of the sizes of the multislabs. This can be used to extend and or pad coordinate grids.

Users may specify redundant ranges of indices in a multislab, e.g.,

```
ncks -d lon,0,4 -d lon,2,9,2 in.nc out.nc
```

This command retrieves the first five longitudes, and then every other longitude value up to the tenth. Elements 0, 2, and 4 are specified by both hyperslab arguments (hence this is redundant) but will count only once if an arithmetic operation is being performed. This example uses index-based (not coordinate-based) multislabs because the *stride* option only supports index-based hyper-slabbing. See Section 3.16 [Stride], page 64, for more information on the *stride* option.

Multislabs are more efficient than the alternative of sequentially performing hyperslab operations and concatenating the results. This is because NCO employs a novel multislab algorithm to minimize the number of I/O operations when retrieving irregularly spaced data from disk. The NCO multislab algorithm retrieves each element from disk once and only once. Thus users may take some shortcuts in specifying multislabs and the algorithm will obtain the intended values. Specifying redundant ranges is not encouraged, but may be useful on occasion and will not result in unintended consequences.

Suppose the *Q* variable contains three dimensional arrays of distinct chemical constituents in no particular order. We are interested in the NOy species in a certain geographic range. Say that NO, NO2, and N2O5 are elements 0, 1, and 5 of the *species* dimension of *Q*. The multislab specification might look something like

```
ncks -d species,0,1 -d species,5 -d lon,0,4 -d lon,2,9,2 in.nc out.nc
```

Multislabs are powerful because they may be specified for every dimension at the same time. Thus multislabs obsolete the need to execute multiple `ncks` commands to gather the desired range of data.

The MSA user-order switch '`--msa_usr_rdr`' (or '`--msa_user_order`', both of which shorten to '`--msa`') requests that the multislabs be output in the user-specified order from the command-line, rather than in the input-file on-disk storage order. This allows the user to perform complex data re-ordering in one operation that would otherwise require cumbersome steps of hyperslabbing, concatenating, and permuting. Consider the example of converting datasets stored with the longitude coordinate `Lon` ranging from [−180,180) to datasets that follow the [0,360) convention.

```
% ncks -H -v Lon in.nc
Lon[0]=-180
Lon[1]=-90
Lon[2]=0
Lon[3]=90
```

What is needed is a simple way to rotate longitudes. Although simple in theory, this task requires both mathematics to change the numerical value of the longitude coordinate, data hyperslabbing to split the input on-disk arrays at Greenwich, and data re-ordering within to stitch the western hemisphere onto the eastern hemisphere at the date-line. The '`--msa`' user-order switch overrides the default that data are output in the same order in which they are stored on-disk in the input file, and instead stores them in the same order as the multi-slabs are given to the command line. This default is intuitive and is not important in most uses. However, the MSA user-order switch allows users to meet their output order needs by specifying multi-slabs in a certain order. Compare the results of default ordering to user-ordering for longitude:

```
% ncks -O -H       -v Lon -d Lon,0.,180. -d Lon,-180.,-1.0 in.nc
Lon[0]=-180
Lon[1]=-90
Lon[2]=0
Lon[3]=90
% ncks -O -H --msa -v Lon -d Lon,0.,180. -d Lon,-180.,-1.0 in.nc
Lon[0]=0
Lon[1]=90
Lon[2]=-180
Lon[3]=-90
```

The two multi-slabs are the same but they can be presented to screen, or to an output file, in either order. The second example shows how to place the western hemisphere after the eastern hemisphere, although they are stored in the opposite order in the input file.

With this background, one sees that the following commands suffice to rotate the input file by 180 degrees longitude:

```
% ncks -O -v LatLon --msa -d Lon,0.,180. -d Lon,-180.,-1.0 in.nc out.nc
% ncap2 -O -s 'where(Lon < 0) Lon=Lon+360' out.nc out.nc
% ncks -C -H -v LatLon ~/nco/data/in.nc
Lat[0]=-45 Lon[0]=-180 LatLon[0]=0
Lat[0]=-45 Lon[1]=-90 LatLon[1]=1
Lat[0]=-45 Lon[2]=0 LatLon[2]=2
Lat[0]=-45 Lon[3]=90 LatLon[3]=3
Lat[1]=45 Lon[0]=-180 LatLon[4]=4
Lat[1]=45 Lon[1]=-90 LatLon[5]=5
Lat[1]=45 Lon[2]=0 LatLon[6]=6
```

```
Lat[1]=45 Lon[3]=90 LatLon[7]=7
% ncks -C -H -v LatLon ~/out.nc
Lat[0]=-45 Lon[0]=0 LatLon[0]=2
Lat[0]=-45 Lon[1]=90 LatLon[1]=3
Lat[0]=-45 Lon[2]=180 LatLon[2]=0
Lat[0]=-45 Lon[3]=270 LatLon[3]=1
Lat[1]=45 Lon[0]=0 LatLon[4]=6
Lat[1]=45 Lon[1]=90 LatLon[5]=7
Lat[1]=45 Lon[2]=180 LatLon[6]=4
Lat[1]=45 Lon[3]=270 LatLon[7]=5
```

There are other workable, valid methods to accomplish this rotation, yet none are simpler nor more efficient than utilizing MSA user-ordering. Some final comments on applying this algorithm: Be careful to specify hemispheres that do not overlap, e.g., by inadvertently specifying coordinate ranges that both include Greenwich. Some users will find using index-based rather than coordinate-based hyperslabs makes this clearer.

## 3.20 Wrapped Coordinates

Availability: `ncks`
Short options: '`-d` *dim*,[*min*][,[*max*][,[*stride*]]]'
Long options: '`--dimension` *dim*,[*min*][,[*max*][,[*stride*]]]',
'`--dmn` *dim*,[*min*][,[*max*][,[*stride*]]]'

A *wrapped coordinate* is a coordinate whose values increase or decrease monotonically (nothing unusual so far), but which represents a dimension that ends where it begins (i.e., wraps around on itself). Longitude (i.e., degrees on a circle) is a familiar example of a wrapped coordinate. Longitude increases to the East of Greenwich, England, where it is defined to be zero. Halfway around the globe, the longitude is 180 degrees East (or West). Continuing eastward, longitude increases to 360 degrees East at Greenwich. The longitude values of most geophysical data are either in the range [0,360), or [−180,180). In either case, the Westernmost and Easternmost longitudes are numerically separated by 360 degrees, but represent contiguous regions on the globe. For example, the Saharan desert stretches from roughly 340 to 50 degrees East. Extracting the hyperslab of data representing the Sahara from a global dataset presents special problems when the global dataset is stored consecutively in longitude from 0 to 360 degrees. This is because the data for the Sahara will not be contiguous in the *input-file* but is expected by the user to be contiguous in the *output-file*. In this case, `ncks` must invoke special software routines to assemble the desired output hyperslab from multiple reads of the *input-file*.

Assume the domain of the monotonically increasing longitude coordinate `lon` is $0 < lon < 360$. `ncks` will extract a hyperslab which crosses the Greenwich meridian simply by specifying the westernmost longitude as *min* and the easternmost longitude as *max*. The following commands extract a hyperslab containing the Saharan desert:

```
ncks -d lon,340.,50. in.nc out.nc
```

```
ncks -d lon,340.,50. -d lat,10.,35. in.nc out.nc
```

The first example selects data in the same longitude range as the Sahara. The second example further constrains the data to having the same latitude as the Sahara. The coordinate `lon` in the *output-file*, `out.nc`, will no longer be monotonic! The values of `lon` will be, e.g., '`340, 350, 0, 10, 20, 30, 40, 50`'. This can have serious implications should you run `out.nc` through another operation which expects the `lon` coordinate to be monotonically increasing. Fortunately, the chances of this happening are slim, since `lon` has already been hyperslabbed, there should be no reason to hyperslab `lon` again. Should you need to hyperslab `lon` again, be sure to give dimensional indices as the hyperslab arguments, rather than coordinate values (see Section 3.15 [Hyperslabs], page 62).

## 3.21 Auxiliary Coordinates

Availability: `ncbo`, `nces`, `ncecat`, `ncflint`, `ncks`, `ncpdq`, `ncra`, `ncrcat`
Short options: '`-X` *`lon_min,lon_max,lat_min,lat_max`*'
Long options: '`--auxiliary` *`lon_min,lon_max,lat_min,lat_max`*'

Utilize auxiliary coordinates specified in values of the coordinate variable's `standard_name` attributes, if any, when interpreting hyperslab and multi-slab options. Also '`--auxiliary`'. This switch supports hyperslabbing cell-based grids (aka unstructured grids) over coordinate ranges. This works on datasets that associate coordinate variables to grid-mappings using the CF-convention (see Section 3.41 [CF Conventions], page 131) `coordinates` and `standard_name` attributes described here (`http://cfconventions.org/1.6.html#coordinate-system`). Currently, NCO understands auxiliary coordinate variables pointed to by the `standard_name` attributes for *latitude* and *longitude*. Cells that contain a value within the user-specified range [*lon_min,lon_max,lat_min,lat_max*] are included in the output hyperslab.

A cell-based or unstructured grid collapses the horizontal spatial information (latitude and longitude) and stores it along a one-dimensional coordinate that has a one-to-one mapping to both latitude and longitude coordinates. Rectangular (in longitude and latitude) horizontal hyperslabs cannot be selected using the typical procedure (see Section 3.15 [Hyperslabs], page 62) of separately specifying '`-d`' arguments for longitude and latitude. Instead, when the '`-X`' is used, NCO learns the names of the latitude and longitude coordinates by searching the `standard_name` attribute of all variables until it finds the two variables whose `standard_name`'s are "latitude" and "longitude", respectively. This `standard_name` attribute for latitude and longitude coordinates follows the CF-convention (see Section 3.41 [CF Conventions], page 131).

Putting it all together, consider a variable *gds_3dvar* output from simulations on a cell-based geodesic grid. Although the variable contains three dimensions of data (time, latitude, and longitude), it is stored in the netCDF file with only two dimensions, `time` and `gds_crd`.

```
% ncks -m -C -v gds_3dvar ~/nco/data/in.nc
gds_3dvar: type NC_FLOAT, 2 dimensions, 4 attributes, chunked? no, \
 compressed? no, packed? no, ID = 41
```

```
gds_3dvar RAM size is 10*8*sizeof(NC_FLOAT) = 80*4 = 320 bytes
gds_3dvar dimension 0: time, size = 10 NC_DOUBLE, dim. ID = 20 \
 (CRD)(REC)
gds_3dvar dimension 1: gds_crd, size = 8 NC_FLOAT, dim. ID = 17 (CRD)
gds_3dvar attribute 0: long_name, size = 17 NC_CHAR, value = \
 Geodesic variable
gds_3dvar attribute 1: units, size = 5 NC_CHAR, value = meter
gds_3dvar attribute 2: coordinates, size = 15 NC_CHAR, value = \
 lat_gds lon_gds
gds_3dvar attribute 3: purpose, size = 64 NC_CHAR, value = \
 Test auxiliary coordinates like those that define geodesic grids
```

The `coordinates` attribute lists the names of the latitude and longitude coordinates, `lat_gds` and `lon_gds`, respectively. The `coordinates` attribute is recommended though optional. With it, the user can immediately identify which variables contain the latitude and longitude coordinates. Without a `coordinates` attribute it would be unclear at first glance whether a variable resides on a cell-based grid. In this example, `time` is a normal record dimension and `gds_crd` is the cell-based dimension.

The cell-based grid file must contain two variables whose `standard_name` attributes are "latitude", and "longitude":

```
% ncks -m -C -v lat_gds,lon_gds ~/nco/data/in.nc
lat_gds: type NC_DOUBLE, 1 dimensions, 4 attributes, \
 chunked? no, compressed? no, packed? no, ID = 37
lat_gds RAM size is 8*sizeof(NC_DOUBLE) = 8*8 = 64 bytes
lat_gds dimension 0: gds_crd, size = 8 NC_FLOAT, dim. ID = 17 (CRD)
lat_gds attribute 0: long_name, size = 8 NC_CHAR, value = Latitude
lat_gds attribute 1: standard_name, size = 8 NC_CHAR, value = latitude
lat_gds attribute 2: units, size = 6 NC_CHAR, value = degree
lat_gds attribute 3: purpose, size = 62 NC_CHAR, value = \
 1-D latitude coordinate referred to by geodesic grid variables

lon_gds: type NC_DOUBLE, 1 dimensions, 4 attributes, \
 chunked? no, compressed? no, packed? no, ID = 38
lon_gds RAM size is 8*sizeof(NC_DOUBLE) = 8*8 = 64 bytes
lon_gds dimension 0: gds_crd, size = 8 NC_FLOAT, dim. ID = 17 (CRD)
lon_gds attribute 0: long_name, size = 9 NC_CHAR, value = Longitude
lon_gds attribute 1: standard_name, size = 9 NC_CHAR, value = longitude
lon_gds attribute 2: units, size = 6 NC_CHAR, value = degree
lon_gds attribute 3: purpose, size = 63 NC_CHAR, value = \
 1-D longitude coordinate referred to by geodesic grid variables
```

In this example `lat_gds` and `lon_gds` represent the latitude or longitude, respectively, of cell-based variables. These coordinates (must) have the same single dimension (`gds_crd`, in this case) as the cell-based variables. And the coordinates must be one-dimensional—multidimensional coordinates will not work.

This infrastructure allows NCO to identify, interpret, and process (e.g., hyperslab) the variables on cell-based grids as easily as it works with regular grids. To time-average all the values between zero and 180 degrees longitude and between plus and minus 30 degress latitude, we use

```
ncra -O -X 0.,180.,-30.,30. -v gds_3dvar in.nc out.nc
```

NCO accepts multiple '-X' arguments for cell-based grid multi-slabs, just as it accepts multiple '-d' arguments for multi-slabs of regular coordinates.

```
ncra -O -X 0.,180.,-30.,30. -X 270.,315.,45.,90. in.nc out.nc
```

The arguments to '-X' are always interpreted as floating-point numbers, i.e., as coordinate values rather than dimension indices so that these two commands produce identical results

```
ncra -X 0.,180.,-30.,30. in.nc out.nc
ncra -X 0,180,-30,30 in.nc out.nc
```

In contrast, arguments to '-d' require decimal places to be recognized as coordinates not indices (see Section 3.15 [Hyperslabs], page 62). We recommend always using decimal points with '-X' arguments to avoid confusion.

## 3.22 Grid Generation

Availability: `ncks`
Short options: None
Long options: '`--rgr` *`key`*=*`val`*' (multiple invocations allowed)

As of NCO version 4.5.2 (August, 2015), `ncks` generates accurate and complete SCRIP-format gridfiles for select grid types, including uniform, capped and Gaussian rectangular latitude/longitude grids. The grids are stored in an external *grid-file*.

All options pertinent to the grid geometry and metadata are passed to NCO via key-value pairs prefixed by the '`--rgr`' option, or its synonym, '`--regridding`'. The option '`--rgr`' (and its long option equivalents such as '`--regridding`') indicates the argument syntax will be *key*=*val*. As such, '`--rgr`' and its synonyms are indicator options that accept arguments supplied one-by-one like '`--rgr key1=val1 --rgr key2=val2`', or aggregated together in multi-argument format like '`--rgr key1=val1#key2=val2`' (see Section 3.4.2 [Multi-arguments], page 32).

The text strings that describe the grid and name the file are important aids to convey the grid geometry to other users. These arguments, and their corresponding keys, are the grid title (*grd_ttl*), and grid filename (*grid*), respectively. The numbers of latitudes (*lat_nbr*) and longitudes (*lon_nbr*) are independent, and together determine the grid storage size. These four options should be considered mandatory, although NCO provides defaults for any arguments omitted.

The remaining arguments depend on the whether the grid is global or regional. For global grids, one should specify only two more arguments, the latitude (*lat_typ*) and longitude (*lon_typ*) grid-types. These types are chosen as described below from a small selection of options that together define the most common rectangular global grids. For regional grids, one must specify the bounding box, i.e., the edges of the rectangular grid on the North (*lat_nrt*), South (*lat_sth*), East (*lat_est*), and West (*lat_nrt*) sides. Specifying a bounding box for global grids is redundant and will cause an error to ensure the user intends a global grid. NCO assumes that regional grids are uniform, though it will attempt to produce regional grids of other types if the user specifies other latitude (*lat_typ*) and longitude (*lon_typ*) grid-types, e.g., Gaussian or Cap. Edges of a regional bounding box may be specified individually, or in the single-argument forms.

The full description of grid-generation arguments, and their corresponding keys, is:

*Grid Title: grd_ttl*

It is surprisingly difficult to discern the geometric configuration of a grid from the coordinates of a SCRIP-format gridfile. A human-readable grid description should be placed in *grd_ttl*. Examples include "CAM-FV scalar grid 129x256" and "T42 Gaussian grid".

*Grid File: grid*

The grid-generation API was bolted-on to NCO and is somewhat primitive, e.g., having to repeat the '`--rgr`' option. Another aspect of this is that the output grid filename is distinct from the output filename of the host `ncks` command. Specify the output gridfile name with *grid*, e.g., `t42_SCRIP.20150901.nc`. It is conventional to include a datestamp in the gridfile name. This helps users identify up-to-date and out-of-date grids. Any valid netCDF file may be named as the source (e.g., `in.nc`). It will not be altered. The destination file (e.g., `foo.nc`) will be overwritten. Its contents are immaterial.

*Grid Types: lat_typ, lon_typ*

The keys that hold the longitude and latitude gridtypes (which are, by the way, independent of eachother) are *lon_typ* and *lat_typ*. The *lat_typ* options for global grids are '`uni`' for Uniform, '`cap`' (or '`fv`') for Capped (equivalent to FV), and '`gss`' for Gaussian. These values are all case-independent, so '`Gss`' and '`gss`' both work.

As its name suggests, the latitudes in a Uniform-latitude grid are uniformly spaced[19]. The Uniform-latitude grid may have any number of latitudes. NCO can only generate longitude grids (below) that are uniformly spaced, so the Uniform-latitude grids we describe are also uniform in the 2D sense. Uniform grids are intuitive, easy to visualize, and simple to program. Hence their popularity in data exchange, visualization, and archives. Moreover, regional grids (unless they include the poles), are free of polar singularities, and thus are well-suited to storage on Uniform grids. Theoretically, a Uniform-latitude

---

[19] A Uniform grid in latitude could be called "equi-angular" in latitude, but NCO reserves the term Equi-angular or "eqa" for grids that have the same uniform spacing in both latitude and longitude, e.g., 1°x1° or 2°x2°. NCO reserves the term Regular to refer to grids that are monotonic and rectangular grids. Confusingly, the angular spacing in a Regular grid need not be uniform, it could be irregular, such as in a Gaussian grid. The term Regular is not too useful in grid-generation, because so many other parameters (spacing, centering) are necessary to disambiguate it.

grid could have non-uniform longitudes, but NCO currently does not implement non-uniform longitude grids.

Their mathematical properties (convergence and excessive resolution at the poles, which can appear as singularities) make Uniform grids fraught for use in global models. One purpose Uniform grids serve in modeling is as "offset" or "staggered" grids, meaning grids whose centers are the interfaces of another grid. The Finite-Volume (FV) method is often used to represent and solve the equations of motion in climate-related fields. Many FV solutions (including the popular Lin-Rood method as used in the CESM CAM-FV atmospheric model) evaluate scalar (i.e., non-vector) fields (e.g., temperature, water vapor) at gridcell centers of what is therefore called the scalar grid. FV methods (like Lin-Rood) that employ an Arakawa C-grid or D-grid formulation define velocities on the edges of the scalar grid. This CAM-FV velocity grid is therefore "staggered" or "offset" from the CAM-FV scalar grid by one-half gridcell. The CAM-FV scalar latitude grid has gridpoints (the "caps") centered on each pole to avoid singularities. The offset of a Cap-grid is a Uniform-grid, so the Uniform grid is often called an FV-"offset" or "staggered" grid. Hence an NCO Uniform grid is equivalent to an NCL "Fixed Offset" grid. For example, a 128x256 Uniform grid is the offset or staggered version of a 129x256 Cap grid (aka FV-grid).

Referring the saucer-like cap-points at the poles, NCO uses the term "Cap grid" to describe the latitude portion of the FV-scalar grid as used by the CAM-FV Lin-Rood dynamics formulation. NCO accepts the shorthand FV, and the more descriptive "Yarmulke", as synonyms for Cap. A Cap-latitude grid differs from a Uniform-latitude grid in many ways:

Most importantly, Cap grids are 2D-representations of numerical grids with cap-midpoints instead of zonal-teeth convergence at the poles. The rectangular 2D-representation of each cap contains gridcells shaped like sharp teeth that converge at the poles similar to the Uniform grid, but the Cap gridcells are meant to be aggregated into a single cell centered at the pole in a dynamical transport algorithm. In other words, the polar teeth are a convenient way to encode a non-rectangular grid in memory into a rectangular array on disk. Hence Cap grids have the unusual property that the poles are labeled as being both the centers and the outer interfaces of all polar gridcells. Second, Cap grids are uniform in angle except at the poles, where the latitudes span half the meridional range of the rest of the gridcells. Even though in the host dynamical model the Cap grid polar points are melded into caps uniform (in angle) with the rest of the grid, the disk representation on disk is not uniform. Nevertheless, some call the Cap grid a uniform-angle grid because the information contained at the poles is aggregated in memory to span twice the range of a single polar gridcell (which has half the normal width). NCL uses the term "Fixed grid" for a Cap grid. The "Fixed" terminology seems broken.

Finally, Gaussian grids are the Cartesian representation of global spectral transform models. Gaussian grids do not have points at the poles, and must have an even number of latitudes. All three latitude grid-type supported by NCO (Uniform, Cap, and Gaussian) are Regular grids in that they are monotonic.

The *lon_typ* options for global grids are '`grn_ctr`' and '`180_ctr`' for the first gridcell centered at Greenwich or 180 degrees, respecitvely. And '`grn_wst`' and '`180_wst`' for Greenwich or 180 degress lying on the western edge of the first gridcell. Many global models use the '`grn_ctr`' longitude grid as their "scalar grid" (where, e.g., temperature, humidity, and other scalars are defined). The "staggered" or "offset" grid (where often the dynamics variables are defined) then must have the '`grn_wst`' longitude convention. That way the centers of the scalar grid are the vertices of the offset grid, and visa versa.

*Grid Resolution: lat_nbr, lon_nbr*
The number of gridcells in the horizontal spatial dimensions are *lat_nbr* and *lon_nbr*, respectively. There are no restrictions on *lon_nbr* for any gridtype. Latitude grids do place some restrictions on *lat_nbr* (see above). As of NCO version 4.5.3, released in October, 2015, the '`--rgr latlon=lat_nbr,lon_nbr`' switch may be used to simultaneously specify both latitude and longitude, e.g., '`--rgr latlon=180,360`'.

*Grid Edges: lon_wst, lon_est, lat_sth, lat_nrt*
The outer edges of a regional rectangular grid are specified by the North (*lat_nrt*), South (*lat_sth*), East (*lat_est*), and West (*lat_nrt*) sides. Latitudes and longigudes must be specified in degrees (not radians). Latitude edges must be between -90 and 90. Longitude edges may be positive or negative and separated by no more than 360 degrees. The edges may be specified individually with four arguments, consecutively separated by the multi-argument delimiter ('`#`' by default), or together in a short list to the pre-ordered options '`wesn`' or '`snwe`'. These three specifications are equivalent:

```
ncks ... --rgr lat_sth=30.0 --rgr lat_nrt=70.0 --rgr lon_wst=-120.0 --r
ncks ... --rgr lat_sth=30.0#lat_nrt=70.0#lon_wst=-120.0#lon_est=-90.0 .
ncks ... --rgr snwe=30.0,70.0,-120.0,-90.0 ...
```

The first example above supplies the bounding box with four *key=val* pairs. The second example above supplies the bounding box with a single option in multi-argument format (see Section 3.4.2 [Multi-arguments], page 32). The third example uses a convenience switch introduced to reduce typing.

Generating common grids:

```
# 180x360 (1x1 degree) Equi-Angular grid, first longitude centered at Greenwich
ncks --rgr grd_ttl='Equi-Angular grid 180x360' --rgr grid=${DATA}/grids/180x360_SC
     --rgr latlon=180,360 --rgr lat_typ=uni --rgr lon_typ=grn_ctr ~zender/nco/data

# 129x256 CAM-FV grid, first longitude centered at Greenwich
ncks --rgr grd_ttl='CAM-FV scalar grid 129x256' --rgr grid=${DATA}/grids/129x256_S
     --rgr latlon=129,256 --rgr lat_typ=fv --rgr lon_typ=grn_ctr ~zender/nco/data/

# 128x256 Equi-Angular grid, Greenwich west edge of first longitude
# This is the CAM-FV offset grid for the 129x256 CAM-FV scalar grid above
ncks --rgr grd_ttl='Equi-Angular grid 128x256' --rgr grid=${DATA}/grids/128x256_SC
     --rgr latlon=128,256 --rgr lat_typ=uni --rgr lon_typ=grn_wst ~zender/nco/data
```

```
# T42 Gaussian grid, first longitude centered at Greenwich
ncks --rgr grd_ttl='T42 Gaussian grid' --rgr grid=${DATA}/grids/t42_SCRIP.20150901.nc
     --rgr latlon=64,128 --rgr lat_typ=gss --rgr lon_typ=grn_ctr ~zender/nco/data/in.n

# NASA Climate Modeling Grid (CMG) 3600x7200 (0.05x0.05 degree) Equi-Angular grid
# Date-line west edge of first longitude, east edge of last longitude
ncks --rgr grd_ttl='Equi-Angular grid 3600x7200 (NASA CMG)' --rgr grid=${DATA}/grids/3
     --rgr latlon=3600,7200 --rgr lat_typ=uni --rgr lon_typ=180_wst ~zender/nco/data/i
```

Often researchers face the problem not of generating a known, idealized grid but of understanding an unknown, possibly irregular or curvilinear grid underlying a dataset produced elsewhere. NCO will *infer* the grid of a datafile by examining its coordinates (and boundaries, if available), reformat that information as necessary to diagnose gridcell areas, and output the results in SCRIP format. As of NCO version 4.5.3, released in October, 2015, the '`--rgr nfr='y'`' switch activates the machinery to infer the grid rather than construct the grid from other user-specified switches. To infer the grid properties, NCO interrogates *input-file* for horizontal coordinate information, such as the presence of dimension names rooted in latitude/longitude-naming traditions and conventions. Once NCO identifies the likely horizontal dimensions it looks for horizontal coordinates and bounds. If bounds are not found, NCO assumes the underlying grid comprises quadrilateral cells whose edges are midway between cell centers, for both rectilinear and curvilinear grids.

```
# Infer the grid of the AIRS swath from input, write it to grd_airs.nc
ncks --rgr nfr=y --rgr grid=${DATA}/sld/rgr/grd_airs.nc \
     ${DATA}/sld/raw/AIRS.2014.10.01.202.L2.TSurfStd.Regrid010.1DLatLon.nc ~/foo.nc
```

When inferring grids, the grid file (`grd_airs.nc`) is written, the input file (`AIRS...nc`) is read, and the output file (`foo.nc`) is overwritten (its contents are immaterial).

Another task that arises in regridding is characterizing new grids. In such cases it can be helpful to have a "skeleton" version of a dataset on the grid, so that grid center and interfaces locations can be assessed, continental outlines can be examined, or the skeleton can be manually populated with data rather than relying on a model. SCRIP files can be difficult to visualize and manipulate, so NCO will provide, if requested, a so-called skeleton file on the user-specified grid. As of NCO version 4.5.3, released in October, 2015, the '`--rgr skl=fl_skl`' switch outputs the skeleton file to *fl_skl*. The skeleton file may then be examined in a dataset viewer, populated with data, and generally serve as a template for what to expect from datasets of the same geometry.

```
# Generate T42 Gaussian grid file t42_SCRIP.nc and skeleton file t42_skl.nc
ncks --rgr skl=${DATA}/grids/t42_skl.nc --rgr grid=${DATA}/grids/t42_SCRIP.nc \
     --rgr latlon=64,128 --rgr lat_typ=gss --rgr lon_typ=Grn_ctr \
     ~zender/nco/data/in.nc ~/foo.nc
```

When generating skeleton files, both the grid file (`t42_SCRIP.nc`) and the skeleton file (`t42_skl.nc`) are written, the input file (`in.nc`) is ignored, and the output file (`foo.nc`) is overwritten (its contents are immaterial).

## 3.23 Regridding

Availability: `ncclimo`, `ncks`, `ncremap`
Short options: None
Long options: '`--map` *map-file*' or '`--rgr_map` *map-file*'
'`--rgr` *key=val*' (multiple invocations allowed)
'`--rnr=`*wgt_thr*' or '`--rgr_rnr=`*wgt_thr*' or '`--renormalize=`*wgt_thr*'

NCO includes extensive regridding features in `ncclimo` (as of version 4.6.0 in May, 2016), `ncremap` (as of version 4.5.4 in November, 2015) and `ncks` (since version 4.5.0 in June, 2015). Regridding can involve many choices, options, inputs, and outputs. The appropriate operator for this workflow is the `ncremap` script which automatically handles many details of regridding and passes the required commands to `ncks` and external programs. Occasionally users need access to lower-level remapping functionality present in `ncks` and not exposed to direct manipulation through `ncremap` or `ncclimo`. This section describes the lower-level functionality and switches as implemented in `ncks`. Knowing what these features are will help `ncremap` and `ncclimo` users understand the full potential of these operators.

`ncks` supports horizontal regridding of datasets where the grids and weights are all stored in an external *map-file*. Use the '`--map`' or '`--rgr_map`' options to specify the *map-file*, and NCO will regrid the *input-file* to a new (or possibly the same, aka, an identity mapping) horizontal grid in the *output-file*, using the input and output grids and mapping weights specified in the ESMF- or SCRIP-format *map-file*. Currently NCO understands only the mapfile format pioneered by SCRIP (`http://oceans11.lanl.gov/svn/SCRIP/trunk/SCRIP`) and later extended by ESMF (`http://www.earthsystemcog.org/projects/regridweightgen`), and adopted (along with Exodus) by TempestRemap (`https://github.com/ClimateGlobalChange/tempestremap.git`). See those references for documentation on map formats, grid specification, and weight generation.

The regridding currently supported by NCO could equally well be called weight-application. NCO reads-in pre-stored weights from the *map-file* and applies them to (almost) every variable, thereby creating a regridded *output-file*. Specify regridding with a standard `ncks` command and options along with the additional specification of a *map-file*:

```
# Regrid entire file, same output format as input:
ncks --map=map.nc in.nc out.nc
# Entire file, netCDF4 output:
ncks -4 --map=map.nc in.nc out.nc
# Deflated netCDF4 output
ncks -4 -L 1 --map=map.nc in.nc out.nc
# Selected variables
ncks -v FS.?,T --map=map.nc in.nc out.nc
# Threading
ncks -t 8 --map=map.nc in.nc out.nc
# Deflated netCDF4 output, threading, selected variables:
ncks -4 -L 1 -t 8 -v FS.?,T --map=map.nc in.nc out.nc
```

OpenMP threading works well with regridding large datasets. Threading improves throughput of regridding 1–10 GB files by factors of 2–5. Options specific to regridding are described below.

NCO supports 1D⇒1D, 1D⇒2D, 2D⇒1D, and 2D⇒2D regridding for any unstructured 1D-grid and any rectangular 2D-grid. This has been tested by converting among and between Gaussian, equiangular, FV, unstructured cubed-sphere grids, and regionally refined grids. Support for irregular 2D- and regional grids (e.g., swath-like data) is planned.

Conservative regridding is, for first-order accurate algorithms, a straightforward procedure of identifying gridcell overlap and apportioning values correctly from source to destination. The presence of missing values forces a decision on how to handle destination gridcells where some but not all source cells are valid. NCO allows the user to choose between two distinct algorithms: "conservative" and "renormalized". The "conservative" algorithm uses all valid data from the input grid on the output grid once and only once. Destination cells receive the weighted valid values of the source cells. This is conservative because the global integrals of the source and destination fields are equal. The "renormalized" algorithm divides the destination value by the sum of the valid weights. This produces values equal to the mean of the valid input values, but extended to the entire destination gridcell. Thus renormalization is equivalent to extrapolating valid data to missing regions. Input and output integrals are unequal and renormalized regridding is not conservative. Both algorithms produce identical answers when no missing data maps to the destination gridcell.

By default, NCO implements the "conservative" algorithm because it has useful properties, is simpler to understand, and requires no additional parameters. To employ the "renormalized" algorithm instead, use the '`--rnr`', '`--rgr_rnr`', or '`--renormalize`' options to supply *wgt_thr*, the threshold weight for valid destination values. Valid values must cover at least the fraction *wgt_thr* of the destination gridcell to meet the threshold for a non-missing destination value. When *wgt_thr* is exceeded, the mean valid value is renormalized by the valid area and placed in the destination gridcell. If the valid area covers less than *wgt_thr*, then the destination gridcell is assigned the missing value. Valid values of *wgt_thr* range from zero to one. Keep in mind though, that this threshold is potentially a divisor, and values of zero or very near to zero can lead to floating-point underflow and divide-by-zero errors. For convenience NCO permits users to specify a *wgt_thr* = 0.0 threshold weight. This indicates that any valid data should be represented and renormalized on the output grid.

```
ncks           --map=map.nc in.nc out.nc # Conservative regridding
ncks --rnr=0.1 --map=map.nc in.nc out.nc # Renormalized regridding
```

The first example uses the default conservative algorithm. The second example specifies that valid values must cover at least 10% of the destination gridcell to meet the threshold for a non-missing destination value. With valid destination areas of, say 25% or 50%, the renormalized algorithm would produce destination values greater than the conservative algorithm by factors of four or two, respectively.

In practice, it may make sense to use the default "conservative" algorithm when performing conservative regridding, and the "renormalized" algorithm when performing other regridding such as bilinear interpolation or nearest-neighbor. Another consideration is whether the fields being regridded are fluxes or state variables. For example, temperature (unlike heat) or concentrations (amount per unit volume) are not physically conserved quantities under areal-regridding so it often makes sense to interpolate them in a non-conservative fashion, to preserve their fine-scale structure. Few researchers can digest the unphysical values of temperature that the "conservative" option will produce in regions rife with missing values. A counter-example is fluxes, which should be physically conserved under areal-regridding. One should consider both the type of field and its conservation properties before choosing a regridding strategy.

NCO automatically annotates the output with relevant metadata such as coordinate bounds, axes, and vertices (à la CF). These annotations include

*Horizontal Dimension Names: lat, lon*
: The name of the horizontal spatial dimensions assumed to represent latitude and longitude in 2D rectangular input files are *lat_nm* and *lon_nm*, which default to `lat` and `lon`, respectively. Variables that contain a *lat_nm*-dimension and a *lon_nm*-dimension on a 2D-rectangular input grid will be regridded, and variables regridded to a 2D-rectangular output grid will all contain the *lat_nm*- and *lon_nm*-dimensions, and variables regridded to a 1D-unstructured output grid will have *lat_nm* and *lon_nm* as auxiliary coordinate variables. To treat different dimensions and variables as latitude and longitude, use the options '`--rgr lat_nm=lat_nm`' and '`--rgr lon_nm=lon_nm`'. Note that, for now at least, *lat_nm* and *lon_nm* indicate both the variable names associated *and*, where applicable (i.e., on 2D-grids), the dimensions of the horizontal coordinates.

*Unstructured Dimension Name: col*
: The name of the horizontal spatial dimension assumed to delineate an unstructured grid is *col_nm*, which defaults to `ncol` (number of columns), the name CAM employs. Other common names for the columns in an unstructured grid include `lndgrid` (used by CLM), and `nCells` (used by MPAS-O). Variables that contain the *col_nm*-dimension on an unstructured input grid will be regridded, and regridded variables written to an unstructured output grid will all contain the *col_nm*-dimension. To treat a different dimension as unstructured, use the option '`--rgr col_nm=col_nm`'. Note: Often there is no coordinate variable for the *col_nm*-dimension, i.e., there is no variable named *col_nm*, although such a coordinate could contain useful information about the unstructured grid.

*Structured Grid Standard Names and Units*
: Longitude and latitude coordinates (both regular and auxiliary, i.e., for unstructured grids) receive CF `standard_name` values of `latitude` and `longitude`, CF `axes` attributes with values `X` and `Y`, and `units` attributes with values `degrees_east` and `degrees_north`, respectively.

*Unstructured Grid Auxiliary Coordinates*
: Unstructured grid auxiliary coordinates for longitude and latitude receive CF `coordinates` attributes with values `lon` and `lat`, respectively.

*Structured Grid Bounds Variables: bnd, lat_bnd, lon_bnd*
: Structured grids with 1D-coordinates use the dimension *bnd_nm* (which defaults to `nbnd`) with the spatial bounds variables in *lat_bnd_nm* and *lon_bnd_nm*

which default to `lon_bnds` and `lat_bnds`, respectively. By default spatial bounds for such structured grids parallel the oft-used temporal bounds dimension (`nbnd=2`) and variable (`time_bnds`). Bounds are attached to the horizontal spatial dimensions via their `bounds` attributes. Change the spatial bounds dimension with the option '`--rgr bnd_nm=bnd_nm`'. Rename the spatial bounds variables with the options '`--rgr lat_bnd_nm=lat_bnd_nm`' and '`--rgr lon_bnd_nm=lon_bnd_nm`'.

*Unstructured Grid Bounds Variables: bnd, lat_bnd, lon_bnd*

Unstructured grids with 1D-coordinates use the dimension *bnd_nm* (which defaults to `nv`, number of vertices) for the spatial bounds variables *lat_bnd_nm* and *lon_bnd_nm* which default to `lat_vertices` and `lon_vertices`, respectively. It may be impossible to re-use the temporal bounds dimension (often `nbnd`) for unstructure grids, because the gridcells are not rectangles, and thus require specification of all vertices for each gridpoint, rather than only two parallel interfaces per dimension. These bounds are attached to the horizontal spatial dimensions via their `bounds` attributes. Change the spatial bounds dimension with the option '`--rgr bnd_nm=bnd_nm`'. Rename the spatial bounds variables with the options '`--rgr lat_bnd_nm=lat_bnd_nm`' and '`--rgr lon_bnd_nm=lon_bnd_nm`'. The temporal bounds dimension in unstructured grid output remains as in the *input-file*, usually `nbnd`.

*Gridcell Area: area*

The variable *area_nm* (which defaults to `area`) is always (re-)created in the *output_file* to hold the gridcell area in steradians. To store the area in a different variable, use the option '`--rgr area=area_nm`'. The *area_nm* variable receives a `standard_name` attribute of `cell_area`, a `units` attribute of `steradian` (the SI unit of solid angle), and a `cell_methods` attribute with value `lat, lon: sum`, which indicates that *area_nm* is *extensive*, meaning that its value depends on the gridcell boundaries. Since *area_nm* is a property of the grid, it is read directly from the *map-file* rather than regridded itself.

*Gridcell Fraction: frc*

The variable *frc_nm* (which defaults to `frac_b`) is automatically copied to the *output_file* to hold the valid fraction of each gridcell when certain conditions are met. First, the regridding method must be conservative. Second, at least one value of *frc_nm* must be non-unity. These conditions ensure that whenever fractional gridcells affect the regridding, they are also placed in the output file. To store the fraction in a different variable, use the option '`--rgr frc_nm=frc_nm`'. The *frc_nm* variable receives a `cell_methods` attribute with value `lat, lon: sum`, which indicates that *frc_nm* is *extensive*, meaning that its value depends on the gridcell boundaries. Since *frc_nm* is a property of the grid, it is read directly from the *map-file* rather than regridded itself.

*Latitude weights: lat_wgt*

Rectangular 2D-grids use the variable *lat_wgt_nm*, which defaults to `gw` (originally for "Gaussian weight"), to store the 1D-weight appropriate for area-weighting the latitude grid. To store the latitude weight in a different variable, use the option '`--rgr lat_wgt=lat_wgt_nm`'. The *lat_wgt_nm* variable will not appear in 1D-grid output. Weighting statistics by latitude (i.e., by *lat_wgt_nm* will produce the same answers (up-to round-off error) as weighting by area (i.e., by *area_nm*) in grids that have both variables. The former requires less memory because *lat_wgt_nm* is 1D), whereas the latter is more general because *area_nm* works on *any* grid.

*Provenance Attributes*
The *map-file* and *input-file* names are stored in the *output-file* global attributes `mapping_file` and `source_file`, respectively.

One may supply muliple '`--rgr key=value`' options to simultaneously customize multiple grid-field names. The following examples may all be assumed to end with the standard options '`--map=map.nc in.nc out.nc`'.

```
ncks --rgr lat_nm=latitude --rgr lon_nm=longitude
ncks --rgr col_nm=column --rgr lat_wgt=lat_wgt
ncks --rgr bnd_nm=bounds --rgr lat_bnd_nm=lat_bounds --rgr lon_bnd_nm=lon_bounds
ncks --rgr bnd_nm=vertices --rgr lat_bnd_nm=lat_vrt --rgr lon_bnd_nm=lon_vrt
```

The first command causes the regridder to associate the latitude and longitude dimensions with the dimension names `latitude` and `longitude` (instead of the defaults, `lat` and `lon`). The second command causes the regridder to associate the independent columns in an unstructured grid with the dimension name `column` (instead of the default, `ncol`) and the variable containing latitude weights to be named `lat_wgt` (instead of the default, `gw`). The third command associates the latitude and longitude bounds with the dimension `bounds` (instead of the default, `nbnd`) and the variables `lat_bounds` and `lon_bounds` (instead of the defaults, `lat_bnds` and `lon_bnds`, respectively). The fourth command associates the latitude and longitude bounds with the dimension `vertices` (instead of the default, `nv`) and the variables `lat_vrt` and `lon_vrt` (instead of the defaults, `lat_vertices` and `lon_vertices`, respectively).

When used with an identity remapping files, regridding can signficantly enhance the metadata and therefore the dataset usability. Consider these selected metadata (those unchanged are not shown for brevity) associated with the variable `FSNT` from typical unstructured grid (CAM-SE cubed-sphere) output before and after an identity regridding:

```
# Raw model output before regridding
netcdf ne30_FSNT {
  dimensions:
    nbnd = 2 ;
    ncol = 48602 ;
    time = UNLIMITED ; // (1 currently)

  variables:
    float FSNT(time,ncol) ;
      FSNT:long_name = "Net solar flux at top of model" ;

    double time(time) ;
      time:long_name = "time" ;
      time:bounds = "time_bnds" ;
```

```
    double time_bnds(time,nbnd) ;
      time_bnds:long_name = "time interval endpoints" ;
} // group /

# Same model output after identity regridding
netcdf dogfood {
  dimensions:
    nbnd = 2 ;
    ncol = 48602 ;
    nv = 5 ;
    time = 1 ;

  variables:
    float FSNT(time,ncol) ;
      FSNT:long_name = "Net solar flux at top of model" ;
      FSNT:coordinates = "lat lon" ;

    double lat(ncol) ;
      lat:long_name = "latitude" ;
      lat:standard_name = "latitude" ;
      lat:units = "degrees_north" ;
      lat:axis = "Y" ;
      lat:bounds = "lat_vertices" ;
      lat:coordinates = "lat lon" ;

    double lat_vertices(ncol,nv) ;
      lat_vertices:long_name = "gridcell latitude vertices" ;

    double lon(ncol) ;
      lon:long_name = "longitude" ;
      lon:standard_name = "longitude" ;
      lon:units = "degrees_east" ;
      lon:axis = "X" ;
      lon:bounds = "lon_vertices" ;
      lon:coordinates = "lat lon" ;

    double lon_vertices(ncol,nv) ;
      lon_vertices:long_name = "gridcell longitude vertices" ;

    double time(time) ;
      time:long_name = "time" ;
      time:bounds = "time_bnds" ;

    double time_bnds(time,nbnd) ;
      time_bnds:long_name = "time interval endpoints" ;
} // group /
```

The raw model output lacks the CF coordinates and bounds attributes that the regridder adds. The metadata turns lat and lon into auxiliary coordinate variables (see Section 3.21 [Auxiliary Coordinates], page 71) which can then be hyperslabbed (with '-X') using latitude/longitude coordinates bounding the region of interest:

```
% ncks -u -H -X 314.6,315.3,-35.6,-35.1 -v FSNT dogfood.nc
time[0]=31 ncol[0] FSNT[0]=344.575 W/m2

ncol[0] lat[0]=-35.2643896828 degrees_north

ncol[0] nv[0] lat_vertices[0]=-35.5977213708
ncol[0] nv[1] lat_vertices[1]=-35.5977213708
ncol[0] nv[2] lat_vertices[2]=-35.0972113817
ncol[0] nv[3] lat_vertices[3]=-35.0972113817
ncol[0] nv[4] lat_vertices[4]=-35.0972113817

ncol[0] lon[0]=315 degrees_east

ncol[0] nv[0] lon_vertices[0]=315
ncol[0] nv[1] lon_vertices[1]=315
ncol[0] nv[2] lon_vertices[2]=315.352825437
ncol[0] nv[3] lon_vertices[3]=314.647174563
ncol[0] nv[4] lon_vertices[4]=314.647174563

time[0]=31 days since 1979-01-01 00:00:00

time[0]=31 nbnd[0] time_bnds[0]=0
time[0]=31 nbnd[1] time_bnds[1]=31
```

Thus auxiliary coordinate variables help to structure unstructured grids. The expanded metadata annotations from an identity regridding may obviate the need to place unstructured data on a rectangular grid. For example, statistics for regions that can be expressed as unions of rectangular regions can now be performed on the native (unstructured) grid.

Here are some quick examples of regridding from common models. All examples require 'in.nc out.nc' at the end.

```
# Identity re-map ACME CAM-SE Cubed-Sphere output (to improve metadata)
ncks --map=${DATA}/maps/map_ne30np4_to_ne30np4_aave.20150603.nc
# Convert ACME CAM-SE Cubed Sphere output to rectangular lat/lon
ncks --map=${DATA}/maps/map_ne30np4_to_fv129x256_aave.150418.nc
# Convert CAM3 T42 output to Cubed-Sphere grid
ncks --map=${DATA}/maps/map_ne30np4_to_t42_aave.20150601.nc
```

## 3.24 UDUnits Support

Availability: ncbo, nces, ncecat, ncflint, ncks, ncpdq, ncra, ncrcat, ncwa
Short options: '-d *dim*, [*min*] [, [*max*] [, [*stride*]]]'
Long options: '--dimension *dim*, [*min*] [, [*max*] [, [*stride*]]]',
'--dmn *dim*, [*min*] [, [*max*] [, [*stride*]]]'

There is more than one way to hyperskin a cat. The UDUnits (http://www.unidata.ucar.edu/software/udunits) package provides a library which, if present, NCO uses to translate user-specified physical dimensions into the physical dimensions of data stored in netCDF files. Unidata provides UDUnits under the same terms as netCDF, so sites should install both. Compiling NCO with UDUnits support is currently optional but may become required in a future version of NCO.

Two examples suffice to demonstrate the power and convenience of UDUnits support. First, consider extraction of a variable containing non-record coordinates with physical dimensions stored in MKS units. In the following example, the user extracts all wavelengths in the visible portion of the spectrum in terms of the units very frequently used in visible spectroscopy, microns:

```
% ncks -C -H -v wvl -d wvl,"0.4 micron","0.7 micron" in.nc
wvl[0]=5e-07 meter
```

The hyperslab returns the correct values because the *wvl* variable is stored on disk with a length dimension that UDUnits recognizes in the units attribute. The automagical algorithm that implements this functionality is worth describing since understanding it helps one avoid some potential pitfalls. First, the user includes the physical units of the hyperslab dimensions she supplies, separated by a simple space from the numerical values of the hyperslab limits. She encloses each coordinate specifications in quotes so that the shell does not break the *value-space-unit* string into separate arguments before passing them to NCO. Double quotes ("*foo*") or single quotes ('*foo*') are equally valid for this purpose. Second, NCO recognizes that units translation is requested because each hyperslab argument contains text characters and non-initial spaces. Third, NCO determines whether the *wvl* is dimensioned with a coordinate variable that has a units attribute. In this case, *wvl* itself is a coordinate variable. The value of its units attribute is meter. Thus *wvl* passes this test so UDUnits conversion is attempted. If the coordinate associated with the variable does not contain a units attribute, then NCO aborts. Fourth, NCO passes the specified and desired dimension strings (microns are specified by the user, meters are required by NCO) to the UDUnits library. Fifth, the UDUnits library that these dimension are commensurate and it returns the appropriate linear scaling factors to convert from microns to meters to NCO. If the units are incommensurate (i.e., not expressible in the same fundamental MKS units), or are not listed in the UDUnits database, then NCO aborts since it cannot determine the user's intent. Finally, NCO uses the scaling information to convert the user-specified hyperslab limits into the same physical dimensions as those of the corresponding cooridinate variable on disk. At this point, NCO can perform a coordinate hyperslab using the same algorithm as if the user had specified the hyperslab without requesting units conversion.

The translation and dimensional interpretation of time coordinates shows a more powerful, and probably more common, UDUnits application. In this example, the user prints all data between 4 PM and 7 PM on December 8, 1999, from a variable whose time dimension is hours since the year 1900:

```
% ncks -u -H -C -v time_udunits -d time_udunits,"1999-12-08 \
  16:00:0.0","1999-12-08 19:00:0.0" in.nc
time_udunits[1]=876018 hours since 1900-01-01 00:00:0.0
```

Here, the user invokes the stride (see Section 3.16 [Stride], page 64) capability to obtain every other timeslice. This is possible because the UDUnits feature is additive, not exclusive—it works in conjunction with all other hyperslabbing (see Section 3.15 [Hyperslabs], page 62) options and in all operators which support hyperslabbing. The following example shows how one might average data in a time period spread across multiple input files

```
ncra -d time,"1939-09-09 12:00:0.0","1945-05-08 00:00:0.0" \
  in1.nc in2.nc in3.nc out.nc
```

Note that there is no excess whitespace before or after the individual elements of the '`-d`' argument. This is important since, as far as the shell knows, '`-d`' takes only *one* command-line argument. Parsing this argument into its component `dim,[min][,[max][,[stride]]]` elements (see Section 3.15 [Hyperslabs], page 62) is the job of NCO. When unquoted whitespace is present between these elements, the shell passes NCO arugment fragments which will not parse as intended.

NCO implemented support for the UDUnits2 library with version 3.9.2 (August, 2007). The UDUnits2 (`http://www.unidata.ucar.edu/software/udunits/udunits-2/udunits2.html`) package supports non-ASCII characters and logarithmic units. We are interested in user-feedback on these features.

One aspect that deserves mention is that UDUnits, and thus NCO, supports run-time definition of the location of the relevant UDUnits databases. With UDUnits version 1, users may specify the directory which contains the UDUnits database, `udunits.dat`, via the `UDUNITS_PATH` environment variable. With UDUnits version 2, users may specify the UDUnits database file itself, `udunits2.xml`, via the `UDUNITS2_XML_PATH` environment variable.

```
# UDUnits1
export UDUNITS_PATH='/unusual/location/share/udunits'
# UDUnits2
export UDUNITS2_XML_PATH='/unusual/location/share/udunits/udunits2.xml'
```

This run-time flexibility can enable the full functionality of pre-built binaries on machines with libraries in different locations.

The UDUnits (`http://www.unidata.ucar.edu/software/udunits`) package documentation describes the supported formats of time dimensions. Among the metadata conventions that adhere to these formats are the Climate and Forecast (CF) Conventions (`http://cf-pcmdi.llnl.gov`) and the Cooperative Ocean/Atmosphere Research Data Service (COARDS) Conventions (`http://ferret.wrc.noaa.gov/noaa_coop/coop_cdf_profile.html`). The following '`-d arguments`' extract the same data using commonly encountered time dimension formats:

```
-d time,'1918-11-11 00:00:0.0','1939-09-09 00:00:0.0'
```

```
-d time,'1918-11-11 00:00:0.0','1939-09-09 00:00:0.0'
-d time,'1918-11-11T00:00:0.0Z','1939-09-09T00:00:0.0Z'
-d time,'1918-11-11','1939-09-09'
-d time,'1918-11-11','1939-9-9'
```

All of these formats include at least one dash - in a non-leading character position (a dash in a leading character position is a negative sign). NCO assumes that a space, colon, or non-leading dash in a limit string indicates that a UDUnits units conversion is requested. Some date formats like YYYYMMDD that are valid in UDUnits are ambiguous to NCO because it cannot distinguish a purely numerical date (i.e., no dashes or text characters in it) from a coordinate or index value:

```
-d time,1918-11-11 # Interpreted as the date November 11, 1918
-d time,19181111   # Interpreted as time-dimension index 19181111
-d time,19181111.  # Interpreted as time-coordinate value 19181111.0
```

Hence, use the YYYY-MM-DD format rather than YYYYMMDD for dates.

As of version 4.0.0 (January, 2010), NCO supports some calendar attributes specified by the CF conventions.

**Supported types:**
"365_day"/"noleap", "360_day", "gregorian", "standard"

**Unsupported types:**
"366_day"/"all_leap","proleptic_gregorian","julian","none"

Unsupported types default to mixed Gregorian/Julian as defined by UDUnits.

An Example: Consider the following netCDF variable

```
variables:
  double lon_cal(lon_cal) ;
    lon_cal:long_name = "lon_cal" ;
    lon_cal:units = "days since 1964-2-28 0:0:0" ;
    lon_cal:calendar = "365_day" ;
data:
  lon_cal = 1,2,3,4,5,6,7,8,9,10;
```

'`ncks -v lon_cal -d lon_cal,'1964-3-1 0:00:0.0','1964-3-4 00:00:0.0'`' results in `lon_cal=1,2,3,4`.

netCDF variables should always be stored with MKS (i.e., God's) units, so that application programs may assume MKS dimensions apply to all input variables. The UDUnits feature is intended to alleviate some of the NCO user's pain when handling MKS units. It connects users who think in human-friendly units (e.g., miles, millibars, days) to extract data which are always stored in God's units, MKS (e.g., meters, Pascals, seconds). The feature is not intended to encourage writers to store data in esoteric units (e.g., furlongs, pounds per square inch, fortnights).

## 3.25 Rebasing Time Coordinate

Availability: `ncra`, `ncrcat` Short options: None

Time rebasing is invoked when numerous files share a common record coordinate, and the record coordinate basetime (not the time increment, e.g., days or hours) changes among input files. The rebasing is performed automatically if and only if UDUnits is installed. Rebasing occurs when the record coordinate is a time-based variable, and times are recorded in units of a time-since-basetime, and the basetime changes from file to file. Since the output file can have only one unit (i.e., one basetime) for the record coordinate, NCO, in such cases, chooses the units of the first input file to be the units of the output file. It is necessary to "rebase" all the input record variables to this output time unit in order for the output file to have the correct values.

For example suppose the time coordinate is in hours and each day in January is stored in its own daily file. Each daily file records the temperature variable `tpt(time)` with an (unadjusted) `time` coordinate value between 0–23 hours, and uses the `units` attribute to advance the base time:

```
file01.nc time:units="hours since 1990-1-1"
file02.nc time:units="hours since 1990-1-2"
...
file31.nc time:units="hours since 1990-1-31"

// Mean noontime temperature in January
ncra -v tpt -d time,"1990-1-1 12:00:00","1990-1-31 23:59:59",24 \
      file??.nc noon.nc

// Concatenate day2 noon through day3 noon records
ncrcat -v tpt -d time,"1990-1-2 12:00:00","1990-1-3 11:59:59" \
      file01.nc file02.nc file03.nc noon.nc

// Results: time is "re-based" to the time units in "file01.nc"
time=36, 37, 38, 39, 40, 41, 42, 43, 44, 45, 46, 47, 48, 49, 50, \
     51, 52, 53, 54, 55, 56, 57, 58, 59 ;

// If we repeat the above command but with only two input files...
ncrcat -v tpt -d time,"1990-1-2 12:00:00","1990-1-3 11:59:59" \
      file02.nc file03 noon.nc

// ...then output time coordinate is based on time units in "file02.nc"
time = 12, 13, 14, 15, 16, 17, 18, 19, 20, 21, 22, 23, 24, 25, \
     26, 27, 28, 29, 30, 31, 32, 33, 34, 35 ;
```

As of NCO version 4.2.1 (August, 2012), NCO automatically rebases not only the record coordinate (`time`, here) but also any cell boundaries associated with the record coordinate (e.g., `time_bnds`) (see Section 3.41 [CF Conventions], page 131).

As of NCO version 4.4.9 (May, 2015), NCO also rebases any climatology boundaries associated with the record coordinate (e.g., `climatology_bounds`) (see Section 3.41 [CF Conventions], page 131).

As of NCO version 4.6.3 (December, 2016), NCO also rebases the time coordinate when the unit between files differ For example the first file may have `units="days since 2014-03-01"` and the second file `units="hours since 2014-03-10 00:00"`.

## 3.26 Multiple Record Dimensions

Availability: `ncecat`, `ncpdq` Short options: None
Long options: '`--mrd`'

The netCDF3 file format allows only one record dimension, and that dimension must be the first dimension (i.e., the least rapidly varying dimension) of any variable in which it appears. This imposes certain rules on how operators must perform operations that alter the ordering of dimensions or the number of record variables. The netCDF4 file format has no such restrictions. Files and variables may have any number of record dimensions in any order. This additional flexibility of netCDF4 can only be realized by selectively abandoning the constraints that would make operations behave completely consistently between netCDF3 and netCDF4 files.

NCO chooses, by default, to impose netCDF3-based constraints on netCDF4 files. This reduces the number of unanticipated consequences and keeps the operators functioning in a familiar way. Put another way, NCO limits production of additional record dimensions so processing netCDF4 files leads to the same results as processing netCDF3 files. Users can override this default with the '`--mrd`' (or '`--multiple_record_dimension`') switch, which enables netCDF4 variables to accumulate additional record dimensions.

How can additional record dimensions be produced? Most commonly `ncecat` (in record-aggregate mode) defines a new leading record dimension. In netCDF4 files this becomes an additional record dimension unless the original record dimension is changed to a fixed dimension (as must be done in netCDF3 files). Also when `ncpdq` reorders dimensions it can preserve the "record" property of record variables. `ncpdq` tries to define as a record dimension whichever dimension ends up first in a record variable, and, in netCDF4 files, this becomes an additional record dimension unless the original record dimension is changed to a fixed dimension (as must be done in netCDF3 files). It it easier if `ncpdq` and `ncecat` do not increase the number of record dimensions in a variable so that is the default. Use '`--mrd`' to override this.

## 3.27 Missing values

Availability: `ncap2`, `ncbo`, `nces`, `ncflint`, `ncpdq`, `ncra`, `ncwa`
Short options: None

The phrase *missing data* refers to data points that are missing, invalid, or for any reason not intended to be arithmetically processed in the same fashion as valid data. The NCO arithmetic operators attempt to handle missing data in an intelligent fashion. There are four steps in the NCO treatment of missing data:

1. Identifying variables that may contain missing data.

   NCO follows the convention that missing data should be stored with the *_FillValue* specified in the variable's `_FillValue` attributes. The *only* way NCO recognizes that a variable *may* contain missing data is if the variable has a `_FillValue` attribute. In this case, any elements of the variable which are numerically equal to the *_FillValue* are treated as missing data.

   NCO adopted the behavior that the default attribute name, if any, assumed to specify the value of data to ignore is `_FillValue` with version 3.9.2 (August, 2007). Prior to that, the `missing_value` attribute, if any, was assumed to specify the value of data to ignore. Supporting both of these attributes simultaneously is not practical. Hence the behavior NCO once applied to *missing_value* it now applies to any *_FillValue*. NCO now treats any *missing_value* as normal data[20].

   It has been and remains most advisable to create both `_FillValue` and `missing_value` attributes with identical values in datasets. Many legacy datasets contain only `missing_value` attributes. NCO can help migrating datasets between these conventions. One may use `ncrename` (see Section 4.13 [ncrename netCDF Renamer], page 278) to rename all `missing_value` attributes to `_FillValue`:

   ```
   ncrename -a .missing_value,_FillValue inout.nc
   ```

   Alternatively, one may use `ncatted` (see Section 4.2 [ncatted netCDF Attribute Editor], page 200) to add a `_FillValue` attribute to all variables

   ```
   ncatted -O -a _FillValue,,o,f,1.0e36 inout.nc
   ```

2. Converting the *_FillValue* to the type of the variable, if neccessary.

   Consider a variable *var* of type *var_type* with a `_FillValue` attribute of type *att_type* containing the value *_FillValue*. As a guideline, the type of the `_FillValue` attribute should be the same as the type of the variable it is attached to. If *var_type* equals *att_type* then NCO straightforwardly compares each value of *var* to *_FillValue* to determine which elements of *var* are to be treated as missing data. If not, then NCO converts *_FillValue* from *att_type* to *var_type* by using the implicit conversion rules of C, or, if *att_type* is `NC_CHAR`[21], by typecasting the results of the C function `strtod(_FillValue)`. You may use the NCO operator `ncatted` to change the `_FillValue` attribute and all data whose data is *_FillValue* to a new value (see Section 4.2 [ncatted netCDF Attribute Editor], page 200).

3. Identifying missing data during arithmetic operations.

   When an NCO arithmetic operator processes a variable *var* with a `_FillValue` attribute, it compares each value of *var* to *_FillValue* before performing an operation. Note the *_FillValue* comparison imposes a performance penalty on the operator. Arithmetic processing of variables which contain the `_FillValue` attribute always incurs this penalty, even when none of the data are missing. Conversely, arithmetic processing of

---

[20] The old functionality, i.e., where the ignored values are indicated by `missing_value` not `_FillValue`, may still be selected *at NCO build time* by compiling NCO with the token definition *CPPFLAGS='-UNCO_USE_FILL_VALUE'*.

[21] For example, the DOE ARM program often uses *att_type* = `NC_CHAR` and *_FillValue* = '`-99999.`'.

variables which do not contain the `_FillValue` attribute never incurs this penalty. In other words, do not attach a `_FillValue` attribute to a variable which does not contain missing data. This exhortation can usually be obeyed for model generated data, but it may be harder to know in advance whether all observational data will be valid or not.

4. Treatment of any data identified as missing in arithmetic operators.

   NCO averagers (`ncra`, `nces`, `ncwa`) do not count any element with the value *_FillValue* towards the average. `ncbo` and `ncflint` define a *_FillValue* result when either of the input values is a *_FillValue*. Sometimes the *_FillValue* may change from file to file in a multi-file operator, e.g., `ncra`. NCO is written to account for this (it always compares a variable to the *_FillValue* assigned to that variable in the current file). Suffice it to say that, in all known cases, NCO does "the right thing".

   It is impossible to determine and store the correct result of a binary operation in a single variable. One such corner case occurs when both operands have differing *_FillValue* attributes, i.e., attributes with different numerical values. Since the output (result) of the operation can only have one *_FillValue*, some information may be lost. In this case, NCO always defines the output variable to have the same *_FillValue* as the first input variable. Prior to performing the arithmetic operation, all values of the second operand equal to the second *_FillValue* are replaced with the first *_FillValue*. Then the arithmetic operation proceeds as normal, comparing each element of each operand to a single *_FillValue*. Comparing each element to two distinct *_FillValue*'s would be much slower and would be no likelier to yield a more satisfactory answer. In practice, judicious choice of *_FillValue* values prevents any important information from being lost.

## 3.28 Chunking

Availability: `ncap2`, `ncbo`, `nces`, `ncecat`, `ncflint`, `ncks`, `ncpdq`, `ncra`, `ncrcat`, `ncwa`
Short options: none
Long options: '`--cnk_byt` *`sz_byt`*', '`--chunk_byte` *`sz_byt`*'
'`--cnk_dmn` *`dmn_nm,sz_lmn`*', '`--chunk_dimension` *`dmn_nm,sz_lmn`*'
, '`--cnk_map` *`cnk_map`*', '`--chunk_map` *`cnk_map`*',
'`--cnk_min` *`sz_byt`*', '`--chunk_min` *`sz_byt`*',
'`--cnk_plc` *`cnk_plc`*', '`--chunk_policy` *`cnk_plc`*',
'`--cnk_scl` *`sz_lmn`*', '`--chunk_scalar` *`sz_lmn`*'

All netCDF4-enabled NCO operators that define variables support a plethora of chunksize options. Chunking can significantly accelerate or degrade read/write access to large datasets. Dataset chunking issues are described by THG and Unidata here (`http://www.hdfgroup.org/HDF5/doc/H5.user/Chunking.html`), here (`http://www.unidata.ucar.edu/blogs/developer/en/entry/chunking_data_why_it_matters`), and here (`http://www.unidata.ucar.edu/blogs/developer/en/entry/chunking_data_choosing_shapes`). NCO authors are working on generalized algorithms and applications of chunking strategies (stay tuned for more in 2017).

The NCO chunking implementation is designed to be flexible. Users control four aspects of the chunking implementation. These are the *chunking policy*, *chunking map*, *chunksize*, and *minimum chunksize*. The chunking policy determines *which* variables to chunk, and the chunking map determines how (with what exact sizes) to chunk those variables. These are high-level mechanisms that apply to an entire file and all variables and dimensions. The chunksize option allows per-dimension specification of sizes that will override the selected (or default) chunking map.

The distinction between elements and bytes is subtle yet crucial to understand. Elements refers to values of an array, whereas bytes refers to the memory size required to hold the elements. These measures differ by a factor of four or eight for `NC_FLOAT` or `NC_DOUBLE`, respectively. The option '`--cnk_scl`' takes an argument *sz_lmn* measured in elements. The options '`--cnk_byt`' and '`--cnk_min`' take arguments *sz_byt* measured in bytes.

Use the '`--cnk_min=sz_byt`' option to set the minimum size in bytes (not elements) of variables to chunk. This threshold is intended to restrict use of chunking to variables for which it is efficient. By default this minimum variable size for chunking is twice the system blocksize (when available) and is 8192 bytes otherwise. Users may set this to any value with the '`--cnk_min=sz_byt`' switch. To guarantee that chunking is performed on all arrays, regardless of size, set the minimum size to one byte (not to zero bytes).

The chunking implementation is similar to a hybrid of the `ncpdq` packing policies (see Section 4.9 [ncpdq netCDF Permute Dimensions Quickly], page 254) and hyperslab specifications (see Section 3.15 [Hyperslabs], page 62). Each aspect is intended to have a sensible default, so that many users only need to set one switch to obtain sensible chunking. Power users can tune chunking with the three switches in tandem to obtain optimal performance.

By default, NCO preserves the chunking characteristics of the input file in the output file[22]. In other words, preserving chunking requires no switches or user intervention.

Users specify the desired chunking policy with the '`-P`' switch (or its long option equivalents, '`--cnk_plc`' and '`--chunk_policy`') and its *cnk_plc* argument. As of August, 2014, six chunking policies are implemented:

*Chunk All Variables*

Definition: Chunk all variables possible. For obvious reasons, scalar variables cannot be chunked.
Alternate invocation: `ncchunk`
*cnk_plc* key values: '`all`', '`cnk_all`', '`plc_all`'
Mnemonic: All

*Chunk Variables with at least Two Dimensions [default]*

Definition: Chunk all variables possible with at least two dimensions
Alternate invocation: none
*cnk_plc* key values: '`g2d`', '`cnk_g2d`', '`plc_g2d`'

[22] This behavior became the default in November 2014 with NCO version 4.4.7. Prior versions would always use netCDF default chunking in the output file when no NCO chunking switches were activated, regardless of the chunking in the input file.

Mnemonic: *G*reater than or equal to *2* *D*imensions

*Chunk Variables with at least Three Dimensions*

Definition: Chunk all variables possible with at least three dimensions
Alternate invocation: none
*cnk_plc* key values: '`g3d`', '`cnk_g3d`', '`plc_g3d`'
Mnemonic: *G*reater than or equal to *3* *D*imensions

*Chunk One-Dimensional Record Variables*

Definition: Chunk all 1-D record variables
Alternate invocation: none
Any specified (with '`--cnk_dmn`') record dimension chunksizes will be applied only to 1-D record variables (and to no other variables). Other dimensions may be chunked with their own '`--cnk_dmn`' options that will apply to all variables.
*cnk_plc* key values: '`r1d`', '`cnk_r1d`', '`plc_r1d`'
Mnemonic: *R*ecord *1-D* variables

*Chunk Variables Containing Explicitly Chunked Dimensions*

Definition: Chunk all variables possible that contain at least one dimension whose chunksize was explicitly set with the '`--cnk_dmn`' option. Alternate invocation: none
*cnk_plc* key values: '`xpl`', '`cnk_xpl`', '`plc_xpl`'
Mnemonic: E*XPL*icitly specified dimensions

*Chunk Variables that are already Chunked*

Definition: Chunk only variables that are already chunked in the input file. When used in conjunction with '`cnk_map=xst`' this option preserves and copies the chunking parameters from the input to the output file. Alternate invocation: none
*cnk_plc* key values: '`xst`', '`cnk_xst`', '`plc_xst`'
Mnemonic: E*X*i*ST*ing chunked variables

*Chunk Variables with NCO recommendations*

Definition: Chunk all variables according to NCO best practices. This is a virtual option that ensures the chunking policy is (in the subjective opinion of the authors) the best policy for typical usage. As of NCO version 4.4.8 (February, 2015), this virtual policy implements '`map_rew`' for 3-D variables and '`map_lfp`' for all other variables.
Alternate invocation: none
*cnk_plc* key values: '`nco`', '`cnk_nco`', '`plc_nco`'
Mnemonic: *N*et*CDF* *O*perator

*Unchunking*

Definition: Unchunk all variables possible. The HDF5 storge layer requires that record variables (i.e., variables that contain at least one record dimension)

must be chunked. Also variables that are compressed or use checksums must be chunked. Such variables cannot be unchunked.
Alternate invocation: `ncunchunk`
*cnk_plc* key values: '`uck`', '`cnk_uck`', '`plc_uck`', '`unchunk`'
Mnemonic: *U*n*C*hun*K*

Equivalent key values are fully interchangeable. Multiple equivalent options are provided to satisfy disparate needs and tastes of NCO users working with scripts and from the command line.

The chunking algorithms must know the chunksizes of each dimension of each variable to be chunked. The correspondence between the input variable shape and the chunksizes is called the *chunking map*. The user specifies the desired chunking map with the '`-M`' switch (or its long option equivalents, '`--cnk_map`' and '`--chunk_map`') and its *cnk_map* argument. Nine chunking maps are currently implemented:

*Chunksize Equals Dimension Size*
Definition: Chunksize defaults to dimension size. Explicitly specify chunksizes for particular dimensions with '`--cnk_dmn`' option.
*cnk_map* key values: '`dmn`', '`cnk_dmn`', '`map_dmn`'
Mnemonic: *D*i*M*e*N*sion

*Chunksize Equals Dimension Size except Record Dimension*
Definition: Chunksize equals dimension size except record dimension has size one. Explicitly specify chunksizes for particular dimensions with '`--cnk_dmn`' option.
*cnk_map* key values: '`rd1`', '`cnk_rd1`', '`map_rd1`'
Mnemonic: *R*ecord *D*imension size *1*

*Chunksize Equals Scalar Size Specified*
Definition: Chunksize for all dimensions is set with the '`--cnk_scl=sz_lmn`' option. For this map *sz_lmn* itself becomes the chunksize of each dimension. This is in contrast to the *cnk_prd* map, where the *r*th root of *sz_lmn*) becomes the chunksize of each dimension.
*cnk_map* key values: '`scl`', '`cnk_scl`', '`map_scl`'
Mnemonic: *SC*a*L*ar
*cnk_map* key values: '`xpl`', '`cnk_xpl`', '`map_xpl`'
Mnemonic: E*XPL*icitly specified dimensions

*Chunksize Product Matches Scalar Size Specified*
Definition: The product of the chunksizes for each variable matches (approximately equals) the size specified with the '`--cnk_scl=sz_lmn`' option. A dimension of size one is said to be *degenerate*. For a variable of rank *R* (i.e., with *R* non-degenerate dimensions), the chunksize in each non-degenerate dimension is (approximately) the *R*th root of *sz_lmn*. This is in contrast to the *cnk_scl*

map, where *sz_lmn* itself becomes the chunksize of each dimension.
*cnk_map* key values: '`prd`', '`cnk_prd`', '`map_prd`'
Mnemonic: *PR*o*D*uct

*Chunksize Lefter Product Matches Scalar Size Specified*

Definition: The product of the chunksizes for each variable (approximately) equals the size specified with the '`--cnk_byt=sz_byt`' (not '`--cnk_dfl`') option. This is accomplished by using dimension sizes as chunksizes for the rightmost (most rapidly varying) dimensions, and then "flexing" the chunksize of the leftmost (least rapidly varying) dimensions such that the product of all chunksizes matches the specified size. All *L*-dimensions to the left of and including the first record dimension define the left-hand side. To be precise, if the total size (in bytes) of the variable is *var_sz*, and if the specified (with '`--cnk_byt`') product of the *R* "righter" dimensions (those that vary more rapidly than the first record dimension) is *sz_byt*, then chunksize (in bytes) of each of the *L* lefter dimensions is (approximately) the *L*th root of *var_sz/sz_byt*. This map was first proposed by Chris Barker.
*cnk_map* key values: '`lfp`', '`cnk_lfp`', '`map_lfp`'
Mnemonic: *LeF*ter *P*roduct

*Chunksize Equals Existing Chunksize*

Definition: Chunksizes are copied from the input to the output file for every variable that is chunked in the input file. Variables not chunked in the input file will be chunked with default mappings.
*cnk_map* key values: '`xst`', '`cnk_xst`', '`map_xst`'
Mnemonic: E*X*i*ST*

*Chunksize Balances 1D and (N-1)-D Access to N-D Variable [default for netCDF4 input]*

Definition: Chunksizes are chosen so that 1-D and (*N-1*)-D hyperslabs of *3*-D variables (e.g., point-timeseries orn latitude/longitude surfaces of 3-D fields) both require approximately the number of chunks. Hence their access time should be balanced. Russ Rew explains the motivation and derivation for this strategy here (`http://www.unidata.ucar.edu/blogs/developer/en/entry/chunking_data_choosing_shapes`).
*cnk_map* key values: '`rew`', '`cnk_rew`', '`map_rew`'
Mnemonic: Russ *REW*

*Chunksizes use netCDF4 defaults*

Definition: Chunksizes are determined by the underlying netCDF library. All variables selected by the current chunking policy have their chunksizes determined by netCDF library defaults. The default algorithm netCDF uses to determine chunksizes has changed through the years, and thus depends on the netCDF library version. This map can be used to reset (portions of) previously chunked files to default chunking values.
*cnk_map* key values: '`nc4`', '`cnk_nc4`', '`map_nc4`'

Mnemonic: *N*et*C*DF*4*

*Chunksizes use NCO recommendations [default for netCDF3 input]*
Definition: Chunksizes are determined by the currently recommended NCO map. This is a virtual option that ensures the chunking map is (in the subjective opinion of the authors) the best map for typical usage. As of NCO version 4.4.9 (May, 2015), this virtual map calls 'map_lfp'.
*cnk_map* key values: 'nco', 'cnk_nco', 'map_nco'
Mnemonic: *N*et*C*DF *O*perator

It is possible to combine the above chunking map algorithms with user-specified per-dimension (though not per-variable) chunksizes that override specific chunksizes determined by the maps above. The user specifies the per-dimension chunksizes with the (equivalent) long options '--cnk_dmn' or '--chunk_dimension'). The option takes two comma-separated arguments, *dmn_nm,sz_lmn*, which are the dimension name and its chunksize (in elements, not bytes), respectively. The '--cnk_dmn' option may be used as many times as necessary.

The default behavior of chunking depends on several factors. As mentioned above, when no chunking options are explicitly specified by the user, then NCO preserves the chunking characteristics of the input file in the output file. This is equivalent to specifying both *cnk_plc* and *cnk_map* as "existing", i.e., '--cnk_plc=xst --cnk_map=xst'. If output netCDF4 files are chunked with the default behavior of the netCDF4 library.

When any chunking parameter *except* 'cnk_plc' or 'cnk_map' is specified (such as 'cnk_dmn' or 'cnk_scl'), then the "existing" policy and map are retained and the output chunksizes are modified where necessary in accord with the user-specified parameter. When 'cnk_map' is specified and 'cnk_plc' is not, then NCO picks (what it thinks is) the optimal chunking policy. This has always been policy 'map_g2d'. When 'cnk_plc' is specified and 'cnk_map' is not, then NCO picks (what it thinks is) the optimal chunking map. This has always been map 'map_rd1'.

To start afresh and return to netCDF4 chunking defaults, select 'cnk_map=nc4'.

```
# Simple chunking and unchunking
ncks -O -4 --cnk_plc=all     in.nc out.nc # Chunk in.nc
ncks -O -4 --cnk_plc=unchunk in.nc out.nc # Unchunk in.nc

# Chunk data then unchunk it, printing informative metadata
ncks -O -4 -D 4 --cnk_plc=all ~/nco/data/in.nc ~/foo.nc
ncks -O -4 -D 4 --cnk_plc=uck ~/foo.nc ~/foo.nc

# Set total chunksize to 8192 B
ncks -O -4 -D 4 --cnk_plc=all --cnk_byt=8192 ~/nco/data/in.nc ~/foo.nc

# More complex chunking procedures, with informative metadata
ncks -O -4 -D 4 --cnk_scl=8 ~/nco/data/in.nc ~/foo.nc
ncks -O -4 -D 4 --cnk_scl=8 dstmch90_clm.nc ~/foo.nc
ncks -O -4 -D 4 --cnk_dmn lat,64 --cnk_dmn lon,128 dstmch90_clm.nc \
```

```
 ~/foo.nc
ncks -O -4 -D 4 --cnk_plc=uck ~/foo.nc ~/foo.nc
ncks -O -4 -D 4 --cnk_plc=g2d --cnk_map=rd1 --cnk_dmn lat,32 \
 --cnk_dmn lon,128 dstmch90_clm_0112.nc ~/foo.nc

# Chunking works with all operators...
ncap2 -O -4 -D 4 --cnk_scl=8 -S ~/nco/data/ncap2_tst.nco \
 ~/nco/data/in.nc ~/foo.nc
ncbo -O -4 -D 4 --cnk_scl=8 -p ~/nco/data in.nc in.nc ~/foo.nc
ncecat -O -4 -D 4 -n 12,2,1 --cnk_dmn lat,32 \
 -p /data/zender/dstmch90 dstmch90_clm01.nc ~/foo.nc
ncflint -O -4 -D 4 --cnk_scl=8 ~/nco/data/in.nc ~/foo.nc
ncpdq -O -4 -D 4 -P all_new --cnk_scl=8 -L 5 ~/nco/data/in.nc ~/foo.nc
ncrcat -O -4 -D 4 -n 12,2,1 --cnk_dmn lat,32 \
 -p /data/zender/dstmch90 dstmch90_clm01.nc ~/foo.nc
ncwa -O -4 -D 4 -a time --cnk_plc=g2d --cnk_map=rd1 --cnk_dmn lat,32 \
 --cnk_dmn lon,128 dstmch90_clm_0112.nc ~/foo.nc
```

Chunking policy '`r1d`' changes the chunksize of 1-D record variables (and no other variables) to that specified (with '`--cnk_dmn`') chunksize. Any specified record dimension chunksizes will be applied to 1-D record variables only. Other dimensions may be chunked with their own '`--cnk_dmn`' options that will apply to all variables. For example,

```
ncks --cnk_plc=r1d --cnk_dmn=time,1000. in.nc out.nc
```

This sets `time` chunks to 1000 only in 1-D record variables. Without the '`r1d`' policy, `time` chunks would change in all variables.

It is appropriate to conclude by informing users about an aspect of chunking that may not be expected. Three types of variables are *always* chunked: Record variables, Deflated (compressed) variables, and Checksummed variables. Hence all variables that contain a record dimension are also chunked (since data must be chunked in all dimensions, not just one). Unless otherwise specified by the user, the other (fixed, non-record) dimensions of record variables are assigned default chunk sizes. The HDF5 layer does all this automatically to optimize the on-disk variable/file storage geometry of record variables. Do not be surprised to learn that files created without any explicit instructions to activate chunking nevertheless contain chunked variables.

## 3.29 Compression

Availability: `ncbo`, `ncecat`, `nces`, `ncflint`, `ncks`, `ncpdq`, `ncra`, `ncrcat`, `ncwa`
Short options: None
Long options: '`--ppc` *var1*`[,`*var2*`[,...]]=`*prc*',
'`--precision_preserving_compression` *var1*`[,`*var2*`[,...]]=`*prc*',
'`--quantize` *var1*`[,`*var2*`[,...]]=`*prc*'

NCO implements or accesses four different compression algorithms, the standard lossless DEFLATE algorithm and three lossy compression algorithms. All four algorithms reduce the on-disk size of a dataset while sacrificing no (lossless) or a tolerable amount (lossy) of precision. First, NCO can access the lossless DEFLATE algorithm, a combination of Lempel-Ziv encoding and Huffman coding, algorithm on any netCDF4 dataset (see Section 3.30 [Deflation], page 107). Because it is lossless, this algorithm re-inflates deflated data to their full original precision. This algorithm is accessed via the HDF5 library layer (which itself calls the `zlib` library also used by `gzip`), and is unavailable with netCDF3.

### 3.29.1 Linear Packing

The three lossy compression algorithms are Linear Packing (see Section 3.34 [Packed data], page 111), and two precision-preserving algorithms. Linear packing quantizes data of a higher precision type into a lower precision type (often `NC_SHORT`) that thus stores a fewer (though constant) number of bytes per value. Linearly packed data unpacks into a (much) smaller dynamic range than the floating-point data can represent. The type-conversion and reduced dynamic range of the data allows packing to eliminate bits typically used to store an exponent, thus improving its packing efficiency. Packed data also can also be deflated for additional space savings.

A limitation of linear packing is that unpacking data stored as integers into the linear range defined by `scale_factor` and `add_offset` rapidly loses precision outside of a narrow range of floating-point values. Variables packed as `NC_SHORT`, for example, can represent only about 64000 discrete values in the range $-32768 * scale_factor + add_offset$ to $32767 * scale_factor + add_offset$. The precision of packed data equals the value of `scale_factor`, and `scale_factor` is usually chosen to span the range of valid data, not to represent the intrinsic precision of the variable. In other words, the precision of packed data cannot be specified in advance because it depends on the range of values to quantize.

### 3.29.2 Precision-Preserving Compression

NCO implemented the final two lossy compression algorithms in version 4.4.8 (February, 2015). These are both *Precision-Preserving Compression* (PPC) algorithms and since standard terminology for precision is remarkably imprecise, so is our nomenclature. The operational definition of "significant digit" in our precision preserving algorithms is that the exact value, before rounding or quantization, is within one-half the value of the decimal place occupied by the *Least Significant Digit* (LSD) of the rounded value. For example, the value $pi = 3.14$ correctly represents the exact mathematical constant *pi* to three significant digits because the LSD of the rounded value (i.e., 4) is in the one-hundredths digit place, and the difference between the exact value and the rounded value is less than one-half of one one-hundredth, i.e., $(3.14159265358979323844 - 3.14 = 0.00159 < 0.005)$.

One PPC algorithm preserves the specified total *Number of Signifcant Digits* (NSD) of the value. For example there is only one significant digit in the weight of most "eight-hundred pound gorillas" that you will encounter, i.e., so *nsd = 1*. This is the most straightforward measure of precision, and thus NSD is the default PPC algorithm.

The other PPC algorithm preserves the number of *Decimal Significant Digits* (DSD), i.e., the number of significant digits following (positive, by convention) or preceding (negative) the decimal point. For example, '`0.008`' and '`800`' have, respectively, three and negative two digits digits following the decimal point, corresponding to *dsd = 3* and *dsd = −2*.

The only justifiable NSD for a given value depends on intrinsic accuracy and error characteristics of the model or measurements, and not on the units with which the value is stored. The appropriate DSD for a given value depends on these intrinsic characteristics and, in addition, the units of storage. This is the fundamental difference between the NSD and DSD approaches. The eight-hundred pound gorilla always has *nsd = 1* regardless of whether the value is stored in pounds or in some other unit. DSD corresponding to this weight is *dsd = −2* if the value is stored in pounds, *dsd = 4* if stored in megapounds.

Users may wish to express the precision to be preserved as either NSD or DSD. Invoke PPC with the long option '`--ppc var=prc`', or give the same arguments to the synonyms '`--precision_preserving_compression`', or to '`--quantize`'. Here *var* is the variable to quantize, and *prc* is its precision. The option '`--ppc`' (and its long option equivalents such as '`--quantize`') indicates the argument syntax will be *key=val*. As such, '`--ppc`' and its synonyms are indicator options that accept arguments supplied one-by-one like '`--ppc key1=val1 --ppc key2=val2`', or aggregated together in multi-argument format like '`--ppc key1=val1#key2=val2`' (see Section 3.4.2 [Multi-arguments], page 32). The default algorithm assumes *prc* specifies NSD precision, e.g., '`T=2`' means *nsd = 2*. Prepend *prc* with a decimal point to specify DSD precision, e.g., '`T=.2`' means *dsd = 2*. NSD precision must be specified as a positive integer. DSD precision may be a positive or negative integer; and is specified as the negative base 10 logarithm of the desired precision, in accord with common usage. For example, specifying '`T=.3`' or '`T=.-2`' tells the DSD algorithm to store only enough bits to preserve the value of $T$ rounded to the nearest thousandth or hundred, respectively.

Setting *var* to `default` has the special meaning of applying the associated NSD or DSD algorithm to all floating point variables except coordinate variables. Variables *not affected* by `default` include integer and non-numeric atomic types, coordinates, and variables mentioned in the `bounds`, `climatology`, or `coordinates` attribute of any variable. NCO applies PPC to coordinate variables only if those variables are explicitly specified (i.e., not with the '`default=prc`' mechanism. NCO applies PPC to integer-type variables only if those variables are explicitly specified (i.e., not with the '`default=prc`', and only if the DSD algorithm is invoked with a negative *prc*. To prevent PPC from applying to certain non-coordinate variables (e.g., `gridcell_area` or `gaussian_weight`), explicitly specify a precision exceeding 7 (for `NC_FLOAT`) or 15 (for `NC_DOUBLE`) for those variables. Since these are the maximum representable precisions in decimal digits, NCO *turns-off* PPC (i.e., does nothing) when more precision is requested.

The time-penalty for compressing and uncompressing data varies according to the algorithm. The Number of Significant Digit (NSD) algorithm quantizes by bitmasking, and employs no floating-point math. The Decimal Significant Digit (DSD) algorithm quantizes by rounding, which does require floating-point math. Hence NSD is likely faster than DSD, though the difference has not been measured. NSD creates a bitmask to alter the *significand* of IEEE 754 floating-point data. The bitmask is one for all bits to be retained and zero or one for all bits to be ignored. The algorithm assumes that the number of binary digits (i.e., bits) necessary to represent a single base-10 digit is $ln(10)/ln(2) = 3.32$. The exact numbers of bits *Nbit* retained for single and double precision values are $ceil(3.32 * nsd) + 1$

and $ceil(3.32 * nsd) + 2$, respectively. Once these reach 23 and 53, respectively, bitmasking is completely ineffective. This occurs at $nsd = 6.3$ and 15.4, respectively.

The DSD algorithm, by contrast, uses rounding to remove undesired precision. The rounding[23] zeroes the greatest number of significand bits consistent with the desired precision.

To demonstrate the change in IEEE representation caused by PPC rounding algorithms, consider again the case of *pi*, represented as an `NC_FLOAT`. The IEEE 754 single precision representations of the exact value (3.141592...), the value with only three significant digits treated as exact (3.140000...), and the value as stored (3.140625) after PPC-rounding with either the NSD ($prc = 3$) or DSD ($prc = 2$) algorithm are, respectively,

```
S Exponent  Fraction (Significand)   Decimal    Notes
0 100000001 0010010000111111011011 # 3.14159265 Exact
0 100000001 0010001111010111000011 # 3.14000000
0 100000001 0010010000000000000000 # 3.14062500 NSD = 3
0 100000001 0010010000000000000000 # 3.14062500 DSD = 2
```

The string of trailing zero-bits in the rounded values facilitates byte-stream compression. Note that the NSD and DSD algorithms do not always produce results that are bit-for-bit identical, although they do in this particular case.

Reducing the preserved precision of NSD-rounding produces increasingly long strings of identical-bits amenable to compression:

```
S Exponent  Fraction (Significand)   Decimal    Notes
0 100000001 0010010000111111011011 # 3.14159265 Exact
0 100000001 0010010000111111011011 # 3.14159265 NSD = 8
0 100000001 0010010000111111011010 # 3.14159262 NSD = 7
0 100000001 0010010000111111011000 # 3.14159203 NSD = 6
0 100000001 0010010000111111000000 # 3.14158630 NSD = 5
0 100000001 0010010000111100000000 # 3.14154053 NSD = 4
0 100000001 0010010000000000000000 # 3.14062500 NSD = 3
0 100000001 0010010000000000000000 # 3.14062500 NSD = 2
0 100000001 0010000000000000000000 # 3.12500000 NSD = 1
```

The consumption of about 3 bits per digit of base-10 precision is evident, as is the coincidence of a quantized value that greatly exceeds the mandated precision for NSD = 2. Although the NSD algorithm generally masks some bits for all $nsd <= 7$ (for `NC_FLOAT`), compression algorithms like DEFLATE may need byte-size-or-greater (i.e., at least eight-bit) bit patterns before their algorithms can take advantage of of encoding such patterns for compression. Do not expect significantly enhanced compression from $nsd > 5$ (for `NC_FLOAT`) or $nsd > 14$ (for `NC_DOUBLE`). Clearly values stored as `NC_DOUBLE` (i.e., eight-bytes) are susceptible to much greater compression than `NC_FLOAT` for a given precision because their significands explicitly contain 53 bits rather than 23 bits.

---

[23] Rounding is performed by the internal math library `rint()` family of functions that were standardized in C99. The exact alorithm employed is $val := rint(scale * val)/scale$ where *scale* is the nearest power of 2 that exceeds $10 * *prc$, and the inverse of *scale* is used when $prc < 0$. For $ppc = 3$ or $ppc = -2$, for example, we have $scale = 1024$ and $scale = 1/128$.

Maintaining non-biased statistical properties during lossy compression requires special attention. The DSD algorithm uses `rint()`, which rounds toward the nearest even integer. Thus DSD has no systematic bias. However, the NSD algorithm uses a bitmask technique susceptible to statistical bias. Zeroing all non-significant bits is guaranteed to produce numbers quantized to the specified tolerance, i.e., half of the decimal value of the position occupied by the LSD. However, always zeroing the non-significant bits results in quantized numbers that never exceed the exact number. This would produce a negative bias in statistical quantities (e.g., the average) subsequently derived from the quantized numbers. To avoid this bias, our NSD implementation rounds non-significant bits down (to zero) or up (to one) in an alternating fashion when processing array data. In general, the first element is rounded down, the second up, and so on. This results in a mean bias quite close to zero. The only exception is that the floating-point value of zero is never quantized upwards. For simplicity, NSD always rounds scalars downwards.

Although NSD or DSD are different algorithms under the hood, they both replace the (unwanted) least siginificant bits of the IEEE significand with a string of consecutive zeroes. Byte-stream compression techniques, such as the `gzip` DEFLATE algorithm compression available in HDF5, always compress zero-strings more efficiently than random digits. The net result is netCDF files that utilize compression can be significantly reduced in size. This feature only works when the data are compressed, either internally (by netCDF) or externally (by another user-supplied mechanism). It is most straightfoward to compress data internally using the built-in compression and decompression supported by netCDF4. For convenience, NCO automatically activates file-wide Lempel-Ziv deflation (see Section 3.30 [Deflation], page 107) level one (i.e., '`-L 1`') when PPC is invoked on any variable in a netCDF4 output file. This makes PPC easier to use effectively, since the user need not explicitly specify deflation. Any explicitly specified deflation (including no deflation, '`-L 0`') will override the PPC deflation default. If the output file is a netCDF3 format, NCO will emit a message suggesting internal netCDF4 or external netCDF3 compression. netCDF3 files compressed by an external utility such as `gzip` accrue approximately the same benefits (shrinkage) as netCDF4, although with netCDF3 the user or provider must uncompress (e.g., `gunzip`) the file before accessing the data. There is no benefit to rounding numbers and storing them in netCDF3 files unless such custom compression/decompression is employed. Without that, one may as well maintain the undesired precision.

The user accesses PPC through a single switch, '`--ppc`', repeated as many times as necessary. To apply the NSD algorithm to variable *u* use, e.g.,

```
ncks -7 --ppc u=2 in.nc out.nc
```

The output file will preserve only two significant digits of *u*. The options '`-4`' or '`-7`' ensure a netCDF4-format output (regardless of the input file format) to support internal compression. It is recommended though not required to write netCDF4 files after PPC. For clarity the '`-4/-7`' switches are omitted in subsequent examples. NCO attaches attributes that indicate the algorithm used and degree of precision retained for each variable affected by PPC. The NSD and DSD algorithms store the attributes `number_of_significant_digits` and `least_significant_digit`[24], respectively.

---

[24] A suggestion by Rich Signell and the `nc3tonc4` tool by Jeff Whitaker inspired NCO to implement PPC. NCO implements a different DSD algorithm than `nc3tonc4`, and produces slightly different (not bit-for-

It is safe to attempt PPC on input that has already been rounded. Variables can be made rounder, not sharper, i.e., variables cannot be "un-rounded". Thus PPC attempted on an input variable with an existing PPC attribute proceeds only if the new rounding level exceeds the old, otherwise no new rounding occurs (i.e., a "no-op"), and the original PPC attribute is retained rather than replaced with the newer value of *prc*.

To request, say, five significant digits (*nsd* = *5*) for all fields, except, say, wind speeds which are only known to integer values (*dsd* = *0*) in the supplied units, requires '--ppc' twice:

```
ncks -4 --ppc default=5 --ppc u,v=.0 in.nc out.nc
```

To preserve five digits in all variables except coordinate variables and *u* and *v*, use the 'default' option and separately specify the exceptions:

```
ncks --ppc default=5 --ppc u,v=20 in.nc out.nc
```

The '--ppc' option may be specified any number of times to support varying precision types and levels, and each option may aggregate all the variables with the same precision

```
ncks --ppc p,w,z=5 --ppc q,RH=4 --ppc T,u,v=3 in.nc out.nc
ncks --ppc p,w,z=5#q,RH=4#T,u,v=3 in.nc out.nc # Multi-argument format
```

Any *var* argument may be a regular expression. This simplifies generating lists of related variables:

```
ncks --ppc Q.?=5 --ppc FS.?,FL.?=4 --ppc RH=.3 in.nc out.nc
ncks --ppc Q.?=5#FS.?,FL.?=4#RH=.3 in.nc out.nc # Multi-argument format
```

Although PPC-rounding instantly reduces data precision, on-disk storage reduction only occurs once the data are compressed.

How can one be sure the lossy data are sufficiently precise? PPC preserves all significant digits of every value. The DSD algorithm uses floating-point math to round each value optimally so that it has the maximum number of zeroed bits that preserve the specified precision. The NSD algorithm uses a theoretical approach (3.2 bits per base-10 digit), tuned and tested to ensure the *worst* case quantization error is less than half the value of the minimum increment in the least significant digit.

We define several metrics to quantify the quantization error. The mean error $\bar{\epsilon}$ and mean absolute error $\bar{\epsilon}^+$ incurred in quantizing a variable from its true values $x_i$ to quantized values $q_i$ are, respectively,

$$\bar{\epsilon} = \frac{\sum_{i=1}^{i=N} \mu_i m_i w_i (x_i - q_i)}{\sum_{i=1}^{i=N} \mu_i m_i w_i} \quad \text{and} \quad \bar{\epsilon}^+ = \frac{\sum_{i=1}^{i=N} \mu_i m_i w_i |x_i - q_i|}{\sum_{i=1}^{i=N} \mu_i m_i w_i}$$

bit) though self-consistent and equivalent results. **nc3tonc4** records the precision of its DSD algorithm in the attribute **least_significant_digit** and NCO does the same for consistency. The Unidata blog here (**http://www.unidata.ucar.edu/blogs/developer/en/entry/compression_by_bit_shaving**) also shows how to compress IEEE floating-point data by zeroing insignificant bits. The author, John Caron, writes that the technique has been called "bit-shaving". When combined with our bias-elimination procedure that rounds-up to one, a more suitable terminology might be "bit-grooming".

where $\mu_i$ is 1 unless $x_i$ equals the missing value, $m_i$ is 1 unless $x_i$ is masked, and $w_i$ is the weight. The maximum and minimum errors $\epsilon_{\text{max}}$ and $\epsilon_{\text{min}}$ are both signed

$$\epsilon_{\text{max}} = \max(x_i - q_i) \qquad \text{and} \qquad \epsilon_{\text{min}} = \min(x_i - q_i)$$

while the maximum and minimum absolute errors $\epsilon^+_{\text{mabs}}$ and $\epsilon^+_{\text{mibs}}$ are positive-definite.

$$\epsilon^+_{\text{mabs}} = \max|x_i - q_i| = \max(|\epsilon_{\text{max}}|, |\epsilon_{\text{min}}|)$$

$$\epsilon^+_{\text{mibs}} = \min|x_i - q_i| = \min(|\epsilon_{\text{max}}|, |\epsilon_{\text{min}}|)$$

Typically $\epsilon^+_{\text{mibs}} = 0$ for quantization, since many exact values need no quantization. Bit-shifting zeros into the least significant bits (LSBs) always underestimates true values so that $\epsilon_{\text{max}} = 0$. Conversely, bit-shifting ones into the LSBs always overestimates true values so that $\epsilon_{\text{min}} = 0$. Our NSD algorithm is balanced because it alternates bit-shifting zeroes and ones. Balanced algorithms should yield $\epsilon_{\text{max}} \approx -\epsilon_{\text{min}}$, $\epsilon^+_{\text{mabs}} \approx \epsilon^+_{\text{mibs}}$, and $\bar{\epsilon} \approx 0$.

The three most important error metrics for quantization are $\epsilon^+_{\text{mabs}}$, $\bar{\epsilon}^+$, and $\bar{\epsilon}$. The upper bound (worst case) quantization performance is $\epsilon^+_{\text{mabs}}$. $\bar{\epsilon}^+$ measures the absolute mean accuracy of quantization, and does not allow positive and negative offsets to compensate eachother and conceal poor performance. The difference bewtween $\epsilon^+_{\text{mabs}}$ and $\bar{\epsilon}^+$ indicates how much of an outlier the worst case is. The mean accuracy $\bar{\epsilon}$ indicates whether statistical properties of quantized numbers will accurately reflect the true values.

All three metrics are expressed in terms of the fraction of the ten's place occupied by the LSD. If the LSD is the hundreds digit or the thousandths digit, then the metrics are fractions of 100, or of 1/100, respectively. PPC algorithms should produce maximum absolute errors no greater than 0.5 in these units. If the LSD is the hundreds digit, then quantized versions of true values will be within fifty of the true value. It is much easier to satisfy this tolerance for a true value of 100 (only 50% accuracy required) than for 999 (5% accuracy required). Thus the minimum accuracy guaranteed for *nsd* = 1 ranges from 5–50%. For this reason, the best and worst cast performance usually occurs for true values whose LSD value is close to one and nine, respectively. Of course most users prefer *prc* > 1 because accuracies increase exponentially with *prc*. Continuing the previous example to *prc* = 2, quantized versions of true values from 1000–9999 will also be within 50 of the true value, i.e., have accuracies from 0.5–5%. In other words, only two significant digits are necessary to guarantee better than 5% accuracy in quantization. We recommend that dataset producers and users consider quantizing datasets with *nsd* = 3. This guarantees accuracy of 0.05–0.5% for individual values. Statistics computed from ensembles of quantized values will, assuming the mean error $\bar{\epsilon}$ is small, have much better accuracy than 0.5%. This accuracy is the most that can be justified for many applications.

To demonstrate these principles we conduct error analyses on an artificial, reproducible dataset, and on an actual dataset of observational analysis values.[25] The table summarizes quantization accuracy based on the three metrics.

`NSD` Number of Significant Digits.

[25] The artificial dataset employed is one million evenly spaced values from 1.0–2.0. The analysis data are $N = 13934592$ values of the temperature field from the NASA MERRA analysis of 20130601.

`Emabs` Maximum absolute error.

`Emebs` Mean absolute error.

`Emean` Mean error.

```
Artificial Data: N=1000000 values in [1.0,2.0) in steps of 1.0e-6
Single-Precision          Double-Precision    Single-Precision
NSD Emabs Emebs Emean     Emabs Emebs Emean   DSD Emabs Emebs Emean
 1  0.31  0.11  4.1e-4    0.31  0.11   4.0e-4  1  0.30  0.11 -8.1e-4
 2  0.39  0.14  6.8e-5    0.39  0.14   5.5e-5  2  0.39  0.14 -1.3e-4
 3  0.49  0.17  1.0e-6    0.49  0.17  -5.5e-7  3  0.49  0.17 -2.0e-5
 4  0.30  0.11  3.2e-7    0.30  0.11  -6.1e-6  4  0.30  0.11  5.1e-8
 5  0.37  0.13  3.1e-7    0.38  0.13  -5.6e-6  5  0.38  0.13  2.6e-6
 6  0.36  0.12 -4.4e-7    0.48  0.17  -4.1e-7  6  0.48  0.17  7.2e-6
 7  0.00  0.00  0.0       0.30  0.10   1.5e-7  7  0.00  0.00  0.0

Observational Analysis: N=13934592 values MERRA Temperature 20130601
Single-Precision
NSD Emabs Emebs Emean
 1  0.31  0.11  2.4e-3
 2  0.39  0.14  3.8e-4
 3  0.49  0.17 -9.6e-5
 4  0.30  0.11  2.3e-3
 5  0.37  0.13  2.2e-3
 6  0.36  0.13  1.7e-2
 7  0.00  0.00  0.0
```

All results show that PPC quantization performs as expected. Absolute maximum errors *Emabs* $< 0.5$ for all *prc*. For $1 <=$ *prc* $<= 6$, quantization results in comparable maximum absolute and mean absolute errors *Emabs* and *Emebs*, respectively. Mean errors *Emean* are orders of magnitude smaller because quantization produces over- and under-estimated values in balance. When *prc* $= 7$, quantization of single-precision values is ineffective, because all available bits are used to represent the maximum precision of seven digits. The maximum and mean absolute errors *Emabs* and *Emebs* are nearly identical across algorithms, precisions, and dataset types. This is consistent with both the artificial data and empirical data being random, and thus exercising equally strengths and weaknesses of the algorithms over the course of millions of input values. We generated artificial arrays with many different starting values and interval spacing and all gave qualitatively similar results. The results presented are the worst obtained.

The artificial data has much smaller mean error *Emean* than the observational analysis. The reason why is unclear. It may be because the temperature field is concentrated in particular ranges of values (and associated quantization errors) prevalent on Earth, e.g., $200 < T < 320$. It is worth noting that the mean error *Emean* $< 0.01$ for $1 <=$ *prc* $< 6$, and that *Emean* is typically at least two or more orders of magnitude less than *Emabs*. Thus quantized values with precisions as low as *prc* $= 1$ still yield highly significant statistics by contemporary scientific standards.

Testing shows that PPC quantization enhances compression of typical climate datasets. The degree of enhancement depends, of course, on the required precision. Model results are often computed as `NC_DOUBLE` then archived as `NC_FLOAT` to save space. This table summarizes the performance of lossless and lossy compression on two typical, or at least random, netCDF data files. The files were taken from representative model-simulated and satellite-retrieved datasets. Only floating-point data were compressed. No attempt was made to compress integer-type variables as they occupy an insignificant fraction of every dataset. The columns are

`Type` File-type: *N3* for netCDF `CLASSIC`, *N4* for `NETCDF4`, *N7* for `NETCDF4_CLASSIC` (which comprises netCDF3 data types and structures with netCDF4 storage features like compression), *H4* for HDF4, and *H5* for HDF5. *N4/7* means results apply to both *N4* and *N7* filetypes.

`LLC` Type of lossless compression employed, if any. Bare numbers refer to the strength of the DEFLATE algorithm employed internally by netCDF4/HDF5, while numbers prefixed with *B* refer to the block size employed by the Burrows-Wheeler algorithm in `bzip2`.

`PPC` Number of significant digits retained by the precision-preserving compression NSD algorithm.

`Pck` *Y* if the default `ncpdq` packing algorithm (convert floating-point types to `NC_SHORT`) was employed.

`Size` Resulting filesize in MB.

`%` Compression ratio, i.e., resulting filesize relative to original size, in percent. In some cases the original files is already losslessly compressed. The compression ratios reported are relative to the size of the original file as distributed, not as optimally losslessly compressed.

A dash (-) indicates the associated compression feature was not employed.

```
# dstmch90_clm.nc
Type LLC PPC Pck  Size    %   Flags and Notes
  N3   -   -   -  34.7 100.0  Original is not compressed
  N3  B1   -   -  28.9  83.2  bzip2 -1
  N3  B9   -   -  29.3  84.4  bzip2 -9
  N7   -   -   -  35.0 101.0
  N7   1   -   -  28.2  81.3  -L 1
  N7   9   -   -  28.0  80.8  -L 9
  N7   -   -   Y  17.6  50.9  ncpdq -L 0
  N7   1   -   Y   7.9  22.8  ncpdq -L 1
  N7   1   7   -  28.2  81.3  --ppc default=7
  N7   1   6   -  27.9  80.6  --ppc default=6
  N7   1   5   -  25.9  74.6  --ppc default=5
  N7   1   4   -  22.3  64.3  --ppc default=4
  N7   1   3   -  18.9  54.6  --ppc default=3
  N7   1   2   -  14.5  43.2  --ppc default=2
  N7   1   1   -  10.0  29.0  --ppc default=1
```

```
# b1850c5cn_doe_polar_merged_0_cesm1_2_0_HD+MAM4+tun2b.hp.e003.cam.h0.0001-01.nc
Type LLC PPC Pck  Size    %    Flags and Notes
  N3   -    -   -  119.8 100.0  Original is not compressed
  N3  B1    -   -   84.2  70.3  bzip2 -1
  N3  B9    -   -   84.8  70.9  bzip2 -9
  N7   -    -   -  120.5 100.7
  N7   1    -   -   82.6  69.0  -L 1
  N7   9    -   -   82.1  68.6  -L 9
  N7   -    -   Y   60.7  50.7  ncpdq -L 0
  N7   1    -   Y   26.0  21.8  ncpdq -L 1
  N7   1    7   -   82.6  69.0  --ppc default=7
  N7   1    6   -   81.9  68.4  --ppc default=6
  N7   1    5   -   77.2  64.5  --ppc default=5
  N7   1    4   -   69.0  57.6  --ppc default=4
  N7   1    3   -   59.3  49.5  --ppc default=3
  N7   1    2   -   49.5  41.3  --ppc default=2
  N7   1    1   -   38.2  31.9  --ppc default=1

# MERRA300.prod.assim.inst3_3d_asm_Cp.20130601.hdf
Type LLC PPC Pck  Size    %    Flags and Notes
  H4   5    -   -  244.3 100.0  Original is compressed
  H4  B1    -   -  244.7 100.1  bzip2 -1
  N4   5    -   -  214.5  87.8
  N7   5    -   -  210.6  86.2
  N4  B1    -   -  215.4  88.2  bzip2 -1
  N4  B9    -   -  214.8  87.9  bzip2 -9
  N3   -    -   -  617.1 252.6
N4/7   -    -   -  694.0 284.0  -L 0
N4/7   1    -   -  223.2  91.3  -L 1
N4/7   9    -   -  207.3  84.9  -L 9
N4/7   -    -   Y  347.1 142.1  ncpdq -L 0
N4/7   1    -   Y  133.6  54.7  ncpdq -L 1
N4/7   1    7   -  223.1  91.3  --ppc default=7
N4/7   1    6   -  225.1  92.1  --ppc default=6
N4/7   1    5   -  221.4  90.6  --ppc default=5
N4/7   1    4   -  201.4  82.4  --ppc default=4
N4/7   1    3   -  185.3  75.9  --ppc default=3
N4/7   1    2   -  150.0  61.4  --ppc default=2
N4/7   1    1   -  100.8  41.3  --ppc default=1

# OMI-Aura_L2-OMIAuraSO2_2012m1222-o44888_v01-00-2014m0107t114720.h5
Type LLC PPC Pck  Size    %    Flags and Notes
  H5   5    -   -   29.5 100.0  Original is compressed
  H5  B1    -   -   29.3  99.6  bzip2 -1
  N4   5    -   -   29.5 100.0
  N4  B1    -   -   29.3  99.6  bzip2 -1
```

```
N4  B9   -  -   29.3  99.4  bzip2 -9
N4   -   -  -   50.7 172.3  -L 0
N4   1   -  -   29.8 101.3  -L 1
N4   9   -  -   29.4  99.8  -L 9
N4   -   -  Y   27.7  94.0  ncpdq -L 0
N4   1   -  Y   12.9  43.9  ncpdq -L 1
N4   1   7  -   29.7 100.7  --ppc default=7
N4   1   6  -   29.7 100.8  --ppc default=6
N4   1   5  -   27.3  92.8  --ppc default=5
N4   1   4  -   23.8  80.7  --ppc default=4
N4   1   3  -   20.3  69.0  --ppc default=3
N4   1   2  -   15.1  51.2  --ppc default=2
N4   1   1  -    9.9  33.6  --ppc default=1
```

A selective, per-variable approach to PPC yields the best balance of precision and compression yet requires the dataset producer to understand the intrinsic precision of each variable. Such a specification for a GCM dataset might look like this (using names for the NCAR CAM model):

```
# Be conservative on non-explicit quantities, so default=5
# Some quantities deserve four significant digits
# Many quantities, such as aerosol optical depths and burdens, are
# highly uncertain and only useful to three significant digits.
ncks -7 -O \
--ppc default=5 \
--ppc AN.?,AQ.?=4 \
--ppc AER.?,AOD.?,ARE.?,AW.?,BURDEN.?=3 \
ncar_cam.nc ~/foo.nc
```

## 3.30 Deflation

Availability: `ncap2`, `ncbo`, `nces`, `ncecat`, `ncflint`, `ncks`, `ncpdq`, `ncra`, `ncrcat`, `ncwa`
Short options: '`-L`'
Long options: '`--dfl_lvl`', '`--deflate`'

All NCO operators that define variables support the netCDF4 feature of storing variables compressed with the lossless DEFLATE compression algorithm. DEFLATE combines the Lempel-Ziv encoding with Huffman coding. The specific version used by netCDF4/HDF5 is that implemented in the `zlib` library used by `gzip`. Activate deflation with the `-L` ***`dfl_lvl`*** short option (or with the same argument to the '`--dfl_lvl`' or '`--deflate`' long options). Specify the deflation level *dfl_lvl* on a scale from no deflation (*dfl_lvl* = *0*) to maximum deflation (*dfl_lvl* = *9*). Under the hood, this selects the compression blocksize. Minimal deflation (*dfl_lvl* = *1*) achieves considerable storage compression with little time penalty. Higher deflation levels require more time for compression. File sizes resulting from minimal (*dfl_lvl* = *1*) and maximal (*dfl_lvl* = *9*) deflation levels typically differ by less than 10% in size.

To compress an entire file using deflation, use

```
ncks -4 -L 0 in.nc out.nc # No deflation (fast, no time penalty)
ncks -4 -L 1 in.nc out.nc # Minimal deflation (little time penalty)
ncks -4 -L 9 in.nc out.nc # Maximal deflation (much slower)
```

Unscientific testing shows that deflation compresses typical climate datasets by 30-60%. Packing, a lossy compression technique available for all netCDF files (see Section 3.34 [Packed data], page 111), can easily compress files by 50%. Packed data may be deflated to squeeze datasets by about 80%:

```
ncks  -4 -L 1 in.nc out.nc # Minimal deflation (~30-60% compression)
ncks  -4 -L 9 in.nc out.nc # Maximal deflation (~31-63% compression)
ncpdq          in.nc out.nc # Standard packing  (~50% compression)
ncpdq -4 -L 9 in.nc out.nc # Deflated packing  (~80% compression)
```

`ncks` prints deflation parameters, if any, to screen (see Section 4.8 [ncks netCDF Kitchen Sink], page 237).

## 3.31 MD5 digests

Availability: `ncecat`, `ncks`, `ncrcat`
Short options:
Long options: '`--md5_dgs`', '`--md5_digest`', '`--md5_wrt_att`', '`--md5_write_attribute`'

As of NCO version 4.1.0 (April, 2012), NCO supports data integrity verification using the MD5 digest algorithm. This support is currently implemented in `ncks` and in the multifile concantenators `ncecat` and `ncrcat`. Activate it with the '`--md5_dgs`' or '`--md5_digest`' long options. As of NCO version 4.3.3 (July, 2013), NCO will write the MD5 digest of each variable as an `NC_CHAR` attribute named `MD5`. This support is currently implemented in `ncks` and in the multifile concantenators `ncecat` and `ncrcat`. Activate it with the '`--md5_wrt_att`' or '`--md5_write_attribute`' long options.

The behavior and verbosity of the MD5 digest is operator-dependent. When activating MD5 digests with `ncks` it is assumed that the user simply wishes to see the digest of every variable and this is done when the debugging level exceeds one. This incurs only the minor overhead of performing the hash algorithm for each variable read. MD5 digests may be activated in both the one- and two-filename argument forms of `ncks`, which are used for printing and for sub-setting, respectively. The MD5 digests are shown as a 32-character hexadecimal string in which each two characters represent one byte of the 16-byte digest:

```
> ncks -O -D 2 -C --md5 -v md5_a,md5_abc ~/nco/data/in.nc
...
ncks: INFO MD5(md5_a) = 0cc175b9c0f1b6a831c399e269772661
md5_a = 'a'
ncks: INFO MD5(md5_abc) = 900150983cd24fb0d6963f7d28e17f72
lev[0]=100 md5_abc[0--2]='abc'
> ncks -O -D 2 -C -d lev,0 --md5 -v md5_a,md5_abc ~/nco/data/in.nc
```

```
...
ncks: INFO MD5(md5_a) = 0cc175b9c0f1b6a831c399e269772661
md5_a = 'a'
ncks: INFO MD5(md5_abc) = 0cc175b9c0f1b6a831c399e269772661
lev[0]=100 md5_abc[0--0]='a'
```

In fact these examples demonstrate the validity of the hash algorithm since the MD5 hashes of the strings "a" and "abc" are widely known. The second example shows that the hyperslab of variable `md5_abc` (= "abc") consisting of only its first letter (= "a") has the same hash as the variable `md5_a` ("a"). This illustrates that MD5 digests act only on variable data, not on metadata.

When activating MD5 digests with `ncecat` or `ncrcat` it is assumed that the user wishes to verify that every variable written to disk has the same MD5 digest as when it is subsequently read from disk. This incurs the major additional overhead of reading in each variable after it is written and performing the hash algorithm again on that to compare to the original hash. Moreover, it is assumed that such operations are generally done "production mode" where the user is not interested in actually examining the digests herself. The digests proceed silently unless the debugging level exceeds three:

```
> ncecat -O -D 4 --md5 -p ~/nco/data in.nc in.nc ~/foo.nc | grep MD5
...
ncecat: INFO MD5(wnd_spd) = bec190dd944f2ce2794a7a4abf224b28
ncecat: INFO MD5 digests of RAM and disk contents for wnd_spd agree
> ncrcat -O -D 4 --md5 -p ~/nco/data in.nc in.nc ~/foo.nc | grep MD5
...
ncrcat: INFO MD5(wnd_spd) = 74699bb0a72b7f16456badb2c995f1a1
ncrcat: INFO MD5 digests of RAM and disk contents for wnd_spd agree
```

Regardless of the debugging level, an error is returned when the digests of the variable read from the source file and from the output file disagree.

These rules are evolving and as NCO pays more attention to data integrity. We welcome feedback and suggestions from users.

## 3.32 Buffer sizes

Availability: All operators
Short options:
Long options: '`--bfr_sz_hnt`', '`--buffer_size_hint`'

As of NCO version 4.2.0 (May, 2012), NCO allows the user to request specific buffer sizes to allocate for reading and writing files. This buffer size determines how many system calls the netCDF layer must invoke to read and write files. By default, netCDF uses the preferred I/O block size returned as the '`st_blksize`' member of the '`stat`' structure returned by the `stat()` system call[26]. Otherwise, netCDF uses twice the system pagesize. Larger sizes can increase access speed by reducing the number of system calls netCDF makes to read/write data from/to disk. Because netCDF cannot guarantee the buffer size request will be met, the actual buffer size granted by the system is printed as an INFO statement.

```
# Request 2 MB file buffer instead of default 8 kB buffer
> ncks -O -D 3 --bfr_sz=2097152 ~/nco/data/in.nc ~/foo.nc
...
ncks: INFO nc__open() will request file buffer size = 2097152 bytes
ncks: INFO nc__open() opened file with buffer size = 2097152 bytes
...
```

## 3.33 RAM disks

Availability: All operators
Short options:
Long options: '`--ram_all`', '`--create_ram`', '`--open_ram`', '`--diskless_all`'

As of NCO version 4.2.1 (August, 2012), NCO supports the use of diskless files, aka RAM disks, for file access and creation. Two independent switches, '`--open_ram`' and '`--create_ram`', control this feature. Before describing the specifics of these switches, we describe why many NCO operations will not benefit from them. Essentially, reading/writing from/to RAM rather than disk only hastens the task when reads/writes to disk are avoided. Most NCO operations are simple enough that they require a single read-from/write-to disk for every block of input/output. Diskless access does not change this, but it does add an extra read-from/write-to RAM. However this extra RAM write/read does avoid contention for limited system resources like disk-head access. Operators which may benefit from RAM disks include `ncwa`, which may need to read weighting variables multiple times, the multi-file operators `ncra`, `ncrcat`, and `ncecat`, which may try to write output at least once per input file, and `ncap2` scripts which may be arbitrarily long and convoluted.

The '`--open_ram`' switch causes input files to copied to RAM when opened. All further metadata and data access occurs in RAM and thus avoids access time delays caused by disk-head movement. Usually input data is read at most once so it is unlikely that requesting input files be stored in RAM will save much time. The likeliest exceptions are files that are accessed numerous times, such as those analyzed extensively analyzed by `ncap2`.

Invoking '`--open_ram`', '`--ram_all`', or '`--diskless_all`' uses much more system memory. To copy the input file to RAM increases the sustained memory use by exactly the on-disk filesize of the input file, i.e., $MS+ = FT$. For large input files this can be a huge memory burden that starves the rest of the NCO analysis of sufficient RAM. To be safe, use '`--open_ram`', '`--ram_all`', or '`--diskless_all`' only on files that are much (say at least a factor of four) smaller than your available system RAM. See Section 2.9 [Memory Requirements], page 24, for further details.

[26] On modern Linux systems the block size defaults to 8192 B. The GLADE filesystem at NCAR has a block size of 512 kB.

The '--create_ram' switch causes output files to be created in RAM, rather than on disk. These files are copied to disk only when closed, i.e., when the operator completes. Creating files in RAM may save time, especially with ncap2 computations that are iterative, e.g., loops, and for multi-file operators that write output every record (timestep) or file. RAM files provide many of the same benefits as RAM variables in such cases (see Section 4.1.13 [RAM variables], page 161).

Two switches, '--ram_all' and '--diskless_all', are convenient shortcuts for specifying both '--create_ram' and '--diskless_ram'. Thus

```
ncks in.nc out.nc # Default: Open in.nc on disk, write out.nc to disk
ncks --open_ram in.nc out.nc # Open in.nc in RAM, write out.nc to disk
ncks --create_ram in.nc out.nc # Create out.nc in RAM, write to disk
# Open in.nc in RAM, create out.nc in RAM, then write out.nc to disk
ncks --open_ram --create_ram in.nc out.nc
ncks --ram_all in.nc out.nc # Same as above
ncks --diskless_all in.nc out.nc # Same as above
```

It is straightforward to demonstrate the efficacy of RAM disks. For NASA we constructed a test that employs ncecat an arbitrary number (set to one hundred thousand) of files are all symbolically linked to the same file. Everything is on the local filesystem (not DAP).

```
# Create symbolic links for benchmark
cd ${DATA}/nco # Do all work here
for idx in {1..99999}; do
  idx_fmt=`printf "%05d" ${idx}`
  /bin/ln -s ${DATA}/nco/LPRM-AMSR_E_L3_D_SOILM3_V002-20120512T111931Z_20020619.nc \
             ${DATA}/nco/${idx_fmt}.nc
done
# Benchmark time to ncecat one hundred thousand files
time ncecat --create_ram -O -u time -v ts -d Latitude,40.0 \
 -d Longitude,-105.0 -p ${DATA}/nco -n 99999,5,1 00001.nc ~/foo.nc
```

Run normally on a laptop in 201303, this completes in 21 seconds. The '--create_ram' reduces the elapsed time to 9 seconds. Some of this speed may be due to using symlinks and caching. However, the efficacy of '--create_ram' is clear. Placing the output file in RAM avoids thousands of disk writes. It is not unreasonable to for NCO to process a million files like this in a few minutes. However, there is no substitute for benchmarking with real files.

A completely independent way to reduce time spent writing files is to refrain from writing temporary output files. This is accomplished with the '--no_tmp_fl' switch (see Section 2.3 [Temporary Output Files], page 17).

## 3.34 Packed data

Availability: `ncap2`, `ncbo`, `nces`, `ncflint`, `ncpdq`, `ncra`, `ncwa`
Short options: None
Long options: '`--hdf_upk`', '`--hdf_unpack`'

The phrase *packed data* refers to data which are stored in the standard netCDF3 lossy linear packing format. See Section 4.8 [ncks netCDF Kitchen Sink], page 237, for a description of deflation, a lossless compression technique available with netCDF4 only. Packed data may be deflated to save additional space.

## Packing Algorithm

*Packing* The standard netCDF linear packing algorithm (described here (`http://www.unidata.ucar.edu/software/netcdf/docs/netcdf/Attribute-Conventions.html`)) produces packed data with the same dynamic range as the original but which requires no more than half the space to store. Like all packing algorithms, linear packing is *lossy*. Just how lossy depends on the values themselves, especially their range. The packed variable is stored (usually) as type `NC_SHORT` with the two attributes required to unpack the variable, `scale_factor` and `add_offset`, stored at the original (unpacked) precision of the variable[27]. Let *min* and *max* be the minimum and maximum values of *x*.

$$\begin{aligned} \text{scale\_factor} &= (\max - \min)/\text{ndrv} \\ \text{add\_offset} &= (\min + \max)/2 \\ \text{pck} &= (\text{upk} - \text{add\_offset})/\text{scale\_factor} \\ &= \frac{\text{ndrv} \times [\text{upk} - (\min + \max)/2]}{\max - \min} \end{aligned}$$

where *ndrv* is the number of discrete representable values for given type of packed variable. The theoretical maximum value for *ndrv* is two raised to the number of bits used to store the packed variable. Thus if the variable is packed into type `NC_SHORT`, a two-byte datatype, then there are at most $2^{16} = 65536$ distinct values representable. In practice, the number of discretely representible values is taken to be two less than the theoretical maximum. This leaves space for a missing value and solves potential problems with rounding that may occur during the unpacking of the variable. Thus for `NC_SHORT`, $ndrv = 65536 - 2 = 65534$. Less often, the variable may be packed into type `NC_CHAR`, where $ndrv = 2^8 - 2 = 256 - 2 = 254$, or type `NC_INT` where where $ndrv = 2^{32} - 2 = 4294967295 - 2 = 4294967293$. One useful feature of (lossy) netCDF packing algorithm is that additional, loss-less packing algorithms perform well on top of it.

## Unpacking Algorithm

*Unpacking* The unpacking algorithm depends on the presence of two attributes, `scale_factor` and `add_offset`. If `scale_factor` is present for a variable, the data are multiplied by the value *scale_factor* after the data are read. If `add_offset` is present for a variable, then the *add_offset* value is added to the data after the data are read. If both `scale_factor` and `add_offset` attributes are present, the data are first scaled by *scale_factor* before the

[27] Although not a part of the standard, NCO enforces the policy that the `_FillValue` attribute, if any, of a packed variable is also stored at the original precision.

offset *add_offset* is added.

$$\begin{aligned}\text{upk} &= \text{scale\_factor} \times \text{pck} + \text{add\_offset}\\ &= \frac{\text{pck} \times (\text{max} - \text{min})}{\text{ndrv}} + \frac{\text{min} + \text{max}}{2}\end{aligned}$$

When `scale_factor` and `add_offset` are used for packing, the associated variable (containing the packed data) is typically of type `byte` or `short`, whereas the unpacked values are intended to be of type `int`, `float`, or `double`. An attribute's `scale_factor` and `add_offset` and `_FillValue`, if any, should all be of the type intended for the unpacked data, i.e., `int`, `float` or `double`.

## Default Handling of Packed Data

Many (most?) files originally written in HDF4 format use poorly documented HDF packing/unpacking algorithms that are incompatible and easily confused with the netCDF packing algorithm described above. The unpacking component of the "conventional" HDF algorithm (described here (`http://www.hdfgroup.org/HDF5/doc/UG/UG_frame10Datasets.html`) and in Section 3.10.6 of the HDF4 Users Guide here (`http://www.hdfgroup.org/release4/doc/UsrGuide_html/UG_PDF.pdf`)) and in the FAQ for MODIS MOD08 data here (`http://modis-atmos.gsfc.nasa.gov/MOD08_D3/faq.html`)) is

$$\text{upk} = \text{scale\_factor} \times (\text{pck} - \text{add\_offset})$$

The unpacking component of the HDF algorithm employed for MODIS MOD13 data is

$$\text{upk} = (\text{pck} - \text{add\_offset})/\text{scale\_factor}$$

The unpacking component of the HDF algorithm employed for MODIS MOD04 data is the same as the netCDF algorithm.

Confusingly, the (incompatible) netCDF and HDF algorithms both store their parameters in attributes with the same names (`scale_factor` and `add_offset`). Data packed with one algorithm should never be unpacked with the other; doing so will result in incorrect answers. Unfortunately, few users are aware that their datasets may be packed, and fewer know the details of the packing algorithm employed. This is what we in the "bizness" call an *interoperability* issue because it hampers data analysis performed on heterogeneous systems.

As described below, NCO automatically unpacks data before performing arithmetic. This automatic unpacking occurs silently since there is usually no reason to bother users with these details. There is as yet no generic way for NCO to know which packing convention was used, so NCO *assumes* the netCDF convention was used. NCO uses the same convention for unpacking unless explicitly told otherwise with the '`--hdf_upk`' (also '`--hdf_unpack`') switch. Until and unless a method of automatically detecting the packing method is devised, it must remain the user's responsibility to tell NCO when to use the HDF convention instead of the netCDF convention to unpack.

If your data originally came from an HDF file (e.g., NASA EOS) then it was likely packed with the HDF convention and must be unpacked with the same convention. Our recommendation is to only request HDF unpacking when you are certain. Most packed datasets encountered by NCO will have used the netCDF convention. Those that were not will hopefully produce noticeably weird values when unpacked by the wrong algorithm. Before or after panicking, treat this as a clue to re-try your commands with the '`--hdf_upk`' switch. See Section 4.9 [ncpdq netCDF Permute Dimensions Quickly], page 254, for an easy technique to unpack data packed with the HDF convention, and then re-pack it with the netCDF convention.

### Default Handling of Packed Data

All NCO arithmetic operators understand packed data. The operators automatically unpack any packed variable in the input file which will be arithmetically processed. For example, `ncra` unpacks all record variables, and `ncwa` unpacks all variable which contain a dimension to be averaged. These variables are stored unpacked in the output file.

On the other hand, arithmetic operators do not unpack non-processed variables. For example, `ncra` leaves all non-record variables packed, and `ncwa` leaves packed all variables lacking an averaged dimension. These variables (called fixed variables) are passed unaltered from the input to the output file. Hence fixed variables which are packed in input files remain packed in output files. Completely packing and unpacking files is easily accomplished with `ncpdq` (see Section 4.9 [ncpdq netCDF Permute Dimensions Quickly], page 254). Pack and unpack individual variables with `ncpdq` and the `ncap2` `pack()` and `unpack()` functions (see Section 4.1.12 [Methods and functions], page 158).

## 3.35 Operation Types

Availability: `ncap2`, `ncra`, `nces`, `ncwa`
Short options: '`-y`'
Long options: '`--operation`', '`--op_typ`'

The '`-y` *op_typ*' switch allows specification of many different types of operations Set *op_typ* to the abbreviated key for the corresponding operation:

`avg` Mean value

`sqravg` Square of the mean

`avgsqr` Mean of sum of squares

`max` Maximum value

`min` Minimum value

`mabs` Maximum absolute value

`mebs` Mean absolute value

`mibs` Minimum absolute value

`rms` Root-mean-square (normalized by $N$)

`rmssdn` Root-mean square (normalized by $N-1$)

`sqrt` Square root of the mean

`tabs` Sum of absolute values

`ttl` Sum of values

NCO assumes coordinate variables represent grid axes, e.g., longitude. The only rank-reduction which makes sense for coordinate variables is averaging. Hence NCO implements the operation type requested with '`-y`' on all non-coordinate variables, not on coordinate variables. When an operation requires a coordinate variable to be reduced in rank, i.e., from one dimension to a scalar or from one dimension to a degenerate (single value) array, then NCO *always averages* the coordinate variable regardless of the arithmetic operation type performed on the non-coordinate variables.

The mathematical definition of each arithmetic operation is given below. See Section 4.14 [ncwa netCDF Weighted Averager], page 283, for additional information on masks and normalization. If an operation type is not specified with '`-y`' then the operator performs an arithmetic average by default. Averaging is described first so the terminology for the other operations is familiar.

The masked, weighted average of a variable $x$ can be generally represented as

$$\bar{x}_j = \frac{\sum_{i=1}^{i=N} \mu_i m_i w_i x_i}{\sum_{i=1}^{i=N} \mu_i m_i w_i}$$

where $\bar{x}_j$ is the $j$'th element of the output hyperslab, $x_i$ is the $i$'th element of the input hyperslab, $\mu_i$ is 1 unless $x_i$ equals the missing value, $m_i$ is 1 unless $x_i$ is masked, and $w_i$ is the weight. This formiddable looking formula represents a simple weighted average whose bells and whistles are all explained below. It is not too early to note, however, that when $\mu_i = m_i = w_i = 1$, the generic averaging expression above reduces to a simple arithmetic average. Furthermore, $m_i = w_i = 1$ for all operators except `ncwa`. These variables are included in the discussion below for completeness, and for possible future use in other operators.

The size $J$ of the output hyperslab for a given variable is the product of all the dimensions of the input variable which are not averaged over. The size $N$ of the input hyperslab contributing to each $\bar{x}_j$ is simply the product of the sizes of all dimensions which are averaged over (i.e., dimensions specified with '`-a`'). Thus $N$ is the number of input elements which *potentially* contribute to each output element. An input element $x_i$ contributes to the output element $x_j$ except in two conditions:

1. $x_i$ equals the *missing value* (see Section 3.27 [Missing Values], page 89) for the variable.
2. $x_i$ is located at a point where the mask condition (see Section 4.14.1 [Mask condition], page 284) is false.

Points $x_i$ in either of these two categories do not contribute to $x_j$—they are ignored. We now define these criteria more rigorously.

Each $x_i$ has an associated Boolean weight $\mu_i$ whose value is 0 or 1 (false or true). The value of $\mu_i$ is 1 (true) unless $x_i$ equals the *missing value* (see Section 3.27 [Missing Values], page 89) for the variable. Thus, for a variable with no `_FillValue` attribute, $\mu_i$ is always 1. All NCO arithmetic operators (`ncbo`, `ncra`, `nces`, `ncflint`, `ncwa`) treat missing values analogously.

Besides (weighted) averaging, `ncwa`, `ncra`, and `nces` also compute some common non-linear operations which may be specified with the '`-y`' switch (see Section 3.35 [Operation Types], page 114). The other rank-reducing operations are simple variations of the generic weighted mean described above. The total value of $x$ (`-y ttl`) is

$$\bar{x}_j = \sum_{i=1}^{i=N} \mu_i m_i w_i x_i$$

Note that the total is the same as the numerator of the mean of $x$, and may also be obtained in `ncwa` by using the '`-N`' switch (see Section 4.14 [ncwa netCDF Weighted Averager], page 283).

The minimum value of $x$ (`-y min`) is

$$\bar{x}_j = \min[\mu_1 m_1 w_1 x_1, \mu_2 m_2 w_2 x_2, \ldots, \mu_N m_N w_N x_N]$$

Analogously, the maximum value of $x$ (`-y max`) is

$$\bar{x}_j = \max[\mu_1 m_1 w_1 x_1, \mu_2 m_2 w_2 x_2, \ldots, \mu_N m_N w_N x_N]$$

Thus the minima and maxima are determined after any weights are applied.

The total absolute value of $x$ (`-y tabs`) is

$$\bar{x}_j = \sum_{i=1}^{i=N} \mu_i m_i w_i |x_i|$$

The minimum absolute value of $x$ (`-y mibs`) is

$$\bar{x}_j = \min[\mu_1 m_1 w_1 |x_1|, \mu_2 m_2 w_2 |x_2|, \ldots, \mu_N m_N w_N |x_N|]$$

Analogously, the maximum absolute value of $x$ (`-y mabs`) is

$$\bar{x}_j = \max[\mu_1 m_1 w_1 |x_1|, \mu_2 m_2 w_2 |x_2|, \ldots, \mu_N m_N w_N |x_N|]$$

Thus the minimum and maximum absolute values are determined after any weights are applied. The mean absolute value of $x$ (`-y mebs`) is

$$\bar{x}_j = \frac{\sum_{i=1}^{i=N} \mu_i m_i w_i |x_i|}{\sum_{i=1}^{i=N} \mu_i m_i w_i}$$

The square of the mean value of $x$ (`-y sqravg`) is

$$\bar{x}_j = \left( \frac{\sum_{i=1}^{i=N} \mu_i m_i w_i x_i}{\sum_{i=1}^{i=N} \mu_i m_i w_i} \right)^2$$

The mean of the sum of squares of $x$ (`-y avgsqr`) is

$$\bar{x}_j = \frac{\sum_{i=1}^{i=N} \mu_i m_i w_i x_i^2}{\sum_{i=1}^{i=N} \mu_i m_i w_i}$$

If $x$ represents a deviation from the mean of another variable, $x_i = y_i - \bar{y}$ (possibly created by `ncbo` in a previous step), then applying `avgsqr` to $x$ computes the approximate variance of $y$. Computing the true variance of $y$ requires subtracting 1 from the denominator, discussed below. For a large sample size however, the two results will be nearly indistinguishable.

The root mean square of $x$ (`-y rms`) is

$$\bar{x}_j = \sqrt{\frac{\sum_{i=1}^{i=N} \mu_i m_i w_i x_i^2}{\sum_{i=1}^{i=N} \mu_i m_i w_i}}$$

Thus `rms` simply computes the squareroot of the quantity computed by `avgsqr`.

The root mean square of $x$ with standard-deviation-like normalization (`-y rmssdn`) is implemented as follows. When weights are not specified, this function is the same as the root mean square of $x$ except one is subtracted from the sum in the denominator

$$\bar{x}_j = \sqrt{\frac{\sum_{i=1}^{i=N} \mu_i m_i x_i^2}{-1 + \sum_{i=1}^{i=N} \mu_i m_i}}$$

If $x$ represents the deviation from the mean of another variable, $x_i = y_i - \bar{y}$, then applying `rmssdn` to $x$ computes the standard deviation of $y$. In this case the $-1$ in the denominator compensates for the degree of freedom already used in computing $\bar{y}$ in the numerator. Consult a statistics book for more details.

When weights are specified it is unclear how to compensate for this extra degree of freedom. Weighting the numerator and denominator of the above by $w_i$ and subtracting one from the denominator is only appropriate when all the weights are 1.0. When the weights are arbitrary (e.g., Gaussian weights), subtracting one from the sum in the denominator does not necessarily remove one degree of freedom. Therefore when `-y rmssdn` is requested and weights are specified, `ncwa` actually implements the `rms` procedure. `nces` and `ncra`, which do not allow weights to be specified, always implement the `rmssdn` procedure when asked.

The square root of the mean of $x$ (`-y sqrt`) is

$$\bar{x}_j = \sqrt{\frac{\sum_{i=1}^{i=N} \mu_i m_i w_i x_i}{\sum_{i=1}^{i=N} \mu_i m_i w_i}}$$

The definitions of some of these operations are not universally useful. Mostly they were chosen to facilitate standard statistical computations within the NCO framework. We are open to redefining and or adding to the above. If you are interested in having other statistical quantities defined in NCO please contact the NCO project (see Section 1.7 [Help Requests and Bug Reports], page 15).

EXAMPLES

Suppose you wish to examine the variable prs_sfc(time,lat,lon) which contains a time series of the surface pressure as a function of latitude and longitude. Find the minimum value of prs_sfc over all dimensions:

```
ncwa -y min -v prs_sfc in.nc foo.nc
```

Find the maximum value of prs_sfc at each time interval for each latitude:

```
ncwa -y max -v prs_sfc -a lon in.nc foo.nc
```

Find the root-mean-square value of the time-series of prs_sfc at every gridpoint:

```
ncra -y rms -v prs_sfc in.nc foo.nc
ncwa -y rms -v prs_sfc -a time in.nc foo.nc
```

The previous two commands give the same answer but ncra is preferred because it has a smaller memory footprint. A dimension of size one is said to be *degenerate*. By default, ncra leaves the (degenerate) time dimension in the output file (which is usually useful) whereas ncwa removes the time dimension (unless '-b' is given).

These operations work as expected in multi-file operators. Suppose that prs_sfc is stored in multiple timesteps per file across multiple files, say jan.nc, feb.nc, march.nc. We can now find the three month maximum surface pressure at every point.

```
nces -y max -v prs_sfc jan.nc feb.nc march.nc out.nc
```

It is possible to use a combination of these operations to compute the variance and standard deviation of a field stored in a single file or across multiple files. The procedure to compute the temporal standard deviation of the surface pressure at all points in a single file in.nc involves three steps.

```
ncwa -O -v prs_sfc -a time in.nc out.nc
ncbo -O -v prs_sfc in.nc out.nc out.nc
ncra -O -y rmssdn out.nc out.nc
```

First construct the temporal mean of prs_sfc in the file out.nc. Next overwrite out.nc with the anomaly (deviation from the mean). Finally overwrite out.nc with the root-mean-square of itself. Note the use of '-y rmssdn' (rather than '-y rms') in the final step. This ensures the standard deviation is correctly normalized by one fewer than the number of time samples. The procedure to compute the variance is identical except for the use of '-y avgsqr' instead of '-y rmssdn' in the final step.

ncap2 can also compute statistics like standard deviations. Brute-force implementation of formulae is one option, e.g.,

```
ncap2 -s 'prs_sfc_sdn=sqrt((prs_sfc-prs_sfc.avg($time)^2). \
      total($time)/($time.size-1))' in.nc out.nc
```

The operation may, of course, be broken into multiple steps in order to archive intermediate quantities, such as the time-anomalies

```
ncap2 -s 'prs_sfc_anm=prs_sfc-prs_sfc.avg($time)' \
      -s 'prs_sfc_sdn=sqrt((prs_sfc_anm^2).total($time)/($time.size-1))' \
```

```
          in.nc out.nc
```

ncap2 supports intrinsic standard deviation functions (see Section 3.35 [Operation Types], page 114) which simplify the above expression to

```
ncap2 -s 'prs_sfc_sdn=(prs_sfc-prs_sfc.avg($time)).rmssdn($time)' in.nc out.nc
```

These instrinsic functions compute the answer quickly and concisely.

The procedure to compute the spatial standard deviation of a field in a single file in.nc involves three steps.

```
ncwa -O -v prs_sfc,gw -a lat,lon -w gw in.nc out.nc
ncbo -O -v prs_sfc,gw in.nc out.nc out.nc
ncwa -O -y rmssdn -v prs_sfc -a lat,lon -w gw out.nc out.nc
```

First the spatially weighted (by '-w gw') mean values are written to the output file, as are the mean weights. The initial output file is then overwritten with the gridpoint deviations from the spatial mean. It is important that the output file after the second line contain the original, non-averaged weights. This will be the case if the weights are named so that NCO treats them like a coordinate (see Section 3.41 [CF Conventions], page 131). One such name is gw, and any variable whose name begins with msk_ (for "mask") or wgt_ (for "weight") will likewise be treated as a coordinate, and will be copied (not differenced) straight from in.nc to out.nc in the second step. When using weights to compute standard deviations one must remember to include the weights in the initial output files so that they may be used again in the final step. Finally the root-mean-square of the appropriately weighted spatial deviations is taken.

No elegant ncap2 solution exists to compute weighted standard deviations. Those brave of heart may try to formulate one. A general formula should allow weights to have fewer than and variables to have more than the minimal spatial dimensions (latitude and longitude).

The procedure to compute the standard deviation of a time-series across multiple files involves one extra step since all the input must first be collected into one file.

```
ncrcat -O -v tpt in.nc in.nc foo1.nc
ncwa -O -a time foo1.nc foo2.nc
ncbo -O -v tpt foo1.nc foo2.nc foo3.nc
ncra -O -y rmssdn foo3.nc out.nc
```

The first step assembles all the data into a single file. Though this may consume a lot of temporary disk space, it is more or less required by the ncbo operation in the third step.

## 3.36 Type Conversion

Availability (automatic type conversion): ncap2, ncbo, nces, ncflint, ncra, ncwa
Short options: None (it's *automatic*)
Availability (manual type conversion): nces, ncra, ncwa
Short options: None
Long options: '--dbl', '--flt', '--rth_dbl', '--rth_flt'

Type conversion refers to the casting or coercion of one fundamental or atomic data type to another, e.g., converting `NC_SHORT` (two bytes) to `NC_DOUBLE` (eight bytes). Type conversion always *promotes* or *demotes* the range and/or precision of the values a variable can hold. Type conversion is automatic when the language carries out this promotion according to an internal set of rules without explicit user intervention. In contrast, manual type conversion refers to explicit user commands to change the type of a variable or attribute. Most type conversion happens automatically, yet there are situations in which manual type conversion is advantageous.

### 3.36.1 Automatic type conversion

There are at least two reasons to avoid type conversions. First, type conversions are expensive since they require creating (temporary) buffers and casting each element of a variable from its storage type to some other type and then, often, converting it back. Second, a dataset's creator perhaps had a good reason for storing data as, say, `NC_FLOAT` rather than `NC_DOUBLE`. In a scientific framework there is no reason to store data with more precision than the observations merit. Normally this is single-precision, which guarantees 6–9 digits of precision. Reasons to engage in type conversion include avoiding rounding errors and out-of-range limitations of less-precise types. This is the case with most integers. Thus NCO defaults to automatically promote integer types to floating-point when performing lengthy arithmetic, yet NCO defaults to not promoting single to double-precision floats.

Before discussing the more subtle floating-point issues, we first examine integer promotion. We will show how following parsimonious conversion rules dogmatically can cause problems, and what NCO does about that. That said, there are situations in which implicit conversion of single- to double-precision is also warranted. Understanding the narrowness of these situations takes time, and we hope the reader appreciates the following detailed discussion.

Consider the average of the two `NC_SHORT`s `17000s` and `17000s`. A straightforward average without promotion results in garbage since the intermediate value which holds their sum is also of type `NC_SHORT` and thus overflows on (i.e., cannot represent) values greater than 32,767[28]. There are valid reasons for expecting this operation to succeed and the NCO philosophy is to make operators do what you want, not what is purest. Thus, unlike C and Fortran, but like many other higher level interpreted languages, NCO arithmetic operators will perform automatic type conversion on integers when all the following conditions are met[29]:

1. The requested operation is arithmetic. This is why type conversion is limited to the operators `ncap2`, `ncbo`, `nces`, `ncflint`, `ncra`, and `ncwa`.
2. The arithmetic operation could benefit from type conversion. Operations that could benefit include averaging, summation, or any "hard" arithmetic that could overflow or underflow. Larger representable sums help avoid overflow, and more precision helps to avoid underflow. Type conversion does not benefit searching for minima and maxima ('`-y min`', or '`-y max`').

---

[28] $32767 = 2^{15} - 1$

[29] Operators began performing automatic type conversions before arithmetic in NCO version 1.2, August, 2000. Previous versions never performed unnecessary type conversion for arithmetic.

3. The variable on disk is of type NC_BYTE, NC_CHAR, NC_SHORT, or NC_INT. Type NC_DOUBLE is not promoted because there is no type of higher precision. Conversion of type NC_FLOAT is discussed in detail below. When it occurs, it follows the same procedure (promotion then arithmetic then demotion) as conversion of integer types.

When these criteria are all met, the operator promotes the variable in question to type NC_DOUBLE, performs all the arithmetic operations, casts the NC_DOUBLE type back to the original type, and finally writes the result to disk. The result written to disk may not be what you expect, because of incommensurate ranges represented by different types, and because of (lack of) rounding. First, continuing the above example, the average (e.g., '-y avg') of 17000s and 17000s is written to disk as 17000s. The type conversion feature of NCO makes this possible since the arithmetic and intermediate values are stored as NC_DOUBLEs, i.e., 34000.0d and only the final result must be represented as an NC_SHORT. Without the type conversion feature of NCO, the average would have been garbage (albeit predictable garbage near -15768s). Similarly, the total (e.g., '-y ttl') of 17000s and 17000s written to disk is garbage (actually -31536s) since the final result (the true total) of 34000 is outside the range of type NC_SHORT.

After arithmetic is computed in double-precision for promoted variables, the intermediate double-precision values must be demoted to the variables' original storage type (e.g., from NC_DOUBLE to NC_SHORT). NCO has handled this demotion in three ways in its history. Prior to October, 2011 (version 4.0.8), NCO employed the C library truncate function, trunc()[30]. Truncation rounds $x$ to the nearest integer not larger in absolute value. For example, truncation rounds 1.0d, 1.5d, and 1.8d to the same value, 1s. Clearly, truncation does not round floating-point numbers to the nearest integer! Yet truncation is how the C language performs implicit conversion of real numbers to integers.

NCO stopped using truncation for demotion when an alert user (Neil Davis) informed us that this caused a small bias in the packing algorithm employed by ncpdq. This led to NCO adopting rounding functions for demotion. Rounding functions eliminated the small bias in the packing algorithm.

From February, 2012 through March, 2013 (versions 4.0.9–4.2.6), NCO employed the C library family of rounding functions, lround(). These functions round $x$ to the nearest integer, halfway cases away from zero. The problem with lround() is that it always rounds real values ending in .5 away from zero. This rounds, for example, 1.5d and 2.5d to 2s and 3s, respectively.

Since April, 2013 (version 4.3.0), NCO has employed the other C library family of rounding functions, lrint(). This algorithm rounds $x$ to the nearest integer, using the current rounding direction. Halfway cases are rounded to the nearest even integer. This rounds, for example, both 1.5d and 2.5d to the same value, 2s, as recommended by the IEEE. This rounding is symmetric: up half the time, down half the time. This is the current and hopefully final demotion algorithm employed by NCO.

Hence because of automatic conversion, NCO will compute the average of 2s and 3s in double-precision arithmetic as (2.0d+3.0d)/2.0d) = 2.5d. It then demotes this intermediate

---

30 The actual type conversions with trunction were handled by intrinsic type conversion, so the trunc() function was never explicitly called, although the results would be the same if it were.

result back to `NC_SHORT` and stores it on disk as `trunc(2.5d)` = `2s` (versions up to 4.0.8), `lround(2.5d)` = `3s` (versions 4.0.9–4.2.6), and `lrint(2.5d)` = `2s` (versions 4.3.0 and later).

### 3.36.2 Promoting Single-precision to Double

Promotion of real numbers from single- to double-precision is fundamental to scientific computing. When it should occur depends on the precision of the inputs and the number of operations. Single-precision (four-byte) numbers contain about seven significant figures, while double-precision contain about sixteen. More, err, precisely, the IEEE single-precision representation gives from 6 to 9 significant decimal digits precision[31]. And the IEEE double-precision representation gives from 15 to 17 significant decimal digits precision[32]. Hence double-precision numbers represent about nine digits more precision than single-precision numbers.

Given these properties, there are at least two possible arithmetic conventions for the treatment of real numbers:

1. Conservative, aka Fortran Convention Automatic type conversion during arithmetic in the Fortran language is, by default, performed only when necessary. All operands in an operation are converted to the most precise type involved the operation before the arithmetic operation. Expressions which involve only single-precision numbers are computed entirely in single-precision. Expressions involving mixed precision types are computed in the type of higher precision. NCO by default employs the Fortan Convention for promotion.
2. Aggressive, aka C Convention The C language is by default much more aggressive (and thus wasteful) than Fortran, and will always implicitly convert single- to double-precision numbers for no good reason. All real-number standard C library functions are double-precision, and C programmers must take extra steps to only utilize single precision arithmetic. The high level interpreted data analysis languages IDL, Matlab, and NCL all adopt the C Convention.

NCO does not automatically promote `NC_FLOAT` because, in our judgement, the performance penalty of always doing so would outweigh the potential benefits. The now-classic text "Numerical Recipes in C" discusses this point under the section "Implicit Conversion of Float to Double"[33]. That said, such promotion is warranted in some circumstances.

---

[31] According to Wikipedia's summary of IEEE standard 754, "If a decimal string with at most 6 significant digits is converted to IEEE 754 single-precision and then converted back to the same number of significant decimal, then the final string should match the original; and if an IEEE 754 single-precision is converted to a decimal string with at leastn 9 significant decimal and then converted back to single, then the final number must match the original".

[32] According to Wikipedia's summary of IEEE standard 754, "If a decimal string with at most 15 significant digits is converted to IEEE 754 double-precision representation and then converted back to a string with the same number of significant digits, then the final string should match the original; and if an IEEE 754 double precision is converted to a decimal string with at least 17 significant digits and then converted back to double, then the final number must match the original".

[33] See page 21 in Section 1.2 of the First edition for this gem:

> One does not need much experience in scientific computing to recognize that the implicit conversion rules are, in fact, sheer madness! In effect, they make it impossible to write efficient numerical programs.

For example, rounding errors can accumulate to worrisome levels during arithmetic performed on large arrays of single-precision floats. This use-case occurs often in geoscientific studies of climate where thousands-to-millions of gridpoints may contribute to a single average. If the inputs are all single-precision, then so should be the output. However the intermediate results where running sums are accumulated may suffer from too much rounding or from underflow unless computed in double-precision.

The order of operations matters to floating-point math even when the analytic expressions are equal. Cautious users feel disquieted when results from equally valid analyses differ in the final bits instead of agreeing bit-for-bit. For example, averaging arrays in multiple stages produces different answers than averaging them in one step. This is easily seen in the computation of ensemble averages by two different methods. The NCO test file `in.nc` contains single- and double-precision representations of the same temperature timeseries as `tpt_flt` and `tpt_dbl`. Pretend each datapoint in this timeseries represents a monthly-mean temperature. We will mimic the derivation of a fifteen-year ensemble-mean January temperature by concatenating the input file five times, and then averaging the datapoints representing January two different ways. In Method 1 we derive the 15-year ensemble January average in two steps, as the average of three five-year averages. This method is naturally used when each input file contains multiple years and multiple input files are needed[34]. In Method 2 we obtain 15-year ensemble January average in a single step, by averaging all 15 Januaries at one time:

```
# tpt_flt and tpt_dbl are identical except for precision
ncks --cdl -C -v tpt_flt,tpt_dbl ~/nco/data/in.nc
# tpt_dbl = 273.1, 273.2, 273.3, 273.4, 273.5, 273.6, 273.7, 273.8, 273.9, 274
# tpt_flt = 273.1, 273.2, 273.3, 273.4, 273.5, 273.6, 273.7, 273.8, 273.9, 274
# Create file with five "ten-month years" (i.e., 50 timesteps) of temperature data
ncrcat -O -v tpt_flt,tpt_dbl -p ~/nco/data in.nc in.nc in.nc in.nc in.nc ~/foo.nc
# Average 1st five "Januaries" (elements 1, 11, 21, 31, 41)
ncra --flt -O -F -d time,1,,10 ~/foo.nc ~/foo_avg1.nc
# Average 2nd five "Januaries" (elements 2, 12, 22, 32, 42)
ncra --flt -O -F -d time,2,,10 ~/foo.nc ~/foo_avg2.nc
# Average 3rd five "Januaries" (elements 3, 13, 23, 33, 43)
ncra --flt -O -F -d time,3,,10 ~/foo.nc ~/foo_avg3.nc
# Method 1: Obtain ensemble January average by averaging the averages
ncra --flt -O ~/foo_avg1.nc ~/foo_avg2.nc ~/foo_avg3.nc ~/foo_avg_mth1.nc
# Method 2: Obtain ensemble January average by averaging the raw data
# Employ ncra's "subcycle" feature (http://nco.sf.net/nco.html#ssc)
ncra --flt -O -F -d time,1,,10,3 ~/foo.nc ~/foo_avg_mth2.nc
# Difference the two methods
ncbo -O ~/foo_avg_mth1.nc ~/foo_avg_mth2.nc ~/foo_avg_dff.nc
ncks --cdl ~/foo_avg_dff.nc
# tpt_dbl = 5.6843418860808e-14 ;
# tpt_flt = -3.051758e-05 ;
```

Although the two methods are arithmetically equivalent, they produce slightly different answers due to the different order of operations. Moreover, it appears at first glance that

[34] For example, the CMIP5 archive tends to distribute monthly average timeseries in 50-year chunks.

the single-precision answers suffer from greater error than the double-precision answers. In fact both precisions suffer from non-zero rounding errors. The answers differ negligibly to machine precision, which is about seven significant figures for single precision floats (`tpt_flt`), and sixteen significant figures for double precision (`tpt_dbl`). The input precision determines the answer precision.

IEEE arithmetic guarantees that two methods will produce bit-for-bit identical answers only if they compute the same operations in the same order. Bit-for-bit identical answers may also occur by happenstance when rounding errors exactly compensate one another. This is demonstrated by repeating the example above with the '`--dbl`' (or '`--rth_dbl`' for clarity) option which forces conversion of single-precision numbers to double-precision prior to arithmetic. Now `ncra` will treat the first value of `tpt_flt`, `273.1000f`, as `273.1000000000000d`. Arithmetic on `tpt_flt` then proceeds in double-precision until the final answer, which is converted back to single-precision for final storage.

```
# Average 1st five "Januaries" (elements 1, 11, 21, 31, 41)
ncra --dbl -O -F -d time,1,,10 ~/foo.nc ~/foo_avg1.nc
# Average 2nd five "Januaries" (elements 2, 12, 22, 32, 42)
ncra --dbl -O -F -d time,2,,10 ~/foo.nc ~/foo_avg2.nc
# Average 3rd five "Januaries" (elements 3, 13, 23, 33, 43)
ncra --dbl -O -F -d time,3,,10 ~/foo.nc ~/foo_avg3.nc
# Method 1: Obtain ensemble January average by averaging the averages
ncra --dbl -O ~/foo_avg1.nc ~/foo_avg2.nc ~/foo_avg3.nc ~/foo_avg_mth1.nc
# Method 2: Obtain ensemble January average by averaging the raw data
# Employ ncra's "subcycle" feature (http://nco.sf.net/nco.html#ssc)
ncra --dbl -O -F -d time,1,,10,3 ~/foo.nc ~/foo_avg_mth2.nc
# Difference the two methods
ncbo -O ~/foo_avg_mth1.nc ~/foo_avg_mth2.nc ~/foo_avg_dff.nc
# Show differences
ncks --cdl ~/foo_avg_dff.nc
# tpt_dbl = 5.6843418860808e-14 ;
# tpt_flt = 0 ;
```

The '`--dbl`' switch has no effect on the results computed from double-precision inputs. But now the two methods produce bit-for-bit identical results from the single-precision inputs! This is due to the happenstance of rounding along with the effects of the '`--dbl`' switch. The '`--flt`' and '`--rth_flt`' switches are provided for symmetry. They enforce the traditional NCO and Fortran convention of keeping single-precision arithmetic in single-precision unless a double-precision number is explicitly involved.

We have shown that forced promotion of single- to double-precision prior to arithmetic has advantages and disadvantages. The primary disadvantages are speed and size. Double-precision arithmetic is 10–60% slower than, and requires twice the memory of single-precision arithmetic. The primary advantage is that rounding errors in double-precision are much less likely to accumulate to values near the precision of the underlying geophysical variable.

For example, if we know temperature to five significant digits, then a rounding error of 1-bit could affect the least precise digit of temperature after 1,000–10,000 consecutive one-sided rounding errors under the worst possible scenario. Many geophysical grids have tens-of-thousands to millions of points that must be summed prior to normalization to compute an average. It is possible for single-precision rouding errors to accumulate and degrade the precision in such situtations. Double-precision arithmetic mititgates this problem, so '`--dbl`' would be warranted.

This can be seen with another example, averaging a global surface temperature field with `ncwa`. The input contains a single-precision global temperature field (stored in `TREFHT`) produced by the CAM3 general circulation model (GCM) run and stored at 1.9 by 2.5 degrees resolution. This requires 94 latitudes and 144 longitudes, or 13,824 total surface gridpoints, a typical GCM resolution in 2008–2013. These input characteristics are provided only to show the context to the interested reader, equivalent results would be found in statistics of any dataset of comparable size. Models often represent Earth on a spherical grid where global averages must be created by weighting each gridcell by its latitude-dependent weight (e.g., a Gaussian weight stored in `gw`), or by the surface area of each contributing gridpoint (stored in `area`).

Like many geophysical models and most GCMs, CAM3 runs completely in double-precision yet stores its archival output in single-precision to save space. In practice such models usually save multi-dimensional prognostic and diagnostic fields (like `TREFHT(lat,lon)`) as single-precision, while saving all one-dimensional coordinates and weights (here `lat`, `lon`, and `gw(lon)`) as double-precision. The gridcell area `area(lat,lon)` is an extensive grid property that should be, but often is not, stored as double-precision. To obtain pure double-precision arithmetic *and* storage of the globla mean temperature, we first create and store double-precision versions of the single-precision fields:

```
ncap2 -O -s 'TREFHT_dbl=double(TREFHT);area_dbl=double(area)' in.nc in.nc
```

The single- and double-precision temperatures may each be averaged globally using four permutations for the precision of the weight and of the intermediate arithmetic representation:

1. Single-precision weight (`area`), single-precision arithmetic
2. Double-precision weight (`gw`), single-precision arithmetic
3. Single-precision weight (`area`), double-precision arithmetic
4. Double-precision weight (`gw`), double-precision arithmetic

```
# NB: Values below are printed with C-format %5.6f using
# ncks -H -C -s '%5.6f' -v TREFHT,TREFHT_dbl out.nc
# Single-precision weight (area), single-precision arithmetic
ncwa --flt -O -a lat,lon -w area in.nc out.nc
# TREFHT     = 289.246735
# TREFHT_dbl = 289.239964
# Double-precision weight (gw),   single-precision arithmetic
ncwa --flt -O -a lat,lon -w gw   in.nc out.nc
# TREFHT     = 289.226135
# TREFHT_dbl = 289.239964
# Single-precision weight (area), double-precision arithmetic
ncwa --dbl -O -a lat,lon -w area in.nc out.nc
```

```
# TREFHT     = 289.239960
# TREFHT_dbl = 289.239964
# Double-precision weight (gw),   double-precision arithmetic
ncwa --dbl -O -a lat,lon -w gw   in.nc out.nc
# TREFHT     = 289.239960
# TREFHT_dbl = 289.239964
```

First note that the `TREFHT_dbl` average never changes because `TREFHT_dbl(lat,lon)` is double-precision in the input file. As described above, NCO automatically converts all operands involving to the highest precision involved in the operation. So specifying '`--dbl`' is redundant for double-precision inputs.

Second, the single-precision arithmetic averages of the single-precision input `TREFHT` differ by $289.246735 - 289.226135 = 0.0206$ from eachother, and, more importantly, by as much as $289.239964 - 289.226135 = 0.013829$ from the correct (double-precision) answer. These averages differ in the fifth digit, i.e., they agree only to four significant figures! Given that climate scientists are concerned about global temperature variations of a tenth of a degree or less, this difference is large. Global mean temperature changes significant to climate scientists are comparable in size to the numerical artifacts produced by the averaging procedure.

Why are the single-precision numerical artifacts so large? Each global average is the result of multiplying almost 15,000 elements each by its weight, summing those, and then dividing by the summed weights. Thus about 50,000 single-precision floating-point operations caused the loss of two to three significant digits of precision. The net error of a series of independent rounding errors is a random walk phenomena[35]. Successive rounding errors displace the answer further from the truth. An ensemble of such averages will, on average, have no net bias. In other words, the expectation value of a series of IEEE rounding errors is zero. And the error of any given sequence of rounding errors obeys, for large series, a Gaussian distribution centered on zero.

Single-precision numbers use three of their four eight-bit bytes to represent the mantissa so the smallest representable single-precision mantissa is $\epsilon \equiv 2^{-23} = 1.19209 \times 10^{-7}$. This $\epsilon$ is the smallest x such that $1.0 + x \neq 1.0$. This is the rounding error for non-exact precision-numbers. Applying random walk theory to rounding, it can be shown that the expected rounding error after $n$ inexact operations is $\sqrt{2n/\pi}$ for large $n$. The expected (i.e., mean absolute) rounding error in our example with 13,824 additions is about $\sqrt{2 \times 13824/\pi} = 91.96$. Hence, addition alone of about fifteen thousand single-precision floats is expected to consume about two significant digits of precision. This neglects the error due to the inner product (weights times values) and normalization (division by tally) aspects of a weighted average. The ratio of two numbers each containing a numerical bias can magnify the size of the bias. In summary, a global mean number computed from about 15,000 gridpoints each with weights can be expected to lose up to three significant digits. Since single-precision starts with about seven significant digits, we should not expect to retain more than four significant digits after computing weighted averages in single-precision. The above example with `TREFHT` shows the expected four digits of agreement.

---

35 Thanks to Michael J. Prather for explaining this to me.

The NCO results have been independently validated to the extent possible in three other languages: C, Matlab, and NCL. C and NCO are the only languages that permit single-precision numbers to be treated with single precision arithmetic:

```
# Double-precision weight (gw),   single-precision arithmetic (C)
ncwa_3528514.exe
# TREFHT     = 289.240112
# Double-precision weight (gw),   double-precision arithmetic (C)
# TREFHT     = 289.239964
# Single-precision weight (area), double-precision arithmetic (Matlab)
# TREFHT     = 289.239964
# Double-precision weight (gw),   double-precision arithmetic (Matlab)
# TREFHT     = 289.239964
# Single-precision weight (area), double-precision arithmetic (NCL)
ncl < ncwa_3528514.ncl
# TREFHT     = 289.239960
# TREFHT_dbl = 289.239964
# Double-precision weight (gw),   double-precision arithmetic (NCL)
# TREFHT     = 289.239960
# TREFHT_dbl = 289.239964
```

All languages tested (C, Matlab, NCL, and NCO) agree to machine precision with double-precision arithmetic. Users are fortunate to have a variety of high quality software that liberates them from the drudgery of coding their own. Many packages are free (as in beer)! As shown above NCO permits one to shift to their float-promotion preferences as desired. No other language allows this with a simple switch.

To summarize, until version 4.3.6 (September, 2013), the default arithmetic convention of NCO adhered to Fortran behavior, and automatically promoted single-precision to double-precision in all mixed-precision expressions, and left-alone pure single-precision expressions. This is faster and more memory efficient than other conventions. However, pure single-precision arithmetic can lose too much precision when used to condense (e.g., average) large arrays. Statistics involving about $n = 10,000$ single-precision inputs will lose about 2–3 digits if not promoted to double-precision prior to arithmetic. The loss scales with the squareroot of $n$. For larger $n$, users should promote floats with the '`--dbl`' option if they want to preserve more than four significant digits in their results.

The '`--dbl`' and '`--flt`' switches are only available with the NCO arithmetic operators that could potentially perform more than a few single-precision floating-point operations per result. These are `nces`, `ncra`, and `ncwa`. Each is capable of thousands to millions or more operations per result. By contrast, the arithmetic operators `ncbo` and `ncflint` perform at most one floating-point operation per result. Providing the '`--dbl`' option for such trivial operations makes little sense, so the option is not currently made available.

We are interested in users' opinions on these matters. The default behavior was changed from '`--flt`' to '`--dbl`' with the release of NCO version 4.3.6 (October 2013). We will change the default back to '`--flt`' if users prefer. Or we could set a threshold (e.g., $n \geq 10000$) after which single- to double-precision promotion is automatically invoked. Or we could make the default promotion convention settable via an environment variable (GSL does this a lot). Please let us know what you think of the selected defaults and options.

### 3.36.3 Manual type conversion

`ncap2` provides intrinsic functions for performing manual type conversions. This, for example, converts variable `tpt` to external type `NC_SHORT` (a C-type `short`), and variable `prs` to external type `NC_DOUBLE` (a C-type `double`).

```
ncap2 -s 'tpt=short(tpt);prs=double(prs)' in.nc out.nc
```

With ncap2 there also is the `convert()` method that takes an integer argument. For example the above statements become:

```
ncap2 -s 'tpt=tpt.convert(NC_SHORT);prs=prs.convert(NC_DOUBLE)' in.nc out.nc
```

Can also use `convert()` in combination with `type()` so to make variable `ilev_new` the same type as `ilev` just do:

```
ncap2 -s 'ilev_new=ilev_new.convert(ilev.type())' in.nc out.nc
```

See Section 4.1 [ncap2 netCDF Arithmetic Processor], page 138, for more details.

## 3.37 Batch Mode

Availability: All operators
Short options: '`-O`', '`-A`'
Long options: '`--ovr`', '`--overwrite`', '`--apn`', '`--append`'

If the *output-file* specified for a command is a pre-existing file, then the operator will prompt the user whether to overwrite (erase) the existing *output-file*, attempt to append to it, or abort the operation. However, interactive questions reduce productivity when processing large amounts of data. Therefore NCO also implements two ways to override its own safety features, the '`-O`' and '`-A`' switches. Specifying '`-O`' tells the operator to overwrite any existing *output-file* without prompting the user interactively. Specifying '`-A`' tells the operator to attempt to append to any existing *output-file* without prompting the user interactively. These switches are useful in batch environments because they suppress interactive keyboard input. NB: As of 20120515, `ncap2` is unable to append to files that already contain the appended dimensions.

## 3.38 Global Attribute Addition

Availability: All operators
Short options: None
Long options: '`--glb`', '`--gaa`', '`--glb_att_add`'
'`--glb att_nm=att_val`' (multiple invocations allowed)

All operators can add user-specified global attributes to output files. As of NCO version 4.5.2 (July, 2015), NCO supports multiple uses of the '`--glb`' (or equivalent '`--gaa`' or '`--glb_att_add`') switch. The option '`--gaa`' (and its long option equivalents such as '`--glb_att_add`') indicates the argument syntax will be *key=val*. As such, '`--gaa`' and its synonyms are indicator options that accept arguments supplied one-by-one like '`--gaa key1=val1 --gaa key2=val2`', or aggregated together in multi-argument format like '`--gaa key1=val1#key2=val2`' (see Section 3.4.2 [Multi-arguments], page 32).

The switch takes mandatory arguments '`--glb att_nm=att_val`' where *att_nm* is the desired name of the global attribute to add, and *att_val* is its value. Currently only text attributes are supported (recorded as type `NC_CHAR`), and regular expressions are not allowed (unlike see Section 4.2 [ncatted netCDF Attribute Editor], page 200). Attributes are added in "Append" mode, meaning that values are appended to pre-existing values, if any. Multiple invocations can simplify the annotation of output file at creation (or modification) time:

```
ncra --glb machine=${HOSTNAME} --glb created_by=${USER} in*.nc out.nc
```

As of NCO version 4.6.2 (October, 2016), one may instead combine the separate invocations into a single list of invocations separated by colons:

```
ncra --glb machine=${HOSTNAME}:created_by=${USER} in*.nc out.nc
```

The list may contain any number of key-value pairs. Special care must be taken should a key or value contain a delimiter (i.e., a colon) otherwise `NCO` will interpret the colon as a delimiter and will attempt to create a new attribute. To protect a colon from being interpreted as an argument delimiter, precede it with a backslash.

The global attribution addition feature helps to avoid the performance penalty incurred by using `ncatted` separately to annotate large files. Should users emit a loud hue and cry, we will consider ading the the functionality of ncatted to the front-end of all operators, i.e., accepting valid `ncatted` arguments to modify attributes of any type and to apply regular expressions.

## 3.39 History Attribute

Availability: All operators
Short options: '`-h`'
Long options: '`--hst`', '`--history`'

All operators automatically append a `history` global attribute to any file they create or modify. The `history` attribute consists of a timestamp and the full string of the invocation command to the operator, e.g., '`Mon May 26 20:10:24 1997: ncks in.nc out.nc`'. The full contents of an existing `history` attribute are copied from the first *input-file* to the *output-file*. The timestamps appear in reverse chronological order, with the most recent timestamp appearing first in the `history` attribute. Since NCO adheres to the `history` convention, the entire data processing path of a given netCDF file may often be deduced from examination of its `history` attribute. As of May, 2002, NCO is case-insensitive to the spelling of the `history` attribute name. Thus attributes named `History` or `HISTORY` (which are non-standard and not recommended) will be treated as valid history attributes. When more than one global attribute fits the case-insensitive search for "history", the first one found is used. To avoid information overkill, all operators have an optional switch ('`-h`', '`--hst`', or '`--history`') to override automatically appending the `history` attribute (see Section 4.2 [ncatted netCDF Attribute Editor], page 200). Note that the '`-h`' switch also turns off writing the `nco_input_file_list`-attribute for multi-file operators (see Section 3.40 [File List Attributes], page 130).

As of NCO version 4.5.0 (June, 2015), NCO supports its own convention to retain the `history`-attribute contents of all files that were appended to a file[36]. This convention stores those contents in the `history_of_appended_files` attribute, which complements the `history`-attribute to provide a more complete provenance. These attributes may appear something like this in output:

```
// global attributes:
:history = "Thu Jun  4 14:19:04 2015: ncks -A /home/zender/foo3.nc /home/zender/t
  "Thu Jun  4 14:19:04 2015: ncks -A /home/zender/foo2.nc /home/zender/tmp.nc\n",
  "Thu Jun  4 14:19:04 2015: ncatted -O -a att1,global,o,c,global metadata only i
  "original history from the ur-file serving as the basis for subsequent appends.
:history_of_appended_files = "Thu Jun  4 14:19:04 2015: Appended file \
  /home/zender/foo3.nc had following \"history\" attribute:\n",
  "Thu Jun  4 14:19:04 2015: ncatted -O -a att2,global,o,c,global metadata only i
  "history from foo3 from which data was appended to foo1 after data from foo2 wa
  "Thu Jun  4 14:19:04 2015: Appended file /home/zender/foo2.nc had following \"h
  "Thu Jun  4 14:19:04 2015: ncatted -O -a att2,global,o,c,global metadata only i
  "history of some totally different file foo2 from which data was appended to fo
:att1 = "global metadata only in foo1" ;
```

Note that the `history_of_appended_files`-attribute is only created, and will only exist, in a file that is, or descends from a file that was, appended to. The optional switch '`-h`' (or '`--hst`' or '`--history`') also overrides automatically appending the `history_of_appended_files` attribute.

## 3.40 File List Attributes

Availability: `nces`, `ncecat`, `ncra`, `ncrcat`
Short options: '`-H`'
Long options: '`--fl_lst_in`', '`--file_list`'

Many methods of specifying large numbers of input file names pass these names via pipes, encodings, or argument transfer programs (see Section 2.7 [Large Numbers of Files], page 21). When these methods are used, the input file list is not explicitly passed on the

[36] Note that before version 4.5.0, NCO could, in append ('`-A`') mode only, inadvertently overwrite the global metadata (including `history`) of the output file with that of the input file. This is opposite the behavior most would want.

command line. This results in a loss of information since the `history` attribute no longer contains the exact command by which the file was created.

NCO solves this dilemma by archiving input file list attributes. When the input file list to a multi-file operator is specified via `stdin`, the operator, by default, attaches two global attributes to any file they create or modify. The `nco_input_file_number` global attribute contains the number of input files, and `nco_input_file_list` contains the file names, specified as standard input to the multi-file operator. This information helps to verify that all input files the user thinks were piped through `stdin` actually arrived. Without the `nco_input_file_list` attribute, the information is lost forever and the "chain of evidence" would be broken.

The '`-H`' switch overrides (turns off) the default behavior of writing the input file list global attributes when input is from `stdin`. The '`-h`' switch does this too, and turns off the `history` attribute as well (see Section 3.39 [History Attribute], page 129). Hence both switches allows space-conscious users to avoid storing what may amount to many thousands of filenames in a metadata attribute.

## 3.41 CF Conventions

Availability: `ncbo`, `nces`, `ncecat`, `ncflint`, `ncpdq`, `ncra`, `ncwa`
Short options: None

NCO recognizes some Climate and Forecast (CF) metadata conventions, and applies special rules to such data. NCO was contemporaneous with COARDS and still contains some rules to handle older model datasets that pre-date CF, such as NCAR CCM and early CCSM datasets. Such datasets may not contain an explicit `Conventions` attribute (e.g., '`CF-1.0`'). Nevertheless, we refer to all such metadata collectively as CF metadata. Skip this section if you never work with CF metadata.

The latest CF netCDF conventions are described here (`http://cfconventions.org/1.6.html`). Most CF netCDF conventions are transparent to NCO. There are no known pitfalls associated with using any NCO operator on files adhering to these conventions. To increase user friendliness, NCO applies special rules to certain variables in CF files. Rules not required by CF are because experience shows that they simplify data analysis.

Here is a general sense of NCO's CF-support: Understanding and implementing NUG recommendations such as the history attribute, packing conventions, and attention to units. Special handling of variables designated as coordinates, bounds, or ancillary variables, so that users subsetting a certain variable automatically obtain all related variables. Special handling and prevention of meaningless operations (e.g., the root-mean-square of latitude) so that coordinates and bounds preserve meaningful information even as normal fields are statistically transformed. Understanding units and certain calendars so that hyperslabs may be specified in physical units, and so that user needs not manually decode per-file time specifications. Understanding auxiliary coordinates so that irregular hyperslabs may be specified on complex geometric grids. Checking for CF-compliance on netCDF3 and netCDF4 and HDF files. Converting netCDF4 and HDF files to netCDF3 for strict CF-compliance. Finally, a main use of NCO is to "produce CF", i.e., to improve CF-compliance by annotating metadata, renaming objects (attributes, variables, and dimensions), permuting and inverting dimensions, recomputing values, and data compression.

Currently, NCO determines whether a datafile is a CF output datafile simply by checking (case-insensitively) whether the value of the global attribute `Conventions` (if any) equals '`CF-1.0`' or '`NCAR-CSM`' Should `Conventions` equal either of these in the (first) *input-file*, NCO will apply special rules to certain variables because of their usual meaning in CF files. NCO will not average the following variables often found in CF files: `ntrm`, `ntrn`, `ntrk`, `ndbase`, `nsbase`, `nbdate`, `nbsec`, `mdt`, `mhisf`. These variables contain scalar metadata such as the resolution of the host geophysical model and it makes no sense to change their values.

Furthermore, the *size and rank-preserving arithmetic operators* try not to operate on certain grid properties. These operators are `ncap2`, `ncbo`, `nces`, `ncflint`, and `ncpdq` (when used for packing, not for permutation). These operators do not operate, by default, on (i.e., add, subtract, pack, etc.) the following variables: `ORO`, `area`, `datesec`, `date`, `gw`, `hyai`, `hyam`, `hybi`. `hybm`, `lat_bnds`, `lon_bnds`, `msk_*`, `wgt_*`. These variables represent Gaussian weights, land/sea masks, time fields, hybrid pressure coefficients, and latititude/longitude boundaries. We call these fields non-coordinate *grid properties*. Coordinate grid properties are easy to identify because they are coordinate variables such as `latitude` and `longitude`.

Users usually want *all* grid properties to remain unaltered in the output file. To be treated as a grid property, the variable name must *exactly* match a name in the above list, or be a coordinate variable. Handling of `msk_*` and `wgt_*` is exceptional in that *any* variable whose name starts with `msk_` or `wgt_` is considered to be a "mask" or a "weight" and is thus preserved (not operated on when arithmetic can be avoided).

As of NCO version 4.5.0 (June, 2015), NCO began to support behavior required for the DOE ACME program, and we refer to these rules collectively as the ACME convention. The first ACME rule implemented is that the contents of *input-file* variables named `date_written` and `time_written`, if any, will be updated to the current system-supplied (with `gmtime()`) GMT-time as the variables are copied to the *output-file*.

You must spoof NCO if you would like any grid properties or other special CF fields processed normally. For example rename the variables first with `ncrename`, or alter the `Conventions` attribute.

As of NCO version 4.0.8 (April, 2011), NCO supports the CF `bounds` convention for cell boundaries described here (`http://cfconventions.org/1.6.html#cell-boundaries`). This convention allows coordinate variables (including multidimensional coordinates) to describe the boundaries of their cells. This is done by naming the variable which contains the bounds in in the `bounds` attribute. Note that coordinates of rank $N$ have bounds of rank $N+1$. NCO-generated subsets of CF-compliant files with `bounds` attributes will include the coordinates specified by the `bounds` attribute, if any. Hence the subsets will themselves be CF-compliant. Bounds are subject to the user-specified override switches (including '`-c`' and '`-C`') described in Section 3.12 [Subsetting Coordinate Variables], page 51.

As of NCO version 4.4.9 (May, 2015), NCO supports the CF `climatology` convention for climatological statistics described here (`http://cfconventions.org/Data/cf-conventions/cf-conventions-1.7/build/cf-conventions.html#`

climatological-statistics). This convention allows coordinate variables (including multidimensional coordinates) to describe the (possibly nested) periods and statistical methods of their associated statistics. This is done by naming the variable which contains the periods and methods in the climatology attribute. Note that coordinates of rank $N$ have climatology bounds of rank $N+1$. NCO-generated subsets of CF-compliant files with climatology attributes will include the variables specified by the climatology attribute, if any. Hence the subsets will themselves be CF-compliant. Climatology variables are subject to the user-specified override switches (including '-c' and '-C') described in Section 3.12 [Subsetting Coordinate Variables], page 51.

As of NCO version 4.4.5 (July, 2014), NCO supports the CF ancillary_variables convention for described here (http://cfconventions.org/1.6.html#ancillary-data). This convention allows ancillary variables to be associated with one or more primary variables. NCO attaches any such variables to the extraction list along with the primary variable and its usual (one-dimensional) coordinates, if any. Ancillary variables are subject to the user-specified override switches (including '-c' and '-C') described in Section 3.12 [Subsetting Coordinate Variables], page 51.

As of NCO version 4.6.4 (January, 2017), NCO supports the CF cell_measures convention described here (http://cfconventions.org/1.6.html#cell-measures). This convention allows variables to indicate which other variable or variables contains area or volume information about a gridcell. These measures variables are pointed to by the cell_measures attribute. The CDL specification of a measures variable for area looks like

```
orog:cell_measures = "area: areacella"
```

where areacella is the name of the measures variable. Unless the default behavior is overridden, NCO attaches any measures variables to the extraction list along with the primary variable and other associated variables. By definition, measures variables are a subset of the rank of the variable they measure. The most common case is that the measures variable for area is the same size as 2D fields (like surface air temperature) and much smaller than 3D fields (like full air temperature). In such cases the measures variable might occupy 50% of the space of a dataset consisting of only one 2D field. Extraction of measures variables is subject to the user-specified override switches (including '-c' and '-C') described in Section 3.12 [Subsetting Coordinate Variables], page 51. To conserve space without sacrificing too much metadata, NCO makes it possible to override the extraction of measures variables independent of extracting other associated variables. Override the default with '--no_cell_measures' or '--no_cll_msr'. These options are available in all operators that perform subsetting (i.e., all operators except ncatted and ncrename).

As of NCO version 4.6.4 (January, 2017), NCO supports the CF formula_terms convention described here (http://cfconventions.org/1.6.html#formula-terms). This convention encodes formulas used to construct (usually vertical) coordinate grids. The CDL specification of a vertical coordinate formula for looks like

```
lev:standard_name = "atmosphere_hybrid_sigma_pressure_coordinate"
lev:formula_terms = "a: hyam b: hybm p0: P0 ps: PS"
```

where standard_name contains the standardized name of the formula variable and formula_terms contains a list of the variables used, called formula variables. Above the formula variables are hyam, hybm, P0, and PS. Unless the default behavior is overridden, NCO attaches any formula variables to the extraction list along with the primary variable and other associated variables. By definition, formula variables are a subset of the rank of the variable they measure. One common case is that the formula variables for constructing a 3D height grid involves a 2D variable (like surface pressure, or elevation). In such cases the formula variables typically constitute only a small fraction of a dataset consisting of one 3D field. Extraction of formula variables is subject to the user-specified override switches (including '-c' and '-C') described in Section 3.12 [Subsetting Coordinate Variables], page 51. To conserve space without sacrificing too much metadata, NCO makes it possible to override the extraction of formula variables independent of extracting other associated variables. Override the default with '--no_formula_terms' or '--no_frm_trm'. These options are available in all operators that perform subsetting (i.e., all operators except ncatted and ncrename).

As of NCO version 4.6.0 (May, 2016), NCO supports the CF grid_mapping convention for described here (http://cfconventions.org/cf-conventions/cf-conventions.html#grid-mappings-and-projections). This convention allows descriptions of map-projections to be associated with variables. NCO attaches any such map-projection variables to the extraction list along with the primary variable and its usual (one-dimensional) coordinates, if any. Map-projection variables are subject to the user-specified override switches (including '-c' and '-C') described in Section 3.12 [Subsetting Coordinate Variables], page 51.

As of NCO version 3.9.6 (January, 2009), NCO supports the CF coordinates convention described here (http://cfconventions.org/1.6.html#coordinate-system). This convention allows variables to specify additional coordinates (including mult-idimensional coordinates) in a space-separated string attribute named coordinates. NCO attaches any such coordinates to the extraction list along with the variable and its usual (one-dimensional) coordinates, if any. These auxiliary coordinates are subject to the user-specified override switches (including '-c' and '-C') described in Section 3.12 [Subsetting Coordinate Variables], page 51.

Elimination of reduced dimensions from the coordinates attribute helps ensure that rank-reduced variables become completely independent from their former dimensions. As of NCO version 4.4.9 (May, 2015), NCO may modify the coordinates attribute to assist this. In particular, ncwa eliminates from the coordinates attribute any dimension that it collapses, e.g., by averaging. The former presence of this dimension will usually be indicated by the CF cell_methods convention described here (http://cfconventions.org/1.6.html#cell-methods). Hence the CF cell_methods and coordinates conventions can be said to work in tandem to characterize the state and history of a variable's analysis.

As of NCO version 4.4.2 (February, 2014), NCO supports some of the CF cell_methods convention (http://cfconventions.org/1.6.html#cell-methods) to describe the analysis procedures that have been applied to data. The convention creates (or appends to an existing) cell_methods attribute a space-separated list of couplets of the form *dmn: op* where *dmn* is a comma-separated list of dimensions previously contained in the variable that have been reduced by the arithmetic operation *op*. For example, the cell_methods value time: mean says that the variable in question was averaged over the time dimension. In such cases time will either be a scalar variable or a degenerate dimension or coordinate.

This simply means that it has been averaged-over. The value `time, lon: mean lat: max` says that the variable in question is the maximum zonal mean of the time averaged original variable. Which is to say that the variable was first averaged over time and longitude, and then the residual latitudinal array was reduced by choosing the maximum value. Since the `cell methods` convention may alter metadata in an undesirable (or possibly incorrect) fashion, we provide switches to ensure it is always or never used. Use long-options '`--cll_mth`' or '`--cell_methods`' to invoke the algorithm (true by default), and options '`--no_cll_mth`' or '`--no_cell_methods`' to turn it off. These options are only available in the operators `ncwa` and `ncra`.

## 3.42 ARM Conventions

Availability: `ncrcat`
Short options: None

`ncrcat` has been programmed to correctly handle data files which utilize the Atmospheric Radiation Measurement (ARM) Program convention (`http://www.arm.gov/data/time.stm`) for time and time offsets. If you do not work with ARM data then you may skip this section. ARM data files store time information in two variables, a scalar, `base_time`, and a record variable, `time_offset`. Subtle but serious problems can arise when these type of files are blindly concatenated without CF or ARM support. `NCO` implements rebasing (see Section 3.25 [Rebasing Time Coordinate], page 87) as necessary on both CF and ARM files. Rebasing chains together consecutive *input-files* and produces an *output-file* which contains the correct time information. For ARM files this is expecially complex because the time coordinates are often stored as type `NC_CHAR`. Currently, `ncrcat` determines whether a datafile is an ARM datafile simply by testing for the existence of the variables `base_time`, `time_offset`, and the dimension `time`. If these are found in the *input-file* then `ncrcat` will automatically perform two non-standard, but hopefully useful, procedures. First, `ncrcat` will ensure that values of `time_offset` appearing in the *output-file* are relative to the `base_time` appearing in the first *input-file* (and presumably, though not necessarily, also appearing in the *output-file*). Second, if a coordinate variable named `time` is not found in the *input-files*, then `ncrcat` automatically creates the `time` coordinate in the *output-file*. The values of `time` are defined by the ARM conventions $time = base\_time + time\_offset$. Thus, if *output-file* contains the `time_offset` variable, it will also contain the `time` coordinate. A short message is added to the `history` global attribute whenever these ARM-specific procedures are executed.

## 3.43 Operator Version

Availability: All operators
Short options: '`-r`'
Long options: '`--revision`', '`--version`', or '`--vrs`'

All operators can be told to print their version information, library version, copyright notice, and compile-time configuration with the '`-r`' switch, or its long-option equivalent '`revision`'. The '`--version`' or '`--vrs`' switches print the operator version information only. The internal version number varies between operators, and indicates the most recent change to a particular operator's source code. This is useful in making sure you are working with the most recent operators. The version of NCO you are using might be, e.g., `3.9.5`. Using '`-r`' on, say, `ncks`, produces something like '`NCO netCDF Operators version "3.9.5" last modified 2008/05/11 built May 12 2008 on neige by zender Copyright (C) 1995--2008 Charlie Zender ncks version 20090918`'. This tells you that `ncks` contains all patches up to version `3.9.5`, which dates from May 11, 2008.

# 4 Reference Manual

This chapter presents reference pages for each of the operators individually. The operators are presented in alphabetical order. All valid command line switches are included in the syntax statement. Recall that descriptions of many of these command line switches are provided only in Chapter 3 [Shared features], page 29, to avoid redundancy. Only options specific to, or most useful with, a particular operator are described in any detail in the sections below.

## 4.1 ncap2 netCDF Arithmetic Processor

ncap2 understands a relatively full-featured language of operations, including loops, conditionals, arrays, and math functions. ncap2 is the most rapidly changing NCO operator and its documentation is incomplete. The distribution file data/ncap2_tst.nco contains an up-to-date overview of its syntax and capabilities. The data/*.nco distribution files (especially bin_cnt.nco, psd_wrf.nco, and rgr.nco) contain in-depth examples of ncap2 solutions to complex problems.

SYNTAX

```
ncap2 [-3] [-4] [-6] [-7] [-A] [-C] [-c]
[-D dbg] [-F] [-f] [--glb ...] [-h] [--hdf] [--hdr_pad nbr] [-L dfl_lvl] [-l path
[--no_tmp_fl] [-O] [-o output-file] [-p path] [-R] [-r] [--ram_all]
[-s algebra] [-S fl.nco] [-t thr_nbr] [-v]
input-file [output-file]
```

DESCRIPTION

ncap2 arithmetically processes netCDF files[1]. The processing instructions are contained either in the NCO script file fl.nco or in a sequence of command line arguments. The options '-s' (or long options '--spt' or '--script') are used for in-line scripts and '-S' (or long options '--fl_spt' or '--script-file') are used to provide the filename where (usually multiple) scripting commands are pre-stored. ncap2 was written to perform arbitrary algebraic transformations of data and archive the results as easily as possible. See Section 3.27 [Missing Values], page 89, for treatment of missing values. The results of the algebraic manipulations are called *derived fields*.

Unlike the other operators, ncap2 does not accept a list of variables to be operated on as an argument to '-v' (see Section 3.11 [Subsetting Files], page 46). Rather, the '-v' switch takes no arguments and indicates that ncap2 should output *only* user-defined variables. ncap2 neither accepts nor understands the -x switch. NB: As of 20120515, ncap2 is unable to append to files that already contain the appended dimensions.

Defining new variables in terms of existing variables is a powerful feature of ncap2. Derived fields inherit the metadata (i.e., attributes) of their ancestors, if any, in the script or input file. When the derived field is completely new (no identically-named ancestors exist), then it inherits the metadata (if any) of the left-most variable on the right hand side of the defining expression. This metadata inheritance is called *attribute propagation*. Attribute propagation is intended to facilitate well-documented data analysis, and we welcome suggestions to improve this feature.

The only exception to this rule of attribute propagation is in cases of left hand casting (see Section 4.1.4 [Left hand casting], page 144). The user must manually define the proper metadata for variables defined using left hand casting.

[1] ncap2 is the successor to ncap which was put into maintenance mode in November, 2006. This documentation refers to ncap2, which has a superset of the ncap functionality. Eventually ncap will be deprecated in favor ncap2. ncap2 may be renamed ncap in 2013.

### 4.1.1 Syntax of ncap2 statements

Mastering `ncap2` is relatively simple. Each valid statement *statement* consists of standard forward algebraic expression. The `fl.nco`, if present, is simply a list of such statements, whitespace, and comments. The syntax of statements is most like the computer language C. The following characteristics of C are preserved:

Array syntax
: Arrays elements are placed within `[]` characters;

Array indexing
: Arrays are 0-based;

Array storage
: Last dimension is most rapidly varying;

Assignment statements
: A semi-colon '`;`' indicates the end of an assignment statement.

Comments
: Multi-line comments are enclosed within `/* */` characters. Single line comments are preceded by `//` characters.

Nesting
: Files may be nested in scripts using `#include` *script*. The `#include` command is not followed by a semi-colon because it is a pre-processor directive, not an assignment statement. The filename `script` is interpreted relative to the run directory.

Attribute syntax
: The at-sign `@` is used to delineate an attribute name from a variable name.

### 4.1.2 Expressions

Expressions are the fundamental building block of `ncap2`. Expressions are composed of variables, numbers, literals, and attributes. The following C operators are "overloaded" and work with scalars and multi-dimensional arrays:

```
Arithmetic Operators: * / % + - ^
Binary Operators:     > >= < <= == != == || && >> <<
Unary Operators:      + - ++ -- !
Conditional Operator: exp1 ? exp2 : exp3
Assign Operators:     = += -= /= *=
```

In the following section a *variable* also refers to a number literal which is read in as a scalar variable:

**Arithmetic and Binary Operators**

Consider *var1 'op' var2*

**Precision**

- When both operands are variables, the result has the precision of the higher precision operand.
- When one operand is a variable and the other an attribute, the result has the precision of the variable.

- When both operands are attributes, the result has the precision of the more precise attribute.
- The exponentiation operator "^" is an exception to the above rules. When both operands have type less than `NC_FLOAT`, the result is `NC_FLOAT`. When either type is `NC_DOUBLE`, the result is also `NC_DOUBLE`.

**Rank**

- The Rank of the result is generally equal to Rank of the operand that has the greatest number of dimensions.
- If the dimensions in var2 are a subset of the dimensions in var1 then its possible to make var2 conform to var1 through broadcasting and or dimension reordering.
- Broadcasting a variable means creating data in non-existing dimensions by copying data in existing dimensions.
- More specifically: If the numbers of dimensions in var1 is greater than or equal to the number of dimensions in var2 then an attempt is made to make var2 conform to var1 ,else var1 is made to conform to var2. If conformance is not possible then an error message will be emitted and script execution will cease.

Even though the logical operators return True(1) or False(0) they are treated in the same way as the arithmetic operators with regard to precision and rank.
Examples:

```
dimensions: time=10, lat=2, lon=4
Suppose we have the two variables:

double  P(time,lat,lon);
float   PZ0(lon,lat);  // PZ0=1,2,3,4,5,6,7,8;

Consider now the expression:
 PZ=P-PZ0

PZ0 is made to conform to P and the result is
PZ0 =
   1,3,5,7,2,4,6,8,
   1,3,5,7,2,4,6,8,
   1,3,5,7,2,4,6,8,
   1,3,5,7,2,4,6,8,
   1,3,5,7,2,4,6,8,
   1,3,5,7,2,4,6,8,
   1,3,5,7,2,4,6,8,
   1,3,5,7,2,4,6,8,
   1,3,5,7,2,4,6,8,
   1,3,5,7,2,4,6,8,

Once the expression is evaluated then PZ will be of type double;
```

```
Consider now
 start=four-att_var@double_att;  // start =-69  and is of type intger;
 four_pow=four^3.0f              // four_pow=64 and is of type float
 three_nw=three_dmn_var_sht*1.0f; // type is now float
 start@n1=att_var@short_att*att_var@int_att;
                                  // start@n1=5329 and is type int
```

**Binary Operators**

Unlike C the binary operators return an array of values. There is no such thing as short circuiting with the AND/OR operators. Missing values are carried into the result in the same way they are with the arithmetic operators. When an expression is evaluated in an if() the missing values are treated as true.

The binary operators are, in order of precedence:

```
!   Logical Not
----------------------------
<<  Less Than Selection
>>  Greater Than Selection
----------------------------
>   Greater than
>=  Greater than or equal to
<   Less than
<=  Less than or equal to
----------------------------
==  Equal to
!=  Not equal to
----------------------------
&&  Logical AND
----------------------------
||  Logical OR
----------------------------
```

To see all operators: see Section 4.1.29 [Operator precedence and associativity], page 197,

Examples:

```
tm1=time>2 && time <7;  // tm1=0, 0, 1, 1, 1, 1, 0, 0, 0, 0 double
tm2=time==3 || time>=6; // tm2=0, 0, 1, 0, 0, 1, 1, 1, 1, 1 double
tm3=int(!tm1);          // tm3=1, 1, 0, 0, 0, 0, 1, 1, 1, 1 int
tm4=tm1 && tm2;         // tm4=0, 0, 1, 0, 0, 1, 0, 0, 0, 0 double
tm5=!tm4;               // tm5=1, 1, 0, 1, 1, 0, 1, 1, 1, 1 double
```

**Regular Assign Operator**

*var1 '=' exp1*

If var1 does not already exist in Input or Output then var1 is written to Output with the values, type and dimensions from expr1. If var1 is in Input only it is copied to Output first. Once the var is in Ouptut then the only reqirement on expr1 is that the number of elements must match the number already on disk. The type of expr1 is converted as necessary to the disk type.

If you wish to change the type or shape of a variable in Input then you have to cast the variable. See see Section 4.1.4 [Left hand casting], page 144,

```
time[time]=time.int();
three_dmn_var_dbl[time,lon,lat]=666L;
```

**Other Assign Operators +=,-=,*=./=**
*var1 'ass_op' exp1*
if exp1 is a variable and it doesn't conform to var1 then an attempt is made to make it conform to var1. If exp1 is an attribute it must have unity size or else have the same number of elements as var1. If expr1 has a different type to var1 the it is converted to the var1 type.

```
z1=four+=one*=10 // z1=14 four=14 one=10;
time-=2          // time= -1,0,1,2,3,4,5,6,7,8
```

**Increment/Decrement Operators**
These work in a similar fashion to their regular C counterparts. If say the variable `four` is input only then the statement `++four` effectively means read `four` from input increment each element by one, then write the new values to Output;

Example:

```
n2=++four;    n2=5, four=5
n3=one--+20; n3=21  one=0;
n4=--time;    n4=time=0.,1.,2.,3.,4.,5.,6.,7.,8.,9.;
```

**Conditional Operator ?:**
*exp1 ? exp2 : exp3*
The conditional operator (or ternary Operator) is a succinct way of writing an if/then/else. If exp1 evaluates to true then exp2 is returned else exp3 is returned.

Example:

```
weight_avg=weight.avg();
weight_avg@units= (weight_avg == 1 ? "kilo" : "kilos");
PS_nw=PS-(PS.min() > 100000 ? 100000 : 0);
```

**Clipping Operators**

<< Less-than Clipping

For arrays, the less-than selection operator selects all values in the left operand that are less than the corresponding value in the right operand. If the value of the left side is greater than or equal to the corresponding value of the right side, then the right side value is placed in the result

>> Greater-than Clipping

For arrays, the greater-than selection operator selects all values in the left operand that are greater than the corresponding value in the right operand. If the value of the left side is less than or equal to the corresponding value of the right side, then the right side value is placed in the result.

Example:

```
RDM2=RDM >> 100.0 // 100,100,100,100,126,126,100,100,100,100 double
RDM2=RDM <<  90s  // 1, 9, 36, 84, 90, 90, 84, 36, 9, 1 int
```

### 4.1.3 Dimensions

Dimensions are defined in Output using the `defdim()` function.

```
defdim("cnt",10); # Dimension size is fixed by default
defdim("cnt",10,NC_UNLIMITED); # Dimension is unlimited (record dimension)
defdim("cnt",10,0); # Dimension is unlimited (record dimension)
defdim("cnt",10,1); # Dimension size is fixed
defdim("cnt",10,737); # All non-zero values indicate dimension size is fixed
```

This dimension name must then be prefixed with a dollar-sign '$' when referred to in method arguments or left-hand-casting, e.g.,

```
new_var[$cnt]=time;
temperature[$time,$lat,$lon]=35.5;
temp_avg=temperature.avg($time);
```

The `size` method allows the dimension size to be used in an arithmetic expression:

```
time_avg=time.total() / $time.size;
```

Increase the size of a new variable by one and set new member to zero:

```
defdim("cnt_new",$cnt.size+1);
new_var[$cnt_new]=0.0;
new_var(0:($cnt_new.size-2))=old_var;
```

To define an unlimited dimension simply set the size to zero

```
defdim("time2",0)
```

**Dimension Abbreviations**

It is possible to use dimension abbreviations as method arguments:
`$0` is the first dimension of a variable
`$1` is the second dimension of a variable
`$n` is the n+1 dimension of a variable

```
float four_dmn_rec_var(time,lat,lev,lon);
double three_dmn_var_dbl(time,lat,lon);

four_nw=four_dmn_rev_var.reverse($time,$lon)
four_nw=four_dmn_rec_var.reverse($0,$3);

four_avg=four_dmn_rec_var.avg($lat,$lev);
four_avg=four_dmn_rec_var.avg($1,$2);

three_mw=three_dmn_var_dbl.permute($time,$lon,$lat);
three_mw=three_dmn_var_dbl.permute($0,$2,$1);
```

**ID Quoting**
If the dimension name contains non-regular characters use ID quoting. See see Section 4.1.30 [ID Quoting], page 197,

```
defdim("a--list.A",10);
A1['$a--list.A']=30.0;
```

**GOTCHA**
It is not possible to manually define in Output any dimensions that exist in Input. When a variable from Input appears in an expression or statement its dimensions in Input are automagically copied to Output (if they are not already present)

### 4.1.4 Left hand casting

The following examples demonstrate the utility of the *left hand casting* ability of `ncap2`. Consider first this simple, artificial, example. If *lat* and *lon* are one dimensional coordinates of dimensions *lat* and *lon*, respectively, then addition of these two one-dimensional arrays is intrinsically ill-defined because whether *lat_lon* should be dimensioned *lat* by *lon* or *lon* by *lat* is ambiguous (assuming that addition is to remain a *commutative* procedure, i.e., one that does not depend on the order of its arguments). Differing dimensions are said to be *orthogonal* to one another, and sets of dimensions which are mutually exclusive are orthogonal as a set and any arithmetic operation between variables in orthogonal dimensional spaces is ambiguous without further information.

The ambiguity may be resolved by enumerating the desired dimension ordering of the output expression inside square brackets on the left hand side (LHS) of the equals sign. This is called *left hand casting* because the user resolves the dimensional ordering of the RHS of the expression by specifying the desired ordering on the LHS.

```
ncap2 -s 'lat_lon[lat,lon]=lat+lon' in.nc out.nc
ncap2 -s 'lon_lat[lon,lat]=lat+lon' in.nc out.nc
```

The explicit list of dimensions on the LHS, `[lat,lon]` resolves the otherwise ambiguous ordering of dimensions in *lat_lon*. In effect, the LHS *casts* its rank properties onto the RHS. Without LHS casting, the dimensional ordering of *lat_lon* would be undefined and, hopefully, `ncap2` would print an error message.

Consider now a slightly more complex example. In geophysical models, a coordinate system based on a blend of terrain-following and density-following surfaces is called a *hybrid coordinate system*. In this coordinate system, four variables must be manipulated to obtain the pressure of the vertical coordinate: *PO* is the domain-mean surface pressure offset (a scalar), *PS* is the local (time-varying) surface pressure (usually two horizontal spatial dimensions, i.e. latitude by longitude), *hyam* is the weight given to surfaces of constant density (one spatial dimension, pressure, which is orthogonal to the horizontal dimensions), and *hybm* is the weight given to surfaces of constant elevation (also one spatial dimension). This command constructs a four-dimensional pressure `prs_mdp` from the four input variables of mixed rank and orthogonality:

```
ncap2 -s 'prs_mdp[time,lat,lon,lev]=P0*hyam+PS*hybm' in.nc out.nc
```

Manipulating the four fields which define the pressure in a hybrid coordinate system is easy with left hand casting.

Finally, we show how to use interface quantities to define midpoint quantities. In particular, we will define interface pressures using the standard CESM output hybrid coordinate parameters, and then difference those interface pressures to obtain the pressure difference between the interfaces. The pressure difference is necessary obtain gridcell mass path and density (which are midpoint quantities). Definitions are as in the above example, with new variables *hyai* and *hybi* defined at grid cell vertical interfaces (rather than midpoints like *hyam* and *hybm*). The approach naturally fits into two lines:

```
cat > ~/pdel.nco << 'EOF'
*prs_ntf[time,lat,lon,ilev]=P0*hyai+PS*hybi;
// Requires NCO 4.5.4 and later:
prs_dlt[time,lat,lon,lev]=prs_ntf(:,:,:,1:$ilev.size-1)-prs_ntf(:,:,:,0:$ilev.size-2);
// Derived variable that require pressure thickness:
// Divide by gravity to obtain total mass path in layer aka mpl [kg m-2]
mpl=prs_dlt/grv_sfc;
// Multiply by mass mixing ratio to obtain mass path of constituent
mpl_CO2=mpl*mmr_CO2;
EOF
ncap2 -O -v -S ~/pdel.nco ~/nco/data/in.nc ~/foo.nc
ncks -O -C -v prs_dlt ~/foo.nc
```

The first line defines the four-dimensional interface pressures `prs_ntf` as a RAM variable because those are not desired in the output file. The second differences each pressure level from the pressure above it to obtain the pressure difference. This line employs both left-hand casting and array hyperslabbing. However, this syntax only works with NCO version 4.5.4 (November, 2015) and later because earlier versions require that LHS and RHS dimension names (not just sizes) match. From the pressure differences, one can obtain the mass path in each layer as shown.

Another reason to cast a variable is to modify the shape or type of a variable already in Input

```
gds_var[gds_crd]=gds_var.double();
three_dmn_var_crd[lat,lon,lev]=10.0d;
four[]=four.int();
```

### 4.1.5 Arrays and hyperslabs

Generating a regularly spaced n-dimensional array with `ncap2` is simple with the `array()` function. The function comes in three (overloaded) forms

```
(A) var_out=array(val_srt, val_inc, $dmn_nm);           // One-dimensional output
(B) var_out=array(val_srt, val_inc, var_tpl);           // Multi-dimensional output
(C) var_out=array(val_srt, val_inc, /dmn1,dmn2..dmnN/); // Multi-dimensional output
```

*val_srt* Starting value of the array. The *type* of the array will be the *type* of this starting value.

*val_inc* Spacing (or increment) between elements.

*var_tpl* Variable from which the array can derive its shape 1D or nD

**One-Dimensional Arrays**
Use form (A) or (B) for 1D arrays

```
In the following var_out is of type NC_DOUBLE
var_out=array(10.0, 2, $time)  //10.5,12.5,14.5,16.5,18.5,20.5,22.5,24.5,26.5,28.

The following is also ID
It gets its "shape" from the var "ilev" and is of type NC_UINT
var_out=array( 0ul, 2, ilev)    // 0,2,4,6

The following is of type NC_FLOAT
var_out=array(99.0f, 2.5, $lon) // 99,101.5,104,106.5

// create an array of zeros
var_out=array(0, 0, $time) // 0,0,0,0,0,0,0,0,0,0

// create an array of ones
var_out=array(1.0, 0.0, $lon) // 1.0,1.0,1.0,1.0
```

**n-Dimensional Arrays**
Use form (B) or (C) for creating n-D arrays.
nb In (C) the final argument is a list of dimensions

```
The following two are equivalent
var_out=array(1.0, 2.0, three_dmn_var)
var_out=array(1.0, 2.0,/$lat, $lev, $lon/)

Below the type is NC_BYTE
var_out=array(20b, -4, /$lat,$lon/)  // 20,16,12,8,4,0,-4,-8

srt=3.14159f; inc=srt/2.0f
var_out(srt,inc, var_2D_rrg)
// 3.14159, 4.712385, 6.28318, 7.853975, 9.42477, 10.99557, 12.56636, 14.13716 ;
```

Hyperslabs in `ncap2` are more limited than hyperslabs with the other NCO operators. `ncap2` does not understand the shell command-line syntax used to specify multi-slabs, wrapped co-ordinates, negative stride or coordinate value limits. However with a bit of syntactic magic they are all are possible. `ncap2` accepts (in fact, it requires) $N$-hyperslab arguments for a variable of rank $N$:

```
var1(arg1,arg2 ... argN);
```

where each hyperslab argument is of the form

```
start:end:stride
```

and the arguments for different dimensions are separated by commas. If *start* is omitted, it defaults to zero. If *end* is omitted, it defaults to dimension size minus one. If *stride* is omitted, it defaults to one.

If a single value is present then it is assumed that that dimension collapses to a single value (i.e., a cross-section). The number of hyperslab arguments MUST equal the variable's rank.

### Hyperslabs on the Right Hand Side of an assign

A simple 1D example:

```
($time.size=10)
od[$time]={20,22,24,26,28,30,32,34,36,38};

od(7);      // 34
od(7:);     // 34,36,38
od(:7);     // 20,22,24,26,28,30,32,34
od(::4);    // 20,28,36
od(1:6:2)   // 22,26,30
od(:)       // 20,22,24,26,28,30,32,34,36,38
```

A more complex three dimensional example:

```
($lat.size=2,$lon.size=4)
th[$time,$lat,$lon]=
                          {1, 2, 3, 4, 5, 6, 7, 8,
                          9,10,11,12,13,14,15,16,
                          17,18,19,20,21,22,23,24,
                          -99,-99,-99,-99,-99,-99,-99,-99,
                          33,34,35,36,37,38,39,40,
                          41,42,43,44,45,46,47,48,
                          49,50,51,52,53,54,55,56,
                          -99,58,59,60,61,62,63,64,
                          65,66,67,68,69,70,71,72,
                          -99,74,75,76,77,78,79,-99 };

th(1,1,3);        // 16
th(2,0,:);        // 17, 18, 19, 20
th(:,1,3);        // 8, 16, 24, -99, 40, 48, 56, 64, 72, -99
th(::5,:,0:3:2); // 1, 3, 5, 7, 41, 43, 45, 47
```

If hyperslab arguments collapse to a single value (a cross-section has been specified), then that dimension is removed from the returned variable. If all the values collapse then a scalar variable is returned. So, for example, the following is valid:

```
th_nw=th(0,:,:)+th(9,:,:);
// th_nw has dimensions $lon,$lat
// NB: the time dimension has become degenerate
```

The following is invalid:

```
th_nw=th(0,:,0:1)+th(9,:,0:1);
```

because the `$lon` dimension now only has two elements. The above can be calculated by using a LHS cast with `$lon_nw` as replacement dim for `$lon`:

```
defdim("lon_nw",2);
th_nw[$lat,$lon_nw]=th(0,:,0:1) +th(9,:,0:1);
```

**Hyperslabs on the Left Hand Side of an assign**
When hyperslabing on the LHS, the expression on the RHS must evaluate to a scalar or a variable/attribute with the same number of elements as the LHS hyperslab. Set all elements of the last record to zero:

```
th(9,:,:)=0.0;
```

Set first element of each lon element to 1.0:

```
th(:,:,0)=1.0;
```

One may hyperslab on both sides of an assign. For example, this sets the last record to the first record:

```
th(9,:,:)=th(0,:,:);
```

Say *th0* represents pressure at height=0 and *th1* represents pressure at height=1. Then it is possible to insert these hyperslabs into the records

```
prs[$time,$height,$lat,$lon]=0.0;
prs(:,0,:,:)=th0;
prs(:,1,:,:)=th1
```

**Reverse method**
Use the `reverse()` method to reverse a dimension's elements in a variable with at least one dimension. This is equivalent to a negative stride, e.g.,

```
th_rv=th(1 ,:,:).reverse($lon); // {12,11,10,9 }, {16,15,14,13}
od_rv=od.reverse($time);          // {38,36,34,32,30,28,26,24,22,20}
```

**Permute methodp**
Use the `permute()` method to swap the dimensions of a variable. The number and names of dimension arguments must match the dimensions in the variable. If the first dimension in the variable is of record type then this must remain the first dimension. If you want to change the record dimension then consider using `ncpdq`.

Consider the variable:

```
float three_dmn_var(lat,lev,lon);
three_dmn_var_prm=three_dmn_var.permute($lon,$lat,$lev);
// The permuted values are
three_dmn_var_prm=
  0,4,8,
  12,16,20,
  1,5,9,
  13,17,21,
  2,6,10,
  14,18,22,
```

```
3,7,11,
15,19,23;
```

### 4.1.6 Attributes

Attributes are referred to by *var_nm@att_nm*
All the following are valid statements:

```
global@text="Test Attributes"; /* Assign a global variable attribute */
a1[$time]=time*20;
a1@long_name="Kelvin";
a1@min=a1.min();
a1@max=a1.max();
a1@min++;
--a1@max;
a1(0)=a1@min;
a1($time.size-1)=a1@max;
```

The netCDF specification allows all attribute types to have a size greater than one. The maximum is defined by `NC_MAX_ATTRS`. The following is an `ncdump` of the metadata for variable *a1*

```
double a1(time) ;
  a1:long_name = "Kelvin" ;
  a1:max = 199. ;
  a1:min = 21. ;
  a1:trip1 = 1, 2, 3 ;
  a1:triplet = 21., 110., 199. ;
```

The following basic methods `size()`, `type()`, `exists()` can be used with attributes. For example, to save an attribute text string in a variable,

```
defdim("sng_len",a1@long_name.size());
sng_arr[$sng_len]=a1@long_name; // sng_arr now contains "Kelvin"
```

Attributes defined in a script are stored in memory and are written to Output after script completion. To stop the attribute being written use the ram_delete() method or use a bogus variable name.

**Attribute Propagation and Inheritance**

- Attribute propagation occurs in a regular assign statement. The variable being defined on the LHS gets copies of the attributes from the leftermost variable on the RHS.
- Attribute Inheritance: The LHS variable “inherits” attributes from an Input variable with the same name
- It is possible to have a regular assign statement for which both propagation and inheritance occur.

```
// prs_mdp inherits attributes from P0:
prs_mdp[time,lat,lon,lev]=P0*hyam+hybm*PS;
// th_min inherits attributes from three_dmn_var_dbl:
th_min=1.0 + 2*three_dmn_var_dbl.min($time);
```

### Attribute Concatenation

The push() function concatenates attributes, or appends an "expression" to a pre-existing attribute. It comes in two forms

```
(A) att_new=push(att_exp, expr)
(B) att_size=push(&att_nm,expr)
```

In form (A) The first argument should be an attribute identifier or an expression that evaluates to an attribute. The second argument can evalute to an attribute or a variable. The second argument is then converted to the the type of *att_exp*; and appended to *att_exp* ; and the resulting attribute is returned.

In form (B) the first argument is a call-by-reference attribute identifier (which may not yet exist). The second argument is then evaluated (and type-converted as needed) and appended to the call-by-reference atttribute. The final size of the attribute is then returned.

```
temp@range=-10.0;
push(&temp@range,12.0); // temp@range=-10.0,12.0

numbers@squares=push(1,4);
numbers@squares=push(numbers@squares,9);
push(&number@squares,16.0);
push(&number@squares,25ull); // numbers@squares=1,4,9,16,25
```

Now some text examples.
Remember, an atttribute identifier that begins with @ implies a global attribute. For example, '@institution' is short for 'global@institution'.

```
global@greetings=push("hello"," world !!");
global@greek={"alpha"s,"beta"s,"gamma"s};
// Append an NC_STRING
push(&@greek,"delta"s);
// Pushing an NC_CHAR to a NC_STRING attribute is allowed, it is converted to an
@e="epsilon";
push(&@greek,@e);
push(&@greek,"zeta");

// Pushing a single NC_STRING to an NC_CHAR is not allowed
@h="hello";
push(&@h," again"s); // BAD PUSH
```

If the attribute name contains non-regular characters use ID quoting.

```
'b..m1@c--lost'=23;
```

See see Section 4.1.30 [ID Quoting], page 197.

### 4.1.7 Value List

A *value list* is a special type of attribute. It can only be used on the RHS of the assign family of statements.
That is =, +=, -=, *=, /=
A value list CAN-NOT be involved in any logical, binary, or arithmetical operations (except those above).
A value list CAN-NOT be used as a function argument.
A value list CANT have nested value lists.
The type of a value list is the type of the member with the highest type.

```
a1@trip={1,2,3};
a1@trip+={3,2,1}; // 4,4,4
a1@triplet={a1@min,(a1@min+a1@max)/2,a1@max};
lon[lon]={0.0,90.0,180.0,270.0};
lon*={1.0,1.1,1.2,1.3}
dlon[lon]={1b,2s,3ull,4.0f}; // final type NC_FLOAT

a1@ind={1,2,3}+{4,4,4};  // BAD
a1@s=sin( {1.0,16.0} );  // BAD
```

One can also use a value_list to create an attribute of type NC_STRING. Remember, a literal string of type NC_STRING has a postfix 's'. A value list of NC_CHAR has no semantic meaning and is plain wrong.

```
array[lon]={1.0,2.,4.0,7.0};
array@numbers={"one"s, "two"s, "four"s, "seven"s}; // GOOD

ar[lat]={0,20}
ar@numbers={"zero","twenty"}; // BAD
```

### 4.1.8 Number literals

The table below lists the postfix character(s) to add to a number literal (aka, a naked constant) for explicit type specification. The same type-specification rules are used for variables and attributes. A floating-point number without a postfix defaults to `NC_DOUBLE`, while an integer without a postfix defaults to type `NC_INT`:

```
var[$rlev]=0.1;     // Variable will be type @code{NC_DOUBLE}
var[$lon_grd]=2.0;  // Variable will be type @code{NC_DOUBLE}
var[$gds_crd]=2e3;  // Variable will be type @code{NC_DOUBLE}
var[$gds_crd]=2.0f; // Variable will be type @code{NC_FLOAT} (note "f")
var[$gds_crd]=2e3f; // Variable will be type @code{NC_FLOAT} (note "f")
var[$gds_crd]=2;    // Variable will be type @code{NC_INT}
var[$gds_crd]=-3;   // Variable will be type @code{NC_INT}
var[$gds_crd]=2s;   // Variable will be type @code{NC_SHORT}
var[$gds_crd]=-3s;  // Variable will be type @code{NC_SHORT}
var@att=41.;        // Attribute will be type @code{NC_DOUBLE}
var@att=41.f;       // Attribute will be type @code{NC_FLOAT}
```

```
var@att=41;           // Attribute will be type @code{NC_INT}
var@att=-21s;         // Attribute will be type @code{NC_SHORT}
var@units="kelvin"; // Attribute will be type @code{NC_CHAR}
```

There is no postfix for characters, use a quoted string instead for `NC_CHAR`. `ncap2` interprets a standard double-quoted string as a value of type `NC_CHAR`. In this case, any receiving variable must be dimensioned as an array of `NC_CHAR` long enough to hold the value.

To use the newer netCDF4 types NCO must be compiled/linked to the netCDF4 library and the output file must be of type `NETCDF4`:

```
var[$time]=1UL;     // Variable will be type @code{NC_UINT}
var[$lon]=4b;       // Variable will be type @code{NC_BYTE}
var[$lat]=5ull;     // Variable will be type @code{NC_UINT64}
var[$lat]=5ll;     // Variable will be type @code{NC_INT64}
var@att=6.0d;       // Attribute will be type @code{NC_DOUBLE}
var@att=-666L;      // Attribute will be type @code{NC_INT}
var@att="kelvin"s; // Attribute will be type @code{NC_STRING} (note the "s")
```

Use a post-quote '`s`' for `NC_STRING`. Place the letter '`s`' immediately following the double-quoted string to indicate that the value is of type `NC_STRING`. In this case, the receiving variable need not have any memory allocated to hold the string because netCDF4 handles that memory allocation.

Suppose one creates a file containing an ensemble of model results, and wishes to label the record coordinate with the name of each model. The `NC_STRING` type is well-suited to this because it facilitates storing arrays of strings of arbitrary length. This is sophisticated, though easy with `ncap2`:

```
% ncecat -O -u model cesm.nc ecmwf.nc giss.nc out.nc
% ncap2 -4 -O -s 'model[$model]={"cesm"s,"ecmwf"s,"giss"s}' out.nc out.nc
```

The key here to place an '`s`' character after each double-quoted string value to indicate an `NC_STRING` type. The '`-4`' ensures the output filetype is netCDF4 in case the input filetype is not.

**netCDF3/4 Types**

b|B
: `NC_BYTE`, a signed 1-byte integer

none
: `NC_CHAR`, an ISO/ASCII character

s|S
: `NC_SHORT`, a signed 2-byte integer

l|L
: `NC_INT`, a signed 4-byte integer

f|F
: `NC_FLOAT`, a single-precision (4-byte) floating-point number

d|D
: `NC_DOUBLE`, a double-precision (8-byte) floating-point number

**netCDF4 Types**

ub|UB
: `NC_UBYTE`, an unsigned 1-byte integer

us|US
: `NC_USHORT`, an unsigned 2-byte integer

u|U|ul|UL
: NC_UINT, an unsigned 4-byte integer

ll|LL
: NC_INT64, a signed 8-byte integer

ull|ULL
: NC_UINT64, an unsigned 8-byte integer

s
: NC_STRING, a string of arbitrary length

### 4.1.9 if statement

The syntax of the if statement is similar to its C counterpart. The *Conditional Operator (ternary operator)* has also been implemented.

```
if(exp1)
   stmt1;
else if(exp2)
   stmt2;
else
   stmt3;

# Can use code blocks as well:
if(exp1){
   stmt1;
   stmt1a;
   stmt1b;
}else if(exp2)
   stmt2;
else{
   stmt3;
   stmt3a;
   stmt3b;
}
```

For a variable or attribute expression to be logically true all its non-missing value elements must be logically true, i.e., non-zero. The expression can be of any type. Unlike C there is no short-circuiting of an expression with the OR (||) and AND (&&) operators. The whole expression is evaluated regardless if one of the AND/OR operands are True/False.

```
# Simple example
if(time>0)
  print("All values of time are greater than zero\n");
else if(time<0)
  print("All values of time are less than zero\n");
else {
  time_max=time.max();
  time_min=time.min();
  print("min value of time=");print(time_min,"%f");
  print("max value of time=");print(time_max,"%f");
}
```

```
# Example from ddra.nco
if(fl_typ==fl_typ_gcm){
  var_nbr_apx=32;
  lmn_nbr=1.0*var_nbr_apx*varsz_gcm_4D; /* [nbr] Variable size */
  if(nco_op_typ==nco_op_typ_avg){
    lmn_nbr_avg=1.0*var_nbr_apx*varsz_gcm_4D; // Block size
    lmn_nbr_wgt=dmnsz_gcm_lat; /* [nbr] Weight size */
  } // !nco_op_typ_avg
}else if(fl_typ==fl_typ_stl){
  var_nbr_apx=8;
  lmn_nbr=1.0*var_nbr_apx*varsz_stl_2D; /* [nbr] Variable size */
  if(nco_op_typ==nco_op_typ_avg){
    lmn_nbr_avg=1.0*var_nbr_apx*varsz_stl_2D; // Block size
    lmn_nbr_wgt=dmnsz_stl_lat; /* [nbr] Weight size */
  } // !nco_op_typ_avg
} // !fl_typ
```

**Conditional Operator**

```
// netCDF4 needed for this example
th_nw=(three_dmn_var_sht >= 0 ? three_dmn_var_sht.uint() : \
       three_dmn_var_sht.int());
```

### 4.1.10 Print & String methods

The print statement comes in a variety of forms

```
(A)   print(variable_name, format string?);
(A1)  print(expression/string, format string?);

(B)   sprint(expression/string, format string?);
(B1)  sprint4(expression/string, format string?);
```

**print()**

If the variable exists in I/O then it is printed in a similar fashion to `ncks -H`.

```
print(lon);
lon[0]=0
lon[1]=90
lon[2]=180
lon[3]=270

print(byt_2D)
lat[0]=-90 lon[0]=0 byt_2D[0]=0
lat[0]=-90 lon[1]=90 byt_2D[1]=1
lat[0]=-90 lon[2]=180 byt_2D[2]=2
lat[0]=-90 lon[3]=270 byt_2D[3]=3
lat[1]=90 lon[0]=0 byt_2D[4]=4
```

```
lat[1]=90 lon[1]=90 byt_2D[5]=5
lat[1]=90 lon[2]=180 byt_2D[6]=6
lat[1]=90 lon[3]=270 byt_2D[7]=7
```

If the first argument is NOT a variable the form (A1) is invoked.

```
print(mss_val_fst@_FillValue);
mss_val_fst@_FillValue, size = 1 NC_FLOAT, value = -999

print("This function \t is monotonic\n");
This function is          monotonic

print(att_var@float_att)
att_var@float_att, size = 7 NC_FLOAT, value = 73, 72, 71, 70.01, 69.001, 68.01, 67.01

print(lon*10.0)
lon, size = 4 NC_DOUBLE, value = 0, 900, 1800, 2700
```

If the format string is specified then the results from (A) and (A1) forms are the same

```
print(lon_2D_rrg,"%3.2f,");
0.00,0.00,180.00,0.00,180.00,0.00,180.00,0.00,

print(lon*10.0, "%g,")
0,900,1800,2700,

print(att_var@float_att,"%g," )
73,72,71,70.01,69.001,68.01,67.01,
```

**sprint() & sprint4()**

These functions work in an identical fashion to (A1) except that `sprint()` outputs a regular netCDF3 `NC_CHAR` attribute and `sprint4()` outputs a netCDF4 `NC_STRING` attribute

```
time@units=sprint(nDays, "%d days since 1970-1-1")
bnd@num=sprint4(bnd_idx,"Band number=%d")

time@arr=sprint4(time,"%.2f,")  // "1.00,2.00,3.00,4.00,5.00,6.00,7.00,8.00,9.00,10.00
```

You can also use `sprint4()` to convert a `NC_CHAR` string to a `NC_STRING` string and `sprint()` to convert a `NC_STRING` to a `NC_CHAR`

```
lat_1D_rct@long_name = "Latitude for 2D rectangular grid stored as 1D arrays"; //

// convert to NC_STRING
lat_1D_rct@long_name = sprint4(lat_1D_rct@long_name)
```

**hyperslab a netCDF string**

Its possible to index-into a NC_CHAR string. Just like a C-String. Remember an

NC_CHAR string is has no terminating null. You CANNOT index into a NC_STRING. You have to convert to an NC_CHAR first.

```
global@greeting="hello world!!!"
@h=@greeting(0:4);  // "hello"
@w=@greeting(6:11); // "world"

// can use negative inidices
@x=@greeting(-3:-1);  // "!!!"

// can  use stride
@n=@greeting(::2);  // "hlowrd!"

// concatenation
global@new_greeting=push(@h, " users !!!"); // "hello users!!!"

@institution="hotel california"s;
@h=@institution(0:4); // BAD

// convert NC_STRING to NC_CHAR
@is=sprint(@institution);
@h=@is(0:4);  // "hotel"

// convert NC_CHAR to NC_STRING
@h=sprint4(@h);
```

**get_vars_in() & get_vars_out()**

```
att_lst=get_vars_in(att_regexp?)
att_lst=get_vars_out(att_regexp?)
```

These functions are used to create a list of vars in Input or Output. The optional arg 'att_regexp'. Can be an NC_CHAR att or a NC_STRING att. If NC_CHAR then only a single reg-exp can be specified. If NC_STRING then multiple reg-exp can be specified. The output is allways an NC_STRING att. The matching works in an identical fashion to the -v switch in ncks. if there is no arg then all vars are returned.

```
@slist=get_vars_in("^time");  // "time", "time_bnds", "time_lon", "time_udunits"
// Use NC_STRINGS
@regExp={".*_bnd"s,".*_grd"s}
@slist=get_vars_in(@regExp);  // "lat_bnd", "lat_grd", "lev_bnd", "lon_grd", "tim
```

### 4.1.11 Missing values ncap2

Missing values operate slightly differently in `ncap2` Consider the expression where op is any of the following operators (excluding '=')

```
Arithmetic operators ( * / % + - ^ )
Binary Operators     ( >, >= <, <= ==, !=,==,||,&&, >>,<< )
Assign Operators     ( +=,-=,/=, *= )
```

```
var1 'op' var2
```

If var1 has a missing value then this is the value used in the operation, otherwise the missing value for var2 is used. If during the element-by-element operation an element from either operand is equal to the missing value then the missing value is carried through. In this way missing values 'percolate' or propagate through an expression.
Missing values associated with Output variables are stored in memory and are written to disk after the script finishes. During script execution its possible (and legal) for the missing value of a variable to take on several different values.

```
# Consider the variable:
int rec_var_int_mss_val_int(time); =-999,2,3,4,5,6,7,8,-999,-999;
rec_var_int_mss_val_int:_FillValue = -999;

n2=rec_var_int_mss_val_int + rec_var_int_mss_val_int.reverse($time);

n2=-999,-999,11,11,11,11,11,11,999,-999;
```

The following methods query or manipulate missing value information associated with a variable. The methods that "manipulate" will only succeed on variables in Output

`set_miss(expr)`
: The numeric argument *expr* becomes the new missing value, overwriting the old missing value, if any. The argument given is converted if necessary to the variable's type. NB: This only changes the missing value attribute. Missing values in the original variable remain unchanged, and thus are no long considered missing values. They are effectively "orphaned". Thus `set_miss()` is normally used only when creating new variables. The intrinsic function `change_miss()` (see below) is typically used to edit values of existing variables.

`change_miss(expr)`
: Sets or changes (any pre-existing) missing value attribute and missing data values to *expr*. NB: This is an expensive function since all values must be examined. Use this function when changing missing values for pre-existing variables.

`get_miss()`
: Returns the missing value of a variable. If the variable exists in Input and Output then the missing value of the variable in Output is returned. If the variable has no missing value then an error is returned.

`delete_miss()`
: Delete the missing value associated with a variable.

`number_miss()`
: Count the number of missing values a variable contains.

`has_miss()`
: Returns 1 (True) if the variable has a missing value associated with it. else returns 0 (False)

```
th=three_dmn_var_dbl;
```

```
th.change_miss(-1e10d);
/* Set values less than 0 or greater than 50 to missing value */
where(th < 0.0 || th > 50.0) th=th.get_miss();

# Another example:
new[$time,$lat,$lon]=1.0;
new.set_miss(-997.0);

// Extract only elements divisible by 3
where (three_dmn_var_dbl%3 == 0)
     new=three_dmn_var_dbl;
elsewhere
     new=new.get_miss();

// Print missing value and variable summary
mss_val_nbr=three_dmn_var_dbl.number_miss();
print(three_dmn_var_dbl@_FillValue);
print("Number of missing values in three_dmn_var_dbl: ");
print(mss_val_nbr,"%d");
print(three_dmn_var_dbl);
```

### 4.1.12 Methods and functions

The convention within this document is that methods can be used as functions. However, functions are not and cannot be used as methods. Methods can be daisy-chained d and their syntax is cleaner than functions. Method names are reserved words and CANNOT be used as variable names. The command `ncap2 -f` shows the complete list of methods available on your build.

```
n2=sin(theta)
n2=theta.sin()
n2=sin(theta)^2 + cos(theta)^2
n2=theta.sin().pow(2) + theta.cos()^2
```

This statement chains together methods to convert three_dmn_var_sht to type double, average it, then convert this back to type short:

```
three_avg=three_dmn_var_sht.double().avg().short();
```

**Aggregate Methods**

These methods mirror the averaging types available in `ncwa`. The arguments to the methods are the dimensions to average over. Specifying no dimensions is equivalent to specifying all dimensions i.e., averaging over all dimensions. A masking variable and a weighting variable can be manually created and applied as needed.

`avg()` Mean value

`sqravg()` Square of the mean

`avgsqr()` Mean of sum of squares

`max()` Maximum value

`min()` Minimum value

`mabs()` Maximum absolute value

`mebs()` Mean absolute value

`mibs()` Minimum absolute value

`rms()` Root-mean-square (normalize by *N*)

`rmssdn()` Root-mean square (normalize by *N-1*)

`tabs()` or `ttlabs()`
: Sum of absolute values

`ttl()` or `total()` or `sum()`
: Sum of values

```
// Average a variable over time
four_time_avg=four_dmn_rec_var($time);
```

**Packing Methods**

For more information see see Section 3.34 [Packed data], page 111, and see Section 4.9 [ncpdq netCDF Permute Dimensions Quickly], page 254,

`pack() & pack_short()`
: The default packing algorithm is applied and variable is packed to `NC_SHORT`

`pack_byte()`
: Variable is packed to `NC_BYTE`

`pack_short()`
: Variable is packed to `NC_SHORT`

`pack_int()`
: Variable is packed to `NC_INT`

`unpack()` The standard unpacking algorithm is applied.

NCO automatically unpacks packed data before arithmetically modifying it. After modification NCO stores the unpacked data. To store it as packed data again, repack it with, e.g., the `pack()` function. To ensure that `temperature` is packed in the output file, regardless of whether it is packed in the input file, one uses, e.g.,

```
ncap2 -s 'temperature=pack(temperature-273.15)' in.nc out.nc
```

**Basic Methods**

These methods work with variables and attributes. They have no arguments

`size()` Total number of elements

`ndims()` Number of dimensions in variable

`type()` Returns the netcdf type (see previous section)

`exists()` Return 1 (true) if var or att is present in I/O else return 0 (false)

`getdims()`
: Returns an NC_STRING attribute of all the dim names of a variable

**Utility Methods**

These functions are used to manipulate missing values and RAM variables. see Section 4.1.11 [Missing values ncap2], page 156,

`set_miss(expr)`
: Takes one argument the missing value. Sets or overwrites the existing missing value. The argument given is converted if necessary to the variable type

`change_miss(expr)`
: Changes the missing value elements of the variable to the new missing value (n.b. an expensive function).

`get_miss()`
: Returns the missing value of a variable in Input or Output

`delete_miss()`
: Deletes the missing value associated with a variable.

`has_miss()`
: Returns 1 (True) if the variable has a missing else returns 0 (False)

`number_miss`
: Returns the number of missing values a variable contains

`ram_write()`
: Writes a RAM variable to disk i.e., converts it to a regular disk type variable

`ram_delete()`
: Deletes a RAM variable or an attribute

**PDQ Methods**

See see Section 4.9 [ncpdq netCDF Permute Dimensions Quickly], page 254,

`reverse(dim args)`
: Reverse the dimension ordering of elements in a variable.

`permute(dim args)`
: Re-shape variables by re-ordering the dimensions. All the dimensions of the variable must be specified in the arguments. A limitation of this permute (unlike `ncpdq`) is that the record dimension cannot be re-assigned.

// Swap dimensions about and reorder along lon

```
lat_2D_rrg_new=lat_2D_rrg.permute($lon,$lat).reverse($lon);
lat_2D_rrg_new=0,90,-30,30,-30,30,-90,0
```

**Type Conversion Methods and Functions**

These methods allow `ncap2` to convert variables and attributes to the different netCDF types. For more details on automatic and manual type conversion see (see Section 3.36 [Type Conversion], page 119). netCDF4 types are only available if you have compiled/links NCO with the netCDF4 library and the Output file is HDF5.

**netCDF3/4 Types**

`byte()` convert to `NC_BYTE`, a signed 1-byte integer

`char()` convert to `NC_CHAR`, an ISO/ASCII character

`short()` convert to `NC_SHORT`, a signed 2-byte integer

`int()` convert to `NC_INT`, a signed 4-byte integer

`float()` convert to `NC_FLOAT`, a single-precision (4-byte) floating-point number

`double()` convert to `NC_DOUBLE`, a double-precision (8-byte) floating-point number

**netCDF4 Types**

`ubyte()` convert to `NC_UBYTE`, an unsigned 1-byte integer

`ushort()` convert to `NC_USHORT`, an unsigned 2-byte integer

`uint()` convert to `NC_UINT`, an unsigned 4-byte integer

`int64()` convert to `NC_INT64`, a signed 8-byte integer

`uint64()` convert to `NC_UINT64`, an unsigned 8-byte integer

You can also use the `convert()` method to do type conversion. This takes an integer agument. For convenience, `ncap2` defines the netCDF pre-processor tokens as RAM variables. For example you may wish to convert a non-floating point variable to the same type as another variable.

```
lon_type=lon.type();
if(time.type() != NC_DOUBLE && time.type() != NC_FLOAT)
   time=time.convert(lon_type);
```

**Intrinsic Mathematical Methods**

The list of mathematical methods is system dependant. For the full list see Section 4.1.28 [Intrinsic mathematical methods], page 195,

All the mathematical methods take a single argument except `atan2()` and `pow()` which take two. If the operand type is less than *float* then the result will be of type *float*. Arguments of type *double* yield results of type *double*. Like the other methods, you are free to use the mathematical methods as functions.

```
n1=pow(2,3.0f)     // n1 type float
n2=atan2(2,3.0)    // n2 type double
n3=1/(three_dmn_var_dbl.cos().pow(2))-tan(three_dmn_var_dbl)^2; // n3 type double
```

### 4.1.13 RAM variables

Unlike regular variables, RAM variables are never written to disk. Hence using RAM variables in place of regular variables (especially within loops) significantly increases execution speed. Variables that are frequently accessed within `for` or `where` clauses provide the greatest opportunities for optimization. To declare and define a RAM variable simply prefix the variable name with an asterisk (*) when the variable is declared/initialized. To delete a RAM variables (and recover their memory) use the `ram_delete()` method. To write a RAM variable to disk (like a regular variable) use `ram_write()`.

```
*temp[$time,$lat,$lon]=10.0;      // Cast
*temp_avg=temp.avg($time);        // Regular assign
temp.ram_delete();                // Delete RAM variable
temp_avg.ram_write();             // Write Variable to output

// Create and increment a RAM variable from "one" in Input
*one++;
// Create RAM variables from the variables three and four in Input.
// Multiply three by 10 and add it to four.
*four+=*three*=10; // three=30, four=34
```

### 4.1.14 Where statement

A `where()` combines the definition and application of a mask all in one go and can lead to succinct code. The full syntax of a `where()` statement is as follows:

```
// Single assign (the 'elsewhere' block is optional)
where(mask)
   var1=expr1;
elsewhere
   var1=expr2;

// Multiple assigns
where(mask){
    var1=expr1;
    var2=expr2;
    ...
}elsewhere{
    var1=expr3
    var2=expr4
    var3=expr5;
    ...
}
```

- The only expression allowed in the predicate of a where is assign, i.e., 'var=expr'. This assign differs from a regular `ncap2` assign. The LHS var must already exist in Input or Output. The RHS expression must evaluate to a scalar or a variable/attribute of the same size as the LHS variable.
- Consider when both the LHS and RHS are variables: For every element where mask condition is True, the corresponding LHS variable element is re-assigned to its partner element on the RHS. In the elsewhere part the mask is logically inverted and the assign process proceeds as before.
- If the mask dimensions are a subset of the LHS variable's dimensions, then it is made to conform; if it cannot be made to conform then script execution halts.

- Missing values in the mask evaluate to False in the where code/block statement and to True in the elsewhere block/statement.
- LHS variable elements set to missing value are treated just like any other elements and can be re-assigned as the mask dictates

Example: Consider the variables `float lon_2D_rct(lat,lon);` and `float var_msk(lat,lon);`. Suppose we wish to multiply by two the elements for which `var_msk` equals 1:

```
where(var_msk==1) lon_2D_rct=2*lon_2D_rct;
```

Suppose that we have the variable `int RDM(time)` and that we want to set its values less than 8 or greater than 80 to 0:

```
where(RDM < 8 || RDM > 80) RDM=0;
```

Consider irregularly gridded data, described using rank 2 coordinates: `double lat(south_north,east_west)`, `double lon(south_north,east_west)`, `double temperature(south_north,east_west)`. This type of structure is often found in regional weather/climate model (such as WRF) output, and in satellite swath data. For this reason we call it "Swath-like Data", or SLD. To find the average temperature in a region bounded by [*lat_min*,*lat_max*] and [*lon_min*,*lon_max*]:

```
temperature_msk[$south_north,$east_west]=0.0;
where((lat >= lat_min && lat <= lat_max) && (lon >= lon_min && lon <= lon_max))
  temperature_msk=temperature;
elsewhere
  temperature_msk=temperature@_FillValue;

temp_avg=temperature_msk.avg();
temp_max=temperature.max();
```

For North American Regional Reanalysis (NARR) data (example dataset (`http://dust.ess.uci.edu/diwg/narr_uwnd.199605.nc`)) the procedure looks like this

```
ncap2 -O -v -S ~/narr.nco ${DATA}/hdf/narr_uwnd.199605.nc ~/foo.nc
```

where `narr.nco` is an `ncap2` script like this:

```
/* North American Regional Reanalysis (NARR) Statistics
   NARR stores grids with 2-D latitude and longitude, aka Swath-like Data (SLD)
   Here we work with three variables:
   lat(y,x), lon(y,x), and uwnd(time,level,y,x);
   To study sub-regions of SLD, we use masking techniques:
   1. Define mask as zero times variable to be masked
      Then mask automatically inherits variable attributes
      And average below will inherit mask attributes
   2. Optionally, create mask as RAM variable (as below with asterisk *)
      NCO does not write RAM variable to output
      Masks are often unwanted, and can be big, so this speeds execution
   3. Example could be extended to preserve mean lat and lon of sub-region
```

```
     Follow uwnd example to do this: lat_msk=0.0*lat ... lat_avg=lat.avg($y,$x)
*uwnd_msk=0.0*uwnd;
where((lat >= 35.6 && lat <= 37.0) && (lon >= -100.5 && lon <= -99.0))
  uwnd_msk=uwnd;
elsewhere
  uwnd_msk=uwnd@_FillValue;

// Average only over horizontal dimensions x and y (preserve level and time)
uwnd_avg=uwnd_msk.avg($y,$x);
```

Stripped of comments and formatting, this example is a three-statement script executed by a one-line command. NCO needs only this meagre input to unpack and copy the input data and attributes, compute the statistics, and then define and write the output file. Unless the comments pointed out that wind variable (`uwnd`) was four-dimensional and the latitude/longitude grid variables were both two-dimensional, there would be no way to tell. This shows how NCO hides from the user the complexity of analyzing multi-dimensional SLD. We plan to extend such SLD features to more operators soon.

### 4.1.15 Loops

`ncap2` supplies `for()` loops and `while()` loops. They are completely unoptimized so use them only with RAM variables unless you want thrash your disk to death. To break out of a loop use the `break` command. To iterate to the next cycle use the `continue` command.

```
// Set elements in variable double temp(time,lat)
// If element < 0 set to 0, if element > 100 set to 100
*sz_idx=$time.size;
*sz_jdx=$lat.size;

for(*idx=0;idx<sz_idx;idx++)
  for(*jdx=0;jdx<sz_jdx;jdx++)
    if(temp(idx,jdx) > 100) temp(idx,jdx)=100.0;
      else if(temp(idx,jdx) < 0) temp(idx,jdx)=0.0;

// Are values of co-ordinate variable double lat(lat) monotonic?
*sz=$lat.size;

for(*idx=1;idx<sz;idx++)
  if(lat(idx)-lat(idx-1) < 0.0) break;

if(idx == sz) print("lat co-ordinate is monotonic\n");
   else print("lat co-ordinate is NOT monotonic\n");

// Sum odd elements
*idx=0;
*sz=$lat_nw.size;
*sum=0.0;

while(idx<sz){
```

```
    if(lat(idx)%2) sum+=lat(idx);
    idx++;
  }

  ram_write(sum);
  print("Total of odd elements ");print(sum);print("\n");
```

### 4.1.16 Include files

The syntax of an *include-file* is:

```
#include "script.nco"
#include "/opt/SOURCES/nco/data/tst.nco"
```

If the filename is relative and not absolute then the directory searched is relative to the run-time directory. It is possible to nest include files to an arbitrary depth. A handy use of inlcude files is to store often used constants. Use RAM variables if you do not want these constants written to nc-file.

*output-file.*

```
// script.nco
// Sample file to #include in ncap2 script
*pi=3.1415926535; // RAM variable, not written to output
*h=6.62607095e-34; // RAM variable, not written to output
e=2.71828; // Regular (disk) variable, written to output
```

As of NCO version 4.6.3 (December, 2016), The user can specify the directory(s) to be searched by specifing them in the UNIX environment var `NCO_PATH`. The format used is identical to the UNIX `PATH`. The directory(s) are only searched if the include filename is relative.

```
export NCO_PATH=":/home/henryb/bin/:/usr/local/scripts:/opt/SOURCES/nco/data:"
```

### 4.1.17 sort methods

In ncap2 there are multiple ways to sort data. Beginning with NCO 4.1.0 (March, 2012), ncap2 support six sorting functions:

```
var_out=sort(var_in,&srt_map); // Ascending sort
var_out=asort(var_in,&srt_map); // Accending sort
var_out=dsort(var_in,&srt_map); // Desending sort
var_out=remap(var_in,srt_map); // Apply srt_map to var_in
var_out=unmap(var_in,srt_map); // Reverse what srt_map did to var_in
dsr_map=invert_map(srt_map); // Produce "de-sort" map that inverts srt_map
```

The first two functions, `sort()` and `asort()` sort, in ascending order, all the elements of *var_in* (which can be a variable or attribute) without regard to any dimensions. The third function, `dsort()` does the same but sorts in descending order. Remember that ascending and descending sorts are specified by `asort()` and `dsort()`, respectively.

These three functions are overloaded to take a second, optional argument called the sort map *srt_map*, which should be supplied as a call-by-reference variable, i.e., preceded with an ampersand. If the sort map does not yet exist, then it will be created and returned as an integer type the same shape as the input variable.

The output *var_out* of each sort function is a sorted version of the input, *var_in*. The output *var_out* of the two mapping functions the result of applying (with `remap()` or unapplying (with `unmap()`) the sort map *srt_map* to the input *var_in*. To apply the sort map with `remap()` the size of the variable must be exactly divisible by the size of the sort map.

The final function `invert_map()` returns the so-called de-sorting map *dsr_map* which is inverse map of the input map *srt_map*. This gives the user access to both the forward and inverse sorting maps which can be useful in special situations.

```
a1[$time]={10,2,3,4,6,5,7,3,4,1};
a1_sort=sort(a1);
print(a1_sort);
// 1, 2, 3, 3, 4, 4, 5, 6, 7, 10;

a2[$lon]={2,1,4,3};
a2_sort=sort(a2,&a2_map);
print(a2);
// 1, 2, 3, 4
print(a2_map);
// 1, 0, 3, 2;
```

If the map variable does not exist prior to the `sort()` call, then it will be created with the same shape as the input variable and be of type `NC_INT`. If the map variable already exists, then the only restriction is that it be of at least the same size as the input variable. To apply a map use `remap(var_in,srt_map)`.

```
defdim("nlat",5);

a3[$lon]={2,5,3,7};
a4[$nlat,$lon]={
 1, 2, 3, 4,
 5, 6, 7, 8,
 9,10,11,12,
 13,14,15,16,
 17,18,19,20};

a3_sort=sort(a3,&a3_map);
print(a3_map);
// 0, 2, 1, 3;

a4_sort=remap(a4,a3_map);
print(a4_sort);
// 1, 3, 2, 4,
// 5, 7, 6, 8,
// 9,11,10,12,
// 13,15,14,16,
```

```
// 17,19,18,20;

a3_map2[$nlat]={4,3,0,2,1};

a4_sort2=remap(a4,a3_map2);
print(a4_sort2);
// 3, 5, 4, 2, 1
// 8, 10, 9,7, 6,
// 13,15,14,12,11,
// 18,20,19,17,16
```

As in the above example you may create your own sort map. To sort in descending order, apply the reverse() method after the sort().

Here is an extended example of how to use ncap2 features to hyperslab an irregular region based on the values of a variable not a coordinate. The distinction is crucial: hyperslabbing based on dimensional indices or coordinate values is straightforward. Using the values of single or multi-dimensional variable to define a hyperslab is quite different.

```
cat > ~/ncap2_foo.nco << 'EOF'
// Purpose: Save irregular 1-D regions based on variable values

// Included in NCO User Guide at http://nco.sf.net/nco.html#sort

/* NB: Single quotes around EOF above turn off shell parameter
    expansion in "here documents". This in turn prevents the
    need for protecting dollarsign characters in NCO scripts with
    backslashes when the script is cut-and-pasted (aka "moused")
    from an editor or e-mail into a shell console window */

/* Copy coordinates and variable(s) of interest into RAM variable(s)
   Benefits:
   1. ncap2 defines writes all variables on LHS of expression to disk
      Only exception is RAM variables, which are stored in RAM only
      Repeated operations on regular variables takes more time,
      because changes are written to disk copy after every change.
      RAM variables are only changed in RAM so script works faster
      RAM variables can be written to disk at end with ram_write()
   2. Script permutes variables of interest during processing
      Safer to work with copies that have different names
      This discourages accidental, mistaken use of permuted versions
   3. Makes this script a more generic template:
      var_in instead of specific variable names everywhere */
*var_in=one_dmn_rec_var;
*crd_in=time;
*dmn_in_sz=$time.size; // [nbr] Size of input arrays

/* Create all other "intermediate" variables as RAM variables
```

```
   to prevent them from cluttering the output file.
   Mask flag and sort map are same size as variable of interest */
*msk_flg=var_in;
*srt_map=var_in;

/* In this example we mask for all values evenly divisible by 3
   This is the key, problem-specific portion of the template
   Replace this where() condition by that for your problem
   Mask variable is Boolean: 1=Meets condition, 0=Fails condition */
where(var_in % 3 == 0) msk_flg=1; elsewhere msk_flg=0;

// print("msk_flg = ");print(msk_flg); // For debugging...

/* The sort() routine is overloaded, and takes one or two arguments
   The second argument (optional) is the "sort map" (srt_map below)
   Pass the sort map by reference, i.e., prefix with an ampersand
   If the sort map does not yet exist, then it will be created and
   returned as an integer type the same shape as the input variable.
   The output of sort(), on the LHS, is a sorted version of the input
   msk_flg is not needed in its original order after sort()
   Hence we use msk_flg as both input to and output from sort()
   Doing this prevents the need to define a new, unneeded variable */
msk_flg=sort(msk_flg,&srt_map);

// Count number of valid points in mask by summing the one's
*msk_nbr=msk_flg.total();

// Define output dimension equal in size to number of valid points
defdim("crd_out",msk_nbr);

/* Now sort the variable of interest using the sort map and remap()
   The output, on the LHS, is the input re-arranged so that all points
   meeting the mask condition are contiguous at the end of the array
   Use same srt_map to hyperslab multiple variables of the same shape
   Remember to apply srt_map to the coordinate variables */
crd_in=remap(crd_in,srt_map);
var_in=remap(var_in,srt_map);

/* Hyperslab last msk_nbr values of variable(s) of interest */
crd_out[crd_out]=crd_in((dmn_in_sz-msk_nbr):(dmn_in_sz-1));
var_out[crd_out]=var_in((dmn_in_sz-msk_nbr):(dmn_in_sz-1));

/* NB: Even though we created all variables possible as RAM variables,
   the original coordinate of interest, time, is written to the ouput.
   I'm not exactly sure why. For now, delete it from the output with:
   ncks -O -x -v time ~/foo.nc ~/foo.nc
   */
```

```
EOF
ncap2 -O -v -S ~/ncap2_foo.nco ~/nco/data/in.nc ~/foo.nc
ncks -O -x -v time ~/foo.nc ~/foo.nc
ncks ~/foo.nc
```

Here is an extended example of how to use ncap2 features to sort multi-dimensional arrays based on the coordinate values along a single dimension.

```
cat > ~/ncap2_foo.nco << 'EOF'
/* Purpose: Sort multi-dimensional array based on coordinate values
   This example sorts the variable three_dmn_rec_var(time,lat,lon)
   based on the values of the time coordinate. */

// Included in NCO User Guide at http://nco.sf.net/nco.html#sort

// Randomize the time coordinate
time=10.0*gsl_rng_uniform(time);
//print("original randomized time =\n");print(time);

/* The sort() routine is overloaded, and takes one or two arguments
   The first argument is a one dimensional array
   The second argument (optional) is the "sort map" (srt_map below)
   Pass the sort map by reference, i.e., prefix with an ampersand
   If the sort map does not yet exist, then it will be created and
   returned as an integer type the same shape as the input variable.
   The output of sort(), on the LHS, is a sorted version of the input */

time=sort(time,&srt_map);
//print("sorted time (ascending order) and associated sort map =\n");print(time);print

/* sort() always sorts in ascending order
   The associated sort map therefore re-arranges the original,
   randomized time array into ascending order.
   There are two methods to obtain the descending order the user wants
   1) We could solve the problem in ascending order (the default)
   and then apply the reverse() method to re-arrange the results.
   2) We could change the sort map to return things in descending
   order of time and solve the problem directly in descending order. */

// Following shows how to do method one:

/* Expand the sort map to srt_map_3d, the size of the data array
   1. Use data array to provide right shape for the expanded sort map
   2. Coerce data array into an integer so srt_map_3d is an integer
   3. Multiply data array by zero so 3-d map elements are all zero
   4. Add the 1-d sort map to the 3-d sort map (NCO automatically resizes)
   5. Add the spatial (lat,lon) offsets to each time index
   6. de-sort using the srt_map_3d
```

```
   7. Use reverse to obtain descending in time order
   Loops could accomplish the same thing (exercise left for reader)
   However, loops are slow for large datasets */

/* Following index manipulation requires understanding correspondence
   between 1-d (unrolled, memory order of storage) and access into that
   memory as a multidimensional (3-d, in this case) rectangular array.
   Key idea to understand is how dimensionality affects offsets */
// Copy 1-d sort map into 3-d sort map
srt_map_3d=(0*int(three_dmn_rec_var))+srt_map;
// Multiply base offset by factorial of lesser dimensions
srt_map_3d*=$lat.size*$lon.size;
lon_idx=array(0,1,$lon);
lat_idx=array(0,1,$lat)*$lon.size;
lat_lon_idx[$lat,$lon]=lat_idx+lon_idx;
srt_map_3d+=lat_lon_idx;

print("sort map 3d =\n");print(srt_map_3d);

// Use remap() to re-map the data
three_dmn_rec_var=remap(three_dmn_rec_var,srt_map_3d);

// Finally, reverse data so time coordinate is descending
time=time.reverse($time);
//print("sorted time (descending order) =\n");print(time);
three_dmn_rec_var=three_dmn_rec_var.reverse($time);

// Method two: Key difference is srt_map=$time.size-srt_map-1;
EOF
ncap2 -O -v -S ~/ncap2_foo.nco ~/nco/data/in.nc ~/foo.nc
```

### 4.1.18 UDUnits script

As of NCO version 4.6.3 (December, 2016), ncap2 includes support for UDUnits conversions. The function is called `udunits`. Its syntax is

```
varOut=udunits(varIn, "UnitsOutString")
```

The `udunits()` function looks for the attribute of `varIn@units` and fails if it is not found. A quirk of this function that due to attribute propagation `varOut@units` will be overwritten by `varIn@units`. It is best to re-initialize this attribute AFTER the call. In addition if `varIn@units` is of the form `"time_interval since basetime"` then the calendar attribute `varIn@calendar` will read it. If it does not exist then the calendar used defaults to mixed Gregorian/Julian as defined by UDUnits.

If `varIn` is not a floating point type then it is promoted to `NC_DOUBLE` for the system call in the Udunits library; and then demoted back to to its original type after.

```
T[lon]={0.0,100.0,150.0,200.0};
T@units="Celsius";
```

```
// Overwrite variable
T=udunits(T,"kelvin");
print(T);
// 273.15, 373.15, 423.15, 473.15 ;
T@units="kelvin";

// Rebase coordinate days to hours
timeOld=time;
print(timeOld);
// 1, 2, 3, 4, 5, 6, 7, 8, 9, 10 ;
timeOld@units="days since 2012-01-30";

@units="hours since 2012-02-01 01:00";
timeNew=udunits(timeOld, @units);
timeNew@units=@units;
print(timeNew);
// -25, -1, 23, 47, 71, 95, 119, 143, 167, 191 ;

tOld=time;
// nb in this calendar NO Leap year
tOld@calendar="365_day";
tOld@units="minutes since 2012-02-28 23:58:00.00";

@units="seconds since 2012-03-01 00:00";
tNew=udunits(tOld, @units);
tNew@units=@units;
print(tNew);
// -60, 0, 60, 120, 180, 240, 300, 360, 420, 480
```

### 4.1.19 Vpointer

A variable-pointer or *vpointer* is a pointer to a variable or attribute. It is most usefull when one needs to apply a set of operations on a list of variables. For example After regular processing one may wish to set the _FillVlaue of all NC_FLOAT variables to a particular value. Or say after processing, create min/max attributes for all 3D variables of type NC_DOUBLE. A vpointer is not a 'pointer' to a memory location in the normal C/C++ sense. Rather the vpointer is a text attribute that contains the name of a variable. To use the pointer simply prefix the pointer with '*'. Most places where you use VAR_ID you can use *vpointer_nm. There is a variety of ways to maintain a list of strings in ncap2. The easiest method is to use a NC_STRING attribute.

Below is a simple illustration using NC_CHAR as the vpointer.
Remember an attribute starting with @ implies 'global'. eg '@vpx' is short for 'global@vpx'

```
idx=9;
idy=20;
t2=time;

global@vpx="idx";
```

```
// lets increment idx by one
*global@vpx++;
print(idx);

// multiply by 5
*@vpx*=5;  // idx now 50
print(idx);

// lets add 200 (long method)
*@vpx=*@vpx+200;  //idx now 250
print(idx);

@vpy="idy";

// lets add together idx and idy
idz=*@vpx+*@vpy;  // idz == 270
print(idz);

// we can also reference variables in  the input file
// can use an existing att pointer as atts are not written
// to the netcdf file until after script has finished
@vpx="three_dmn_var";

// we can convert the above var to type NC_DOUBLE and
// write  it to ouptut all in one go
*@vpx=*@vpx.double();
```

The following script writes to Output all vars that are of type NC_DOUBLE and and have at least 2 dimesions; It then changes their _FillValue to '1.0 E-9'. The function `get_vars_in()` creates an NC_STRING attribue that contains all the var names in Input. It is important to note that That a vpointer must a plain attribute and NOT an a attribute expression. So in the below script using `*all(idx)` would be a fundamental mistake. In the above example the vpointer `var_nm` is of type NC_STRING.

```
@all=get_vars_in();

*sz=@all.size();
*idx=0;

for(idx=0;idx<sz;idx++)
{
  // remember @var_nm is of type NC_STRING
  @var_nm=@all(idx);

  if( *@var_nm.type()==NC_DOUBLE && *@var_nm.ndims()>=2  )
  {
     *@var_nm=*@var_nm;
```

```
      *@var_nm.change_miss(1e-9d);
    }
  }
```

The following script, writes to Output all 3D/4D vars as type NC_FLOAT. Then for each var it calculates a range att that contains min & max; and a total att that is the sum of all elements. Note that in this example vpointer are used to 'point' to attributes

```
@all=get_vars_in();
*sz=@all.size();

for(*idx=0;idx<sz;idx++)
{
  @var_nm=@all(idx);
  if(*@var_nm.ndims()>=3 )
  {

    *@var_nm=*@var_nm.float();
    // The push function also takes a call-by-ref att -if it  doesnt already exist the
    // the call below is pushing a NC_STRING to an att so the end result is a list of
    push(&@prc,@var_nm);
  }
}

*sz=@prc.size();

for(*idx=0;idx<sz;idx++)
{
  @var_nm=@prc(idx);

  // we can work with att pointers as well
  // sprint - ouptut is of type NC_CHAR
  @att_total=sprint(@var_nm,"%s@total");
  @att_range=sprint(@var_nm,"%s@range");

  // if you are still confused then print out the atts
  print(@att_total);
  print(@att_range);

  *@att_total= *@var_nm.total();
  *@att_range={ min(*@var_nm), max(*@var_nm)};
}
```

This is an ncdump of one of the variables that has been processed by the above script

```
float three_dmn_var_int(time, lat, lon) ;
three_dmn_var_int:_FillValue = -99.f ;
three_dmn_var_int:long_name = "three dimensional record variable of type int" ;
```

```
three_dmn_var_int:range = 1.f, 80.f ;
three_dmn_var_int:total = 2701.f ;
three_dmn_var_int:units = "watt meter-2" ;
```

### 4.1.20 Irregular Grids

NCO is capable of analyzing datasets for many different underlying coordinate grid types. netCDF was developed for and initially used with grids comprised of orthogonal dimensions forming a rectangular coordinate system. We call such grids *standard* grids. It is increasingly common for datasets to use metadata to describe much more complex grids. Let us first define three important coordinate grid properties: rectangularity, regularity, and fxm.

Grids are *regular* if the spacing between adjacent is constant. For example, a 4-by-5 degree latitude-longitude grid is regular because the spacings between adjacent latitudes (4 degrees) are constant as are the (5 degrees) spacings between adjacent longitudes. Spacing in *irregular* grids depends on the location along the coordinate. Grids such as Gaussian grids have uneven spacing in latitude (points cluster near the equator) and so are irregular.

Grids are *rectangular* if the number of elements in any dimension is not a function of any other dimension. For example, a T42 Gaussian latitude-longitude grid is rectangular because there are the same number of longitudes (128) for each of the (64) latitudes. Grids are *non-rectangular* if the elements in any dimension depend on another dimension. Non-rectangular grids present many special challenges to analysis software like NCO.

Wrapped coordinates (see Section 3.20 [Wrapped Coordinates], page 70), such as longitude, are independent of these grid properties (regularity, rectangularity).

The preferred NCO technique to analyze data on non-standard coordinate grids is to create a region mask with `ncap2`, and then to use the mask within `ncap2` for variable-specific processing, and/or with other operators (e.g., `ncwa`, `ncdiff`) for entire file processing.

Before describing the construction of masks, let us review how irregularly gridded geoscience data are described. Say that latitude and longitude are stored as $R$-dimensional arrays and the product of the dimension sizes is the total number of elements N in the other variables. Geoscience applications tend to use $R = 1$, $R = 2$, and $R = 3$.

If the grid is has no simple representation (e.g., discontinuous) then it makes sense to store all coordinates as 1D arrays with the same size as the number of grid points. These gridpoints can be completely independent of all the other (own weight, area, etc.).

$R$=1: lat(number_of_gridpoints) and lon(number_of_gridpoints)

If the horizontal grid is time-invariant then $R$=2 is common:

$R$=2: lat(south_north,east_west) and lon(south_north,east_west)

The Weather and Research Forecast (WRF) model uses $R$=3:

$R$=3: lat(time,south_north,east_west), lon(time,south_north,east_west)

and so supports grids that change with time.

Grids with $R$ > 1 often use missing values to indicated empty points. For example, so-called "staggered grids" will use fewer east_west points near the poles and more near the equator. netCDF only accepts rectangular arrays so space must be allocated for the maximum number of east_west points at all latitudes. Then the application writes missing values into the unused points near the poles.

We demonstrate the `ncap2` analysis technique for irregular regions by constructing a mask for an $R$=2 grid. We wish to find, say, the mean temperature within [*lat_min*,*lat_max*] and [*lon_min*,*lon_max*]:

```
ncap2 -s 'mask_var= (lat >= lat_min && lat <= lat_max) && \
                    (lon >= lon_min && lon <= lon_max);' in.nc out.nc
```

Arbitrarily shaped regions can be defined by more complex conditional statements. Once defined, masks can be applied to specific variables, and to entire files:

```
ncap2 -s 'temperature_avg=(temperature*mask_var).avg()' in.nc out.nc
ncwa -a lat,lon -m mask_var -w area in.nc out.nc
```

Crafting such commands on the command line is possible though unwieldy. In such cases, a script is often cleaner and allows you to document the procedure:

```
cat > ncap2.in << 'EOF'
mask_var = (lat >= lat_min && lat <= lat_max) && (lon >= lon_min && > lon <= lon_max);
if(mask_var.total() > 0){ // Check that mask contains some valid values
  temperature_avg=(temperature*mask_var).avg(); // Average temperature
  temperature_max=(temperature*mask_var).max(); // Maximum temperature
}
EOF
ncap2 -S ncap2.in in.nc out.nc
```

Grids like those produced by the WRF model are complex because one must use global metadata to determine the grid staggering and offsets to translate `XLAT` and `XLONG` into real latitudes, longitudes, and missing points. The WRF grid documentation should describe this. For WRF files creating regional masks looks, in general, like

```
mask_var = (XLAT >= lat_min && XLAT <= lat_max) && (XLONG >= lon_min && XLONG <= lon_m
```

A few notes: Irregular regions are the union of arrays lat/lon_min/max's. The mask procedure is identical for all $R$.

### 4.1.21 Bilinear interpolation

As of version 4.0.0 NCO has internal routines to perform bilinear interpolation on gridded data sets. In mathematics, bilinear interpolation is an extension of linear interpolation for interpolating functions of two variables on a regular grid. The idea is to perform linear interpolation first in one direction, and then again in the other direction.

Suppose we have an irregular grid of data `temperature[lat,lon]`, with co-ordinate vars `lat[lat], lon[lon]`. We wish to find the temperature at an arbitary point $[X,Y]$ within the grid. If we can locate lat_min,lat_max and lon_min,lon_max such that `lat_min <= X <= lat_max` and `lon_min <= Y <= lon_max` then we can interpolate in two dimensions the temperature at $[X,Y]$.

The general form of the `ncap2` interpolation function is

```
var_out=bilinear_interp(grid_in,grid_out,grid_out_x,grid_out_y,grid_in_x,grid_in_y)
```

where

`grid_in` Input function data. Usually a two dimensional variable. It must be of size `grid_in_x.size()*grid_in_y.size()`

`grid_out` This variable is the shape of `var_out`. Usually a two dimensional variable. It must be of size `grid_out_x.size()*grid_out_y.size()`

`grid_out_x`
: $X$ output values

`grid_out_y`
: $Y$ output values

`grid_in_x`
: $X$ input values values. Must be monotonic (increasing or decreasing).

`grid_in_y`
: $Y$ input values values. Must be monotonic (increasing or decreasing).

Prior to calculations all arguments are converted to type `NC_DOUBLE`. After calculations `var_out` is converted to the input type of `grid_in`.

Suppose the first part of an `ncap2` script is

```
defdim("X",4);
defdim("Y",5);

// Temperature
T_in[$X,$Y]=
 {100, 200, 300, 400, 500,
  101, 202, 303, 404, 505,
  102, 204, 306, 408, 510,
  103, 206, 309, 412, 515.0 };

// Coordinate variables
x_in[$X]={0.0,1.0,2.0,3.01};
y_in[$Y]={1.0,2.0,3.0,4.0,5};
```

Now we interpolate with the following variables:

```
defdim("Xn",3);
defdim("Yn",4);
T_out[$Xn,$Yn]=0.0;
x_out[$Xn]={0.0,0.02,3.01};
y_out[$Yn]={1.1,2.0,3,4};

var_out=bilinear_interp(T_in,T_out,x_out,y_out,x_in,y_in);
print(var_out);
// 110, 200, 300, 400,
// 110.022, 200.04, 300.06, 400.08,
// 113.3, 206, 309, 412 ;
```

It is possible to interpolate a single point:

```
var_out=bilinear_interp(T_in,0.0,3.0,4.99,x_in,y_in);
print(var_out);
// 513.920594059406
```

**Wrapping and Extrapolation**
The function `bilinear_interp_wrap()` takes the same arguments as `bilinear_interp()` but performs wrapping ($Y$) and extrapolation ($X$) for points off the edge of the grid. If the given range of longitude is say (25-335) and we have a point at 20 degrees, then the endpoints of the range are used for the interpolation. This is what wrapping means. For wrapping to occur $Y$ must be longitude and must be in the range (0,360) or (-180,180). There are no restrictions on the longitude ($X$) values, though typically these are in the range (-90,90). This `ncap2` script illustrates both wrapping and extrapolation of end points:

```
defdim("lat_in",6);
defdim("lon_in",5);

// Coordinate input vars
lat_in[$lat_in]={-80,-40,0,30,60.0,85.0};
lon_in[$lon_in]={30, 110, 190, 270, 350.0};

T_in[$lat_in,$lon_in]=
  {10,40,50,30,15,
    12,43,52,31,16,
    14,46,54,32,17,
    16,49,56,33,18,
    18,52,58,34,19,
    20,55,60,35,20.0 };

defdim("lat_out",4);
defdim("lon_out",3);

// Coordinate variables
lat_out[$lat_out]={-90,0,70,88.0};
lon_out[$lon_out]={0,190,355.0};

T_out[$lat_out,$lon_out]=0.0;

T_out=bilinear_interp_wrap(T_in,T_out,lat_out,lon_out,lat_in,lon_in);
print(T_out);
// 13.4375, 49.5, 14.09375,
// 16.25, 54, 16.625,
// 19.25, 58.8, 19.325,
// 20.15, 60.24, 20.135 ;
```

### 4.1.22 GSL special functions

As of version 3.9.6 (released January, 2009), NCO can link to the GNU Scientific Library (GSL). `ncap2` can access most GSL special functions including Airy, Bessel, error, gamma, beta, hypergeometric, and Legendre functions and elliptical integrals. GSL must be version 1.4 or later. To list the GSL functions available with your NCO build, use `ncap2 -f | grep ^gsl`.

The function names used by ncap2 mirror their GSL names. The NCO wrappers for GSL functions automatically call the error-handling version of the GSL function when available[2]. This allows NCO to return a missing value when the GSL library encounters a domain error or a floating-point exception. The slow-down due to calling the error-handling version of the GSL numerical functions was found to be negligible (please let us know if you find otherwise).

Consider the gamma function.
The GSL function prototype is
`int gsl_sf_gamma_e(const double x, gsl_sf_result * result)` The `ncap2` script would be:

```
lon_in[lon]={-1,0.1,0,2,0.3};
lon_out=gsl_sf_gamma(lon_in);
lon_out= _, 9.5135, 4.5908, 2.9915
```

The first value is set to `_FillValue` since the gamma function is undefined for negative integers. If the input variable has a missing value then this value is used. Otherwise, the default double fill value is used (defined in the netCDF header `netcdf.h` as `NC_FILL_DOUBLE = 9.969e+36`).

Consider a call to a Bessel function with GSL prototype
`int gsl_sf_bessel_Jn_e(int n, double x, gsl_sf_result * result)`

An `ncap2` script would be

```
lon_out=gsl_sf_bessel_Jn(2,lon_in);
lon_out=0.11490, 0.0012, 0.00498, 0.011165
```

This computes the Bessel function of order *n=2* for every value in `lon_in`. The Bessel order argument, an integer, can also be a non-scalar variable, i.e., an array.

```
n_in[lon]={0,1,2,3};
lon_out=gsl_sf_bessel_Jn(n_in,0.5);
lon_out= 0.93846, 0.24226, 0.03060, 0.00256
```

Arguments to GSL wrapper functions in `ncap2` must conform to one another, i.e., they must share the same sub-set of dimensions. For example: `three_out=gsl_sf_bessel_Jn(n_in,three_dmn_var_dbl)` is valid because the variable `three_dmn_var_dbl` has a *lon* dimension, so `n_in` in can be broadcast to conform to `three_dmn_var_dbl`. However `time_out=gsl_sf_bessel_Jn(n_in,time)` is invalid.

---

[2] These are the GSL standard function names postfixed with `_e`. NCO calls these functions automatically, without the NCO command having to specifically indicate the `_e` function suffix.

Consider the elliptical integral with prototype `int gsl_sf_ellint_RD_e(double x, double y, double z, gsl_mode_t mode, gsl_sf_result * result)`

```
three_out=gsl_sf_ellint_RD(0.5,time,three_dmn_var_dbl);
```

The three arguments are all conformable so the above `ncap2` call is valid. The mode argument in the function prototype controls the convergence of the algorithm. It also appears in the Airy Function prototypes. It can be set by defining the environment variable `GSL_PREC_MODE`. If unset it defaults to the value `GSL_PREC_DOUBLE`. See the GSL manual for more details.

```
export GSL_PREC_MODE=0 // GSL_PREC_DOUBLE
export GSL_PREC_MODE=1 // GSL_PREC_SINGLE
export GSL_PREC_MODE=2 // GSL_PREC_APPROX
```

The `ncap2` wrappers to the array functions are slightly different. Consider the following GSL prototype
`int gsl_sf_bessel_Jn_array(int nmin, int nmax, double x, double *result_array)`

```
b1=lon.double();
x=0.5;
status=gsl_sf_bessel_Jn_array(1,4,x,&b1);
print(status);
b1=0.24226,0.0306,0.00256,0.00016;
```

This calculates the Bessel function of $x$=0.5 for $n$=1 to 4. The first three arguments are scalar values. If a non-scalar variable is supplied as an argument then only the first value is used. The final argument is the variable where the results are stored (NB: the `&` indicates this is a call by reference). This final argument must be of type `double` and must be of least size *nmax-nmin+1*. If either of these conditions is not met then then the function returns an error message. The function/wrapper returns a status flag. Zero indicates success.

Consider another array function
`int gsl_sf_legendre_Pl_array(int lmax, double x, double *result_array);`

```
a1=time.double();
x=0.3;
status=gsl_sf_legendre_Pl_array(a1.size()-1, x,&a1);
print(status);
```

This call calculates *P_l*(0.3) for *l*=0..9. Note that |*x*|<=*1*, otherwise there will be a domain error. See the GSL documentation for more details.

The GSL functions implemented in NCO are listed in the table below. This table is correct for GSL version 1.10. To see what functions are available on your build run the command `ncap2 -f |grep ^gsl` . To see this table along with the GSL C-function prototypes look at the spreadsheet **doc/nco_gsl.ods**.

| GSL NAME | I | NCAP FUNCTION CALL |
|---|---|---|
| gsl_sf_airy_Ai_e | Y | gsl_sf_airy_Ai(dbl_expr) |
| gsl_sf_airy_Bi_e | Y | gsl_sf_airy_Bi(dbl_expr) |

| | | |
|---|---|---|
| gsl_sf_airy_Ai_scaled_e | Y | gsl_sf_airy_Ai_scaled(dbl_expr) |
| gsl_sf_airy_Bi_scaled_e | Y | gsl_sf_airy_Bi_scaled(dbl_expr) |
| gsl_sf_airy_Ai_deriv_e | Y | gsl_sf_airy_Ai_deriv(dbl_expr) |
| gsl_sf_airy_Bi_deriv_e | Y | gsl_sf_airy_Bi_deriv(dbl_expr) |
| gsl_sf_airy_Ai_deriv_scaled_e | Y | gsl_sf_airy_Ai_deriv_scaled(dbl_expr) |
| gsl_sf_airy_Bi_deriv_scaled_e | Y | gsl_sf_airy_Bi_deriv_scaled(dbl_expr) |
| gsl_sf_airy_zero_Ai_e | Y | gsl_sf_airy_zero_Ai(uint_expr) |
| gsl_sf_airy_zero_Bi_e | Y | gsl_sf_airy_zero_Bi(uint_expr) |
| gsl_sf_airy_zero_Ai_deriv_e | Y | gsl_sf_airy_zero_Ai_deriv(uint_expr) |
| gsl_sf_airy_zero_Bi_deriv_e | Y | gsl_sf_airy_zero_Bi_deriv(uint_expr) |
| gsl_sf_bessel_J0_e | Y | gsl_sf_bessel_J0(dbl_expr) |
| gsl_sf_bessel_J1_e | Y | gsl_sf_bessel_J1(dbl_expr) |
| gsl_sf_bessel_Jn_e | Y | gsl_sf_bessel_Jn(int_expr,dbl_expr) |
| gsl_sf_bessel_Jn_array | Y | status=gsl_sf_bessel_Jn_array(int,int,double,&var_out) |
| gsl_sf_bessel_Y0_e | Y | gsl_sf_bessel_Y0(dbl_expr) |
| gsl_sf_bessel_Y1_e | Y | gsl_sf_bessel_Y1(dbl_expr) |
| gsl_sf_bessel_Yn_e | Y | gsl_sf_bessel_Yn(int_expr,dbl_expr) |
| gsl_sf_bessel_Yn_array | Y | gsl_sf_bessel_Yn_array |
| gsl_sf_bessel_I0_e | Y | gsl_sf_bessel_I0(dbl_expr) |
| gsl_sf_bessel_I1_e | Y | gsl_sf_bessel_I1(dbl_expr) |
| gsl_sf_bessel_In_e | Y | gsl_sf_bessel_In(int_expr,dbl_expr) |
| gsl_sf_bessel_In_array | Y | status=gsl_sf_bessel_In_array(int,int,double,&var_out) |
| gsl_sf_bessel_I0_scaled_e | Y | gsl_sf_bessel_I0_scaled(dbl_expr) |
| gsl_sf_bessel_I1_scaled_e | Y | gsl_sf_bessel_I1_scaled(dbl_expr) |
| gsl_sf_bessel_In_scaled_e | Y | gsl_sf_bessel_In_scaled(int_expr,dbl_expr) |
| gsl_sf_bessel_In_scaled_array | Y | staus=gsl_sf_bessel_In_scaled_array(int,int,double,&var_out) |
| gsl_sf_bessel_K0_e | Y | gsl_sf_bessel_K0(dbl_expr) |
| gsl_sf_bessel_K1_e | Y | gsl_sf_bessel_K1(dbl_expr) |
| gsl_sf_bessel_Kn_e | Y | gsl_sf_bessel_Kn(int_expr,dbl_expr) |
| gsl_sf_bessel_Kn_array | Y | status=gsl_sf_bessel_Kn_array(int,int,double,&var_out) |
| gsl_sf_bessel_K0_scaled_e | Y | gsl_sf_bessel_K0_scaled(dbl_expr) |
| gsl_sf_bessel_K1_scaled_e | Y | gsl_sf_bessel_K1_scaled(dbl_expr) |
| gsl_sf_bessel_Kn_scaled_e | Y | gsl_sf_bessel_Kn_scaled(int_expr,dbl_expr) |
| gsl_sf_bessel_Kn_scaled_array | Y | status=gsl_sf_bessel_Kn_scaled_array(int,int,double,&var_out) |
| gsl_sf_bessel_j0_e | Y | gsl_sf_bessel_J0(dbl_expr) |
| gsl_sf_bessel_j1_e | Y | gsl_sf_bessel_J1(dbl_expr) |
| gsl_sf_bessel_j2_e | Y | gsl_sf_bessel_j2(dbl_expr) |
| gsl_sf_bessel_jl_e | Y | gsl_sf_bessel_jl(int_expr,dbl_expr) |
| gsl_sf_bessel_jl_array | Y | status=gsl_sf_bessel_jl_array(int,double,&var_out) |
| gsl_sf_bessel_jl_steed_array | Y | gsl_sf_bessel_jl_steed_array |
| gsl_sf_bessel_y0_e | Y | gsl_sf_bessel_Y0(dbl_expr) |
| gsl_sf_bessel_y1_e | Y | gsl_sf_bessel_Y1(dbl_expr) |
| gsl_sf_bessel_y2_e | Y | gsl_sf_bessel_y2(dbl_expr) |
| gsl_sf_bessel_yl_e | Y | gsl_sf_bessel_yl(int_expr,dbl_expr) |
| gsl_sf_bessel_yl_array | Y | status=gsl_sf_bessel_yl_array(int,double,&var_out) |
| gsl_sf_bessel_i0_scaled_e | Y | gsl_sf_bessel_I0_scaled(dbl_expr) |
| gsl_sf_bessel_i1_scaled_e | Y | gsl_sf_bessel_I1_scaled(dbl_expr) |

| | | |
|---|---|---|
| gsl_sf_bessel_i2_scaled_e | Y | gsl_sf_bessel_i2_scaled(dbl_expr) |
| gsl_sf_bessel_il_scaled_e | Y | gsl_sf_bessel_il_scaled(int_expr,dbl_expr) |
| gsl_sf_bessel_il_scaled_array | Y | status=gsl_sf_bessel_il_scaled_array(int,double,&var_out) |
| gsl_sf_bessel_k0_scaled_e | Y | gsl_sf_bessel_K0_scaled(dbl_expr) |
| gsl_sf_bessel_k1_scaled_e | Y | gsl_sf_bessel_K1_scaled(dbl_expr) |
| gsl_sf_bessel_k2_scaled_e | Y | gsl_sf_bessel_k2_scaled(dbl_expr) |
| gsl_sf_bessel_kl_scaled_e | Y | gsl_sf_bessel_kl_scaled(int_expr,dbl_expr) |
| gsl_sf_bessel_kl_scaled_array | Y | status=gsl_sf_bessel_kl_scaled_array(int,double,&var_out) |
| gsl_sf_bessel_Jnu_e | Y | gsl_sf_bessel_Jnu(dbl_expr,dbl_expr) |
| gsl_sf_bessel_Ynu_e | Y | gsl_sf_bessel_Ynu(dbl_expr,dbl_expr) |
| gsl_sf_bessel_sequence_Jnu_e | N | gsl_sf_bessel_sequence_Jnu |
| gsl_sf_bessel_Inu_scaled_e | Y | gsl_sf_bessel_Inu_scaled(dbl_expr,dbl_expr) |
| gsl_sf_bessel_Inu_e | Y | gsl_sf_bessel_Inu(dbl_expr,dbl_expr) |
| gsl_sf_bessel_Knu_scaled_e | Y | gsl_sf_bessel_Knu_scaled(dbl_expr,dbl_expr) |
| gsl_sf_bessel_Knu_e | Y | gsl_sf_bessel_Knu(dbl_expr,dbl_expr) |
| gsl_sf_bessel_lnKnu_e | Y | gsl_sf_bessel_lnKnu(dbl_expr,dbl_expr) |
| gsl_sf_bessel_zero_J0_e | Y | gsl_sf_bessel_zero_J0(uint_expr) |
| gsl_sf_bessel_zero_J1_e | Y | gsl_sf_bessel_zero_J1(uint_expr) |
| gsl_sf_bessel_zero_Jnu_e | N | gsl_sf_bessel_zero_Jnu |
| gsl_sf_clausen_e | Y | gsl_sf_clausen(dbl_expr) |
| gsl_sf_hydrogenicR_1_e | N | gsl_sf_hydrogenicR_1 |
| gsl_sf_hydrogenicR_e | N | gsl_sf_hydrogenicR |
| gsl_sf_coulomb_wave_FG_e | N | gsl_sf_coulomb_wave_FG |
| gsl_sf_coulomb_wave_F_array | N | gsl_sf_coulomb_wave_F_array |
| gsl_sf_coulomb_wave_FG_array | N | gsl_sf_coulomb_wave_FG_array |
| gsl_sf_coulomb_wave_FGp_array | N | gsl_sf_coulomb_wave_FGp_array |
| gsl_sf_coulomb_wave_sphF_array | N | gsl_sf_coulomb_wave_sphF_array |
| gsl_sf_coulomb_CL_e | N | gsl_sf_coulomb_CL |
| gsl_sf_coulomb_CL_array | N | gsl_sf_coulomb_CL_array |
| gsl_sf_coupling_3j_e | N | gsl_sf_coupling_3j |
| gsl_sf_coupling_6j_e | N | gsl_sf_coupling_6j |
| gsl_sf_coupling_RacahW_e | N | gsl_sf_coupling_RacahW |
| gsl_sf_coupling_9j_e | N | gsl_sf_coupling_9j |
| gsl_sf_coupling_6j_INCORRECT_e | N | gsl_sf_coupling_6j_INCORRECT |
| gsl_sf_dawson_e | Y | gsl_sf_dawson(dbl_expr) |
| gsl_sf_debye_1_e | Y | gsl_sf_debye_1(dbl_expr) |
| gsl_sf_debye_2_e | Y | gsl_sf_debye_2(dbl_expr) |
| gsl_sf_debye_3_e | Y | gsl_sf_debye_3(dbl_expr) |
| gsl_sf_debye_4_e | Y | gsl_sf_debye_4(dbl_expr) |
| gsl_sf_debye_5_e | Y | gsl_sf_debye_5(dbl_expr) |
| gsl_sf_debye_6_e | Y | gsl_sf_debye_6(dbl_expr) |
| gsl_sf_dilog_e | N | gsl_sf_dilog |
| gsl_sf_complex_dilog_xy_e | N | gsl_sf_complex_dilog_xy_e |
| gsl_sf_complex_dilog_e | N | gsl_sf_complex_dilog |
| gsl_sf_complex_spence_xy_e | N | gsl_sf_complex_spence_xy_e |
| gsl_sf_multiply_e | N | gsl_sf_multiply |
| gsl_sf_multiply_err_e | N | gsl_sf_multiply_err |

| | | |
|---|---|---|
| gsl_sf_ellint_Kcomp_e | Y | gsl_sf_ellint_Kcomp(dbl_expr) |
| gsl_sf_ellint_Ecomp_e | Y | gsl_sf_ellint_Ecomp(dbl_expr) |
| gsl_sf_ellint_Pcomp_e | Y | gsl_sf_ellint_Pcomp(dbl_expr,dbl_expr) |
| gsl_sf_ellint_Dcomp_e | Y | gsl_sf_ellint_Dcomp(dbl_expr) |
| gsl_sf_ellint_F_e | Y | gsl_sf_ellint_F(dbl_expr,dbl_expr) |
| gsl_sf_ellint_E_e | Y | gsl_sf_ellint_E(dbl_expr,dbl_expr) |
| gsl_sf_ellint_P_e | Y | gsl_sf_ellint_P(dbl_expr,dbl_expr,dbl_expr) |
| gsl_sf_ellint_D_e | Y | gsl_sf_ellint_D(dbl_expr,dbl_expr,dbl_expr) |
| gsl_sf_ellint_RC_e | Y | gsl_sf_ellint_RC(dbl_expr,dbl_expr) |
| gsl_sf_ellint_RD_e | Y | gsl_sf_ellint_RD(dbl_expr,dbl_expr,dbl_expr) |
| gsl_sf_ellint_RF_e | Y | gsl_sf_ellint_RF(dbl_expr,dbl_expr,dbl_expr) |
| gsl_sf_ellint_RJ_e | Y | gsl_sf_ellint_RJ(dbl_expr,dbl_expr,dbl_expr,dbl_expr) |
| gsl_sf_elljac_e | N | gsl_sf_elljac |
| gsl_sf_erfc_e | Y | gsl_sf_erfc(dbl_expr) |
| gsl_sf_log_erfc_e | Y | gsl_sf_log_erfc(dbl_expr) |
| gsl_sf_erf_e | Y | gsl_sf_erf(dbl_expr) |
| gsl_sf_erf_Z_e | Y | gsl_sf_erf_Z(dbl_expr) |
| gsl_sf_erf_Q_e | Y | gsl_sf_erf_Q(dbl_expr) |
| gsl_sf_hazard_e | Y | gsl_sf_hazard(dbl_expr) |
| gsl_sf_exp_e | Y | gsl_sf_exp(dbl_expr) |
| gsl_sf_exp_e10_e | N | gsl_sf_exp_e10 |
| gsl_sf_exp_mult_e | Y | gsl_sf_exp_mult(dbl_expr,dbl_expr) |
| gsl_sf_exp_mult_e10_e | N | gsl_sf_exp_mult_e10 |
| gsl_sf_expm1_e | Y | gsl_sf_expm1(dbl_expr) |
| gsl_sf_exprel_e | Y | gsl_sf_exprel(dbl_expr) |
| gsl_sf_exprel_2_e | Y | gsl_sf_exprel_2(dbl_expr) |
| gsl_sf_exprel_n_e | Y | gsl_sf_exprel_n(int_expr,dbl_expr) |
| gsl_sf_exp_err_e | Y | gsl_sf_exp_err(dbl_expr,dbl_expr) |
| gsl_sf_exp_err_e10_e | N | gsl_sf_exp_err_e10 |
| gsl_sf_exp_mult_err_e | N | gsl_sf_exp_mult_err |
| gsl_sf_exp_mult_err_e10_e | N | gsl_sf_exp_mult_err_e10 |
| gsl_sf_expint_E1_e | Y | gsl_sf_expint_E1(dbl_expr) |
| gsl_sf_expint_E2_e | Y | gsl_sf_expint_E2(dbl_expr) |
| gsl_sf_expint_En_e | Y | gsl_sf_expint_En(int_expr,dbl_expr) |
| gsl_sf_expint_E1_scaled_e | Y | gsl_sf_expint_E1_scaled(dbl_expr) |
| gsl_sf_expint_E2_scaled_e | Y | gsl_sf_expint_E2_scaled(dbl_expr) |
| gsl_sf_expint_En_scaled_e | Y | gsl_sf_expint_En_scaled(int_expr,dbl_expr) |
| gsl_sf_expint_Ei_e | Y | gsl_sf_expint_Ei(dbl_expr) |
| gsl_sf_expint_Ei_scaled_e | Y | gsl_sf_expint_Ei_scaled(dbl_expr) |
| gsl_sf_Shi_e | Y | gsl_sf_Shi(dbl_expr) |
| gsl_sf_Chi_e | Y | gsl_sf_Chi(dbl_expr) |
| gsl_sf_expint_3_e | Y | gsl_sf_expint_3(dbl_expr) |
| gsl_sf_Si_e | Y | gsl_sf_Si(dbl_expr) |
| gsl_sf_Ci_e | Y | gsl_sf_Ci(dbl_expr) |
| gsl_sf_atanint_e | Y | gsl_sf_atanint(dbl_expr) |
| gsl_sf_fermi_dirac_m1_e | Y | gsl_sf_fermi_dirac_m1(dbl_expr) |
| gsl_sf_fermi_dirac_0_e | Y | gsl_sf_fermi_dirac_0(dbl_expr) |

| | | |
|---|---|---|
| gsl_sf_fermi_dirac_1_e | Y | gsl_sf_fermi_dirac_1(dbl_expr) |
| gsl_sf_fermi_dirac_2_e | Y | gsl_sf_fermi_dirac_2(dbl_expr) |
| gsl_sf_fermi_dirac_int_e | Y | gsl_sf_fermi_dirac_int(int_expr,dbl_expr) |
| gsl_sf_fermi_dirac_mhalf_e | Y | gsl_sf_fermi_dirac_mhalf(dbl_expr) |
| gsl_sf_fermi_dirac_half_e | Y | gsl_sf_fermi_dirac_half(dbl_expr) |
| gsl_sf_fermi_dirac_3half_e | Y | gsl_sf_fermi_dirac_3half(dbl_expr) |
| gsl_sf_fermi_dirac_inc_0_e | Y | gsl_sf_fermi_dirac_inc_0(dbl_expr,dbl_expr) |
| gsl_sf_lngamma_e | Y | gsl_sf_lngamma(dbl_expr) |
| gsl_sf_lngamma_sgn_e | N | gsl_sf_lngamma_sgn |
| gsl_sf_gamma_e | Y | gsl_sf_gamma(dbl_expr) |
| gsl_sf_gammastar_e | Y | gsl_sf_gammastar(dbl_expr) |
| gsl_sf_gammainv_e | Y | gsl_sf_gammainv(dbl_expr) |
| gsl_sf_lngamma_complex_e | N | gsl_sf_lngamma_complex |
| gsl_sf_taylorcoeff_e | Y | gsl_sf_taylorcoeff(int_expr,dbl_expr) |
| gsl_sf_fact_e | Y | gsl_sf_fact(uint_expr) |
| gsl_sf_doublefact_e | Y | gsl_sf_doublefact(uint_expr) |
| gsl_sf_lnfact_e | Y | gsl_sf_lnfact(uint_expr) |
| gsl_sf_lndoublefact_e | Y | gsl_sf_lndoublefact(uint_expr) |
| gsl_sf_lnchoose_e | N | gsl_sf_lnchoose |
| gsl_sf_choose_e | N | gsl_sf_choose |
| gsl_sf_lnpoch_e | Y | gsl_sf_lnpoch(dbl_expr,dbl_expr) |
| gsl_sf_lnpoch_sgn_e | N | gsl_sf_lnpoch_sgn |
| gsl_sf_poch_e | Y | gsl_sf_poch(dbl_expr,dbl_expr) |
| gsl_sf_pochrel_e | Y | gsl_sf_pochrel(dbl_expr,dbl_expr) |
| gsl_sf_gamma_inc_Q_e | Y | gsl_sf_gamma_inc_Q(dbl_expr,dbl_expr) |
| gsl_sf_gamma_inc_P_e | Y | gsl_sf_gamma_inc_P(dbl_expr,dbl_expr) |
| gsl_sf_gamma_inc_e | Y | gsl_sf_gamma_inc(dbl_expr,dbl_expr) |
| gsl_sf_lnbeta_e | Y | gsl_sf_lnbeta(dbl_expr,dbl_expr) |
| gsl_sf_lnbeta_sgn_e | N | gsl_sf_lnbeta_sgn |
| gsl_sf_beta_e | Y | gsl_sf_beta(dbl_expr,dbl_expr) |
| gsl_sf_beta_inc_e | N | gsl_sf_beta_inc |
| gsl_sf_gegenpoly_1_e | Y | gsl_sf_gegenpoly_1(dbl_expr,dbl_expr) |
| gsl_sf_gegenpoly_2_e | Y | gsl_sf_gegenpoly_2(dbl_expr,dbl_expr) |
| gsl_sf_gegenpoly_3_e | Y | gsl_sf_gegenpoly_3(dbl_expr,dbl_expr) |
| gsl_sf_gegenpoly_n_e | N | gsl_sf_gegenpoly_n |
| gsl_sf_gegenpoly_array | Y | gsl_sf_gegenpoly_array |
| gsl_sf_hyperg_0F1_e | Y | gsl_sf_hyperg_0F1(dbl_expr,dbl_expr) |
| gsl_sf_hyperg_1F1_int_e | Y | gsl_sf_hyperg_1F1_int(int_expr,int_expr,dbl_expr) |
| gsl_sf_hyperg_1F1_e | Y | gsl_sf_hyperg_1F1(dbl_expr,dbl_expr,dbl_expr) |
| gsl_sf_hyperg_U_int_e | Y | gsl_sf_hyperg_U_int(int_expr,int_expr,dbl_expr) |
| gsl_sf_hyperg_U_int_e10_e | N | gsl_sf_hyperg_U_int_e10 |
| gsl_sf_hyperg_U_e | Y | gsl_sf_hyperg_U(dbl_expr,dbl_expr,dbl_expr) |
| gsl_sf_hyperg_U_e10_e | N | gsl_sf_hyperg_U_e10 |
| gsl_sf_hyperg_2F1_e | Y | gsl_sf_hyperg_2F1(dbl_expr,dbl_expr,dbl_expr,dbl_expr) |
| gsl_sf_hyperg_2F1_conj_e | Y | gsl_sf_hyperg_2F1_conj(dbl_expr,dbl_expr,dbl_expr,dbl_expr) |
| gsl_sf_hyperg_2F1_renorm_e | Y | gsl_sf_hyperg_2F1_renorm(dbl_expr,dbl_expr,dbl_expr,dbl_expr) |
| gsl_sf_hyperg_2F1_conj_renorm_e | Y | gsl_sf_hyperg_2F1_conj_renorm(dbl_expr,dbl_expr,dbl_expr,dbl_expr) |

| | | |
|---|---|---|
| gsl_sf_hyperg_2F0_e | Y | gsl_sf_hyperg_2F0(dbl_expr,dbl_expr,dbl_expr) |
| gsl_sf_laguerre_1_e | Y | gsl_sf_laguerre_1(dbl_expr,dbl_expr) |
| gsl_sf_laguerre_2_e | Y | gsl_sf_laguerre_2(dbl_expr,dbl_expr) |
| gsl_sf_laguerre_3_e | Y | gsl_sf_laguerre_3(dbl_expr,dbl_expr) |
| gsl_sf_laguerre_n_e | Y | gsl_sf_laguerre_n(int_expr,dbl_expr,dbl_expr) |
| gsl_sf_lambert_W0_e | Y | gsl_sf_lambert_W0(dbl_expr) |
| gsl_sf_lambert_Wm1_e | Y | gsl_sf_lambert_Wm1(dbl_expr) |
| gsl_sf_legendre_Pl_e | Y | gsl_sf_legendre_Pl(int_expr,dbl_expr) |
| gsl_sf_legendre_Pl_array | Y | status=gsl_sf_legendre_Pl_array(int,double,&var_out) |
| gsl_sf_legendre_Pl_deriv_array | N | gsl_sf_legendre_Pl_deriv_array |
| gsl_sf_legendre_P1_e | Y | gsl_sf_legendre_P1(dbl_expr) |
| gsl_sf_legendre_P2_e | Y | gsl_sf_legendre_P2(dbl_expr) |
| gsl_sf_legendre_P3_e | Y | gsl_sf_legendre_P3(dbl_expr) |
| gsl_sf_legendre_Q0_e | Y | gsl_sf_legendre_Q0(dbl_expr) |
| gsl_sf_legendre_Q1_e | Y | gsl_sf_legendre_Q1(dbl_expr) |
| gsl_sf_legendre_Ql_e | Y | gsl_sf_legendre_Ql(int_expr,dbl_expr) |
| gsl_sf_legendre_Plm_e | Y | gsl_sf_legendre_Plm(int_expr,int_expr,dbl_expr) |
| gsl_sf_legendre_Plm_array | Y | status=gsl_sf_legendre_Plm_array(int,int,double,&var_out) |
| gsl_sf_legendre_Plm_deriv_array | N | gsl_sf_legendre_Plm_deriv_array |
| gsl_sf_legendre_sphPlm_e | Y | gsl_sf_legendre_sphPlm(int_expr,int_expr,dbl_expr) |
| gsl_sf_legendre_sphPlm_array | Y | status=gsl_sf_legendre_sphPlm_array(int,int,double,&var_out) |
| gsl_sf_legendre_sphPlm_deriv_array | N | gsl_sf_legendre_sphPlm_deriv_array |
| gsl_sf_legendre_array_size | N | gsl_sf_legendre_array_size |
| gsl_sf_conicalP_half_e | Y | gsl_sf_conicalP_half(dbl_expr,dbl_expr) |
| gsl_sf_conicalP_mhalf_e | Y | gsl_sf_conicalP_mhalf(dbl_expr,dbl_expr) |
| gsl_sf_conicalP_0_e | Y | gsl_sf_conicalP_0(dbl_expr,dbl_expr) |
| gsl_sf_conicalP_1_e | Y | gsl_sf_conicalP_1(dbl_expr,dbl_expr) |
| gsl_sf_conicalP_sph_reg_e | Y | gsl_sf_conicalP_sph_reg(int_expr,dbl_expr,dbl_expr) |
| gsl_sf_conicalP_cyl_reg_e | Y | gsl_sf_conicalP_cyl_reg(int_expr,dbl_expr,dbl_expr) |
| gsl_sf_legendre_H3d_0_e | Y | gsl_sf_legendre_H3d_0(dbl_expr,dbl_expr) |
| gsl_sf_legendre_H3d_1_e | Y | gsl_sf_legendre_H3d_1(dbl_expr,dbl_expr) |
| gsl_sf_legendre_H3d_e | Y | gsl_sf_legendre_H3d(int_expr,dbl_expr,dbl_expr) |
| gsl_sf_legendre_H3d_array | N | gsl_sf_legendre_H3d_array |
| gsl_sf_legendre_array_size | N | gsl_sf_legendre_array_size |
| gsl_sf_log_e | Y | gsl_sf_log(dbl_expr) |
| gsl_sf_log_abs_e | Y | gsl_sf_log_abs(dbl_expr) |
| gsl_sf_complex_log_e | N | gsl_sf_complex_log |
| gsl_sf_log_1plusx_e | Y | gsl_sf_log_1plusx(dbl_expr) |
| gsl_sf_log_1plusx_mx_e | Y | gsl_sf_log_1plusx_mx(dbl_expr) |
| gsl_sf_mathieu_a_array | N | gsl_sf_mathieu_a_array |
| gsl_sf_mathieu_b_array | N | gsl_sf_mathieu_b_array |
| gsl_sf_mathieu_a | N | gsl_sf_mathieu_a |
| gsl_sf_mathieu_b | N | gsl_sf_mathieu_b |
| gsl_sf_mathieu_a_coeff | N | gsl_sf_mathieu_a_coeff |
| gsl_sf_mathieu_b_coeff | N | gsl_sf_mathieu_b_coeff |
| gsl_sf_mathieu_ce | N | gsl_sf_mathieu_ce |
| gsl_sf_mathieu_se | N | gsl_sf_mathieu_se |

| | | |
|---|---|---|
| gsl_sf_mathieu_ce_array | N | gsl_sf_mathieu_ce_array |
| gsl_sf_mathieu_se_array | N | gsl_sf_mathieu_se_array |
| gsl_sf_mathieu_Mc | N | gsl_sf_mathieu_Mc |
| gsl_sf_mathieu_Ms | N | gsl_sf_mathieu_Ms |
| gsl_sf_mathieu_Mc_array | N | gsl_sf_mathieu_Mc_array |
| gsl_sf_mathieu_Ms_array | N | gsl_sf_mathieu_Ms_array |
| gsl_sf_pow_int_e | N | gsl_sf_pow_int |
| gsl_sf_psi_int_e | Y | gsl_sf_psi_int(int_expr) |
| gsl_sf_psi_e | Y | gsl_sf_psi(dbl_expr) |
| gsl_sf_psi_1piy_e | Y | gsl_sf_psi_1piy(dbl_expr) |
| gsl_sf_complex_psi_e | N | gsl_sf_complex_psi |
| gsl_sf_psi_1_int_e | Y | gsl_sf_psi_1_int(int_expr) |
| gsl_sf_psi_1_e | Y | gsl_sf_psi_1(dbl_expr) |
| gsl_sf_psi_n_e | Y | gsl_sf_psi_n(int_expr,dbl_expr) |
| gsl_sf_synchrotron_1_e | Y | gsl_sf_synchrotron_1(dbl_expr) |
| gsl_sf_synchrotron_2_e | Y | gsl_sf_synchrotron_2(dbl_expr) |
| gsl_sf_transport_2_e | Y | gsl_sf_transport_2(dbl_expr) |
| gsl_sf_transport_3_e | Y | gsl_sf_transport_3(dbl_expr) |
| gsl_sf_transport_4_e | Y | gsl_sf_transport_4(dbl_expr) |
| gsl_sf_transport_5_e | Y | gsl_sf_transport_5(dbl_expr) |
| gsl_sf_sin_e | N | gsl_sf_sin |
| gsl_sf_cos_e | N | gsl_sf_cos |
| gsl_sf_hypot_e | N | gsl_sf_hypot |
| gsl_sf_complex_sin_e | N | gsl_sf_complex_sin |
| gsl_sf_complex_cos_e | N | gsl_sf_complex_cos |
| gsl_sf_complex_logsin_e | N | gsl_sf_complex_logsin |
| gsl_sf_sinc_e | N | gsl_sf_sinc |
| gsl_sf_lnsinh_e | N | gsl_sf_lnsinh |
| gsl_sf_lncosh_e | N | gsl_sf_lncosh |
| gsl_sf_polar_to_rect | N | gsl_sf_polar_to_rect |
| gsl_sf_rect_to_polar | N | gsl_sf_rect_to_polar |
| gsl_sf_sin_err_e | N | gsl_sf_sin_err |
| gsl_sf_cos_err_e | N | gsl_sf_cos_err |
| gsl_sf_angle_restrict_symm_e | N | gsl_sf_angle_restrict_symm |
| gsl_sf_angle_restrict_pos_e | N | gsl_sf_angle_restrict_pos |
| gsl_sf_angle_restrict_symm_err_e | N | gsl_sf_angle_restrict_symm_err |
| gsl_sf_angle_restrict_pos_err_e | N | gsl_sf_angle_restrict_pos_err |
| gsl_sf_zeta_int_e | Y | gsl_sf_zeta_int(int_expr) |
| gsl_sf_zeta_e | Y | gsl_sf_zeta(dbl_expr) |
| gsl_sf_zetam1_e | Y | gsl_sf_zetam1(dbl_expr) |
| gsl_sf_zetam1_int_e | Y | gsl_sf_zetam1_int(int_expr) |
| gsl_sf_hzeta_e | Y | gsl_sf_hzeta(dbl_expr,dbl_expr) |
| gsl_sf_eta_int_e | Y | gsl_sf_eta_int(int_expr) |
| gsl_sf_eta_e | Y | gsl_sf_eta(dbl_expr) |

### 4.1.23 GSL interpolation

As of version 3.9.9 (released July, 2009), NCO has wrappers to the GSL interpolation functions.

Given a set of data points (x1,y1)...(xn, yn) the GSL functions computes a continuous interpolating function Y(x) such that Y(xi) = yi. The interpolation is piecewise smooth, and its behavior at the end-points is determined by the type of interpolation used. For more information consult the GSL manual.

Interpolation with `ncap2` is a two stage process. In the first stage, a RAM variable is created from the chosen interpolating function and the data set. This RAM variable holds in memory a GSL interpolation object. In the second stage, points along the interpolating function are calculated. If you have a very large data set or are interpolating many sets then consider deleting the RAM variable when it is redundant. Use the command `ram_delete(var_nm)`.

A simple example

```
x_in[$lon]={1.0,2.0,3.0,4.0};
y_in[$lon]={1.1,1.2,1.5,1.8};

// Ram variable is declared and defined here
gsl_interp_cspline(&ram_sp,x_in,y_in);

x_out[$lon_grd]={1.1,2.0,3.0,3.1,3.99};

y_out=gsl_spline_eval(ram_sp,x_out);
y2=gsl_spline_eval(ram_sp,1.3);
y3=gsl_spline_eval(ram_sp,0.0);
ram_delete(ram_sp);

print(y_out); // 1.10472, 1.2, 1.4, 1.42658, 1.69680002
print(y2);    // 1.12454
print(y3);    // '_'
```

Note in the above example y3 is set to 'missing value' because 0.0 isn't within the input X range.

**GSL Interpolation Types**

All the interpolation functions have been implemented. These are:
gsl_interp_linear()
gsl_interp_polynomial()
gsl_interp_cspline()
gsl_interp_cspline_periodic()
gsl_interp_akima()
gsl_interp_akima_periodic()

**Evaluation of Interpolating Types**

**Implemented**
gsl_spline_eval()
**Unimplemented**
gsl_spline_deriv()
gsl_spline_deriv2()
gsl_spline_integ()

### 4.1.24 GSL least-squares fitting

Least Squares fitting is a method of calculating a straight line through a set of experimental data points in the XY plane. The data maybe weighted or unweighted. For more information please refer to the GSL manual.

These GSL functions fall into three categories:
**A**) Fitting data to Y=c0+c1*X
**B**) Fitting data (through the origin) Y=c1*X
**C**) Multi-parameter fitting (not yet implemented)

**Section A**

`status=`**gsl_fit_linear**
`(data_x,stride_x,data_y,stride_y,n,&co,&c1,&cov00,&cov01,&cov11,&sumsq)`

**Input variables**: data_x, stride_x, data_y, stride_y, n
From the above variables an X and Y vector both of length 'n' are derived. If data_x or data_y is less than type double then it is converted to type `double`. It is up to you to do bounds checking on the input data. For example if stride_x=3 and n=8 then the size of data_x must be at least 24

**Output variables**: c0, c1, cov00, cov01, cov11,sumsq
The '&' prefix indicates that these are call-by-reference variables. If any of the output variables don't exist prior to the call then they are created on the fly as scalar variables of type `double`. If they already exist then their existing value is overwritten. If the function call is successful then `status=0`.

`status=` **gsl_fit_wlinear**`(data_x,stride_x,data_w,stride_w,data_y,stride_y,n,&co,&c1,&cov00,&cov01,&cov11,&chisq)`

Similar to the above call except it creates an additional weighting vector from the variables data_w, stride_w, n

`data_y_out=`**gsl_fit_linear_est**`(data_x,c0,c1,cov00,cov01,cov11)`

This function calculates y values along the line Y=c0+c1*X

**Section B**

`status=`**gsl_fit_mul**`(data_x,stride_x,data_y,stride_y,n,&c1,&cov11,&sumsq)`

**Input variables**: data_x, stride_x, data_y, stride_y, n
From the above variables an X and Y vector both of length 'n' are derived. If data_x or data_y is less than type `double` then it is converted to type `double`.

**Output variables**: c1,cov11,sumsq

`status=` **gsl_fit_wmul**`(data_x,stride_x,data_w,stride_w,data_y,stride_y,n,&c1,&cov11,&sumsq)`

Similar to the above call except it creates an additional weighting vector from the variables data_w, stride_w, n

`data_y_out=`**gsl_fit_mul_est**`(data_x,c0,c1,cov11)`

This function calculates y values along the line Y=c1*X

The below example shows **gsl_fit_linear()** in action

```
defdim("d1",10);
xin[d1]={1,2,3,4,5,6,7,8,9,10.0};
yin[d1]={3.1,6.2,9.1,12.2,15.1,18.2,21.3,24.0,27.0,30.0};
gsl_fit_linear(xin,1,yin,1,$d1.size,&c0,&c1,&cov00,&cov01,&cov11,&sumsq);
print(c0);  // 0.2
print(c1);  // 2.98545454545


defdim("e1",4);
xout[e1]={1.0,3.0,4.0,11};
yout[e1]=0.0;

yout=gsl_fit_linear_est(xout, c0,c1, cov00,cov01, cov11, sumsq);

print(yout);  // 3.18545454545 ,9.15636363636, ,12.1418181818 ,33.04
```

### 4.1.25 GSL statistics

Wrappers for most of the GSL Statistical functions have been implemented. The GSL function names include a type specifier (except for type double functions). To obtain the equivalent NCO name simply remove the type specifier; then depending on the data type the appropriate GSL function is called. The weighed statistical functions e.g., `gsl_stats_wvariance()` are only defined in GSL for floating-point types; so your data must of type `float` or `double` otherwise ncap2 will emit an error message. To view the implemented functions use the shell command `ncap2 -f|grep _stats`

GSL Functions

```
short gsl_stats_max (short data[], size_t stride, size_t n);
double gsl_stats_int_mean (int data[], size_t stride, size_t n);
double gsl_stats_short_sd_with_fixed_mean (short data[], size_t stride, size_t n, doub
double gsl_stats_wmean (double w[], size_t wstride, double data[], size_t stride, size
double gsl_stats_quantile_from_sorted_data (double sorted_data[], size_t stride, size_
```

Equivalent ncap2 wrapper functions

```
short gsl_stats_max (var_data, data_stride, n);
double gsl_stats_mean (var_data, data_stride, n);
double gsl_stats_sd_with_fixed_mean (var_data, data_stride, n, var_mean);
double gsl_stats_wmean (var_weight, weight_stride, var_data, data_stride, n, var_mean)
double gsl_stats_quantile_from_sorted_data (var_sorted_data, data_stride, n, var_f) ;
```

GSL has no notion of missing values or dimensionality beyond one. If your data has missing values which you want ignored in the calculations then use the ncap2 built in aggregate functions( Section 4.1.12 [Methods and functions], page 158, ). The GSL functions operate on a vector of values created from the var_data/stride/n arguments. The ncap wrappers check that there is no bounding error with regard to the size of the data and the final value in the vector.

Some examples

```
a1[time]={1,2,3,4,5,6,7,8,9,10};

a1_avg=gsl_stats_mean(a1,1,10);
print(a1_avg); // 5.5

a1_var=gsl_stats_variance(a1,4,3);
print(a1_var); // 16.0

// bounding error, vector attempts to access element a1(10)
a1_sd=gsl_stats_sd(a1,5,3);
```

For functions with the signature **func_nm(var_data,data_stride,n)**, one may omit the second or third arguments. The default value for *stride* is 1. The default value for *n* is 1+(data.size()-1)/stride.

```
// Following statements are equvalent
n2=gsl_stats_max(a1,1,10)
n2=gsl_stats_max(a1,1);
n2=gsl_stats_max(a1);

// Following statements are equvalent
n3=gsl_stats_median_from_sorted_data(a1,2,5);
n3=gsl_stats_median_from_sorted_data(a1,2);

// Following statements are NOT equvalent
n4=gsl_stats_kurtosis(a1,3,2);
```

```
n4=gsl_stats_kurtosis(a1,3); //default n=4
```

The following example illustrates some of the weighted functions. The data are randomly generated. In this case the value of the weight for each datum is either 0.0 or 1.0

```
defdim("r1",2000);
data[r1]=1.0;

// Fill with random numbers [0.0,10.0)
data=10.0*gsl_rng_uniform(data);

// Create a weighting variable
weight=(data>4.0);

wmean=gsl_stats_wmean(weight,1,data,1,$r1.size);
print(wmean);

wsd=gsl_stats_wsd(weight,1,data,1,$r1.size);
print(wsd);

// number of values in data that are greater than 4
weight_size=weight.total();
print(weight_size);

// print min/max of data
dmin=data.gsl_stats_min();
dmax=data.gsl_stats_max();
print(dmin);print(dmax);
```

### 4.1.26 GSL random number generation

The GSL library has a large number of random number generators. In addition there are a large set of functions for turning uniform random numbers into discrete or continuous probabilty distributions. The random number generator algorithms vary in terms of quality numbers output, speed of execution and maximum number output. For more information see the GSL documentation. The algorithm and seed are set via environment variables, these are picked up by the `ncap2` code.

**Setup**

The number algorithm is set by the environment variable `GSL_RNG_TYPE`. If this variable isn't set then the default rng algorithm is gsl_rng_19937. The seed is set with the environment variable `GSL_RNG_SEED`. The following wrapper functions in ncap2 provide information about the chosen algorithm.

`gsl_rng_min()`
: the minimum value returned by the rng algorithm.

`gsl_rng_max()`
: the maximum value returned by the rng algorithm.

### Uniformly Distributed Random Numbers

`gsl_rng_get(var_in)`
: This function returns var_in with integers from the chosen rng algorithm. The min and max values depend uoon the chosen rng algorthm.

`gsl_rng_uniform_int(var_in)`
: This function returns var_in with random integers from 0 to n-1. The value n must be less than or equal to the maximum value of the chosen rng algorithm.

`gsl_rng_uniform(var_in)`
: This function returns var_in with double-precision numbers in the range [0.0,1). The range includes 0.0 and excludes 1.0.

`gsl_rng_uniform_pos(var_in)`
: This function returns var_in with double-precision numbers in the range (0.0,1), excluding both 0.0 and 1.0.

Below are examples of `gsl_rng_get()` and `gsl_rng_uniform_int()` in action.

```
export GSL_RNG_TYPE=ranlux
export GSL_RNG_SEED=10
ncap2 -v -O -s 'a1[time]=0;a2=gsl_rng_get(a1);' in.nc foo.nc
// 10 random numbers from the range 0 - 16777215
// a2=9056646, 12776696, 1011656, 13354708, 5139066, 1388751, 11163902, 7730127, 15531

ncap2 -v -O -s 'a1[time]=21;a2=gsl_rng_uniform_int(a1).sort();' in.nc foo.nc
// 10 random numbers from the range 0 - 20
a2 = 1, 1, 6, 9, 11, 13, 13, 15, 16, 19 ;
```

The following example produces an `ncap2` runtime error. This is because the chose rng algorithm has a maximum value greater than `NC_MAX_INT=2147483647` ; the wrapper functions to `gsl_rng_get()` and `gsl_rng_uniform_int()` return variable of type `NC_INT`. Please be aware of this when using random number distribution functions functions from the GSL library which return `unsigned int`. Examples of these are `gsl_ran_geometric()` and `gsl_ran_pascal()`.

```
export GSL_RNG_TYPE=mt19937
ncap2 -v -O -s 'a1[time]=0;a2=gsl_rng_get(a1);' in.nc foo.nc
```

To find the maximum value of the chosen rng algorithm use the following code snippet.

```
ncap2 -v -O -s 'rng_max=gsl_rng_max();print(rng_max)' in.nc foo.nc
```

### Random Number Distributions

The GSL library has a rich set of random number disribution functions. The library also provides cumulative distribution functions and inverse cumulative distribution functions sometimes referred to a quantile functions. To see whats available on your build use the shell command `ncap2 -f|grep -e _ran -e _cdf`.

The following examples all return variables of type `NC_INT`

```
defdim("out",15);
a1[$out]=0.5;
a2=gsl_ran_binomial(a1,30).sort();
//a2 = 10, 11, 12, 12, 13, 14, 14, 15, 15, 16, 16, 16, 16, 17, 22 ;
a3=gsl_ran_geometric(a2).sort();
//a2 = 1, 1, 1, 1, 1, 1, 1, 1, 2, 2, 2, 2, 3, 4, 5 ;
a4=gsl_ran_pascal(a2,50);
//a5 = 37, 40, 40, 42, 43, 45, 46, 49, 52, 58, 60, 62, 62, 65, 67 ;
```

The following all return variables of type `NC_DOUBLE`;

```
defdim("b1",1000);
b1[$b1]=0.8;
b2=gsl_ran_exponential(b1);
b2_avg=b2.avg();
print(b2_avg);
// b2_avg = 0.756047976787

b3=gsl_ran_gaussian(b1);
b3_avg=b3.avg();
b3_rms=b3.rms();
print(b3_avg);
// b3_avg = -0.00903446534258;
print(b3_rms);
// b3_rms = 0.81162979889;

b4[$b1]=10.0;
b5[$b1]=20.0;
b6=gsl_ran_flat(b4,b5);
b6_avg=b6.avg();
print(b6_avg);
// b6_avg=15.0588129413
```

### 4.1.27 Examples ncap2

See the `ncap.in` and `ncap2.in` scripts released with NCO for more complete demonstrations of `ncap2` functionality (script available on-line at `http://nco.sf.net/ncap2.in`).

Define new attribute *new* for existing variable *one* as twice the existing attribute *double_att* of variable *att_var*:

```
ncap2 -s 'one@new=2*att_var@double_att' in.nc out.nc
```

Average variables of mixed types (result is of type `double`):

```
ncap2 -s 'average=(var_float+var_double+var_int)/3' in.nc out.nc
```

Multiple commands may be given to `ncap2` in three ways. First, the commands may be placed in a script which is executed, e.g., `tst.nco`. Second, the commands may be individually specified with multiple '`-s`' arguments to the same `ncap2` invocation. Third, the commands may be chained into a single '`-s`' argument to `ncap2`. Assuming the file tst.nco contains the commands a=3;b=4;c=sqrt(a^2+b^2);, then the following ncap2 invocations produce identical results:

```
ncap2 -v -S tst.nco in.nc out.nc
ncap2 -v -s 'a=3' -s 'b=4' -s 'c=sqrt(a^2+b^2)' in.nc out.nc
ncap2 -v -s 'a=3;b=4;c=sqrt(a^2+b^2)' in.nc out.nc
```

The second and third examples show that ncap2 does not require that a trailing semi-colon ';' be placed at the end of a '-s' argument, although a trailing semi-colon ';' is always allowed. However, semi-colons are required to separate individual assignment statements chained together as a single '-s' argument.

ncap2 may be used to "grow" dimensions, i.e., to increase dimension sizes without altering existing data. Say in.nc has ORO(lat,lon) and the user wishes a new file with new_ORO(new_lat,new_lon) that contains zeros in the undefined portions of the new grid.

```
defdim("new_lat",$lat.size+1); // Define new dimension sizes
defdim("new_lon",$lon.size+1);
new_ORO[$new_lat,$new_lon]=0.0f; // Initialize to zero
new_ORO(0:$lat.size-1,0:$lon.size-1)=ORO; // Fill valid data
```

The commands to define new coordinate variables new_lat and new_lon in the output file follow a similar pattern. One would might store these commands in a script grow.nco and then execute the script with

```
ncap2 -v -S grow.nco in.nc out.nc
```

Imagine you wish to create a binary flag based on the value of an array. The flag should have value 1.0 where the array exceeds 1.0, and value 0.0 elsewhere. This example creates the binary flag ORO_flg in out.nc from the continuous array named ORO in in.nc.

```
ncap2 -s 'ORO_flg=(ORO > 1.0)' in.nc out.nc
```

Suppose your task is to change all values of ORO which equal 2.0 to the new value 3.0:

```
ncap2 -s 'ORO_msk=(ORO==2.0);ORO=ORO_msk*3.0+!ORO_msk*ORO' in.nc out.nc
```

This creates and uses ORO_msk to mask the subsequent arithmetic operation. Values of ORO are only changed where ORO_msk is true, i.e., where ORO equals 2.0
Using the where statement the above code simplifies to :

```
ncap2 -s 'where(ORO==2.0) ORO=3.0;' in.nc foo.nc
```

This example uses ncap2 to compute the covariance of two variables. Let the variables *u* and *v* be the horizontal wind components. The *covariance* of *u* and *v* is defined as the time mean product of the deviations of *u* and *v* from their respective time means. Symbolically, the covariance $[u'v'] = [uv] - [u][v]$ where $[x]$ denotes the time-average of $x$, $[x] \equiv \frac{1}{\tau}\int_{t=0}^{t=\tau} x(t)\,dt$ and $x'$ denotes the deviation from the time-mean. The covariance tells us how much of the correlation of two signals arises from the signal fluctuations versus the mean signals. Sometimes this is called the *eddy covariance*. We will store the covariance in the variable uprmvprm.

```
ncwa -O -a time -v u,v in.nc foo.nc # Compute time mean of u,v
ncrename -O -v u,uavg -v v,vavg foo.nc # Rename to avoid conflict
```

```
ncks -A -v uavg,vavg foo.nc in.nc # Place time means with originals
ncap2 -O -s 'uprmvprm=u*v-uavg*vavg' in.nc in.nc # Covariance
ncra -O -v uprmvprm in.nc foo.nc # Time-mean covariance
```

The mathematically inclined will note that the same covariance would be obtained by replacing the step involving `ncap2` with

```
ncap2 -O -s 'uprmvprm=(u-uavg)*(v-vavg)' foo.nc foo.nc # Covariance
```

As of NCO version 3.1.8 (December, 2006), `ncap2` can compute averages, and thus covariances, by itself:

```
ncap2 -s 'uavg=u.avg($time);vavg=v.avg($time);uprmvprm=u*v-uavg*vavg' \
      -s 'uprmvrpmavg=uprmvprm.avg($time)' in.nc foo.nc
```

We have not seen a simpler method to script and execute powerful arithmetic than `ncap2`.

`ncap2` utilizes many meta-characters (e.g., '`$`', '`?`', '`;`', '`()`', '`[]`') that can confuse the command-line shell if not quoted properly. The issues are the same as those which arise in utilizing extended regular expressions to subset variables (see Section 3.11 [Subsetting Files], page 46). The example above will fail with no quotes and with double quotes. This is because shell globbing tries to *interpolate* the value of `$time` from the shell environment unless it is quoted:

```
ncap2 -s 'uavg=u.avg($time)'  in.nc foo.nc # Correct (recommended)
ncap2 -s  uavg=u.avg('$time') in.nc foo.nc # Correct (and dangerous)
ncap2 -s  uavg=u.avg($time)   in.nc foo.nc # Wrong ($time = '')
ncap2 -s "uavg=u.avg($time)"  in.nc foo.nc # Wrong ($time = '')
```

Without the single quotes, the shell replaces `$time` with an empty string. The command `ncap2` receives from the shell is `uavg=u.avg()`. This causes `ncap2` to average over all dimensions rather than just the *time* dimension, and unintended consequence.

We recommend using single quotes to protect `ncap2` command-line scripts from the shell, even when such protection is not strictly necessary. Expert users may violate this rule to exploit the ability to use shell variables in `ncap2` command-line scripts (see Chapter 9 [CCSM Example], page 323). In such cases it may be necessary to use the shell backslash character '`\`' to protect the `ncap2` meta-character.

A dimension of size one is said to be *degenerate*. Whether a degenerate record dimension is desirable or not depends on the application. Often a degenerate *time* dimension is useful, e.g., for concatentating, but it may cause problems with arithmetic. Such is the case in the above example, where the first step employs `ncwa` rather than `ncra` for the time-averaging. Of course the numerical results are the same with both operators. The difference is that, unless '`-b`' is specified, `ncwa` writes no *time* dimension to the output file, while `ncra` defaults to keeping *time* as a degenerate (size 1) dimension. Appending `u` and `v` to the output file would cause `ncks` to try to expand the degenerate time axis of `uavg` and `vavg` to the size of the non-degenerate *time* dimension in the input file. Thus the append (`ncks -A`) command would be undefined (and should fail) in this case. Equally important is the '`-C`' argument (see Section 3.12 [Subsetting Coordinate Variables], page 51) to `ncwa` to prevent any scalar *time* variable from being written to the output file. Knowing when to use `ncwa -a time` rather than the default `ncra` for time-averaging takes, well, time.

### 4.1.28 Intrinsic mathematical methods

`ncap2` supports the standard mathematical functions supplied with most operating systems. Standard calculator notation is used for addition `+`, subtraction `-`, multiplication `*`, division `/`, exponentiation `^`, and modulus `%`. The available elementary mathematical functions are:

`abs(x)` *Absolute value* Absolute value of $x$, $|x|$. Example: $\text{abs}(-1) = 1$

`acos(x)` *Arc-cosine* Arc-cosine of x where x is specified in radians. Example: acos(1.0) = 0.0

`acosh(x)` *Hyperbolic arc-cosine* Hyperbolic arc-cosine of x where x is specified in radians. Example: acosh(1.0) = 0.0

`asin(x)` *Arc-sine* Arc-sine of x where x is specified in radians. Example: asin(1.0) = 1.57079632679489661922

`asinh(x)` *Hyperbolic arc-sine* Hyperbolic arc-sine of x where x is specified in radians. Example: asinh(1.0) = 0.88137358702

`atan(x)` *Arc-tangent* Arc-tangent of x where x is specified in radians between $-\pi/2$ and $\pi/2$. Example: atan(1.0) = 0.78539816339744830961

`atan2(y,x)`
*Arc-tangent2* Arc-tangent of y/x

`atanh(x)` *Hyperbolic arc-tangent* Hyperbolic arc-tangent of x where x is specified in radians between $-\pi/2$ and $\pi/2$. Example: atanh(3.14159265358979323844) = 1.0

`ceil(x)` *Ceil* Ceiling of x. Smallest integral value not less than argument. Example: ceil(0.1) = 1.0

`cos(x)` *Cosine* Cosine of x where x is specified in radians. Example: cos(0.0) = 1.0

`cosh(x)` *Hyperbolic cosine* Hyperbolic cosine of x where x is specified in radians. Example: cosh(0.0) = 1.0

`erf(x)` *Error function* Error function of x where x is specified between $-1$ and 1. Example: erf(1.0) = 0.842701

`erfc(x)` *Complementary error function* Complementary error function of x where x is specified between $-1$ and 1. Example: erfc(1.0) = 0.15729920705

`exp(x)` *Exponential* Exponential of x, $e^x$. Example: exp(1.0) = 2.71828182845904523536

`floor(x)` *Floor* Floor of x. Largest integral value not greater than argument. Example: floor(1.9) = 1

`gamma(x)` *Gamma function* Gamma function of x, $\Gamma(x)$. The well-known and loved continuous factorial function. Example: gamma(0.5) = $\sqrt{\pi}$

`gamma_inc_P(x)`
: *Incomplete Gamma function* Incomplete Gamma function of parameter a and variable x, $P(a,x)$. One of the four incomplete gamma functions. Example: $\mathrm{gamma\_inc\_P}(1,1) = 1 - \mathrm{e}^{-1}$

`ln(x)`
: *Natural Logarithm* Natural logarithm of x, $\ln(x)$. Example: $\ln(2.71828182845904523536) = 1.0$

`log(x)`
: *Natural Logarithm* Exact synonym for `ln(x)`.

`log10(x)`
: *Base 10 Logarithm* Base 10 logarithm of x, $\log_{10}(x)$. Example: $\log(10.0) = 1.0$

`nearbyint(x)`
: *Round inexactly* Nearest integer to x is returned in floating-point format. No exceptions are raised for *inexact conversions*. Example: $\mathrm{nearbyint}(0.1) = 0.0$

`pow(x,y)`
: *Power* Value of x is raised to the power of y. Exceptions are raised for *domain errors*. Due to type-limitations in the C language `pow` function, integer arguments are promoted (see Section 3.36 [Type Conversion], page 119) to type `NC_FLOAT` before evaluation. Example: $\mathrm{pow}(2,3) = 8$

`rint(x)`
: *Round exactly* Nearest integer to x is returned in floating-point format. Exceptions are raised for *inexact conversions*. Example: $\mathrm{rint}(0.1) = 0$

`round(x)`
: *Round* Nearest integer to x is returned in floating-point format. Round halfway cases away from zero, regardless of current IEEE rounding direction. Example: $\mathrm{round}(0.5) = 1.0$

`sin(x)`
: *Sine* Sine of x where x is specified in radians. Example: $\sin(1.57079632679489661922) = 1.0$

`sinh(x)`
: *Hyperbolic sine* Hyperbolic sine of x where x is specified in radians. Example: $\sinh(1.0) = 1.1752$

`sqrt(x)`
: *Square Root* Square Root of x, $\sqrt{x}$. Example: $\mathrm{sqrt}(4.0) = 2.0$

`tan(x)`
: *Tangent* Tangent of x where x is specified in radians. Example: $\tan(0.78539816339744830961) = 1.0$

`tanh(x)`
: *Hyperbolic tangent* Hyperbolic tangent of x where x is specified in radians. Example: $\tanh(1.0) = 0.761594155956$

`trunc(x)`
: *Truncate* Nearest integer to x is returned in floating-point format. Round halfway cases toward zero, regardless of current IEEE rounding direction. Example: $\mathrm{trunc}(0.5) = 0.0$

The complete list of mathematical functions supported is platform-specific. Functions mandated by ANSI C are *guaranteed* to be present and are indicated with an asterisk [3]. and

[3] ANSI C compilers are guaranteed to support double-precision versions of these functions. These functions normally operate on netCDF variables of type `NC_DOUBLE` without having to perform intrinsic conversions. For example, ANSI compilers provide `sin` for the sine of C-type `double` variables. The ANSI standard does not require, but many compilers provide, an extended set of mathematical functions that apply to single (`float`) and quadruple (`long double`) precision variables. Using these functions (e.g., `sinf` for `float`, `sinl` for `long double`), when available, is (presumably) more efficient than casting variables to type `double`, performing the operation, and then re-casting. NCO uses the faster intrinsic functions when they are available, and uses the casting method when they are not.

are indicated with an asterisk. Use the '-f' (or 'fnc_tbl' or 'prn_fnc_tbl') switch to print a complete list of functions supported on your platform. [4]

### 4.1.29 Operator precedence and associativity

This page lists the ncap2 operators in order of precedence (highest to lowest). Their associativity indicates in what order operators of equal precedence in an expression are applied.

| Operator | Description | Associativity |
|---|---|---|
| ++ -- | Postfix Increment/Decrement | Right to Left |
| () | Parentheses (function call) | |
| . | Method call | |
| ++ -- | Prefix Increment/Decrement | Right to Left |
| + - | Unary Plus/Minus | |
| ! | Logical Not | |
| ^ | Power of Operator | Right to Left |
| * / % | Multiply/Divide/Modulus | Left To Right |
| + - | Addition/Subtraction | Left To Right |
| >> << | Fortran style array clipping | Left to Right |
| < <= | Less than/Less than or equal to | Left to Right |
| > >= | Greater than/Greater than or equal to | |
| == != | Equal to/Not equal to | Left to Right |
| && | Logical AND | Left to Right |
| \|\| | Logical OR | Left to Right |
| ?: | Ternary Operator | Right to Left |
| = | Assignment | Right to Left |
| += -= | Addition/subtraction assignment | |
| *= /= | Multiplication/division assignment | |

### 4.1.30 ID Quoting

In this section when I refer to a name I mean a variable name, attribute name or a dimension name The allowed characters in a valid netCDF name vary from release to release. (See end section). If you want to use metacharacters in a name or use a method name as a variable name then the name has to be quoted wherever it occurs.

The default NCO name is specified by the regular expressions:

```
DGT:     ('0'..'9');
LPH:     ( 'a'..'z' | 'A'..'Z' | '_' );
name:    (LPH)(LPH|DGT)+
```

The first character of a valid name must be alphabetic or the underscore. Any subsequent characters must be alphanumeric or underscore. ( e.g., a1,_23, hell_is_666 )

The valid characters in a quoted name are specified by the regular expressions:

```
LPHDGT:  ( 'a'..'z' | 'A'..'Z' | '_' | '0'..'9');
name:    (LPHDGT|'-'|'+'|'.'|'('|')'|':' )+  ;
```

---

[4] Linux supports more of these intrinsic functions than other OSs.

Quote a variable:
'avg' , '10_+10','set_miss' '+-90field' , '–test'=10.0d

Quote a attribute:
'three@10', 'set_mss@+10', '666@hell', 't1@+units'="kelvin"

Quote a dimension:
'$10', '$t1–', '$–odd', c1['$10','$t1–']=23.0d

The following comments are from the netCDF library definitions and detail the naming conventions for each release. netcdf-3.5.1
netcdf-3.6.0-p1
netcdf-3.6.1
netcdf-3.6.2

```
/*
 * ( [a-zA-Z]|[0-9]|'_'|'-'|'+'|'.'|'|':'|'@'|'('|')' )+
 * Verify that name string is valid CDL syntax, i.e., all characters are
 * alphanumeric, '-', '_', '+', or '.'.
 * Also permit ':', '@', '(', or ')' in names for chemists currently making
 * use of these characters, but don't document until ncgen and ncdump can
 * also handle these characters in names.
 */
```

netcdf-3.6.3
netcdf-4.0 Final 2008/08/28

```
/*
 * Verify that a name string is valid syntax.  The allowed name
 * syntax (in RE form) is:
 *
 * ([a-zA-Z_]|{UTF8})([^\x00-\x1F\x7F/]|{UTF8})*
 *
 * where UTF8 represents a multibyte UTF-8 encoding.  Also, no
 * trailing spaces are permitted in names.  This definition
 * must be consistent with the one in ncgen.l.  We do not allow '/'
 * because HDF5 does not permit slashes in names as slash is used as a
 * group separator.  If UTF-8 is supported, then a multi-byte UTF-8
 * character can occur anywhere within an identifier.  We later
 * normalize UTF-8 strings to NFC to facilitate matching and queries.
 */
```

### 4.1.31 create_bounds() function

The `ncap2` custom function 'create_bounds()' takes any monotonic 1D coordinate variable with regular or irregular (e.g., Gaussian) spacing and creates a bounds variable.

*<bounds_var_out>=create_bounds( <coordinate_var_in>, <dim in>, <string>)*

*1st Argument*
The name of the input coordinate variable.

*2nd Argument*
The dimension name of the second dimension of the output variable. The size of this dimension should always be 2. If the dimension does not exist create it using `defdim()`.

*3rd Argument*
The string value of a "bounds" attribute that is created in the input coordinate variable. This must be the variable name to contain the bounds.

Typical usage:

```
defdim("nv",2);
longitude_bounds=create_bounds(longitude,$nv,"longitude_bounds");
```

Another common CF convention:

```
defdim("nv",2);
climatology_bounds=create_bounds(time,$nv,"climatology_bounds");
```

## 4.2 ncatted netCDF Attribute Editor

SYNTAX

```
ncatted [-a att_dsc] [-a ...] [-D dbg] [-h] [--hdr_pad nbr]
[-l path] [-O] [-o output-file] [-p path] [-R] [-r]
[--ram_all] [-t] input-file [[output-file]]
```

DESCRIPTION

`ncatted` edits attributes in a netCDF file. If you are editing attributes then you are spending too much time in the world of metadata, and `ncatted` was written to get you back out as quickly and painlessly as possible. `ncatted` can *append*, *create*, *delete*, *modify*, and *overwrite* attributes (all explained below). `ncatted` allows each editing operation to be applied to every variable in a file. This saves time when changing attribute conventions throughout a file. `ncatted` is for *writing* attributes. To *read* attribute values in plain text, use `ncks -m -M`, or define something like `ncattget` as a shell command (see Section 4.8.2 [Filters for `ncks`], page 248).

Because repeated use of `ncatted` can considerably increase the size of the `history` global attribute (see Section 3.39 [History Attribute], page 129), the '`-h`' switch is provided to override automatically appending the command to the `history` global attribute in the *output-file*.

According to the *netCDF User Guide*, altering metadata in netCDF files does not incur the penalty of recopying the entire file when the new metadata occupies less space than the old metadata. Thus `ncatted` may run much faster (at least on netCDF3 files) if judicious use of header padding (see Section 3.2 [Metadata Optimization], page 29) was made when producing the *input-file*. Similarly, using the '`--hdr_pad`' option with `ncatted` helps ensure that future metadata changes to *output-file* occur as swiftly as possible.

When `ncatted` is used to change the `_FillValue` attribute, it changes the associated missing data self-consistently. If the internal floating-point representation of a missing value, e.g., 1.0e36, differs between two machines then netCDF files produced on those machines will have incompatible missing values. This allows `ncatted` to change the missing values in files from different machines to a single value so that the files may then be concatenated, e.g., by `ncrcat`, without losing information. See Section 3.27 [Missing Values], page 89, for more information.

To master `ncatted` one must understand the meaning of the structure that describes the attribute modification, *att_dsc* specified by the required option '`-a`' or '`--attribute`'. This option is repeatable and may be used multiple time in a single `ncatted` invocation to increase the efficiency of altering multiple attributes. Each *att_dsc* contains five elements. This makes using `ncatted` somewhat complicated, though powerful. The *att_dsc* fields are in the following order:

*att_dsc* = *att_nm*, *var_nm*, *mode*, *att_type*, *att_val*

*att_nm* Attribute name. Example: `units` As of NCO 4.5.1 (July, 2015), `ncatted` accepts regular expressions (see Section 3.11 [Subsetting Files], page 46) for attribute names (it has "always" accepted regular expressions for variable names). Regular expressions will select all matching attribute names.

*var_nm* Variable name. Example: `pressure`, `'^H2O'`. Regular expressions (see Section 3.11 [Subsetting Files], page 46) are accepted and will select all matching variable (and/or group) names. The names `global` and `group` have special meaning.

*mode* Edit mode abbreviation. Example: `a`. See below for complete listing of valid values of *mode*.

*att_type* Attribute type abbreviation. Example: `c`. See below for complete listing of valid values of *att_type*.

*att_val* Attribute value. Example: `pascal`.

There should be no empty space between these five consecutive arguments. The description of these arguments follows in their order of appearance.

The value of *att_nm* is the name of the attribute to edit. This meaning of this should be clear to all `ncatted` users. Both *att_nm*) and *var_nm* may be specified as regular expressions. If *att_nm* is omitted (i.e., left blank) and *Delete* mode is selected, then all attributes associated with the specified variable will be deleted.

The value of *var_nm* is the name of the variable containing the attribute (named *att_nm*) that you want to edit. There are three very important and useful exceptions to this rule. The value of *var_nm* can also be used to direct `ncatted` to edit global attributes, or to repeat the editing operation for every group or variable in a file. A value of *var_nm* of `global` indicates that *att_nm* refers to a global (i.e., root-level) attribute, rather than to a particular variable's attribute. This is the method `ncatted` supports for editing global attributes. A value of *var_nm* of `group` indicates that *att_nm* refers to all groups, rather than to a particular variable's or group's attribute. The operation will proceed to edit group metadata for every group. Finally, if *var_nm* is left blank, then `ncatted` attempts to perform the editing operation on every variable in the file. This option may be convenient to use if you decide to change the conventions you use for describing the data. As of NCO 4.6.0 (May, 2016), `ncatted` accepts the '`-t`' (or long-option equivalent '`--typ_mch`' or '`--type_match`') option. This causes `ncatted` to perform the editing operation only on variables that are the same type as the specified attribute.

The value of *mode* is a single character abbreviation (`a`, `c`, `d`, `m`, `n`, or `o`) standing for one of five editing modes:

`a` *Append*. Append value *att_val* to current *var_nm* attribute *att_nm* value *att_val*, if any. If *var_nm* does not already have an existing attribute *att_nm*, it is created with the value *att_val*.

`c` *Create*. Create variable *var_nm* attribute *att_nm* with *att_val* if *att_nm* does not yet exist. If *var_nm* already has an attribute *att_nm*, there is no effect, so the existing attribute is preserved without change.

`d` *Delete*. Delete current *var_nm* attribute *att_nm*. If *var_nm* does not have an attribute *att_nm*, there is no effect. If *att_nm* is omitted (left blank), then all attributes associated with the specified variable are automatically deleted. When *Delete* mode is selected, the *att_type* and *att_val* arguments are superfluous and may be left blank.

`m` *Modify*. Change value of current *var_nm* attribute *att_nm* to value *att_val*. If *var_nm* does not have an attribute *att_nm*, there is no effect.

`n` *Nappend*. Append value *att_val* to *var_nm* attribute *att_nm* value *att_val* if *att_nm* already exists. If *var_nm* does not have an attribute *att_nm*, there is no effect. In other words, if *att_nm* already exist, Nappend behaves like Append otherwise it does nothing. The mnemonic is "non-create append". Nappend mode was added to `ncatted` in version 4.6.0 (May, 2016).

`o` *Overwrite*. Write attribute *att_nm* with value *att_val* to variable *var_nm*, overwriting existing attribute *att_nm*, if any. This is the default mode.

The value of *att_type* is a single character abbreviation (`f`, `d`, `l`, `i`, `s`, `c`, `b`, `u`) or a short string standing for one of the twelve primitive netCDF data types:

`f` *Float*. Value(s) specified in *att_val* will be stored as netCDF intrinsic type `NC_FLOAT`.

`d` *Double*. Value(s) specified in *att_val* will be stored as netCDF intrinsic type `NC_DOUBLE`.

`i, l` *Integer* or (its now deprecated synonym) *Long*. Value(s) specified in *att_val* will be stored as netCDF intrinsic type `NC_INT`.

`s` *Short*. Value(s) specified in *att_val* will be stored as netCDF intrinsic type `NC_SHORT`.

`c` *Char*. Value(s) specified in *att_val* will be stored as netCDF intrinsic type `NC_CHAR`.

`b` *Byte*. Value(s) specified in *att_val* will be stored as netCDF intrinsic type `NC_BYTE`.

`ub` *Unsigned Byte*. Value(s) specified in *att_val* will be stored as netCDF intrinsic type `NC_UBYTE`.

`us` *Unsigned Short*. Value(s) specified in *att_val* will be stored as netCDF intrinsic type `NC_USHORT`.

`u, ui, ul` *Unsigned Int*. Value(s) specified in *att_val* will be stored as netCDF intrinsic type `NC_UINT`.

`ll, int64` *Int64*. Value(s) specified in *att_val* will be stored as netCDF intrinsic type `NC_INT64`.

`ull, uint64`
*Uint64*. Value(s) specified in *att_val* will be stored as netCDF intrinsic type `NC_UINT64`.

`sng, string`
: *String*. Value(s) specified in *att_val* will be stored as netCDF intrinsic type `NC_STRING`. Note that `ncatted` handles type `NC_STRING` attributes correctly beginning with version 4.3.3 released in July, 2013. Earlier versions fail when asked to handle `NC_STRING` attributes.

In *Delete* mode the specification of *att_type* is optional (and is ignored if supplied).

The value of *att_val* is what you want to change attribute *att_nm* to contain. The specification of *att_val* is optional in *Delete* (and is ignored) mode. Attribute values for all types besides `NC_CHAR` must have an attribute length of at least one. Thus *att_val* may be a single value or one-dimensional array of elements of type `att_type`. If the *att_val* is not set or is set to empty space, and the *att_type* is `NC_CHAR`, e.g., `-a units,T,o,c,""` or `-a units,T,o,c,,` then the corresponding attribute is set to have zero length. When specifying an array of values, it is safest to enclose *att_val* in single or double quotes, e.g., `-a levels,T,o,s,"1,2,3,4"` or `-a levels,T,o,s,'1,2,3,4'`. The quotes are strictly unnecessary around *att_val* except when *att_val* contains characters which would confuse the calling shell, such as spaces, commas, and wildcard characters.

NCO processing of `NC_CHAR` attributes is a bit like Perl in that it attempts to do what you want by default (but this sometimes causes unexpected results if you want unusual data storage). If the *att_type* is `NC_CHAR` then the argument is interpreted as a string and it may contain C-language escape sequences, e.g., `\n`, which NCO will interpret before writing anything to disk. NCO translates valid escape sequences and stores the appropriate ASCII code instead. Since two byte escape sequences, e.g., `\n`, represent one-byte ASCII codes, e.g., ASCII 10 (decimal), the stored string attribute is one byte shorter than the input string length for each embedded escape sequence. The most frequently used C-language escape sequences are `\n` (for linefeed) and `\t` (for horizontal tab). These sequences in particular allow convenient editing of formatted text attributes. The other valid ASCII codes are `\a`, `\b`, `\f`, `\r`, `\v`, and `\\`. See Section 4.8 [ncks netCDF Kitchen Sink], page 237, for more examples of string formatting (with the `ncks` '`-s`' option) with special characters.

Analogous to `printf`, other special characters are also allowed by `ncatted` if they are "protected" by a backslash. The characters `"`, `'`, `?`, and `\` may be input to the shell as `\"`, `\'`, `\?`, and `\\`. NCO simply strips away the leading backslash from these characters before editing the attribute. No other characters require protection by a backslash. Backslashes which precede any other character (e.g., `3`, `m`, `$`, `|`, `&`, `@`, `%`, `{`, and `}`) will not be filtered and will be included in the attribute.

Note that the NUL character `\0` which terminates C language strings is assumed and need not be explicitly specified. If `\0` is input, it is translated to the NUL character. However, this will make the subsequent portion of the string, if any, invisible to C standard library string functions. And that may cause unintended consequences. Because of these context-sensitive rules, one must use `ncatted` with care in order to store data, rather than text strings, in an attribute of type `NC_CHAR`.

Note that `ncatted` interprets character attributes (i.e., attributes of type `NC_CHAR`) as strings. EXAMPLES

Append the string `Data version 2.0.\n` to the global attribute `history`:

```
ncatted -a history,global,a,c,'Data version 2.0\n' in.nc
```

Note the use of embedded C language `printf()`-style escape sequences.

Change the value of the `long_name` attribute for variable `T` from whatever it currently is to "temperature":

```
ncatted -a long_name,T,o,c,temperature in.nc
```

Many model and observational datasets use missing values that are not annotated in the standard manner. For example, the MPAS ocean and ice models use $-9.99999979021476795361e+33$ as the missing value. To prevent arithmetic from treating these values as normal, designate this value as the `_FillValue` attribute:

```
ncatted    -a _FillValue,,o,d,-9.99999979021476795361e+33 in.nc
ncatted -t -a _FillValue,,o,d,-9.99999979021476795361e+33 in.nc
ncatted -t -a _FillValue,,o,d,-9.99999979021476795361e+33 \
           -a _FillValue,,o,f,1.0e36 -a _FillValue,,o,i,-999 in.nc
```

The first example adds the attribute to all variables. The '`-t`' switch causes the second example to add the attribute only to double precision variables. This is often more useful, and can be used to provide distinct missing value attributes to each numeric type, as in the third example.

NCO arithmetic operators may not work as expected on IEEE NaN (short for Not-a-Number) and NaN-like numbers such as positive infinity and negative infinity[1]. One way to work-around this problem is to change IEEE NaNs to normal missing values. As of NCO 4.1.0 (March, 2012), `ncatted` works with NaNs (though none of the arithmetic operators do). This limited support enables users to change NaN to a normal number before performing arithmetic or propagating a NaN-tainted dataset. First set the missing value (i.e., the value of the `_FillValue` attribute) for the variable(s) in question to the IEEE NaN value.

```
ncatted -a _FillValue,,o,f,NaN in.nc
```

Then change the missing value from the IEEE NaN value to a normal IEEE number, like 1.0e36 (or to whatever the original missing value was).

```
ncatted -a _FillValue,,m,f,1.0e36 in.nc
```

Some NASA MODIS datasets provide a real-world example.

```
ncatted -O -a _FillValue,,m,d,1.0e36 -a missing_value,,m,d,1.0e36 \
        MODIS_L2N_20140304T1120.nc MODIS_L2N_20140304T1120_noNaN.nc
```

---

[1] NaN is a special floating point value (not a string). Arithmetic comparisons to NaN and NaN-like numbers always return False, contrary to the behavior of all other numbers. This behavior is difficult to intuit, yet IEEE 754 mandates it. To correctly handle NaNs during arithmetic, code must use special math library macros (e.g., `isnormal()`) to determine whether any operand is special. If so, additional special logic must handle the arithmetic. This is in addition to the normal handling incurred to correctly handle missing values. Handling field and missing values (either or both of which may be NaN) in binary operators thus incurs four-to-eight extra code paths. Each code path slows down arithmetic relative to normal numbers. This makes supporting NaN arithmetic costly and inefficient. Hence NCO supports NaN only to the extent necessary to replace it with a normal number. Although using NaN for the missing value (or any value) in datasets is legal in netCDF, we strongly discourage it. We recommend avoiding NaN entirely.

Delete all existing units attributes:

```
ncatted -a units,,d,, in.nc
```

The value of *var_nm* was left blank in order to select all variables in the file. The values of *att_type* and *att_val* were left blank because they are superfluous in *Delete* mode.

Delete all attributes associated with the tpt variable, and delete all global attributes

```
ncatted -a ,tpt,d,, -a ,global,d,, in.nc
```

The value of *att_nm* was left blank in order to select all attributes associated with the variable. To delete all global attributes, simply replace tpt with global in the above.

Modify all existing units attributes to meter second-1:

```
ncatted -a units,,m,c,'meter second-1' in.nc
```

Add a units attribute of kilogram kilogram-1 to all variables whose first three characters are 'H2O':

```
ncatted -a units,'^H2O',c,c,'kilogram kilogram-1' in.nc
```

Overwrite the quanta attribute of variable energy to an array of four integers.

```
ncatted -a quanta,energy,o,s,'010,101,111,121' in.nc
```

As of NCO 3.9.6 (January, 2009), ncatted accepts *extended regular expressions* as arguments for variable names, and, since NCO 4.5.1 (July, 2015), for attribute names.

```
ncatted -a isotope,'^H2O*',c,s,'18' in.nc
ncatted -a '.?_iso19115$','^H2O*',d,, in.nc
```

The first example creates isotope attributes for all variables whose names contain 'H2O'. The second deletes all attributes whose names end in _iso19115 from all variables whose names contain 'H2O'. See Section 3.11 [Subsetting Files], page 46, for more details on using regular expressions.

As of NCO 4.3.8 (November, 2013), ncatted accepts full and partial group paths in names of attributes, variables, dimensions, and groups.

```
# Overwrite units attribute of specific 'lon' variable
ncatted -O -a units,/g1/lon,o,c,'degrees_west' in_grp.nc
# Overwrite units attribute of all 'lon' variables
ncatted -O -a units,lon,o,c,'degrees_west' in_grp.nc
# Delete units attribute of all 'lon' variables
ncatted -O -a units,lon,d,, in_grp.nc
# Overwrite units attribute with new type for specific 'lon' variable
ncatted -O -a units,/g1/lon,o,sng,'degrees_west' in_grp.nc
# Add new_att attribute to all variables
ncatted -O -a new_att,,c,sng,'new variable attribute' in_grp.nc
# Add new_grp_att group attribute to all groups
ncatted -O -a new_grp_att,group,c,sng,'new group attribute' in_grp.nc
# Add new_grp_att group attribute to single group
ncatted -O -a g1_grp_att,g1,c,sng,'new group attribute' in_grp.nc
```

```
# Add new_glb_att global attribute to root group
ncatted -O -a new_glb_att,global,c,sng,'new global attribute' in_grp.nc
```

Note that regular expressions work well in conjuction with group path support. In other words, the variable name (including group path component) and the attribute names may both be extended regular expressions.

Demonstrate input of C-language escape sequences (e.g., `\n`) and other special characters (e.g., `\"`)

```
ncatted -h -a special,global,o,c,
'\nDouble quote: \"\nTwo consecutive double quotes: \"\"\n
Single quote: Beyond my shell abilities!\nBackslash: \\\n
Two consecutive backslashes: \\\\\nQuestion mark: \?\n' in.nc
```

Note that the entire attribute is protected from the shell by single quotes. These outer single quotes are necessary for interactive use, but may be omitted in batch scripts.

## 4.3 ncbo netCDF Binary Operator

SYNTAX

```
ncbo [-3] [-4] [-6] [-7] [-A] [-C] [-c]
[--cnk_byt sz_byt] [--cnk_dmn nm,sz_lmn] [--cnk_map map]
[--cnk_min sz_byt] [--cnk_plc plc] [--cnk_scl sz_lmn]
[-D dbg] [-d dim,[min][,[max][,[stride]]] [-F]
[-G gpe_dsc] [-g grp[,...]] [--glb ...] [-h] [--hdr_pad nbr]
[-L dfl_lvl] [-l path] [--no_cll_msr] [--no_frm_trm] [--no_tmp_fl]
[-O] [-o file_3] [-p path] [-R] [-r] [--ram_all]
[-t thr_nbr] [--unn] [-v var[,...]] [-X ...] [-x] [-y op_typ]
file_1 file_2 [file_3]
```

DESCRIPTION

ncbo performs binary operations on variables in *file_1* and the corresponding variables (those with the same name) in *file_2* and stores the results in *file_3*. The binary operation operates on the entire files (modulo any excluded variables). See Section 3.27 [Missing Values], page 89, for treatment of missing values. One of the four standard arithmetic binary operations currently supported must be selected with the '-y *op_typ*' switch (or long options '--op_typ' or '--operation'). The valid binary operations for ncbo, their definitions, corresponding values of the *op_typ* key, and alternate invocations are:

*Addition*
: Definition: *file_3 = file_1 + file_2*
Alternate invocation: ncadd
*op_typ* key values: 'add', '+', 'addition'
Examples: 'ncbo --op_typ=add 1.nc 2.nc 3.nc', 'ncadd 1.nc 2.nc 3.nc'

*Subtraction*
: Definition: *file_3 = file_1 - file_2*
Alternate invocations: ncdiff, ncsub, ncsubtract
*op_typ* key values: 'sbt', '-', 'dff', 'diff', 'sub', 'subtract', 'subtraction'
Examples: 'ncbo --op_typ=- 1.nc 2.nc 3.nc', 'ncdiff 1.nc 2.nc 3.nc'

*Multiplication*
: Definition: *file_3 = file_1 * file_2*
Alternate invocations: ncmult, ncmultiply
*op_typ* key values: 'mlt', '*', 'mult', 'multiply', 'multiplication'
Examples: 'ncbo --op_typ=mlt 1.nc 2.nc 3.nc', 'ncmult 1.nc 2.nc 3.nc'

*Division*
: Definition: *file_3 = file_1 / file_2*
Alternate invocation: ncdivide
*op_typ* key values: 'dvd', '/', 'divide', 'division'
Examples: 'ncbo --op_typ=/ 1.nc 2.nc 3.nc', 'ncdivide 1.nc 2.nc 3.nc'

Care should be taken when using the shortest form of key values, i.e., '+', '-', '*', and '/'. Some of these single characters may have special meanings to the shell [1]. Place these characters inside quotes to keep them from being interpreted (globbed) by the shell[2]. For example, the following commands are equivalent

```
ncbo --op_typ=* 1.nc 2.nc 3.nc # Dangerous (shell may try to glob)
ncbo --op_typ='*' 1.nc 2.nc 3.nc # Safe ('*' protected from shell)
ncbo --op_typ="*" 1.nc 2.nc 3.nc # Safe ('*' protected from shell)
ncbo --op_typ=mlt 1.nc 2.nc 3.nc
ncbo --op_typ=mult 1.nc 2.nc 3.nc
ncbo --op_typ=multiply 1.nc 2.nc 3.nc
ncbo --op_typ=multiplication 1.nc 2.nc 3.nc
ncmult 1.nc 2.nc 3.nc # First do 'ln -s ncbo ncmult'
ncmultiply 1.nc 2.nc 3.nc # First do 'ln -s ncbo ncmultiply'
```

No particular argument or invocation form is preferred. Users are encouraged to use the forms which are most intuitive to them.

Normally, `ncbo` will fail unless an operation type is specified with '`-y`' (equivalent to '`--op_typ`'). You may create exceptions to this rule to suit your particular tastes, in conformance with your site's policy on *symbolic links* to executables (files of a different name point to the actual executable). For many years, `ncdiff` was the main binary file operator. As a result, many users prefer to continue invoking `ncdiff` rather than memorizing a new command ('`ncbo -y` *`sbt`*') which behaves identically to the original `ncdiff` command. However, from a software maintenance standpoint, maintaining a distinct executable for each binary operation (e.g., `ncadd`) is untenable, and a single executable, `ncbo`, is desirable. To maintain backward compatibility, therefore, NCO automatically creates a symbolic link from `ncbo` to `ncdiff`. Thus `ncdiff` is called an *alternate invocation* of `ncbo`. `ncbo` supports many additional alternate invocations which must be manually activated. Should users or system adminitrators decide to activate them, the procedure is simple. For example, to use '`ncadd`' instead of '`ncbo --op_typ=add`', simply create a symbolic link from `ncbo` to `ncadd`[3]. The alternatate invocations supported for each operation type are listed above. Alternatively, users may always define '`ncadd`' as an *alias* to '`ncbo --op_typ=add`'[4].

It is important to maintain portability in NCO scripts. Therefore we recommend that site-specfic invocations (e.g., '`ncadd`') be used only in interactive sessions from the command-line. For scripts, we recommend using the full invocation (e.g., '`ncbo --op_typ=add`'). This ensures portability of scripts between users and sites.

`ncbo` operates (e.g., adds) variables in *file_2* with the corresponding variables (those with the same name) in *file_1* and stores the results in *file_3*. Variables in *file_1* or *file_2*

---

[1] A naked (i.e., unprotected or unquoted) '`*`' is a wildcard character. A naked '`-`' may confuse the command line parser. A naked '`+`' and '`/`' are relatively harmless.

[2] The widely used shell Bash correctly interprets all these special characters even when they are not quoted. That is, Bash does not prevent NCO from correctly interpreting the intended arithmetic operation when the following arguments are given (without quotes) to `ncbo`: '`--op_typ=+`', '`--op_typ=-`', '`--op_typ=*`', and '`--op_typ=/`'

[3] The command to do this is '`ln -s -f ncbo ncadd`'

[4] The command to do this is '`alias ncadd='ncbo --op_typ=add'`'

are *broadcast* to conform to the corresponding variable in the other input file if necessary[5]. Now `ncbo` is completely symmetric with respect to *file_1* and *file_2*, i.e., $\mathrm{file}_1 - \mathrm{file}_2 = -(\mathrm{file}_2 - \mathrm{file}_1)$.

Broadcasting a variable means creating data in non-existing dimensions by copying data in existing dimensions. For example, a two dimensional variable in *file_2* can be subtracted from a four, three, or two (not one or zero) dimensional variable (of the same name) in `file_1`. This functionality allows the user to compute anomalies from the mean. In the future, we will broadcast variables in *file_1*, if necessary to conform to their counterparts in *file_2*. Thus, presently, the number of dimensions, or *rank*, of any processed variable in *file_1* must be greater than or equal to the rank of the same variable in *file_2*. Of course, the size of all dimensions common to both *file_1* and *file_2* must be equal.

When computing anomalies from the mean it is often the case that *file_2* was created by applying an averaging operator to a file with initially the same dimensions as *file_1* (often *file_1* itself). In these cases, creating *file_2* with `ncra` rather than `ncwa` will cause the `ncbo` operation to fail. For concreteness say the record dimension in `file_1` is `time`. If *file_2* was created by averaging *file_1* over the `time` dimension with the `ncra` operator (rather than with the `ncwa` operator), then *file_2* will have a `time` dimension of size 1 rather than having no `time` dimension at all [6]. In this case the input files to `ncbo`, *file_1* and *file_2*, will have unequally sized `time` dimensions which causes `ncbo` to fail. To prevent this from occurring, use `ncwa` to remove the `time` dimension from *file_2*. See the example below.

`ncbo` never operates on coordinate variables or variables of type `NC_CHAR` or `NC_STRING`. This ensures that coordinates like (e.g., latitude and longitude) are physically meaningful in the output file, *file_3*. This behavior is hardcoded. `ncbo` applies special rules to some CF-defined (and/or NCAR CCSM or NCAR CCM fields) such as `ORO`. See Section 3.41 [CF Conventions], page 131, for a complete description. Finally, we note that `ncflint` (see Section 4.7 [ncflint netCDF File Interpolator], page 234) is designed for file interpolation. As such, it also performs file subtraction, addition, multiplication, albeit in a more convoluted way than `ncbo`.

Beginning with NCO version 4.3.1 (May, 2013), `ncbo` supports *group broadcasting*. Group broadcasting means processing data based on group patterns in the input file(s) and automatically transferring or transforming groups to the output file. Consider the case where *file_1* contains multiple groups each with the variable *v1*, while *file_2* contains *v1* only in its top-level (i.e., root) group. Then `ncbo` will replicate the group structure of *file_1* in the output file, *file_3*. Each group in *file_3* contains the output of the corresponding group in *file_1* operating on the data in the single group in *file_2*. An example is provided below.

EXAMPLES

Say files `85_0112.nc` and `86_0112.nc` each contain 12 months of data. Compute the change in the monthly averages from 1985 to 1986:

---

5 Prior to NCO version 4.3.1 (May, 2013), `ncbo` would only broadcast variables in *file_2* to conform to *file_1*. Variables in *file_1* were *never* broadcast to conform to the dimensions in *file_2*.

6 This is because `ncra` collapses the record dimension to a size of 1 (making it a *degenerate* dimension), but does not remove it, while, unless '`-b`' is given, `ncwa` removes all averaged dimensions. In other words, by default `ncra` changes variable size though not rank, while, `ncwa` changes both variable size and rank.

```
ncbo   86_0112.nc 85_0112.nc 86m85_0112.nc
ncdiff 86_0112.nc 85_0112.nc 86m85_0112.nc
ncbo --op_typ=sub 86_0112.nc 85_0112.nc 86m85_0112.nc
ncbo --op_typ='-' 86_0112.nc 85_0112.nc 86m85_0112.nc
```

These commands are all different ways of expressing the same thing.

The following examples demonstrate the broadcasting feature of ncbo. Say we wish to compute the monthly anomalies of T from the yearly average of T for the year 1985. First we create the 1985 average from the monthly data, which is stored with the record dimension time.

```
ncra 85_0112.nc 85.nc
ncwa -O -a time 85.nc 85.nc
```

The second command, ncwa, gets rid of the time dimension of size 1 that ncra left in 85.nc. Now none of the variables in 85.nc has a time dimension. A quicker way to accomplish this is to use ncwa from the beginning:

```
ncwa -a time 85_0112.nc 85.nc
```

We are now ready to use ncbo to compute the anomalies for 1985:

```
ncdiff -v T 85_0112.nc 85.nc t_anm_85_0112.nc
```

Each of the 12 records in t_anm_85_0112.nc now contains the monthly deviation of T from the annual mean of T for each gridpoint.

Say we wish to compute the monthly gridpoint anomalies from the zonal annual mean. A *zonal mean* is a quantity that has been averaged over the longitudinal (or $x$) direction. First we use ncwa to average over longitudinal direction lon, creating 85_x.nc, the zonal mean of 85.nc. Then we use ncbo to subtract the zonal annual means from the monthly gridpoint data:

```
ncwa -a lon 85.nc 85_x.nc
ncdiff 85_0112.nc 85_x.nc tx_anm_85_0112.nc
```

This examples works assuming 85_0112.nc has dimensions time and lon, and that 85_x.nc has no time or lon dimension.

Group broadcasting simplifies evaluation of multiple models against observations. Consider the input file cmip5.nc which contains multiple top-level groups cesm, ecmwf, and giss, each of which contains the surface air temperature field tas. We wish to compare these models to observations stored in obs.nc which contains tas only in its top-level (i.e., root) group. It is often the case that many models and/or model simulations exist, whereas only one observational dataset does. We evaluate the models and obtain the bias (difference) between models and observations by subtracting obs.nc from cmip5.nc. Then ncbo "broadcasts" (i.e., replicates) the observational data to match the group structure of cmip5.nc, subtracts, and then stores the results in the output file, bias.nc which has the same group structure as cmip5.nc.

```
% ncbo -O cmip5.nc obs.nc bias.nc
% ncks -H -v tas -d time,3 bias.nc
/cesm/tas
```

```
time[3] tas[3]=-1
/ecmwf/tas
time[3] tas[3]=0
/giss/tas
time[3] tas[3]=1
```

As a final example, say we have five years of monthly data (i.e., 60 months) stored in 8501_8912.nc and we wish to create a file which contains the twelve month seasonal cycle of the average monthly anomaly from the five-year mean of this data. The following method is just one permutation of many which will accomplish the same result. First use ncwa to create the five-year mean:

```
ncwa -a time 8501_8912.nc 8589.nc
```

Next use ncbo to create a file containing the difference of each month's data from the five-year mean:

```
ncbo 8501_8912.nc 8589.nc t_anm_8501_8912.nc
```

Now use ncks to group together the five January anomalies in one file, and use ncra to create the average anomaly for all five Januarys. These commands are embedded in a shell loop so they are repeated for all twelve months:

```
for idx in {1..12}; do # Bash Shell (version 3.0+)
  idx=`printf "%02d" ${idx}` # Zero-pad to preserve order
  ncks -F -d time,${idx},,12 t_anm_8501_8912.nc foo.${idx}
  ncra foo.${idx} t_anm_8589_${idx}.nc
done
for idx in 01 02 03 04 05 06 07 08 09 10 11 12; do # Bourne Shell
  ncks -F -d time,${idx},,12 t_anm_8501_8912.nc foo.${idx}
  ncra foo.${idx} t_anm_8589_${idx}.nc
done
foreach idx (01 02 03 04 05 06 07 08 09 10 11 12) # C Shell
  ncks -F -d time,${idx},,12 t_anm_8501_8912.nc foo.${idx}
  ncra foo.${idx} t_anm_8589_${idx}.nc
end
```

Note that ncra understands the stride argument so the two commands inside the loop may be combined into the single command

```
ncra -F -d time,${idx},,12 t_anm_8501_8912.nc foo.${idx}
```

Finally, use ncrcat to concatenate the 12 average monthly anomaly files into one twelve-record file which contains the entire seasonal cycle of the monthly anomalies:

```
ncrcat t_anm_8589_??.nc t_anm_8589_0112.nc
```

## 4.4 ncclimo netCDF Climatology Generator

SYNTAX

```
ncclimo [-a dec_md] [-C clm_md] [-c caseid] [-d dbg_lvl]
[-E yr_prv] [-e yr_end] [-f fml_nm] [-h hst_nm] [-i drc_in]
[-j job_nbr] [-l lnk_flg] [-m mdl_nm] [-n nco_opt]
[-O drc_rgr] [-o drc_out] [-p par_typ] [-R rgr_opt] [-r rgr_map]
[-S yr_prv] [-s yr_srt] [--stdin] [--tpd=tpd_dly] [-t thr_nbr] [--tpd=tpd_dly]
[-v var_lst] [-x cf_flg] [-X drc_xtn] [-x drc_prv] [-Y rgr_xtn] [-y rgr_prv]
[--ypf=ypf_max]
```

DESCRIPTION

In climatology generation mode, `ncclimo` ingests "raw" data consisting of a monthly or annual timeseries of files and from these produces climatological monthly means, seasonal means, and/or annual means. Alternatively, in timeseries reshaping mode, `ncclimo` will subset and temporally split the input raw data timeseries into per-variable files spanning the entire period. `ncclimo` can optionally regrid all output files in either mode.

There are five required options ('-c', '-s', '-e', '-i', and '-o')) to generate climatologies, and many more options are available to customize the processing. Options are similar to `ncremap` options. Standard `ncclimo` usage for climatology generation looks like

```
ncclimo             -c caseid -s srt_yr -e end_yr -i drc_in -o drc_out
ncclimo -m mdl_nm   -c caseid -s srt_yr -e end_yr -i drc_in -o drc_out
ncclimo -v var_lst -c caseid -s srt_yr -e end_yr -i drc_in -o drc_out
ncclimo --case=caseid --start=srt_yr --end=end_yr --input=drc_in --output=drc_out
```

In climatology generation mode, `ncclimo` constructs the list of input filenames from the argument to the date and model-type options. `ncclimo` automatically switches to timeseries reshaping mode if it receives a list of files from `stdin`, or, alternatively, placed as positional arguments (after the last command-line option), or if neither of these is done and no *caseid* is specified, in which case it assumes all `*.nc` files in *drc_in* constitute the input file list.

Options come in both short (single-letter) and long forms. The handful of long-option synonyms for each option allows the user to imbue the commands with a level of verbosity and precision that suits her taste. A complete description of all options is given below, in alphabetical order of the short option letter. Long option synonyms are given just after the letter. When invoked without options, `ncclimo` prints a succinct table of all options and some examples.

`-a` *dec_md* `(--dec_md, --december_mode, --dec_mode)`
: December mode determines the type of DJF average. The two valid options are `scd` (default) and `sdd`. SCD-mode stands for "Seasonally Continuous December". The first month used is December of the year before the start year specified with '-s'. The last month is November of the end year specified with '-e'. SDD-mode stands for "Seasonally Discontinuous December". The first month used is January of the specified start year. The last month is December of the end year specified with '-e'.

-C *clm_md* (--clm_md, --climatology_mode, --mode, --climatology)
: Climatology mode. Valid values are 'ann' and 'mth'. The value indicates the timespan of the averages in each input file. The default mode is 'mth', which means input files are monthly averages. Use 'ann' if the input files are a series of annual means.

-c *caseid* (--case, --caseid, --case_id)
: Simulation name, or any input filename for non-CESM'ish files. The use of *caseid* is required in climate generation mode (unless equivalent information is provided through other options), where *caseid* is used to construct both input and output filenames. For CESM'ish input files like famipc5_ne30_v0.3_00001.cam.h0.1980-01.nc, specify '-c famipc5_ne30_v0.3_00001'. The '.cam.' and '.h0.' bits are added internally to produce the input filenames. These can be modified via the -m *mdl_nm* and -h *hst_nm* switches if needed. For input files like merra2_198001.nc, specify '-c merra2_198001.nc'. In timeseries reshaping mode, *caseid* will be used, if supplied, as an additional string in the output filename. For example, specifying '-c control' would cause T_000101_000912.nc to be instead named T_control_000101_000912.nc.

-D *dbg_lvl* (--dbg_lvl, --dbg, --debug, --debug_level)
: Specifies a debugging level similar to the rest of NCO. If *dbg_lvl* = 1, ncclimo prints more extensive diagnostics of its behavior. If *dbg_lvl* = 2, ncclimo prints the commands it would execute at any higher or lower debugging level, but does not execute these commands. If *dbg_lvl* > 2, ncclimo prints the diagnostic information, executes all commands, and passes-through the debugging level to the regridder (ncks) for additional diagnostics.

-e *end_yr* (--end_yr, --yr_end, --end_year, --year_end, --end)
: End year (example: 2000). Unless the option '-a sdd' is specified, the last month used is November of the specified end year. If '-a sdd' is specified, the last month is December of the specified end year.

-f *fml_nm* (--fml_nm, --family, --family_name)
: Family name (nickname) of output files. In climate generation mode, output climo file names are constructed by default with the same *caseid* as the input files. The *fml_nm*, if supplied, replaces *caseid* in output climo names, which are of the form *fml_nm*_XX_YYYYMM_YYYYMM.nc where *XX* is the month or seasonal abbreviation. Use '-f *fml_nm*' to simplify long names, avoid overlap, etc. Example values of *fml_nm* are 'control', 'experiment', and (for a single-variable climo) 'FSNT'. In timeseries reshaping mode, *fml_nm* will be used, if supplied, as an additional string in the output filename. For example, specifying '-f control' would cause T_000101_000912.nc to be instead named T_control_000101_000912.nc.

-h *hst_nm* (--hst_nm, --history_name, --history)
: History volume name of file used to generate climatologies. This referring to the *hst_nm* character sequence used to construct input file names: caseid.mdl_nm.*hst_nm*.YYYY-MM.nc. By default input climo file names are constructed from the *caseid* of the input files, together with the model name *mdl_nm* (specified with '-m') and the date range. Use '-h *hst_nm*' to specify alternative

history volumes. Examples include 'h0' (default, works for CAM, ALM/CLM), 'h1', and 'h' (for CISM).

`-i` *drc_in* `(--drc_in, --in_drc, --dir_in, --input)`
: Directory containing all monthly mean files to read as input to the climatology. The use of *drc_in* is mandatory in climate generation mode but is optional in timeseries reshaping mode. In timeseries reshaping mode, `ncclimo` uses all netCDF files (meaning files with suffixes `.nc`, `.nc3`, `.nc4`, `.cdf`, `.hdf`, `.he5`, or `.h5`) in *drc_in* to create the list of input files when no list is provided through `stdin` or as positional arguments to the command-line.

`-j` *job_nbr* `(--job_nbr, --job_number, --jobs)`
: Specifies the number of simultaneous subsetting processes to spawn during parallel execution for both Background and MPI modes. This applies to timeseries reshaping mode only, and has no effect in climatology generation mode. In both parallel modes `ncclimo` spawns processes in batches of *job_nbr* jobs, then waits for those processes to complete. Once a batch finishes, `ncclimo` spawns the next batch. In Background mode, all jobs are spawned to the local node. In MPI mode, all jobs are spawned in round-robin fashion to all available nodes until *job_nbr* jobs are running.

  If subsetting consumes so much RAM (e.g., because variables are large and/or the number of threads is large) that a single node can perform only one subsetting job at a time, then a reasonable value for *job_nbr* is the number of nodes, *node_nbr*. Often, however, nodes can usually subset (and then regrid, if requested) multiple variables simultaneously.

  By default *job_nbr* = 2 in Background mode, and *job_nbr* = *node_nbr* in MPI mode. This helps prevent users from overloading nodes with too many jobs. Subject to the availability of adequate RAM, expand the number of jobs per node by increasing *job_nbr* until, ideally, each core on the node is used.

  The main throughput bottleneck in timeseries reshaping mode is I/O. It is possible that each node can write to only one file at a time, in which case increasing *job_nbr* may have little effect. Regridding requires math that can relieve some I/O contention and allows for some throughput gains with increasing *job_nbr*. In general, though, increasing *job_nbr* is expected to improve throughput much more in `ncremap` than in `ncclimo`.

`-l (--lnk_flg, --link_flag, --no_amwg_links)`
: This switch (which takes no argument) turns-off the default linking of ACME-climo to AMWG-climo filenames. AMWG omits the YYYYMM components of climo filenames, resulting in shorter names. By default `ncclimo` symbolically links the full (ACME) filename to the shorter (AMWG) name. AMWG diagnostics scripts can produce plots directly from these linked filenames. Use this switch to turn-off that linking and reduce filename proliferation if you do not need AMWG filenames.

`-m` *mdl_nm* `(--mdl_nm, --model_name, --model)`
: Model name (as embedded in monthly input filenames). Default is 'cam'. Other options are 'clm2', 'ocn', 'ice', 'cism', 'cice', 'pop'.

`-n` *nco_opt* `(nco_opt, nco, nco_options)`
Specifies a string of options to pass-through unaltered to `ncks`. *nco_opt* defaults to '`-O --no_tmp_fl`'.

`-O` *drc_rgr* `(--drc_rgr, --rgr_drc, --dir_rgr, --regrid)`
Directory to hold regridded climo files. Regridded climos are placed in *drc_out* unless a separate directory for them is specified with '`-O`' (NB: capital "O").

`-o` *drc_out* `(--drc_out, --out_drc, --dir_out, --output)`
Directory to hold computed (output) native grid climo files. Regridded climos are also placed here unless a separate directory for them is specified with '`-O`' (NB: capital "O").

`-p` *par_typ* `(--par_typ, --par_md, --parallel_type, --parallel_mode, --parallel)`
Specifies the parallelism mode desired. The options are serial mode ('`-p nil`' or '`-p serial`'), background mode parallelism ('`-p bck`'), and MPI parallelism '`-p mpi`'. The default is background-mode parallelism. The default *par_typ* is '`bck`', which means `ncclimo` runs spawns up to twelve (one for each month) parallel processes at a time. See discussion below under Memory Considerations.

`-R` *rgr_opt* `(rgr_opt, regrid_options)`
Specifies a string of options to pass-through unaltered to `ncks`. *rgr_opt* defaults to '`-O --no_tmp_fl`'.

`-r` *rgr_map* `(--rgr_map, --regrid_map, --map)`
Regridding map. Unless '`-r`' is specified `ncclimo` produces only a climatology on the native grid of the input datasets. The *rgr_map* specifies how to (quickly) transform the native grid into the desired analysis grid. `ncclimo` will (call `ncremap` to) apply the given map to the native grid climatology and produce a second climatology on the analysis grid. Options intended exclusively for the regridder may be passed as arguments to the '`-R`' switch. See below the discussion on regridding.

`-s` *srt_yr* `(--srt_yr, --yr_srt, --start_year, --year_start, --start)`
Start year (example: 1980). Unless the option '`-a sdd`' is specified, the first month used will be December of the year before the start year (to allow for contiguous DJF climos). If '`-a sdd`' is specified, the first month used is January of the specified start year.

`--stdin (--stdin, --inp_std, --std_flg, --redirect, --standard_input)`
This switch (which takes no argument) explicitly indicates that input file lists are provided via `stdin`, i.e., standard input. In interactive environments, `ncclimo` can automatically (i.e., without any switch) detect whether input is provided via `stdin`. This switch is never required for jobs run in an interactive shell. However, non-interactive batch jobs (such as those submitted to the SLURM and PBS schedulers) make it impossible to unambiguously determine whether input has been provided via `stdin`. Specifically, the '`--stdin`' switch *must* be used in non-interactive batch jobs on PBS when the input files are piped to `stdin`, and on SLURM when the input files are redirected from a file

to `stdin`. Using this switch in any other context (e.g., interactive shells) is optional.

`-t` *thr_nbr* (`--thr_nbr`, `--threads`, `--thread_number`)
: Specifies the number of threads used per regridding process (see Section 3.3 [OpenMP Threading], page 29). The NCO regridder scales well to 8–16 threads. However, regridding with the maximum number of threads can interfere with climatology generation in parallel climatology mode (i.e., when *par_typ* = `mpi` or `bck`). Hence `ncclimo` defaults to *thr_nbr*=2.

`--tpd_out` *tpd_out* (`--tpd_out`, `--tpd`, `--timesteps_per_day`)
: The number of timesteps-per-day in output created by `ncclimo`'s climatology generator in daily average mode. The climatology output from input files at daily or sub-daily resolution is, by default, averaged to daily resolution, i.e., *tpd_out*=1. If the number of timesteps per day in each input file is *tpd_in*, then the user may select any value of *tpd_out* that is smaller than and integrally divides *tpd_in*. For example, an input timeseries with *tpd_in*=8 (i.e., 3-hourly resolution), can be used to produce climatological output at 3, 6, or 12-hourly resolution by setting *tpd_out* to 8, 4, or 2, respectively. This option only takes effect in daily-average climatology mode.

`-v` *var_lst* (`--var_lst`, `--var`, `--vars`, `--variables`, `--variable_list`)
: Variables to subset or split. Same behavior as Section 3.11 [Subsetting Files], page 46. The use of *var_lst* is optional in climate generation mode but is mandatory in timeseries reshaping mode (to prevent inadvertently copying the results of an entire model simulation). Regular expressions are allowed so, e.g., '`PREC.?`' extracts the variables '`PRECC,PRECL,PRECSC,PRECSL`' if present. Note that in reshaping mode all matches to a regular expression are placed in the same output file.

`--ypf_max` *ypf_max* (`--ypf`, `--years`, `--years_per_file`)
: The maximum number of years-per-file output by `ncclimo`'s splitting operation. When `ncclimo` subsets and splits a collection of input files spanning a timerseries, it places each subset variable in its own output file. The maximum length, in years, of each output file is *ypf_max*, which defaults to *ypf_max*=50. If an input timeseries spans 237 years and *ypf_max*=50, then `ncclimo` will generate four output files of length 50 years and one output file of length 37 years. This option only takes effect in timeseries reshaping mode.

## Timeseries Reshaping mode, aka Splitting

This section of the `ncclimo` documentation applies only to resphaping mode, whereas all subsequent sections apply to climatology generation mode. As mentioned above, `ncclimo` automatically switches to timeseries reshaping mode if it receives a list of files through `stdin`, or, alternatively, placed as positional arguments (after the last command-line option), or if neither of these is done and no *caseid* is specified, in which case it assumes all `*.nc` files in *drc_in* constitute the input file list. These examples invoke reshaping mode in the three possible ways:

```
# Pipe list to stdin
```

```
cd $drc_in;ls *mdl*000[1-9]*.nc | ncclimo -v T,Q,RH -s 1 -e 9 -o $drc_out
# Redirect list from file to stdin
cd $drc_in;ls *mdl*000[1-9]*.nc > foo;ncclimo -v T,Q,RH -s 1 -e 9 -o $drc_out < foo
# List as positional arguments
ncclimo -v T,Q,RH -s 1 -e 9 -o $drc_out $drc_in/*mdl*000[1-9]*.nc
# Glob directory
ncclimo -v T,Q,RH -s 1 -e 9 -i $drc_in -o $drc_out
```

Assuming each input file is a monthly average comprising the variables *T*, *Q*, and *RH*, then the output will be files `T_000101_000912.nc`, `Q_000101_000912.nc`, and `RH_000101_000912.nc`. `ncclimo` *reshapes* the input so that the outputs are continuous timeseries of each variable taken from all input files. When necessary, the output is split into segments each containing no more than *ypf_max* (default 50) years of input, i.e., `T_000101_005012.nc`, `T_005101_009912.nc`, `T_010001_014912.nc`, etc.

## MPAS-O/I considerations

MPAS ocean and ice models currently have their own (non-CESM'ish) naming convention that guarantees output files have the same names for all simulations. By default `ncclimo` analyzes the "timeSeriesStatsMonthly" analysis member output (tell us if you want options for other analysis members). `ncclimo` recognizes input files as being MPAS-style when invoked with '`-m mpaso`' or '`-m mpascice`' like this:

```
ncclimo -m mpaso    -s 1980 -e 1983 -i $drc_in -o $drc_out # MPAS-O
ncclimo -m mpascice -s 1980 -e 1983 -i $drc_in -o $drc_out # MPAS-I
```

MPAS climos are unaware of missing values until/unless input files are "fixed". We recommend that simulation producers annotate all floating point variables with the appropriate `_FillValue` prior to invoking `ncclimo`. Run something like this once in the history-file directory:

```
for fl in `ls hist.*` ; do
  ncatted -O -t -a _FillValue,,o,d,-9.99999979021476795361e+33 ${fl}
done
```

If/when MPAS-O/I generates the `_FillValue` attributes itself, this step can and should be skipped. All other `ncclimo` features like regridding (below) are invoked identically for MPAS as for CAM/CLM users although under-the-hood `ncclimo` does do some special pre-processing (dimension permutation, metadata annotation) for MPAS. A five-year oEC60to30 MPAS-O climo with regridding to T62 takes less than 10 minutes on the machine `rhea`.

## Annual climos

Not all model or observed history files are created as monthly means. To create a climatological annual mean from a series of annual mean inputs, select `ncclimo`'s annual climatology mode with the '`-C ann`' option:

```
ncclimo -C ann -m cism -h h -c caseid -s 1851 -e 1900 -i drc_in -o drc_out
```

The options '`-m mdl_nm`' and '`-h hst_nm`' (that default to `cam` and `h0`, respectively) tell `ncclimo` how to construct the input filenames. The above formula names the files `caseid.cism.h.1851-01-01-00000.nc`, `caseid.cism.h.1852-01-01-00000.nc`, and so on. Annual climatology mode produces a single output file (or two if regridding is selected), and in all other respects behaves the same as monthly climatology mode.

## Regridding Climos and Other Files

`ncclimo` will (optionally) regrid during climatology generation and produce climatology files on both native and analysis grids. This regridding is virtually free, because it is performed on idle nodes/cores after monthly climatologies have been computed and while seasonal climatologies are being computed. This load-balancing can save half-an-hour on ne120 datasets. To regrid, simply pass the desired mapfile name with '`-r map.nc`', e.g., '`-r maps/map_ne120np4_to_fv257x512_aave.20150901.nc`'. Although this should not be necessary for normal use, you may pass any options specific to regridding with '`-R opt1 opt2`'.

Specifying '`-O` *`drc_rgr`*' (NB: uppercase '`O`') causes `ncclimo` to place the regridded files in the directory *drc_rgr*. These files have the same names as the native grid climos from which they were derived. There is no namespace conflict because they are in separate directories. These files also have symbolic links to their AMWG filenames. If '`-O` *`drc_rgr`*' is not specified, `ncclimo` places all regridded files in the native grid climo output directory, *drc_out*, specified by '`-o` *`drc_out`*' (NB: lowercase '`o`'). To avoid namespace conflicts when both climos are stored in the same directory, the names of regridded files are suffixed by the destination geometry string obtained from the mapfile, e.g., `*_climo_fv257x512_bilin.nc`. These files also have symbolic links to their AMWG filenames.

```
ncclimo -c amip_xpt -s 1980 -e 1983 -i drc_in -o drc_out
ncclimo -c amip_xpt -s 1980 -e 1983 -i drc_in -o drc_out -r map_fl
ncclimo -c amip_xpt -s 1980 -e 1983 -i drc_in -o drc_out -r map_fl -O drc_rgr
```

The above commands perform a climatology without regridding, then with regridding (all climos stored in *drc_out*), then with regridding and storing regridded files separately. Paths specified by *drc_in*, *drc_out*, and *drc_rgr* may be relative or absolute. An alternative to regridding during climatology generation is to regrid afterwards with `ncremap`, which has more special features built-in for regridding. To use `ncremap` to regrid a climatology in *drc_out* and place the results in *drc_rgr*, use something like

```
ncremap -I drc_out -m map.nc -O drc_rgr
ls drc_out/*climo* | ncremap -m map.nc -O drc_rgr
```

See Section 4.12 [ncremap netCDF Remapper], page 267, for more details (including MPAS!).

## Extended Climatologies

`ncclimo` supports two methods for generating extended climatologies: Binary and Incremental. Both methods lengthen a climatology without requiring access to all the raw monthly data spanning the time period. The binary method combines, with appropriate weighting, two previously computed climatologies into a single climatology. No raw monthly data are employed. The incremental method computes a climatology from raw monthly data and (with appropriate weighting) combines that with a previously computed climatology that ends the month prior to raw data. The incremental method was introduced in NCO version

4.6.1 (released August, 2016), and the binary method was introduced in NCO version 4.6.3 (released December, 2016).

Both methods, binary and incremental, compute the so-called "extended climo" as a weighted mean of two shorter climatologies, called the "previous" and "current" climos. The incremental method uses the original monthly input to compute the curent climo, which must immediately follow in time the previous climo which has been pre-computed. The binary method use pre-computed climos for both the previous and current climos, and these climos need not be sequential nor chronological. Both previous and current climos for both binary and incremental methods may be of any length (in years); their weights will be automatically adjusted in computing the extended climo.

The use of pre-computed climos permits ongoing simulations (or lengthy observations) to be analyzed in shorter segments combined piecemeal, instead of requiring all raw, native-grid data to be simultaneously accessible. Without extended climatology capability, generating a one-hundred year climatology requires that one-hundred years of monthly data be available on disk. Disk-space requirements for large datasets may make this untenable. Extended climo methods permits a one-hundred year climo to be generated as the weighted mean of, say, the current ten year climatology (weighted at 10%) combined with the pre-computed climatology of the previous 90-years (weighted at 90%). The 90-year climo could itself have been generated incrementally or binary-wise, and so on. Climatologies occupy at most $17/(12N)$ the amount of space of $N$ years of monthly data, so the extended methods vastly reduce disk-space requirements.

Incremental mode is selected by specifying '`-S`', the start year of the pre-computed, previous climo. The argument to '`-S`') is the previous climo start year. That, together with the current climo end year, determines the extended climo range. `ncclimo` assumes that the previous climo ends the month before the current climo begins. In incremental mode, `ncclimo` first generates the current climatology from the current monthly input files then weights that current climo with the previous climo to produce the extended climo.

Binary mode is selected by specifying both '`-S`' and '`-E`', the end year of the pre-computed, previous climo. In binary mode, the previous and current climatologies can be of any length, and from any time-period, even overlapping. Most users will run extended clmos the same way they run regular climos in terms of parallelism and regridding, although that is not required. Both climos must treat Decembers same way (or else previous climo files will not be found), and if subsetting (i.e., '`-v var_lst`') is performed, then the subset must remain the same, and if nicknames (i.e., '`-f fml_nm`') are employed, then the nickname must remain the same.

As of 20161129, the `climatology_bounds` attributes of extended climo are incorrect. This is a work in progress...

Options:

`-E` *yr_end_prv* `(--yr_end_prv, --prv_yr_end, --previous_end)`
: The ending year of the previous climo. This argument is required to trigger binary climatologies, and should not be used for incremental climatologies.

`-S` *yr_srt_prv* `(--yr_srt_prv, --prv_yr_srt, --previous_start)`
: The starting year of the previous climo. This argument is required to trigger incremental climatologies, and is also mandatory for binary climatologies.

`-X` *drc_xtn* `(--drc_xtn, --xtn_drc, --extended)`
: Directory in which the extended native grid climo files will be stored for an extended climatology. Default value is *drc_prv*. Unless a separate directory is specified (with '`-Y`') for the extended climo on the analysis grid, it will be stored in *drc_xtn*, too.

`-x` *drc_prv* `(--drc_prv, --prv_drc, --previous)`
: Directory in which the previous native grid climo files reside for an incremental climatology. Default value is *drc_out*. Unless a separate directory is specified (with '`-y`') for the previous climo on the analysis grid, it is assumed to reside in *drc_prv*, too.

`-Y` *drc_rgr_xtn* `(--drc_rgr_xtn, --drc_xtn_rgr, --extended_regridded, --regridded_extended)`
: Directory in which the extended analysis grid climo files will be stored in an incremental climatology. Default value is *drc_xtn*.

`-y` *drc_rgr_prv* `(--drc_rgr_prv, --drc_prv_rgr, --regridded_previous, --previous_regridded)`
: Directory in which the previous climo on the analysis grid resides in an incremental climatology. Default value is *drc_prv*.

Incremental method climatologies can be as simple as providing a start year for the previous climo, e.g.,

```
ncclimo -v FSNT,AODVIS -c caseid -s 1980 -e 1981 -i raw -o clm -
r map.nc
ncclimo -v FSNT,AODVIS -c caseid -s 1982 -e 1983 -i raw -o clm -
r map.nc -S 1980
```

By default `ncclimo` stores all native and analysis grid climos in one directory so the above "just works". There are no namespace clashes because all climos are for distinct years, and regridded files have a suffix based on their grid resolution. However, there can be only one set of AMWG filename links due to AMWG filename convention. Thus AMWG filename links, if any, point to the latest extended climo in a given directory.

Many researchers segregate (with '`-O` ***drc_rgr***') native-grid from analysis-grid climos. Incrementally generated climos must be consistent in this regard. In other words, all climos contributing to an extended climo must have their native-grid and analysis-grid files in the same (per-climo) directory, or all climos must segregate their native from their analysis grid files. Do not segregate the grids in one climo, and combine them in another. Such climos cannot be incrementally aggregated. Thus incrementing climos can require from zero to four additional options that specify all the previous and extended climatologies for both native and analysis grids. The example below constructs the current climo in *crr*, then combines the weighted average of that with the previous climo in *prv*, and places the resulting extended climatology in *xtn*. Here the native and analysis climos are combined in one directory per climo:

```
ncclimo -v FSNT,AODVIS -c caseid -s 1980 -e 1981 -i raw -o prv -r map.nc
ncclimo -v FSNT,AODVIS -c caseid -s 1982 -e 1983 -i raw -o clm -r map.nc \
        -S 1980 -x prv -X xtn
```

If the native and analysis grid climo directories are segregated, then those directories must be specified, too:

```
ncclimo -v FSNT,AODVIS -c caseid -s 1980 -e 1981 -i raw -o prv -O rgr_prv -r map.nc
ncclimo -v FSNT,AODVIS -c caseid -s 1982 -e 1983 -i raw -o clm -O rgr -r map.nc \
        -S 1980 -x prv -X xtn -y rgr_prv -Y rgr_xtn
```

`ncclimo` does not know whether a pre-computed climo is on a native grid or an analysis grid, i.e., whether it has been regridded. In binary mode, `ncclimo` may be pointed to two pre-computed native grid climatologies, or to two pre-computed analysis grid climatologies. In other words, it is not necessary to maintain native grid climatologies for use in creating extended climatologies. It is sufficient to generate climatologies on the analysis grid, and feed them to `ncclimo` in binary mode, without a mapping file:

```
ncclimo -c caseid -S 1980 -E 1981 -x prv -s 1980 -e 1981 -i crr -o clm
```

## Coupled Runs

`ncclimo` works on all ACME and CESM models. It can simultaneously generate climatologies for a coupled run, where climatologies mean both native and regridded monthly, seasonal, and annual averages as per ACME specifications (which mandate the inclusion of certain helpful metadata and provenance information). Here are template commands for a recent simulation:

```
caseid=20160121.A_B2000ATMMOD.ne30_oEC.titan.a00
drc_in=/scratch/simulations/$caseid/run
drc_out=${DATA}/acme
map_atm=${DATA}/maps/map_ne30np4_to_fv129x256_aave.20150901.nc
map_lnd=$map_atm
map_ocn=${DATA}/maps/map_oEC60to30_to_t62_bilin.20160301.nc
map_ice=$map_ocn
ncclimo -p mpi -c $caseid -m cam  -s 2 -e 5 -i $drc_in -r $map_atm -o $drc_out/atm
ncclimo        -c $caseid -m clm2 -s 2 -e 5 -i $drc_in -r $map_lnd -o $drc_out/lnd
ncclimo -p mpi -m mpaso           -s 2 -e 5 -i $drc_in -r $map_ocn -o $drc_out/ocn
ncclimo        -m mpascice        -s 2 -e 5 -i $drc_in -r $map_ice -o $drc_out/ice
```

Atmosphere and ocean model output is typically larger than land and ice model output. These commands recognize that by using different parallelization strategies that may (`rhea` standard queue) or may not (`cooley`, or `rhea`'s `bigmem` queue) be required, depending on the fatness of the analysis nodes, as explained below.

## Memory Considerations

It is important to employ the optimal `ncclimo` parallelization strategy for your computer hardware resources. Select from the three available choices with the `-p` *`par_typ`* switch. The options are serial mode ('`-p nil`' or '`-p serial`'), background mode parallelism ('`-p bck`'), and MPI parallelism '`-p mpi`'. The default is background-mode parallelism. This is appropriate for lower resolution (e.g., ne30L30) simulations on most nodes at high-performance computer centers. Use (or at least start with) serial mode on personal laptops/workstations. Serial mode requires twelve times less RAM than the parallel modes, and is much less likely to deadlock or cause OOM (out-of-memory) conditions on your personal computer. If the available RAM (plus swap) is $< 12 * 4*$`sizeof(monthly input file)`, then try serial mode first (12 is the optimal number of parallel processes for monthly climos, the computational overhead is a factor of four). CAM-SE ne30L30 output is about 1 GB/month so each month requires about 4 GB of RAM. CAM-SE ne30L72 output (with LINOZ) is about 10 GB/month so each month requires about 40 GB RAM. CAM-SE ne120 output is about 12 GB/month so each month requires about 48 GB RAM. The computer does not actually use all this memory at one time, and many kernels compress RAM usage to below what top reports, so the actual physical usage is hard to pin-down, but may be a factor of 2.5–3.0 (rather than a factor of four) times the size of the input file. For instance, my 16 GB 2014 MacBookPro successfully runs an ne30L30 climatology (that requests 48 GB RAM) in background mode. However the laptop is slow and unresponsive for other uses until it finishes (in 6–8 minutes) the climos. Experiment and choose the parallelization option that performs best.

Serial-mode, as its name implies, uses one core at a time for climos, and proceeds sequentially from months to seasons to annual climatologies. Serial mode means that climos are performed serially, while regridding still employs OpenMP threading (up to 16 cores) on platforms that support it. By design each month and each season is independent of the others, so all months can be computed in parallel, then each season can be computed in parallel (using monthly climatologies), from which annual average is computed. Background parallelization mode exploits this parallelism and executes the climos in parallel as background processes on a single node, so that twelve cores are simultaneously employed for monthly climatologies, four for seasonal, and one for annual. The optional regridding will employ, by default, up to two cores per process. The MPI parallelism mode executes the climatologies on different nodes so that up to (optimally) twelve nodes compute monthly climos. The full memory of each node is available for each individual climo. The optional regridding employs, by default, up to eight cores per node in MPI-mode. MPI-mode or serial-mode must be used to process ne30L72 and ne120L30 climos on all but the fattest DOE nodes. An ne120L30 climo in background mode on `rhea` (i.e., on one 128 GB compute node) fails due to OOM. (Unfortunately OOM errors do not produce useful return codes so if your climo processes die without printing useful information, the cause may be OOM). However the same climo in background-mode succeeds when executed on a single big-memory (1 TB) node on `rhea` (use '`-lpartition=gpu`', as shown below). Or MPI-mode can be used for any climatology. The same ne120L30 climo will also finish blazingly fast in background mode on `cooley` (i.e., on one 384 GB compute node), so MPI-mode is unnecessary on `cooley`. In general, the fatter the memory, the better the performance.

## Single, Dedicated Nodes at LCFs

The basic approach above (running the script from a standard terminal window) that works well for small cases can be unpleasantly slow on login nodes of LCFs and for longer or higher resolution (e.g., ne120) climatologies. As a baseline, generating a climatology of 5 years of ne30 (~1x1 degree) CAM-SE output with `ncclimo` takes 1–2 minutes on `rhea` (at a time with little contention), and 6–8 minutes on a 2014 MacBook Pro. To make things a bit faster at LCFs, request a dedicated node (this only makes sense on supercomputers or clusters with job-schedulers). On `rhea` or `titan`, which use the PBS scheduler, do this with

```
# Standard node (128 GB), PBS scheduler
qsub -I -A CLI115 -V -l nodes=1 -l walltime=00:10:00 -N ncclimo
# Bigmem node (1 TB), PBS scheduler
qsub -I -A CLI115 -V -l nodes=1 -l walltime=00:10:00 -lpartition=gpu -N ncclimo
```

The equivalent requests on `cooley` or `mira` (Cobalt scheduler) and `cori` or `titan` (SLURM scheduler) are:

```
# Cooley node (384 GB) with Cobalt
qsub -I -A HiRes_EarthSys --nodecount=1 --time=00:10:00 --jobname=ncclimo
# Cori node (128 GB) with SLURM
salloc  -A acme --nodes=1 --partition=debug --time=00:10:00 --job-name=ncclimo
```

Flags used and their meanings:

`-I` Submit in interactive mode. This returns a new terminal shell rather than running a program.

`--time` How long to keep this dedicated node for. Unless you kill the shell created by the `qsub` command, the shell will exist for this amount of time, then die suddenly. In the above examples, 10 minutes is requested.

`-l nodes=1`
PBS syntax (e.g., on `rhea`) for nodes.

`--nodecount 1`
Cobalt syntax (e.g., on `cooley`) for nodes.

`--nodes=1`
SLURM syntax (e.g., on `cori` or `edison`) for nodes. These scheduler-dependent variations request a quantity of nodes. Request 1 node for Serial or Background-mode, and up to 12 nodes for MPI-mode parallelism. In all cases `ncclimo` will use multiple cores per node if available.

`-V` Export existing environmental variables into the new interactive shell. This may not actually be needed.

`-q name` Queue name. This is needed for locations like `edison` that have multiple queues with no default queue.

`-A` Name of account to charge for time used.

Acquiring a dedicated node is useful for any workflow, not just creating climos. This command returns a prompt once nodes are assigned (the prompt is returned in your home directory so you may then have to `cd` to the location you meant to run from). Then run your code with the basic `ncclimo` invocation. The is faster because the node is exclusively dedicated to `ncclimo`. Again, ne30L30 climos only require < 2 minutes, so the 10 minutes requested in the example is excessive and conservative. Tune it with experience.

## 12 node MPI-mode Jobs

The above parallel approaches will fail when a single node lacks enough RAM (plus swap) to store all twelve monthly input files, plus extra RAM for computations. One should employ MPI multinode parallelism '`-p mpi`' on nodes with less RAM than $12 * 3*$`sizeof`(input).

The longest an ne120 climo will take is less than half an hour (~25 minutes on **edison** or **rhea**), so the simplest method to run MPI jobs is to request 12-interactive nodes using the above commands (though remember to add '`-p mpi`'), then execute the script at the command line.

It is also possible, and sometimes preferable, to request non-interactive compute nodes in a batch queue. Executing an MPI-mode climo (on machines with job scheduling and, optimally, 12 nodes) in a batch queue can be done in two commands. First, write an executable file which calls the `ncclimo` script with appropriate arguments. We do this below by echoing to a file, `ncclimo.pbs`.

```
echo "ncclimo -p mpi -c $caseid -s 1 -e 20 -i $drc_in -o $drc_out" > ncclimo.pbs
```

The only new argument here is '`-p mpi`' that tells `ncclimo` to use MPI parallelism. Then execute this command file with a 12 node non-interactive job:

```
qsub -A CLI115 -V -l nodes=12 -l walltime=00:30:00 -j oe -m e -N ncclimo \
     -o ncclimo.out ncclimo.pbs
```

This script adds new flags: '`-j oe`' (combine output and error streams into standard error), '`-m e`' (send email to the job submitter when the job ends), '`-o ncclimo.out`' (write all output to `ncclimo.out`). The above commands are meant for PBS schedulers like on `rhea`. Equivalent commands for `cooley/mira` (Cobalt) and `cori/edison` (SLURM) are

```
# Cooley (Cobalt scheduler)
/bin/rm -f ncclimo.err ncclimo.out
echo '#!/bin/bash' > ncclimo.cobalt
echo "ncclimo -p mpi -c $caseid -s 1 -e 20 -i $drc_in -o $drc_out" >> ncclimo.cob
chmod a+x ncclimo.cobalt
qsub -A HiRes_EarthSys --nodecount=12 --time=00:30:00 --jobname ncclimo \
     --error ncclimo.err --output ncclimo.out --notify zender@uci.edu ncclimo.cob

# Cori/Edison (SLURM scheduler)
echo "ncclimo -p mpi -c $caseid -s 1 -e 20 -i $drc_in -o $drc_out -r $map_fl" \
      > ncclimo.pbs
chmod a+x ncclimo.slurm
sbatch -A acme --nodes=12 --time=03:00:00 --partition=regular --job-name=ncclimo
       --mail-type=END --error=ncclimo.err --output=ncclimo.out ncclimo.slurm
```

Notice that Cobalt and SLURM require the introductory shebang-interpreter line (`#!/bin/bash`) which PBS does not need. Set only the scheduler batch queue parameters mentioned above. In MPI-mode, `ncclimo` determines the appropriate number of tasks-per-node based on the number of nodes available and script internals (like load-balancing for regridding). Hence do not set a tasks-per-node parameter with scheduler configuration parameters as this could cause conflicts.

## What does `ncclimo` do?

For monthly climatologies (e.g., JAN), `ncclimo` passes the list of all relevant January monthly files to NCO's `ncra` command, which averages each variable in these monthly files over their time-dimension (if it exists) or copies the value from the first month unchanged (if no time-axis exists). Seasonal climos are then created by taking the average of the monthly climo files using `ncra`. To account for differing numbers of days per month, the `ncra` '`-w`' flag is used, followed by the number of days in the relevant months. For example, the MAM climo is computed with '`ncra -w 31,30,31 MAR_climo.nc APR_climo.nc MAY_climo.nc MAM_climo.nc`' (details about file names and other optimization flags have been stripped here to make the concept easier to follow). The annual (ANN) climo is then computed as a weighted average of the seasonal climos.

## Assumptions, Approximations, and Algorithms (AAA) Employed:

A climatology embodies many algorithmic choices, and regridding from the native to the analysis grid involves still more choices. A separate method should reproduce the `ncclimo` and NCO answers to round-off precision if it implements the same algorithmic choices. For example, `ncclimo` agrees to round-off with AMWG diagnostics when making the same (sometimes questionable) choices. The most important choices have to do with converting single- to double-precision (SP and DP, respectively), treatment of missing values, and generation/application of regridding weights. For concreteness and clarity we describe the algorithmic choices made in processing a CAM-SE monthly output into a climatological annual mean (ANN) and then regridding that. Other climatologies (e.g., daily to monthly, or annual-to-climatological) involve similar choices.

ACME (and CESM) computes fields in DP and outputs history (not restart) files as monthly means in SP. The NCO climatology generator (`ncclimo`) processes these data in four stages. Stage $N$ accesses input only from stage $N-1$, never from stage $N-2$ or earlier. Thus the (on-disk) files from stage $N$ determine the highest precision achievable by stage $N+1$. The general principal is to perform math (addition, weighting, normalization) in DP and output results to disk in the same precision in which they were input from disk (usually SP). In Stage 1, NCO ingests Stage 0 monthly means (raw CAM-SE output), converts SP input to DP, performs the average across all years, then converts the answer from DP to SP for storage on-disk as the climatological monthly mean. In Stage 2, NCO ingests Stage 1 climatological monthly means, converts SP input to DP, performs the average across all months in the season (e.g., DJF), then converts the answer from DP to SP for storage on-disk as the climatological seasonal mean. In Stage 3, NCO ingests Stage 2 climatological seasonal means, converts SP input to DP, performs the average across all four seasons (DJF, MAM, JJA, SON), then converts the answer from DP to SP for storage on-disk as the climatological annual mean.

Stage 2 weights each input month by its number of days (e.g., 31 for January), and Stage 3 weights each input season by its number of days (e.g., 92 for MAM). ACME runs CAM-SE with a 365-day calendar, so these weights are independent of year and never change. The treatment of missing values in Stages 1–3 is limited by the lack of missing value tallies provided by Stage 0 (model) output. Stage 0 records a value as missing if it is missing for the entire month, and present if the value is valid for one or more timesteps. Stage 0 does not record the missing value tally (number of valid timesteps) for each spatial point. Thus a point with a single valid timestep during a month is weighted the same in Stages 1–4 as a point with 100% valid timesteps during the month. The absence of tallies inexorably degrades the accuracy of subsequent statistics by an amount that varies in time and space. On the positive side, it reduces the output size (by a factor of two) and complexity of analyzing fields that contain missing values. Due to the ambiguous nature of missing values, it is debatable whether they merit efforts to treat them more exactly.

The vast majority of fields undergo three promotion/demotion cycles between CAM-SE and ANN. No promotion/demotion cycles occur for history fields that CAM-SE outputs in DP rather than SP, nor for fields without a time dimension. Typically these fields are grid coordinates (e.g., longitude, latitude) or model constants (e.g., $CO_2$ mixing ratio). NCO never performs any arithmetic on grid coordinates or non-time-varying input, regardless of whether they are SP or DP. Instead, NCO copies these fields directly from the first input file. Stage 4 uses a mapfile to regrid climos from the native to the desired analysis grid. ACME currently uses mapfiles generated by `ESMF_RegridWeightGen` (ERWG) and by TempestRemap.

The algorithmic choices, approximations, and commands used to generate mapfiles from input gridfiles are separate issues. We mention only some of these issues here for brevity. Input gridfiles used by ACME until ~20150901, and by CESM (then and currently, at least for Gaussian grids) contained flaws that effectively reduced their precision, especially at regional scales, and especially for Gaussian grids. ACME (and CESM) mapfiles continue to approximate grids as connected by great circles, whereas most analysis grids (and some models) use great circles for longitude and small circles for latitude. The great circle assumption may be removed in the future. Constraints imposed by ERWG during weight-generation ensure that global integrals of fields undergoing conservative regridding are exactly conserved.

Application of weights from the mapfile to regrid the native data to the analysis grid is straightforward. Grid fields (e.g., latitude, longitude, area) are not regridded. Instead they are copied (and area is reconstructed if absent) directly from the mapfile. NCO ingests all other native grid (source) fields, converts SP to DP, and accumulates destination gridcell values as the sum of the DP weight (from the sparse matrix in the mapfile) times the (usually SP-promoted-to-DP) source values. Fields without missing values are then stored to disk in their original precision. Fields with missing values are treated (by default) with what NCO calls the "conservative" algorithm. This algorithm uses all valid data from the source grid on the destination grid once and only once. Destination cells receive the weighted valid values of the source cells. This is conservative because the global integrals of the source and destination fields are equal. See Section 4.12 [ncremap netCDF Remapper], page 267, for more description of the conservative and of the optional ("renormalized") algorithm.

EXAMPLES

How to create a climo from a collection of monthly non-CESM'ish files? This is a two-step procedure: First be sure the names are arranged with a YYYYMM-format date preceding the suffix (usually '`.nc`'). Then give *any* monthly input filename to `ncclimo`. Consider the MERRA2 collection, for example. As retrieved from NASA, MERRA2 files have names like `svc_MERRA2_300.tavgM_2d_aer_Nx.200903.nc4`. While the sub-string '200903' is easy to recognize as a month in YYYYMM format, other parts (specifically the '300' code) of the filename also change with date. We can use Bash regular expressions to extract dates and create symbolic links to simpler filenames with regularly patterned YYYYMM strings like `merra2_200903.nc4`:

```
for fl in 'ls *.nc4' ; do
# Convert svc_MERRA2_300.tavgM_2d_aer_Nx.YYYYMM.nc4 to merra2_YYYYMM.nc4
```

```
        sfx_out=`expr match "${fl}" '.*_Nx.\(.*.nc4\)'`
        fl_out="merra2_${sfx_out}"
        ln -s ${fl} ${fl_out}
    done
```

Then call `ncclimo` with `merra2_200903.nc4` as *caseid*:

```
ncclimo -c merra2_200903.nc4 -s 1980 -e 2016 -i $drc_in -o $drc_out
```

Often one wishes to create a climatology of a single variable. The '`-f` *fml_nm*' option to `ncclimo` makes this easy. Consider a series of single-variable climos for the fields `FSNT`, and `FLNT`

```
ncclimo -v FSNT -f FSNT -c amip_xpt -s 1980 -e 1983 -i drc_in -o drc_out
ncclimo -v FLNT -f FLNT -c amip_xpt -s 1980 -e 1983 -i drc_in -o drc_out
```

These climos use the '`-f`' option and so there output files will have no namespace conflicts. Moreover, the climatologies can be generated in parallel.

## 4.5 ncecat netCDF Ensemble Concatenator

SYNTAX

```
ncecat [-3] [-4] [-6] [-7] [-A] [-C] [-c]
[--cnk_byt sz_byt] [--cnk_dmn nm,sz_lmn] [--cnk_map map]
[--cnk_min sz_byt] [--cnk_plc plc] [--cnk_scl sz_lmn]
[-D dbg] [-d dim,[min][,[max][,[stride]]] [-F]
[-G gpe_dsc] [-g grp[,...]] [--gag] [--glb ...] [-h] [--hdf] [--hdr_pad nbr]
[-L dfl_lvl] [-l path] [-M] [--md5_digest] [--mrd] [-n loop]
[--no_cll_msr] [--no_frm_trm] [--no_tmp_fl]
[-O] [-o output-file] [-p path] [--ppc ...] [-R] [-r] [--ram_all]
[-t thr_nbr] [-u ulm_nm] [--unn] [-v var[,...]] [-X ...] [-x]
[input-files] [output-file]
```

DESCRIPTION

`ncecat` aggregates an arbitrary number of input files into a single output file using using one of two methods. *Record AGgregation* (RAG), the traditional method employed on (flat) netCDF3 files and still the default method, stores *input-files* as consecutive records in the *output-file*. *Group AGgregation* (GAG) stores *input-files* as top-level groups in the netCDF4 *output-file*. Record Aggregation (RAG) makes numerous assumptions about the structure of input files whereas Group Aggregation (GAG) makes none. Both methods are described in detail below. Since `ncecat` aggregates all the contents of the input files, it can easily produce large output files so it is often helpful to invoke subsetting simultaneously (see Section 3.11 [Subsetting Files], page 46).

RAG makes each variable (except coordinate variables) in each input file into a single record of the same variable in the output file. Coordinate variables are not concatenated, they are instead simply copied from the first input file to the *output-file*. All *input-files* must contain all extracted variables (or else there would be "gaps" in the output file).

A new record dimension is the glue which binds together the input file data. The new record dimension is defined in the root group of the output file so it is visible to all subgroups. Its name is, by default, "record". This default name can be overridden with the '`-u ulm_nm`' short option (or the '`--ulm_nm`' or '`rcd_nm`' long options).

Each extracted variable must be constant in size and rank across all *input-files*. The only exception is that `ncecat` allows files to differ in the record dimension size if the requested record hyperslab (see Section 3.15 [Hyperslabs], page 62) resolves to the same size for all files. This allows easier gluing/averaging of unequal length timeseries from simulation ensembles (e.g., the CMIP rchive).

Classic (i.e., all netCDF3 and `NETCDF4_CLASSIC`) output files can contain only one record dimension. `ncecat` makes room for the new glue record dimension by changing the pre-existing record dimension, if any, in the input files into a fixed dimension in the output file. netCDF4 output files may contain any number of record dimensions, so `ncecat` need not and does not alter the record dimensions, if any, of the input files as it copies them to the output file.

*Group AGgregation* (GAG) stores *input-files* as top-level groups in the *output-file*. No assumption is made about the size or shape or type of a given object (variable or dimension or group) in the input file. The entire contents of the extracted portion of each input file is placed in its own top-level group in *output-file*, which is automatically made as a netCDF4-format file.

GAG has two methods to specify group names for the *output-file*. The '-G' option, or its long-option equivalent '--gpe', takes as argument a group path editing description *gpe_dsc* of where to place the results. Each input file needs a distinct output group name to avoid namespace conflicts in the *output-file*. Hence ncecat automatically creates unique output group names based on either the input filenames or the *gpe_dsc* arguments. When the user provides *gpe_dsc* (i.e., with '-G'), then the output groups are formed by enumerating sequential two-digit numeric suffixes starting with zero, and appending them to the specified group path (see Section 3.13 [Group Path Editing], page 52). When *gpe_dsc* is not provided (i.e., user requests GAG with '--gag' instead of '-G'), then ncecat forms the output groups by stripping the input file name of any type-suffix (e.g., .nc), and all but the final component of the full filename.

```
ncecat --gag 85.nc 86.nc 87.nc 8587.nc # Output groups 85, 86, 87
ncecat -G 85_ a.nc b.nc c.nc 8589.nc # Output groups 85_00, 85_01, 85_02
ncecat -G 85/ a.nc b.nc c.nc 8589.nc # Output groups 85/00, 85/01, 85/02
```

With both RAG and GAG the *output-file* size is the sum of the sizes of the extracted variables in the input files. See Section 2.6 [Statistics vs. Concatenation], page 20, for a description of the distinctions between the various statistics tools and concatenators. As a multi-file operator, ncecat will read the list of *input-files* from stdin if they are not specified as positional arguments on the command line (see Section 2.7 [Large Numbers of Files], page 21).

Suppress global metadata copying. By default NCO's multi-file operators copy the global metadata from the first input file into *output-file*. This helps to preserve the provenance of the output data. However, the use of metadata is burgeoning and sometimes one encounters files with excessive amounts of extraneous metadata. Extracting small bits of data from such files leads to output files which are much larger than necessary due to the automatically copied metadata. ncecat supports turning off the default copying of global metadata via the '-M' switch (or its long option equivalents, '--no_glb_mtd' and '--suppress_global_metadata').

Consider five realizations, 85a.nc, 85b.nc, ... 85e.nc of 1985 predictions from the same climate model. Then ncecat 85?.nc 85_ens.nc glues together the individual realizations into the single file, 85_ens.nc. If an input variable was dimensioned [lat,lon], it will by default have dimensions [record,lat,lon] in the output file. A restriction of ncecat is that the hyperslabs of the processed variables must be the same from file to file. Normally this means all the input files are the same size, and contain data on different realizations of the same variables.

Concatenating a variable packed with different scales across multiple datasets is beyond the capabilities of ncecat (and ncrcat, the other concatenator (Section 2.6.1 [Concatenation], page 20). ncecat does not unpack data, it simply *copies* the data from the *input-files*, and the metadata from the *first input-file*, to the *output-file*. This means that data compressed with a packing convention must use the identical packing parameters (e.g., `scale_factor` and `add_offset`) for a given variable across *all* input files. Otherwise the concatenated dataset will not unpack correctly. The workaround for cases where the packing parameters differ across *input-files* requires three steps: First, unpack the data using `ncpdq`. Second, concatenate the unpacked data using `ncecat`, Third, re-pack the result with `ncpdq`.

EXAMPLES

Consider a model experiment which generated five realizations of one year of data, say 1985. You can imagine that the experimenter slightly perturbs the initial conditions of the problem before generating each new solution. Assume each file contains all twelve months (a seasonal cycle) of data and we want to produce a single file containing all the seasonal cycles. Here the numeric filename suffix denotes the experiment number (*not* the month):

```
ncecat 85_01.nc 85_02.nc 85_03.nc 85_04.nc 85_05.nc 85.nc
ncecat 85_0[1-5].nc 85.nc
ncecat -n 5,2,1 85_01.nc 85.nc
```

These three commands produce identical answers. See Section 3.5 [Specifying Input Files], page 33, for an explanation of the distinctions between these methods. The output file, `85.nc`, is five times the size as a single *input-file*. It contains 60 months of data.

One often prefers that the (new) record dimension have a more descriptive, context-based name than simply "record". This is easily accomplished with the '`-u` *ulm_nm*' switch. To add a new record dimension named "time" to all variables

```
ncecat -u time in.nc out.nc
```

To glue together multiple files with a new record variable named "reaalization"

```
ncecat -u realization 85_0[1-5].nc 85.nc
```

Users are more likely to understand the data processing history when such descriptive coordinates are used.

Consider a file with an existing record dimension named `time`. and suppose the user wishes to convert `time` from a record dimension to a non-record dimension. This may be useful, for example, when the user has another use for the record variable. The simplest method is to use '`ncks --fix_rec_dmn`' but another possibility is to use `ncecat` followed by `ncwa`:

```
ncecat in.nc out.nc # Convert time to non-record dimension
ncwa -a record in.nc out.nc # Remove new degenerate record dimension
```

The second step removes the degenerate record dimension. See Section 4.9 [ncpdq netCDF Permute Dimensions Quickly], page 254, and Section 4.8 [ncks netCDF Kitchen Sink], page 237, for other methods of of changing variable dimensionality, including the record dimension.

## 4.6 nces netCDF Ensemble Statistics

SYNTAX

```
nces [-3] [-4] [-6] [-7] [-A] [-C] [-c]
[--cnk_byt sz_byt] [--cnk_dmn nm,sz_lmn] [--cnk_map map]
[--cnk_min sz_byt] [--cnk_plc plc] [--cnk_scl sz_lmn]
[-D dbg] [-d dim,[min][,[max][,[stride]]] [-F]
[-G gpe_dsc] [-g grp[,...]] [--glb ...] [-h] [--hdf] [--hdr_pad nbr]
[-L dfl_lvl] [-l path] [-n loop]
[--no_cll_msr] [--no_frm_trm] [--no_tmp_fl] [--nsm_fl|grp] [--nsm_sfx sfx]
[-O] [-o output-
file] [-p path] [--ppc ...] [-R] [-r] [--ram_all] [--rth_dbl|flt]
[-t thr_nbr] [--unn] [-v var[,...]] [-X ...] [-x] [-y op_typ]
[input-files] [output-file]
```

DESCRIPTION

`nces` performs gridpoint statistics (including, but not limited to, averages) on variables across an arbitrary number (an *ensemble*) of *input-files* and/or of input groups within each file. Each file (or group) receives an equal weight. `nces` was formerly (until NCO version 4.3.9, released December, 2013) known as `ncea` (netCDF Ensemble Averager)[1]. For example, `nces` will average a set of files or groups, weighting each file or group evenly. This is distinct from `ncra`, which performs statistics only over the record dimension(s) (e.g., *time*), and weights each record in each record dimension evenly.

The file or group is the logical unit of organization for the results of many scientific studies. Often one wishes to generate a file or group which is the statistical product (e.g., average) of many separate files or groups. This may be to reduce statistical noise by combining the results of a large number of experiments, or it may simply be a step in a procedure whose goal is to compute anomalies from a mean state. In any case, when one desires to generate a file whose statistical properties are equally influenced by all the inputs, then `nces` is the operator to use.

Variables in the *output-file* are the same size as the variable hyperslab in each input file or group, and each input file or group must be the same size after hyperslabbing[2] `nces` does allow files to differ in the record dimension size if the requested record hyperslab (see Section 3.15 [Hyperslabs], page 62) resolves to the same size for all files. `nces` recomputes the record dimension hyperslab limits for each input file so that coordinate limits may be used to select equal length timeseries from unequal length files. This simplifies analysis of unequal length timeseries from simulation ensembles (e.g., the CMIP3 IPCC AR4 archive).

---

[1] The old ncea command was deprecated in NCO version 4.3.9, released December, 2013. NCO will attempt to maintain back-compatibility and work as expected with invocations of `ncea` for as long as possible. Please replace `ncea` by `nces` in all future work.

[2] As of NCO version 4.4.2 (released February, 2014) `nces` allows hyperslabs in all dimensions so long as the hyperslabs resolve to the same size. The fixed (i.e., non-record) dimensions should be the same size in all ensemble members both before and after hyperslabbing, although the hyperslabs may (and usually do) change the size of the dimensions from the input to the output files. Prior to this, `nces` was only guaranteed to work on hyperslabs in the record dimension that resolved to the same size.

`nces` works in one of two modes, file ensembles or group ensembles. File ensembles are the default (equivalent to the old `ncea`) and may also be explicitly specified by the '`--nsm_fl`' or '`--ensemble_file`' switches. To perform statistics on ensembles of groups, a newer feature, use '`--nsm_grp`' or '`--ensemble_group`'. Members of a group ensemble are groups that share the same structure, parent group, and nesting level. Members must be *leaf groups*, i.e., not contain any sub-groups. Their contents usually have different values because they are realizations of replicated experiments. In group ensemble mode `nces` computes the statistics across the ensemble, which may span multiple input files. Files may contain members of multiple, distinct ensembles. However, all ensembles must have at least one member in the first input file. Group ensembles behave as an unlimited dimension of datasets: they may contain an arbitrary and extensible number of realizations in each file, and may be composed from multiple files.

Output statistics in group ensemble mode are stored in the parent group by default. If the ensemble members are `/cesm/cesm_01` and `/cesm/cesm_02`, then the computed statistic will be in `/cesm` in the output file. The '`--nsm_sfx`' option instructs nces to instead store output in a new child group of the parent created by attaching the suffix to the parent group's name, e.g., '`--nsm_sfx='_avg'`' would store results in the output group `/cesm/cesm_avg`:

```
nces --nsm_grp                    mdl1.nc mdl2.nc mdl3.nc out.nc
nces --nsm_grp --nsm_sfx='_avg'   mdl1.nc mdl2.nc mdl3.nc out.nc
```

See Section 2.6 [Statistics vs. Concatenation], page 20, for a description of the distinctions between the statistics tools and concatenators. As a multi-file operator, `nces` will read the list of *input-files* from `stdin` if they are not specified as positional arguments on the command line (see Section 2.7 [Large Numbers of Files], page 21).

Like `ncra` and `ncwa`, `nces` treats coordinate variables as a special case. Coordinate variables are assumed to be the same in all ensemble members, so `nces` simply copies the coordinate variables that appear in ensemble members directly to the output file. This has the same effect as averaging the coordinate variable across the ensemble, yet does not incur the time- or precision- penalties of actually averaging them. `ncra` and `ncwa` allow coordinate variables to be processed only by the linear average operation, regardless of the arithmetic operation type performed on the non-coordinate variables (see Section 3.35 [Operation Types], page 114). Thus it can be said that the three operators (`ncra`, `ncwa`, and `nces`) all average coordinate variables (even though `nces` simply copies them). All other requested arithmetic operations (e.g., maximization, square-root, RMS) are applied only to non-coordinate variables. In these cases the linear average of the coordinate variable will be returned.

EXAMPLES

Consider a model experiment which generated five realizations of one year of data, say 1985. Imagine that the experimenter slightly perturbs the initial conditions of the problem before generating each new solution. Assume each file contains all twelve months (a seasonal cycle) of data and we want to produce a single file containing the ensemble average (mean) seasonal cycle. Here the numeric filename suffix denotes the realization number (*not* the month):

```
nces 85_01.nc 85_02.nc 85_03.nc 85_04.nc 85_05.nc 85.nc
```

```
nces 85_0[1-5].nc 85.nc
nces -n 5,2,1 85_01.nc 85.nc
```

These three commands produce identical answers. See Section 3.5 [Specifying Input Files], page 33, for an explanation of the distinctions between these methods. The output file, `85.nc`, is the same size as the inputs files. It contains 12 months of data (which might or might not be stored in the record dimension, depending on the input files), but each value in the output file is the average of the five values in the input files.

In the previous example, the user could have obtained the ensemble average values in a particular spatio-temporal region by adding a hyperslab argument to the command, e.g.,

```
nces -d time,0,2 -d lat,-23.5,23.5 85_??.nc 85.nc
```

In this case the output file would contain only three slices of data in the *time* dimension. These three slices are the average of the first three slices from the input files. Additionally, only data inside the tropics is included.

As of NCO version 4.3.9 (released December, 2013) `nces` also works with groups (rather than files) as the fundamental unit of the ensemble. Consider two ensembles, `/ecmwf` and `/cesm` stored across three input files `mdl1.nc`, `mdl2.nc`, and `mdl3.nc`. Ensemble members would be leaf groups with names like `/ecmwf/01`, `/ecmwf/02` etc. and `/cesm/01`, `/cesm/02`, etc. These commands average both ensembles:

```
nces --nsm_grp mdl1.nc mdl2.nc mdl3.nc out.nc
nces --nsm_grp --nsm_sfx='_min' --op_typ=min -n 3,1,1 mdl1.nc out.nc
nces --nsm_grp -g cesm -v tas -d time,0,3 -n 3,1,1 mdl1.nc out.nc
```

The first command stores averages in the output groups `/cesm` and `/ecmwf`, while the second stores minima in the output groups `/cesm/cesm_min` and `/ecmwf/ecmwf_min`: The third command demonstrates that sub-setting and hyperslabbing work as expected. Note that each input file may contain different numbers of members of each ensemble, as long as all distinct ensembles contain at least one member in the first file.

## 4.7 ncflint netCDF File Interpolator

SYNTAX

```
ncflint [-3] [-4] [-6] [-7] [-A] [-C] [-c]
[--cnk_byt sz_byt] [--cnk_dmn nm,sz_lmn] [--cnk_map map]
[--cnk_min sz_byt] [--cnk_plc plc] [--cnk_scl sz_lmn]
[-D dbg] [-d dim,[min][,[max][,[stride]]]
[-F] [--fix_rec_crd] [-G gpe_dsc] [-g grp[,...]] [--glb ...] [-h] [--hdr_pad nbr]
[-i var,val3] [-L dfl_lvl] [-l path] [-N]
[--no_cll_msr] [--no_frm_trm] [--no_tmp_fl]
[-O] [-o file_3] [-p path] [--ppc ...] [-R] [-r] [--ram_all]
[-t thr_nbr] [--unn] [-v var[,...]] [-w wgt1[,wgt2]] [-X ...] [-x]
file_1 file_2 [file_3]
```

DESCRIPTION

`ncflint` creates an output file that is a linear combination of the input files. This linear combination is a weighted average, a normalized weighted average, or an interpolation of the input files. Coordinate variables are not acted upon in any case, they are simply copied from *file_1*.

There are two conceptually distinct methods of using `ncflint`. The first method is to specify the weight each input file contributes to the output file. In this method, the value *val3* of a variable in the output file *file_3* is determined from its values *val1* and *val2* in the two input files according to $val3 = wgt1 \times val1 + wgt2 \times val2$ . Here at least *wgt1*, and, optionally, *wgt2*, are specified on the command line with the '`-w`' (or '`--weight`' or '`--wgt_var`') switch. If only *wgt1* is specified then *wgt2* is automatically computed as $wgt2 = 1 - wgt1$. Note that weights larger than 1 are allowed. Thus it is possible to specify $wgt1 = 2$ and $wgt2 = -3$. One can use this functionality to multiply all the values in a given file by a constant.

As of NCO version 4.6.1 (July, 2016), the '`-N`' switch (or long-option equivalents '`--nrm`' or '`--normalize`') implements a variation of this method. This switch instructs `ncflint` to internally normalize the two supplied (or one supplied and one inferred) weights so that $wgt1 = wgt1/(wgt1+wgt2)$ and $wgt2 = wgt2/(wgt1+wgt2)$ . This allows the user to input integral weights, say, and to delegate the chore of normalizing them to `ncflint`. Be careful that '`-N`' means what you think, since the same switch means something quite different in `ncwa`.

The second method of using `ncflint` is to specify the interpolation option with '`-i`' (or with the '`--ntp`' or '`--interpolate`' long options). This is the inverse of the first method in the following sense: When the user specifies the weights directly, `ncflint` has no work to do besides multiplying the input values by their respective weights and adding together the results to produce the output values. It makes sense to use this when the weights are known *a priori*.

Another class of problems has the *arrival value* (i.e., *val3*) of a particular variable *var* known *a priori*. In this case, the implied weights can always be inferred by examining the values of *var* in the input files. This results in one equation in two unknowns, *wgt1* and *wgt2*: $val3 = wgt1 \times val1 + wgt2 \times val2$ . Unique determination of the weights requires imposing the additional constraint of normalization on the weights: $wgt1 + wgt2 = 1$. Thus, to use the interpolation option, the user specifies *var* and *val3* with the '`-i`' option. `ncflint` then computes *wgt1* and *wgt2*, and uses these weights on all variables to generate the output file. Although *var* may have any number of dimensions in the input files, it must represent a single, scalar value. Thus any dimensions associated with *var* must be *degenerate*, i.e., of size one.

If neither '`-i`' nor '`-w`' is specified on the command line, `ncflint` defaults to weighting each input file equally in the output file. This is equivalent to specifying '`-w 0.5`' or '`-w 0.5,0.5`'. Attempting to specify both '`-i`' and '`-w`' methods in the same command is an error.

`ncflint` does not interpolate variables of type `NC_CHAR` and `NC_STRING`. This behavior is hardcoded.

By default `ncflint` interpolates or multiplies record coordinate variables (e.g., time is often stored as a record coordinate) not other coordinate variables (e.g., latitude and longitude). This is because `ncflint` is often used to time-interpolate between existing files, but is rarely used to spatially interpolate. Sometimes however, users wish to multiply entire files by a constant that does not multiply any coordinate variables. The '`--fix_rec_crd`' switch was implemented for this purpose in NCO version 4.2.6 (March, 2013). It prevents `ncflint` from multiplying or interpolating any coordinate variables, including record coordinate variables.

Depending on your intuition, `ncflint` may treat missing values unexpectedly. Consider a point where the value in one input file, say *val1*, equals the missing value *mss_val_1* and, at the same point, the corresponding value in the other input file *val2* is not misssing (i.e., does not equal *mss_val_2*). There are three plausible answers, and this creates ambiguity.

Option one is to set $val3 = mss\_val\_1$. The rationale is that `ncflint` is, at heart, an interpolator and interpolation involving a missing value is intrinsically undefined. `ncflint` currently implements this behavior since it is the most conservative and least likely to lead to misinterpretation.

Option two is to output the weighted valid data point, i.e., $val3 = wgt2 \times val2$ . The rationale for this behavior is that interpolation is really a weighted average of known points, so `ncflint` should weight the valid point.

Option three is to return the *unweighted* valid point, i.e., $val3 = val2$. This behavior would appeal to those who use `ncflint` to estimate data using the closest available data. When a point is not bracketed by valid data on both sides, it is better to return the known datum than no datum at all.

The current implementation uses the first approach, Option one. If you have strong opinions on this matter, let us know, since we are willing to implement the other approaches as options if there is enough interest.

EXAMPLES

Although it has other uses, the interpolation feature was designed to interpolate *file_3* to a time between existing files. Consider input files `85.nc` and `87.nc` containing variables describing the state of a physical system at times `time` = 85 and `time` = 87. Assume each file contains its timestamp in the scalar variable `time`. Then, to linearly interpolate to a file `86.nc` which describes the state of the system at time at `time` = 86, we would use

```
ncflint -i time,86 85.nc 87.nc 86.nc
```

Say you have observational data covering January and April 1985 in two files named `85_01.nc` and `85_04.nc`, respectively. Then you can estimate the values for February and March by interpolating the existing data as follows. Combine `85_01.nc` and `85_04.nc` in a 2:1 ratio to make `85_02.nc`:

```
ncflint -w 0.667 85_01.nc 85_04.nc 85_02.nc
ncflint -w 0.667,0.333 85_01.nc 85_04.nc 85_02.nc
```

Multiply `85.nc` by 3 and by −2 and add them together to make `tst.nc`:

```
ncflint -w 3,-2 85.nc 85.nc tst.nc
```

This is an example of a null operation, so `tst.nc` should be identical (within machine precision) to `85.nc`.

Multiply all the variables except the coordinate variables in the file `emissions.nc` by by 0.8:

```
ncflint --fix_rec_crd -w 0.8,0.0 emissions.nc emissions.nc scaled_emissions.nc
```

The use of '`--fix_rec_crd`' ensures, e.g., that the `time` coordinate, if any, is not scaled (i.e., multiplied).

Add `85.nc` to `86.nc` to obtain `85p86.nc`, then subtract `86.nc` from `85.nc` to obtain `85m86.nc`

```
ncflint -w 1,1 85.nc 86.nc 85p86.nc
ncflint -w 1,-1 85.nc 86.nc 85m86.nc
ncdiff 85.nc 86.nc 85m86.nc
```

Thus `ncflint` can be used to mimic some `ncbo` operations. However this is not a good idea in practice because `ncflint` does not broadcast (see Section 4.3 [ncbo netCDF Binary Operator], page 207) conforming variables during arithmetic. Thus the final two commands would produce identical results except that `ncflint` would fail if any variables needed to be broadcast.

Rescale the dimensional units of the surface pressure `prs_sfc` from Pascals to hectopascals (millibars)

```
ncflint -C -v prs_sfc -w 0.01,0.0 in.nc in.nc out.nc
ncatted -a units,prs_sfc,o,c,millibar out.nc
```

## 4.8 ncks netCDF Kitchen Sink

SYNTAX

```
ncks [-3] [-4] [-5] [-6] [-7] [-A] [-a] [-b fl_bnr] [-C] [-c] [--cdl]
[--cnk_byt sz_byt] [--cnk_dmn nm,sz_lmn] [--cnk_map map]
[--cnk_min sz_byt] [--cnk_plc plc] [--cnk_scl sz_lmn]
[-D dbg] [-d dim,[min][,[max][,[stride]]] [-F] [--fix_rec_dmn dim]
[-G gpe_dsc] [-g grp[,...]] [--glb ...] [--grp_xtr_var_xcl]
[-H] [-h] [--hdn] [--hdr_pad nbr] [--jsn] [--jsn_fmt lvl]
[-L dfl_lvl] [-l path] [-M] [-m] [--map map-file]
[--md5] [--mk_rec_dmn dim] [--no_blank] [--no_cll_msr] [--no_frm_trm] [--no_tmp_fl]
[-O] [-o output-file] [-P] [-p path] [--ppc ...]
[-Q] [-q] [-R] [-r] [--rad] [--ram_all] [--rgr ...] [--rnr=wgt] [-s format]
[-u] [--unn] [-V] [-v var[,...]] [-X ...] [-x] [--xml]
input-file [[output-file]]
```

DESCRIPTION

The nickname "kitchen sink" is a catch-all because `ncks` combines most features of `ncdump` and `nccopy` with extra features to extract, hyperslab, multi-slab, sub-set, and translate into one versatile utility. `ncks` extracts (a subset of the) data from *input-file*, regrids it according to *map-file* if specified, then writes in netCDF format to *output-file*, and optionally writes it in flat binary format to `fl_bnr`, and optionally prints it to screen.

`ncks` prints netCDF input data in ASCII, CDL, JSON, or NcML/XML text formats to `stdout`, like (an extended version of) `ncdump`. By default `ncks` prints data in a tabular format intended to be easy to search for the data you want, one datum per screen line, with all dimension subscripts and coordinate values (if any) preceding the datum. Option '`-s`' (or long options '`--sng_fmt`' and '`--string`') permits the user to format data using C-style format strings, while option '`--cdl`' outputs CDL, option '`--jsn`' (or '`json`') outputs JSON, and option '`--xml`' (or '`ncml`') outputs NcML. `ncks` exposes many flexible controls over printed output, including CDL, JSON, and NcML.

Options '`-a`', '`--cdl`', '`-F`' , '`-H`', '`--hdn`', '`--jsn`', '`-M`', '`-m`', '`-P`', '`-Q`', '`-q`', '`-s`', '`-u`', '`-V`', and '`--xml`' (and their long option counterparts) control the formatted appearance of the data.

`ncks` extracts (and optionally creates a new netCDF file comprised of) only selected variables from the input file (similar to the old `ncextr` specification). Only variables and coordinates may be specifically included or excluded—all global attributes and any attribute associated with an extracted variable are copied to the screen and/or output netCDF file. Options '`-c`', '`-C`', '`-v`', and '`-x`' (and their long option synonyms) control which variables are extracted.

`ncks` extracts hyperslabs from the specified variables (`ncks` implements the original `nccut` specification). Option '`-d`' controls the hyperslab specification. Input dimensions that are not associated with any output variable do not appear in the output netCDF. This feature removes superfluous dimensions from netCDF files.

`ncks` will append variables and attributes from the *input-file* to *output-file* if *output-file* is a pre-existing netCDF file whose relevant dimensions conform to dimension sizes of *input-file*. The append features of `ncks` are intended to provide a rudimentary means of adding data from one netCDF file to another, conforming, netCDF file. If naming conflicts exist between the two files, data in *output-file* is usually overwritten by the corresponding data from *input-file*. Thus, when appending, the user should backup *output-file* in case valuable data are inadvertantly overwritten.

If *output-file* exists, the user will be queried whether to *overwrite*, *append*, or *exit* the `ncks` call completely. Choosing *overwrite* destroys the existing *output-file* and create an entirely new one from the output of the `ncks` call. Append has differing effects depending on the uniqueness of the variables and attributes output by `ncks`: If a variable or attribute extracted from *input-file* does not have a name conflict with the members of *output-file* then it will be added to *output-file* without overwriting any of the existing contents of *output-file*. In this case the relevant dimensions must agree (conform) between the two files; new dimensions are created in *output-file* as required. When a name conflict occurs, a global attribute from *input-file* will overwrite the corresponding global attribute from *output-file*. If the name conflict occurs for a non-record variable, then the dimensions and type of the variable (and of its coordinate dimensions, if any) must agree (conform) in both files. Then the variable values (and any coordinate dimension values) from *input-file* will overwrite the corresponding variable values (and coordinate dimension values, if any) in *output-file*[1].

Since there can only be one record dimension in a file, the record dimension must have the same name (though not necessarily the same size) in both files if a record dimension variable is to be appended. If the record dimensions are of differing sizes, the record dimension of *output-file* will become the greater of the two record dimension sizes, the record variable from *input-file* will overwrite any counterpart in *output-file* and fill values will be written to any gaps left in the rest of the record variables (I think). In all cases variable attributes in *output-file* are superseded by attributes of the same name from *input-file*, and left alone if there is no name conflict.

Some users may wish to avoid interactive `ncks` queries about whether to overwrite existing data. For example, batch scripts will fail if `ncks` does not receive responses to its queries. Options '`-O`' and '`-A`' are available to force overwriting existing files and variables, respectively.

## Options specific to `ncks`

The following summarizes features unique to `ncks`. Features common to many operators are described in Chapter 3 [Shared features], page 29.

'`-a`' Do not alphabetize extracted fields. By default, the specified output variables are extracted, printed, and written to disk in alphabetical order. This tends to make long output lists easier to search for particular variables. Specifying `-a` results in the variables being extracted, printed, and written to disk in the

[1] Those familiar with netCDF mechanics might wish to know what is happening here: `ncks` does not attempt to redefine the variable in *output-file* to match its definition in *input-file*, `ncks` merely copies the values of the variable and its coordinate dimensions, if any, from *input-file* to *output-file*.

order in which they were saved in the input file. Thus -a retains the original ordering of the variables. Also '--abc' and '--alphabetize'.

'-b file' Activate native machine binary output writing to binary file file. Also '--fl_bnr' and '--binary-file'. Writing packed variables in binary format is not supported. Metadata is never output to the binary file. Examine the netCDF output file to see the variables in the binary file. Use the '-C' switch, if necessary, to avoid wanting unwanted coordinates to the binary file:

```
% ncks -O -v one_dmn_rec_var -b bnr.dat -p ~/nco/data in.nc out.nc
% ls -l bnr.dat | cut -d ' ' -f 5 # 200 B contains time and one_dmn_rec_var
200
% ls -l bnr.dat
% ncks -C -O -v one_dmn_rec_var -b bnr.dat -p ~/nco/data in.nc out.nc
% ls -l bnr.dat | cut -d ' ' -f # 40 B contains one_dmn_rec_var only
40
```

'--fix_rec_dmn'
Change record dimension *dim* in the input file into a fixed dimension in the output file. Also '--no_rec_dmn'. Before NCO version 4.2.5 (January, 2013), the syntax for --fix_rec_dmn did not permit or require the specification of the dimension name *dim*. This is because the feature only worked on netCDF3 files, which support only one record dimension, so specifying its name was not necessary. netCDF4 files allow an arbitrary number of record dimensions, so the user must specify which record dimension to fix. The decision was made that starting with NCO version 4.2.5 (January, 2013), it is always required to specify the dimension name to fix regardless of the netCDF file type. This keeps the code simple, and is symmetric with the syntax for --mk_rec_dmn, described next.

As of NCO version 4.4.0 (January, 2014), the argument all may be given to '--fix_rec_dmn' to convert *all* record dimensions to fixed dimensions in the output file. Previously, '--fix_rec_dmn' only allowed one option, the name of a single record dimension to be fixed. Now it is simple to simultaneously fix all record dimensions. This is useful (and nearly mandatory) when flattening netCDF4 files that have multiple record dimensions per group into netCDF3 files (which are limited to at most one record dimension) (see Section 3.13 [Group Path Editing], page 52).

'--hdn' As of NCO version 4.4.0 (January, 2014), the '--hdn' or '--hidden' options print hidden (aka special) attributes. This is equivalent to 'ncdump -s'. Hidden attributes include: _Format, _DeflateLevel, _Shuffle, _Storage, _ChunkSizes, _Endianness, _Fletcher32, and _NOFILL. Previously ncks ignored all these attributes in CDL/XML modes. Now it prints these attributes as appropriate in all modes. As of NCO version 4.4.6 (September, 2014), '--hdn' also prints the extended file format (i.e., the format of the file or server supplying the data) as _SOURCE_FORMAT. As of NCO version 4.6.1 (August, 2016), '--hdn' also prints the hidden attributes _NCProperties, _IsNetcdf4, and _SuperblockVersion for netCDF4 files so long as NCO is linked against netCDF library version 4.4.1 or later. Users are referred to the Unidata netCDF Documentation (http://www.unidata.ucar.edu/software/netcdf/docs), or the man pages for ncgen or ncdump, for detailed descriptions of the meanings of these hidden attributes.

'--cdl' As of NCO version 4.3.3 (July, 2013), ncks can print extracted data and metadata to screen (i.e., stdout) as valid CDL (network Common data form Description Language). CDL is the human-readable "lingua franca" of netCDF ingested by ncgen and excreted by ncdump. Compare ncks "traditional" with CDL printing:

```
zender@roulee:~$ ncks -v one ~/nco/data/in.nc
one: type NC_FLOAT, 0 dimensions, 1 attribute, chunked? no, compressed?
one size (RAM) = 1*sizeof(NC_FLOAT) = 1*4 = 4 bytes
one attribute 0: long_name, size = 3 NC_CHAR, value = one

one = 1

zender@roulee:~$ ncks --cdl -v one ~/nco/data/in.nc
netcdf in {

  variables:
    float one ;
    one:long_name = "one" ;

  data:
    one = 1 ;

} // group /
```

ncgen converts CDL-mode output into a netCDF file:

```
ncks --cdl -v one ~/nco/data/in.nc > ~/in.cdl
ncgen -k netCDF-4 -b -o ~/in.nc ~/in.cdl
ncks -v one ~/in.nc
```

The HDF version of ncgen, often named hncgen or ncgen-hdf, converts netCDF3 CDL into an HDF file:

```
/usr/hdf4/bin/ncgen -b -o ~/in.hdf ~/in.cdl # HDF ncgen (local builds)
/usr/bin/hncgen     -b -o ~/in.hdf ~/in.cdl # Same as HDF ncgen (RPM pa
/usr/bin/ncgen-hdf  -b -o ~/in.hdf ~/in.cdl # Same as HDF ncgen (Debian
hdp dumpsds ~/in.hdf                        # ncdump/h5dump-equivalent
```

Note that HDF4 does not support netCDF-style groups, so the above commands fail when the input file contains groups. Only netCDF4 and HDF5 support groups. In our experience the HDF ncgen command, by whatever name installed, is not robust and can fail on valid netCDF3 CDL.

'--mk_rec_dmn *dim*'

Change existing dimension *dim* to a record dimension in the output file. This is the most straightforward way of changing a dimension to a/the record dimension, and works fine in most cases. See Section 4.5 [ncecat netCDF Ensemble Concatenator], page 228, and Section 4.9 [ncpdq netCDF Permute Dimensions

Quickly], page 254, for other methods of changing variable dimensionality, including the record dimension.

'-H' Toggle default behavior of printing to screen or copying data (not metadata). Also activated using '--print' or '--prn'. By default ncks prints all metadata but no data to screen when no netCDF *output-file* when one is specified. And if *output-file* is specified, ncks copies all metadata and all data to it. In other words, the printing/copying default is context-sensitive, and '-H' toggles the default behavior. Hence, use '-H' to turn-off copying data (not metadata) to an output file. And use '-H' to turn-on printing data (not metadata) to screen. Unless otherwise specified (with -s), each element of the data hyperslab prints on a separate line containing the names, indices, and, values, if any, of all of the variables dimensions. The dimension and variable indices refer to the location of the corresponding data element with respect to the variable as stored on disk (i.e., not the hyperslab).

```
% ncks -C -v three_dmn_var in.nc
lat[0]=-90 lev[0]=100 lon[0]=0 three_dmn_var[0]=0
lat[0]=-90 lev[0]=100 lon[1]=90 three_dmn_var[1]=1
lat[0]=-90 lev[0]=100 lon[2]=180 three_dmn_var[2]=2
...
lat[1]=90 lev[2]=1000 lon[1]=90 three_dmn_var[21]=21
lat[1]=90 lev[2]=1000 lon[2]=180 three_dmn_var[22]=22
lat[1]=90 lev[2]=1000 lon[3]=270 three_dmn_var[23]=23
```

Printing the same variable with the '-F' option shows the same variable indexed with Fortran conventions

```
% ncks -F -C -v three_dmn_var in.nc
lon(1)=0 lev(1)=100 lat(1)=-90 three_dmn_var(1)=0
lon(2)=90 lev(1)=100 lat(1)=-90 three_dmn_var(2)=1
lon(3)=180 lev(1)=100 lat(1)=-90 three_dmn_var(3)=2
...
```

Printing a hyperslab does not affect the variable or dimension indices since these indices are relative to the full variable (as stored in the input file), and the input file has not changed. However, if the hyperslab is saved to an output file and those values are printed, the indices will change:

```
% ncks -H -d lat,90.0 -d lev,1000.0 -v three_dmn_var in.nc out.nc
...
lat[1]=90 lev[2]=1000 lon[0]=0 three_dmn_var[20]=20
lat[1]=90 lev[2]=1000 lon[1]=90 three_dmn_var[21]=21
lat[1]=90 lev[2]=1000 lon[2]=180 three_dmn_var[22]=22
lat[1]=90 lev[2]=1000 lon[3]=270 three_dmn_var[23]=23
% ncks -C -v three_dmn_var out.nc
lat[0]=90 lev[0]=1000 lon[0]=0 three_dmn_var[0]=20
lat[0]=90 lev[0]=1000 lon[1]=90 three_dmn_var[1]=21
lat[0]=90 lev[0]=1000 lon[2]=180 three_dmn_var[2]=22
lat[0]=90 lev[0]=1000 lon[3]=270 three_dmn_var[3]=23
```

'--jsn, --json'

As of NCO version 4.6.2 (November, 2016), ncks can print extracted metadata and data to screen (i.e., stdout) as JSON, JavaScript Object Notation, defined here (http://www.json.org). ncks supports JSON output more completely, flexibly, and robustly than any other tools to our knowledge. With ncks one can translate entire netCDF3 and netCDF4 files into JSON, including metadata and data, using all NCO's subsetting and hyperslabbing capabilities. Behold JSON output in default mode:

```
zender@aerosol:~$ ncks --jsn -v one ~/nco/data/in.nc
{
    "one": {
      "type": "float",
      "long_name": "one",
      "data": 1.0
    }
}
```

NCO converts to (using commonsense rules) and prints all NC_TYPEs as one of three atomic types distinguishable as JSON values: float, string, and int[2]. Floating-point types (NC_FLOAT and NC_DOUBLE) are printed with a decimal point and at least one signficant digit following the decimal point, e.g., 1.0 rather than 1. or 1. Integer types (e.g., NC_INT, NC_UINT64) are printed with no decimal point. String types (NC_CHAR and NC_STRING) are enclosed in double-quotes.

The JSON specification allows many possible output formats for netCDF files. NCO developers implemented a working prototype in Octoboer, 2016 and, after discussing options with interested parties here (https://sourceforge.net/p/nco/discussion/9829/thread/8c4d7e72), finalized the emitted JSON syntax a few weeks later. The resulting JSON backend supports three levels of pedanticness, ordered from more concise, flexible, and human-readable to more verbose, restrictive, and 1-to-1 reproducible. JSON-specific switches access these modes and other features. Each JSON configuration option automatically triggers JSON printing, so that specifying '--json' in addition to a JSON configuration option is redundant and unnecessary.

Request a specific format level with the pedantic level argument to the '--jsn_fmt *lvl*' option. As of NCO version 4.6.3 (December, 2016), the option formerly known as '--jsn_att_fmt' was renamed simply '--jsn_fmt'. The more general name reflects the fact that the option controls all JSON formatting, not just attribute formatting. As of version 4.6.3, NCO defaults to demarcate inner dimensions of variable data with (nested) square brackets rather than printing data as an unrolled single dimensional array. An array with C-ordered dimensionality [2,3,4] prints as:

```
% ncks --jsn -v three_dmn_var ~/nco/data/in.nc
...
```

[2] The JSON boolean atomic type is not (yet) supported as there is no obvious netCDF-equivalent to this type.

```
"data": [[[0.0, 1.0, 2.0, 3.0], [4.0, 5.0, 6.0, 7.0], [8.0, 9.0, 10.0,11.0]]
...
% ncks --jsn_fmt=4 -v three_dmn_var ~/nco/data/in.nc
...
"data": [0.0, 1.0, 2.0, 3.0, 4.0, 5.0, 6.0, 7.0, 8.0, 9.0, 10.0, 11.0, 12.0,
...
```

One can recover the former behavior (and omit the brackets) by adding four to the base pedantic level *lvl* (as shown above). Besides the potential offset of four, *lvl* may take one of three values between 0–2:

- *lvl* = 0 is the default mode, and is also explicitly selectable with '`--jsn_fmt=0`'. All values are output without the original NC_TYPE token. This allows attributes to print as JSON name-value pairs, rather than as more complex objects:

  ```
  % ncks --jsn_fmt=0 -v att_var ~/nco/data/in_grp.nc
  ...
  "att_var": {
    "dims": ["time"],
    "type": "float",
    "attributes": {
      "byte_att": [0, 1, 2, 127, -128, -127, -2, -1],
      "char_att": "Sentence one.\nSentence two.\n",
      "short_att": 37,
      "int_att": 73,
      "long_att": 73,
      "float_att": [73.0, 72.0, 71.0, 70.010, 69.0010, 68.010, 67.010],
      "double_att": [73.0, 72.0, 71.0, 70.010, 69.0010, 68.010, 67.0100010
    },
    "data": [10.0, 10.10, 10.20, 10.30, 10.40101, 10.50, 10.60, 10.70, 10.
  ...
  ```

  This least pedantic mode produces the most easily read results, and suffices for many (most?) purposes. Any downstream parser is expected to assign an appropriate type as indicated by JSON syntax rules. Because the original attribute's `NC_TYPE` is not output, it is not guaranteed that a downstream parser can exactly reproduce the input file datatypes. For example, whether the original attribute string was stored as `NC_CHAR` or `NC_STRING` will be unknown to a downstream parser. Distinctions between `NC_FLOAT` and `NC_DOUBLE` are similarly lost, as are all distinctions among the integer types.

  In our experience, these distinctions are immaterial for attributes, which are intended for metadata not for large-scale storage. Type-distinctions can, however, significantly impact the size of variable data, responsible for nearly all the storage required by datasets. For instance, storing or transferring an `NC_SHORT` field as `NC_DOUBLE` would waste a factor of four in space or bandwidth. This is why NCO *always* prints the `NC_TYPE` of variable data. Downstream parsers can (but are not required to) take advantage of the variable's NC_TYPE to choose the most efficient storage type.

- *lvl* = 1 is a medium-pedantic level that prints all attributes as objects (with explicit types) *except* those attributes whose types match the simplest default JSON value types (NC_FLOAT, NC_CHAR/NC_STRING, NC_INT). double, string, and int attributes are printed as JSON arrays, as in the *lvl* = 0 above:

```
% ncks --jsn_fmt=1 -v att_var ~/nco/data/in.nc
...
"att_var": {
  "dims": ["time"],
  "type": "float",
  "attributes": {
    "byte_att": { "type": "byte", "data": [0, 1, 2, 127, -128, -127
    "char_att": "Sentence one.\nSentence two.\n",
    "short_att": { "type": "short", "data": 37},
    "int_att": 73,
    "long_att": 73,
    "float_att": [73.0, 72.0, 71.0, 70.010, 69.0010, 68.010, 67.010]
    "double_att": { "type": "double", "data": [73.0, 72.0, 71.0, 70
  },
  "data": [10.0, 10.10, 10.20, 10.30, 10.40101, 10.50, 10.60, 10.70
...
```

  The attributes of type NC_BYTE, NC_SHORT, and NC_DOUBLE are printed as JSON objects that comprise an NC_TYPE and a value list, because their values could conceivably not be representable, or would waste space, if interpreted as NC_INT or NC_FLOAT, respectively. All other attributes may be naturally mapped to the type indicated by the JSON syntax of the value, where numbers are assumed to correspond to NC_FLOAT for floating-point, NC_INT for integers, and NC_CHAR or NC_STRING for strings. This minimal increase in verbosity allows a downstream parser to re-construct the original dataset with nearly identical attributes types to the original.

- *lvl* = 2 is the most pedantic mode, and should be used when preserving all input types (e.g., to ensure exact reproducibility of the input file) is important. This mode always prints attributes as JSON objects with a type value so that any downstream parser can (though it need not) guarantee exact reproduction of the original dataset:

```
% ncks --jsn_fmt=2 -v att_var ~/nco/data/in.nc
...
"att_var": {
  "dims": ["time"],
  "type": "float",
  "attributes": {
    "byte_att": { "type": "byte", "data": [0, 1, 2, 127, -128, -127,
    "char_att": { "type": "char", "data": "Sentence one.\nSentence t
    "short_att": { "type": "short", "data": 37},
```

```
          "int_att": { "type": "int", "data": 73},
          "long_att": { "type": "int", "data": 73},
          "float_att": { "type": "float", "data": [73.0, 72.0, 71.0, 70.010, 6
          "double_att": { "type": "double", "data": [73.0, 72.0, 71.0, 70.010,
        },
        "data": [10.0, 10.10, 10.20, 10.30, 10.40101, 10.50, 10.60, 10.70, 10.
      ...
```

That ncks produces correct translations of for all supported datatypes may be verified by JSON syntax checker command like `jsonlint`. Please let us know how to improve JSON features for your application.

'-M' Turn-on printing to screen or turn-off copying global and group metadata. This includes file summary information and global and group attributes. Also '--Mtd' and '--Metadata'. By default `ncks` prints global metadata to screen if no netCDF output file and no variable extraction list is specified (with '-v'). Use '-M' to print global metadata to screen if a netCDF output is specified, or if a variable extraction list is specified (with '-v'). Use '-M' to turn-off copying of global and group metadata when copying, subsetting, or appending to an output file.

The various combinations of printing switches can be confusing. In an attempt to anticipate what most users want to do, `ncks` uses context-sensitive defaults for printing. Our goal is to minimize the use of switches required to accomplish the common operations. We assume that users creating a new file or overwriting (e.g., with '-O') an existing file usually wish to copy all global and variable-specific attributes to the new file. In contrast, we assume that users appending (e.g., with '-A' an explicit variable list from one file to another usually wish to copy only the variable-specific attributes to the output file. The switches '-H', '-M', and '-m' switches are implemented as toggles which reverse the default behavior. The most confusing aspect of this is that '-M' inhibits copying global metadata in overwrite mode and causes copying of global metadata in append mode.

```
ncks                   in.nc        # Print  VAs and GAs
ncks             -v one in.nc        # Print  VAs not GAs
ncks     -M      -v one in.nc        # Print  GAs only
ncks          -m -v one in.nc        # Print  VAs only
ncks     -M -m -v one in.nc        # Print  VAs and GAs
ncks -O                in.nc out.nc # Copy   VAs and GAs
ncks -O          -v one in.nc out.nc # Copy   VAs and GAs
ncks -O -M       -v one in.nc out.nc # Copy   VAs not GAs
ncks -O       -m -v one in.nc out.nc # Copy   GAs not VAs
ncks -O -M -m -v one in.nc out.nc # Copy   only data (no atts)
ncks -A                in.nc out.nc # Append VAs and GAs
ncks -A          -v one in.nc out.nc # Append VAs not GAs
ncks -A -M       -v one in.nc out.nc # Append VAs and GAs
ncks -A       -m -v one in.nc out.nc # Append only data (no atts)
ncks -A -M -m -v one in.nc out.nc # Append GAs not VAs
```

where VAs and GAs denote variable and group/global attributes, respectively.

'-m' Turn-on printing to screen or turn-off copying variable metadata. Using '-m' will print variable metadata to screen (similar to *ncdump -h*). This displays all metadata pertaining to each variable, one variable at a time. This includes information on the storage properties of the variable, such as whether it employs chunking, compression, or packing. Also activated using '--mtd' and '--metadata'. The ncks default behavior is to print variable metadata to screen if no netCDF output file is specified. Use '-m' to print variable metadata to screen if a netCDF output is specified. Also use '-m' to turn-off copying of variable metadata to an output file.

'--no_blank'
Print numeric representation of missing values. As of NCO version 4.2.2 (October, 2012), NCO prints missing values as blanks (i.e., the underscore character '_') by default. To enable the old behavior of printing the numeric representation of missing values (e.g., 1.0e36), use the '--no_blank' switch. Also activated using '--noblank' or '--no-blank'.

'-P' Print data, metadata, and units to screen. The '-P' switch is a convenience abbreviation for '-C -H -M -m -u'. Also activated using '--print' or '--prn'. This set of switches is useful for exploring file contents.

'-Q' Print quietly, meaning omit dimension names, indices, and coordinate values when printing arrays. Variable (not dimension) indices are printed. Variable names appear flush left in the output:

```
zender@roulee:~$ ncks -Q -v three_dmn_rec_var -C -H ~/nco/data/in.nc
three_dmn_rec_var[0]=1
...
```

This helps locate specific variables in lists with many variables and different dimensions. See also the '-V' option, which omits all names and indices and prints only variable values.

'-q' Quench (turn-off) all printing to screen. This overrides the setting of all print-related switches, equivalent to *-H -M -m* when in single-file printing mode. When invoked with -R (see Section 3.8 [Retaining Retrieved Files], page 40), ncks automatically sets -q. This allows ncks to retrieve remote files without automatically trying to print them. Also '--quench'.

'--rad' Retain all dimensions. When invoked with --rad (Retain All Dimensions), ncks copies each dimension in the input file to the output file, regardless of whether the dimension is utilized by any variables. Normally ncks discards "orphan dimensions", i.e., dimensions not referenced by any variables. This switch allows users to keep non-referenced dimensions in the workflow. When invoked in printing mode, causes orphaned dimensions to be printed (they are not printed by default). Also '--retain_all_dimensions', '--orphan_dimensions', and '--rph_dmn'.

'-s *format*'
String format for text output. Accepts C language escape sequences and printf() formats. Also '--string' and '--sng_fmt'.

'--secret'

Print summary of `ncks` hidden features. These hidden or secret features are used mainly by developers. They are not supported for general use and may change at any time. This demonstrates conclusively that I cannot keep a secret. Also '--ssh' and '--scr'.

'-u'

Toggle the printing of a variable's `units` attribute, if any, with its values. Also '--units'.

'-V'

Print variable values only. Do not print variable and dimension names, indices, and coordinate values when printing arrays.

```
zender@roulee:~$ ncks -V -v three_dmn_rec_var -C -H ~/nco/data/in.nc
1
...
```

See also the '-Q' option, which prints variable names and indices, but not dimension names, indices, or coordinate values when printing arrays. Using '-V' is the same as specifying '-Q --no_nm_prn'.

'--xml, --ncml'

As of NCO version 4.3.3 (July, 2013), `ncks` can print extracted data and metadata to screen (i.e., `stdout`) as XML in NcML, the netCDF Markup Language. `ncks` supports XML more completely than 'ncdump -x'. With `ncks` one can translate entire netCDF3 and netCDF4 files into NcML, including metadata and data, using all NCO's subsetting and hyperslabbing capabilities. Compare `ncks` "traditional" with XML printing:

```
zender@roulee:~$ ncks -v one ~/nco/data/in.nc
one: type NC_FLOAT, 0 dimensions, 1 attribute, chunked? no, compressed? no,
one size (RAM) = 1*sizeof(NC_FLOAT) = 1*4 = 4 bytes
one attribute 0: long_name, size = 3 NC_CHAR, value = one

one = 1

zender@roulee:~$ ncks --xml -v one ~/nco/data/in.nc
<?xml version="1.0" encoding="UTF-8"?>
<netcdf xmlns="http://www.unidata.ucar.edu/namespaces/netcdf/ncml-2.2" locat
  <variable name="one" type="float" shape="">
    <attribute name="long_name" separator="*" value="one" />
    <values>1.</values>
  </variable>
</netcdf>
```

XML-mode prints variable metadata and, as of NCO version 4.3.7 (October, 2013), variable data and, as of NCO version 4.4.0 (January, 2014), hidden attributes. That ncks produces correct NcML translations of CDM files for all supported datatypes is verified by comparison to output from Unidata's `toolsUI` Java program. Please let us know how to improve XML/NcML features.

`ncks` provides additional options to configure NcML output: '--xml_no_location', '--xml_spr_chr', and '--xml_spr_nmr'. Every NcML configuration option automatically triggers NcML printing, so that specifying

'--xml' in addition to a configuration option is redundant and unnecessary. The '--xml_no_location' switch prevents output of the NcML location element. By default the location element is printed with a value equal to the location of the input dataset, e.g., location="/home/zender/in.nc". The '--xml_spr_chr' and '--xml_spr_nmr' options customize the strings used as NcML separators for attributes and variables of character-type and numeric-type, respectively. Their default separators are * and " " (a space):

```
zender@roulee:~$ ncks --xml -d time,0,3 -v two_dmn_rec_var_sng in.nc
...
   <values separator="*">abc*bcd*cde*def</values>
 ...
 zender@roulee:~$ ncks --xml_spr_chr=', ' -v two_dmn_rec_var_sng in.nc
...
<values separator=", ">abc, bcd, cde, def, efg, fgh, ghi, hij, jkl, klm
...
zender@roulee:~$ ncks --xml -v one_dmn_rec_var in.nc
...
<values>1 2 3 4 5 6 7 8 9 10</values>
...
zender@roulee:~$ ncks --xml_spr_nmr=', ' -v one_dmn_rec_var in.nc
...
<values separator=", ">1, 2, 3, 4, 5, 6, 7, 8, 9, 10</values>
...
```

Separator elements for strings are a thorny issue. One must be sure that the separator element is not mistaken as a portion of the string. NCO attempts to produce valid NcML and supplies the '--xml_spr_chr' option to work around any difficulties. NCO performs precautionary checks with strstr(*val*,*spr*) to identify presence of the separator string (*spr*) in data (*val*) and, when it detects a match, automatically switches to a backup separator string (*|*). However limitations of strstr() may lead to false negatives when the separator string occurs in data beyond the first string in multi-dimensional NC_CHAR arrays. Hence, results may be ambiguous to NcML parsers. If problems arise, use '--xml_spr_chr' to specify a multi-character separator that does not appear in the string array and that does not include an NcML formatting characters (e.g., commas, angles, quotes).

### 4.8.2 Filters for ncks

We encourage the use of standard UNIX pipes and filters to narrow the verbose output of ncks into more precise targets. For example, to obtain an uncluttered listing of the variables in a file try

```
ncks -m in.nc | grep -E ': type' | cut -f 1 -d ' ' | sed 's/://' | sort
```

A Bash user could alias the previous filter to the shell command nclist as shown below. More complex examples could involve command line arguments. For example, a user may frequently be interested in obtaining the value of an attribute, e.g., for textual file examination or for passing to another shell command. Say the attribute is purpose, the variable is `z`, and the file is `in.nc`. In this example, `ncks -m -v z` is too verbose so a robust `grep` and `cut` filter is desirable, such as

```
ncks -M -m in.nc | grep -E -i "^z attribute [0-9]+: purpose" | cut -f 11- -d ' ' | sor
```

The filters are clearly too complex to remember on-the-fly so the entire procedure could be implemented as a shell command or function called, say, `ncattget`

```
function ncattget { ncks -M -m ${3} | grep -E -i "^${2} attribute [0-9]+: ${1}" | cut
```

The shell `ncattget` is invoked with three arugments that are, in order, the names of the attribute, variable, and file to examine. Global attributes are indicated by using a variable name of `global`. This definition yields the following results

```
% ncattget purpose z in.nc
Height stored with a monotonically increasing coordinate
% ncattget Purpose Z in.nc
Height stored with a monotonically increasing coordinate
% ncattget history z in.nc
% ncattget history global in.nc
History global attribute.
```

Note that case sensitivity has been turned off for the variable and attribute names (and could be turned on by removing the '`-i`' switch to `grep`). Furthermore, extended regular expressions may be used for both the variable and attribute names. The next two commands illustrate this by searching for the values of attribute `purpose` in all variables, and then for all attributes of the variable `z`:

```
% ncattget purpose .+ in.nc
1-D latitude coordinate referred to by geodesic grid variables
1-D longitude coordinate referred to by geodesic grid variables
...
% ncattget .+ Z in.nc
Height
Height stored with a monotonically increasing coordinate
meter
```

Extended filters are best stored as shell commands if they are used frequently. Shell commands may be re-used when they are defined in shell configuration files. These files are usually named `.bashrc`, `.cshrc`, and `.profile` for the Bash, Csh, and Sh shells, respectively.

```
# NB: Untested on Csh, Ksh, Sh, Zsh! Send us feedback!
# Bash shell (/bin/bash) users place these in .bashrc
# ncattget $att_nm $var_nm $fl_nm : What attributes does variable have?
function ncattget { ncks -M -m ${3} | grep -E -i "^${2} attribute [0-9]+: ${1}" | cut
# ncunits $att_val $fl_nm : Which variables have given units?
function ncunits { ncks -m ${2} | grep -E -i " attribute [0-9]+: units.+ ${1}" | cut -
# ncavg $var_nm $fl_nm : What is mean of variable?
function ncavg { ncwa -y avg -O -C -v ${1} ${2} ~/foo.nc ; ncks -H -C -v ${1} ~/foo.nc
# ncavg $var_nm $fl_nm : What is mean of variable?
```

```
function ncavg { ncap2 -O -C -v -s "foo=${1}.avg();print(foo)" ${2} ~/foo.nc | cu
# ncdmnlist $fl_nm : What dimensions are in file?
ncdmnlist { ncks --cdl -m ${1} | cut -d ':' -f 1 | cut -d '=' -s -f 1 ; }
# ncdmnsz $dmn_nm $fl_nm : What is dimension size?
function ncdmnsz { ncks -m -M ${2} | grep -E -i ": ${1}, size =" | cut -f 7 -d '
# nclist $fl_nm : What variables are in file?
function nclist { ncks -m ${1} | grep -E ': type' | cut -f 1 -d ' ' | sed 's/://'
# ncmax $var_nm $fl_nm : What is maximum of variable?
function ncmax { ncwa -y max -O -C -v ${1} ${2} ~/foo.nc ; ncks -H -C -v ${1} ~/f
# ncmax $var_nm $fl_nm : What is maximum of variable?
function ncmax { ncap2 -O -C -v -s "foo=${1}.max();print(foo)" ${2} ~/foo.nc | cu
# ncmdn $var_nm $fl_nm : What is median of variable?
function ncmdn { ncap2 -O -C -v -s "foo=gsl_stats_median_from_sorted_data(${1}.so
# ncrng $var_nm $fl_nm : What is range of variable?
function ncrng { ncap2 -O -C -v -s "foo_min=${1}.min();foo_max=${1}.max();print(f
# ncmode $var_nm $fl_nm : What is mode of variable?
function ncmode { ncap2 -O -C -v -s "foo=gsl_stats_median_from_sorted_data(${1}.s
# ncrecsz $fl_nm : What is record dimension size?
function ncrecsz { ncks -M ${1} | grep -E -i "^Record dimension:" | cut -f 8- -d
# nctypget $var_nm $fl_nm : What type is variable?
function nctypget { ncks -m -v ${1} ${2} | grep -E -i "^${1}: type" | cut -f 3 -d
# Csh shell (/bin/csh) users place these in .cshrc
ncattget() { ncks -M -m -v ${3} | grep -E -i "^${2} attribute [0-9]+: ${1}" | cut
ncdmnsz() { ncks -m -M ${2} | grep -E -i ": ${1}, size =" | cut -f 7 -d ' ' | uni
nclist() { ncks -m ${1} | grep -E ': type' | cut -f 1 -d ' ' | sed 's/://' | sort
ncrecsz() { ncks -M ${1} | grep -E -i "^Record dimension:" | cut -f 8- -d ' ' ; }
# Sh shell (/bin/sh) users place these in .profile
ncattget() { ncks -M -m ${3} | grep -E -i "^${2} attribute [0-9]+: ${1}" | cut -f
ncdmnsz() { ncks -m -M ${2} | grep -E -i ": ${1}, size =" | cut -f 7 -d ' ' | uni
nclist() { ncks -m ${1} | grep -E ': type' | cut -f 1 -d ' ' | sed 's/://' | sort
ncrecsz() { ncks -M ${1} | grep -E -i "^Record dimension:" | cut -f 8- -d ' ' ; }
```

EXAMPLES

View all data in netCDF `in.nc`, printed with Fortran indexing conventions:

```
ncks -F in.nc
```

Copy the netCDF file `in.nc` to file `out.nc`.

```
ncks in.nc out.nc
```

Now the file `out.nc` contains all the data from `in.nc`. There are, however, two differences between `in.nc` and `out.nc`. First, the `history` global attribute (see Section 3.39 [History Attribute], page 129) will contain the command used to create `out.nc`. Second, the variables in `out.nc` will be defined in alphabetical order. Of course the internal storage of variable in a netCDF file should be transparent to the user, but there are cases when alphabetizing a file is useful (see description of `-a` switch).

Copy all global attributes (and no variables) from `in.nc` to `out.nc`:

```
ncks -A -x ~/nco/data/in.nc ~/out.nc
```

The '-x' switch tells NCO to use the complement of the extraction list (see Section 3.11 [Subsetting Files], page 46). Since no extraction list is explicitly specified (with '-v'), the default is to extract all variables. The complement of all variables is no variables. Without any variables to extract, the append ('-A') command (see Section 2.4 [Appending Variables], page 19) has only to extract and copy (i.e., append) global attributes to the output file.

Copy/append metadata (not data) from variables in one file to variables in a second file. When copying/subsetting/appending files (as opposed to printing them), the copying of data, variable metadata, and global/group metadata are now turned OFF by '-H', '-m', and '-M', respectively. This is the opposite sense in which these switches work when *printing* a file. One can use these switches to easily replace data or metadata in one file with data or metadata from another:

```
# Extract naked (data-only) copies of two variables
ncks -h -M -m -O -C -v one,three_dmn_rec_var ~/nco/data/in.nc ~/out.nc
# Change values to be sure original values are not copied in following step
ncap2 -O -v -s 'one*=2;three_dmn_rec_var*=0' ~/nco/data/in.nc ~/in2.nc
# Append in2.nc metadata (not data!) to out.nc
ncks -A -C -H -v one,three_dmn_rec_var ~/in2.nc ~/out.nc
```

Variables in `out.nc` now contain data (not metadata) from `in.nc` and metadata (not data) from `in2.nc`.

Print variable `three_dmn_var` from file `in.nc` with default notations. Next print `three_dmn_var` as an un-annotated text column. Then print `three_dmn_var` signed with very high precision. Finally, print `three_dmn_var` as a comma-separated list.

```
% ncks -C -v three_dmn_var in.nc
lat[0]=-90 lev[0]=100 lon[0]=0 three_dmn_var[0]=0
lat[0]=-90 lev[0]=100 lon[1]=90 three_dmn_var[1]=1
...
lat[1]=90 lev[2]=1000 lon[3]=270 three_dmn_var[23]=23
% ncks -s '%f\n' -C -v three_dmn_var in.nc
0.000000
1.000000
...
23.000000
% ncks -s '%+16.10f\n' -C -v three_dmn_var in.nc
   +0.0000000000
   +1.0000000000
...
  +23.0000000000
% ncks -s '%f, ' -C -v three_dmn_var in.nc
0.000000, 1.000000, ..., 23.000000,
```

Programmers will recognize these as the venerable C language `printf()` formatting strings. The second and third options are useful when pasting data into text files like reports or papers. See Section 4.2 [ncatted netCDF Attribute Editor], page 200, for more details on string formatting and special characters.

As of NCO version 4.2.2 (October, 2012), NCO prints missing values as blanks (i.e., the underscore character '_') by default:

```
% ncks -C -H -v mss_val in.nc
lon[0]=0 mss_val[0]=73
lon[1]=90 mss_val[1]=_
lon[2]=180 mss_val[2]=73
lon[3]=270 mss_val[3]=_
% ncks -s '%+5.1f, ' -H -C -v mss_val in.nc
+73.0, _, +73.0, _,
```

To print the numeric value of the missing value instead of a blank, use the '--no_blank' option.

ncks prints in a verbose fashion by default and supplies a number of switches to pare-down (or even spruce-up) the output. The interplay of the '-Q', '-V', and (otherwise undocumented) '--no_nm_prn' switches yields most desired verbosities:

```
% ncks -v three_dmn_rec_var -C -H ~/nco/data/in.nc
time[0]=1 lat[0]=-90 lon[0]=0 three_dmn_rec_var[0]=1
% ncks -Q -v three_dmn_rec_var -C -H ~/nco/data/in.nc
three_dmn_rec_var[0]=1
% ncks -V -v three_dmn_rec_var -C -H ~/nco/data/in.nc
1
% ncks -Q --no_nm_prn -v three_dmn_rec_var -C -H ~/nco/data/in.nc
1
% ncks --no_nm_prn -v three_dmn_rec_var -C -H ~/nco/data/in.nc
1 -90 0 1
```

One dimensional arrays of characters stored as netCDF variables are automatically printed as strings, whether or not they are NUL-terminated, e.g.,

```
ncks -v fl_nm in.nc
```

The %c formatting code is useful for printing multidimensional arrays of characters representing fixed length strings

```
ncks -s '%c' -v fl_nm_arr in.nc
```

Using the %s format code on strings which are not NUL-terminated (and thus not technically strings) is likely to result in a core dump.

Create netCDF out.nc containing all variables, and any associated coordinates, except variable time, from netCDF in.nc:

```
ncks -x -v time in.nc out.nc
```

As a special case of this, consider how to remove a variable such as time_bounds that is identified in a CF Convention (see Section 3.41 [CF Conventions], page 131) compliant ancillary_variables, bounds, climatology, coordinates, or grid_mapping attribute. NCO subsetting assumes the user wants all ancillary variables, axes, bounds and coordinates associated with all extracted variables (see Section 3.12 [Subsetting Coordinate Variables], page 51). Hence to exclude a `ancillary_variables`, `bounds`, `climatology`, `coordinates`, or `grid_mapping` variable while retaining the "parent" variable (here `time`), one must use the '`-C`' switch:

```
ncks -C -x -v time_bounds in.nc out.nc
```

The '`-C`' switch tells the operator *NOT* to necessarily include all the CF ancillary variables, axes, bounds, and coordinates. Hence the output file will contain `time` and not `time_bounds`.

Extract variables `time` and `pressure` from netCDF `in.nc`. If `out.nc` does not exist it will be created. Otherwise the you will be prompted whether to append to or to overwrite `out.nc`:

```
ncks -v time,pressure in.nc out.nc
ncks -C -v time,pressure in.nc out.nc
```

The first version of the command creates an `out.nc` which contains `time`, `pressure`, and any coordinate variables associated with *pressure*. The `out.nc` from the second version is guaranteed to contain only two variables `time` and `pressure`.

Create netCDF `out.nc` containing all variables from file `in.nc`. Restrict the dimensions of these variables to a hyperslab. The specified hyperslab is: the fifth value in dimension `time`; the half-open range $lat > 0.$ in coordinate `lat`; the half-open range $lon < 330.$ in coordinate `lon`; the closed interval $0.3 < band < 0.5$ in coordinate `band`; and cross-section closest to 1000. in coordinate `lev`. Note that limits applied to coordinate values are specified with a decimal point, and limits applied to dimension indices do not have a decimal point See Section 3.15 [Hyperslabs], page 62.

```
ncks -d time,5 -d lat,,0.0 -d lon,330.0, -d band,0.3,0.5
-d lev,1000.0 in.nc out.nc
```

Assume the domain of the monotonically increasing longitude coordinate `lon` is $0 < lon < 360$. Here, `lon` is an example of a wrapped coordinate. `ncks` will extract a hyperslab which crosses the Greenwich meridian simply by specifying the westernmost longitude as *min* and the easternmost longitude as *max*, as follows:

```
ncks -d lon,260.0,45.0 in.nc out.nc
```

For more details See Section 3.20 [Wrapped Coordinates], page 70.

## 4.9 ncpdq netCDF Permute Dimensions Quickly

SYNTAX

```
ncpdq [-3] [-4] [-6] [-7] [-A] [-a [-]dim[,...]] [-C] [-c]
[--cnk_byt sz_byt] [--cnk_dmn nm,sz_lmn] [--cnk_map map]
[--cnk_min sz_byt] [--cnk_plc plc] [--cnk_scl sz_lmn]
[-D dbg] [-d dim,[min][,[max][,[stride]]]
[-F] [-G gpe_dsc] [-g grp[,...]] [--glb ...] [-h] [--hdf] [--hdr_pad nbr]
[-L dfl_lvl] [-l path] [-M pck_map] [--mrd]
[--no_cll_msr] [--no_frm_trm] [--no_tmp_fl]
[-O] [-o output-file] [-P pck_plc] [-p path] [--ppc ...]
[-R] [-r] [--ram_all] [-t thr_nbr] [-U] [--unn] [-v var[,...]] [-X ...] [-x]
input-file [output-file]
```

DESCRIPTION

ncpdq performs one (not both) of two distinct functions: packing or dimension permutation. ncpdq is optimized to perform these actions in a parallel fashion with a minimum of time and memory. The *pdq* may stand for "Permute Dimensions Quickly", "Pack Data Quietly", "Pillory Dan Quayle", or other silly uses.

### Packing and Unpacking Functions

The ncpdq packing (and unpacking) algorithms are described in Section 4.1.12 [Methods and functions], page 158, and are also implemented in ncap2. ncpdq extends the functionality of these algorithms by providing high level control of the *packing policy* so that users can consistently pack (and unpack) entire files with one command. The user specifies the desired packing policy with the '-P' switch (or its long option equivalents, '--pck_plc' and '--pack_policy') and its *pck_plc* argument. Four packing policies are currently implemented:

*Packing (and Re-Packing) Variables [default]*

Definition: Pack unpacked variables, re-pack packed variables
Alternate invocation: ncpack
*pck_plc* key values: 'all_new', 'pck_all_new_att'

*Packing (and not Re-Packing) Variables*

Definition: Pack unpacked variables, copy packed variables
Alternate invocation: none
*pck_plc* key values: 'all_xst', 'pck_all_xst_att'

*Re-Packing Variables*

Definition: Re-pack packed variables, copy unpacked variables
Alternate invocation: none
*pck_plc* key values: 'xst_new', 'pck_xst_new_att'

*Unpacking*

Definition: Unpack packed variables, copy unpacked variables
Alternate invocation: `ncunpack`
*pck_plc* key values: '`upk`', '`unpack`', '`pck_upk`'

Equivalent key values are fully interchangeable. Multiple equivalent options are provided to satisfy disparate needs and tastes of NCO users working with scripts and from the command line.

Regardless of the packing policy selected, `ncpdq` no longer (as of NCO version 4.0.4 in October, 2010) packs coordinate variables, or the special variables, weights, and other grid properties described in Section 3.41 [CF Conventions], page 131. Prior `ncpdq` versions treated coordinate variables and grid properties no differently from other variables. However, coordinate variables are one-dimensional, so packing saves little space on large files, and the resulting files are difficult for humans to read. `ncpdq` will, of course, *unpack* coordinate variables and weights, for example, in case some other, non-NCO software packed them in the first place.

Concurrently, Gaussian and area weights and other grid properties are often used to derive fields in re-inflated (unpacked) files, so packing such grid properties causes a considerable loss of precision in downstream data processing. If users express strong wishes to pack grid properties, we will implement new packing policies. An immediate workaround for those needing to pack grid properties now, is to use the `ncap2` packing functions or to rename the grid properties prior to calling `ncpdq`. We welcome your feedback.

To reduce required memorization of these complex policy switches, `ncpdq` may also be invoked via a synonym or with switches that imply a particular policy. `ncpack` is a synonym for `ncpdq` and behaves the same in all respects. Both `ncpdq` and `ncpack` assume a default packing policy request of '`all_new`'. Hence `ncpack` may be invoked without any '`-P`' switch, unlike `ncpdq`. Similarly, `ncunpack` is a synonym for `ncpdq` except that `ncpack` implicitly assumes a request to unpack, i.e., '`-P pck_upk`'. Finally, the `ncpdq` '`-U`' switch (or its long option equivalents '`--unpack`') requires no argument. It simply requests unpacking.

Given the menagerie of synonyms, equivalent options, and implied options, a short list of some equivalent commands is appropriate. The following commands are equivalent for packing: `ncpdq -P all_new`, `ncpdq --pck_plc=all_new`, and `ncpack`. The following commands are equivalent for unpacking: `ncpdq -P upk`, `ncpdq -U`, `ncpdq --pck_plc=unpack`, and `ncunpack`. Equivalent commands for other packing policies, e.g., '`all_xst`', follow by analogy. Note that `ncpdq` synonyms are subject to the same constraints and recommendations discussed in the secion on `ncbo` synonyms (see Section 4.3 [ncbo netCDF Binary Operator], page 207). That is, symbolic links must exist from the synonym to `ncpdq`, or else the user must define an `alias`.

The `ncpdq` packing algorithms must know to which type particular types of input variables are to be packed. The correspondence between the input variable type and the output, packed type, is called the *packing map*. The user specifies the desired packing map with the '`-M`' switch (or its long option equivalents, '`--pck_map`' and '`--map`') and its *pck_map* argument. Five packing maps are currently implemented:

*Pack Floating Precisions to* `NC_SHORT` *[default]*
: Definition: Pack floating precision types to `NC_SHORT`
Map: Pack [`NC_DOUBLE`,`NC_FLOAT`] to `NC_SHORT`
Types copied instead of packed: [`NC_INT64`,`NC_UINT64`,`NC_INT`,`NC_UINT`,`NC_SHORT`,`NC_USHORT`,`NC_CHAR`,`NC_BYTE`,`NC_UBYTE`]
*pck_map* key values: '`flt_sht`', '`pck_map_flt_sht`'

*Pack Floating Precisions to* `NC_BYTE`
: Definition: Pack floating precision types to `NC_BYTE`
Map: Pack [`NC_DOUBLE`,`NC_FLOAT`] to `NC_BYTE`
Types copied instead of packed: [`NC_INT64`,`NC_UINT64`,`NC_INT`,`NC_UINT`,`NC_SHORT`,`NC_USHORT`,`NC_CHAR`,`NC_BYTE`,`NC_UBYTE`]
*pck_map* key values: '`flt_byt`', '`pck_map_flt_byt`'

*Pack Higher Precisions to* `NC_SHORT`
: Definition: Pack higher precision types to `NC_SHORT`
Map: Pack [`NC_DOUBLE`,`NC_FLOAT`,`NC_INT64`,`NC_UINT64`,`NC_INT`,`NC_UINT`] to `NC_SHORT`
Types copied instead of packed: [`NC_SHORT`,`NC_USHORT`,`NC_CHAR`,`NC_BYTE`,`NC_UBYTE`]
*pck_map* key values: '`hgh_sht`', '`pck_map_hgh_sht`'

*Pack Higher Precisions to* `NC_BYTE`
: Definition: Pack higher precision types to `NC_BYTE`
Map: Pack [`NC_DOUBLE`,`NC_FLOAT`,`NC_INT64`,`NC_UINT64`,`NC_INT`,`NC_UINT`,`NC_SHORT`,`NC_USHORT`] to `NC_BYTE`
Types copied instead of packed: [`NC_CHAR`,`NC_BYTE`,`NC_UBYTE`]
*pck_map* key values: '`hgh_byt`', '`pck_map_hgh_byt`'

*Pack to Next Lesser Precision*
: Definition: Pack each type to type of next lesser size
Map: Pack [`NC_DOUBLE`,`NC_INT64`,`NC_UINT64`], to `NC_INT`. Pack [`NC_FLOAT`,`NC_INT`,`NC_UINT`] to `NC_SHORT`. Pack [`NC_SHORT`,`NC_USHORT`] to `NC_BYTE`.
Types copied instead of packed: [`NC_CHAR`,`NC_BYTE`,`NC_UBYTE`]
*pck_map* key values: '`nxt_lsr`', '`pck_map_nxt_lsr`'

The default '`all_new`' packing policy with the default '`flt_sht`' packing map reduces the typical `NC_FLOAT`-dominated file size by about 50%. '`flt_byt`' packing reduces an `NC_DOUBLE`-dominated file by about 87%.

The netCDF packing algorithm (see Section 4.1.12 [Methods and functions], page 158) is lossy—once packed, the exact original data cannot be recovered without a full backup. Hence users should be aware of some packing caveats: First, the interaction of packing and data equal to the *_FillValue* is complex. Test the `_FillValue` behavior by performing a pack/unpack cycle to ensure data that are missing *stay* missing and data that are not misssing do not join the Air National Guard and go missing. This may lead you to elect a new *_FillValue*. Second, `ncpdq` actually allows packing into `NC_CHAR` (with, e.g., '`flt_chr`'). However, the intrinsic conversion of `signed char` to higher precision types is tricky for values equal to zero, i.e., for `NUL`. Hence packing to `NC_CHAR` is not documented or advertised. Pack into `NC_BYTE` (with, e.g., '`flt_byt`') instead.

## Dimension Permutation

`ncpdq` re-shapes variables in *input-file* by re-ordering and/or reversing dimensions specified in the dimension list. The dimension list is a whitespace-free, comma separated list of dimension names, optionally prefixed by negative signs, that follows the '`-a`' (or long options '`--arrange`', '`--permute`', '`--re-order`', or '`--rdr`') switch. To re-order variables by a subset of their dimensions, specify these dimensions in a comma-separated list following '`-a`', e.g., '`-a lon,lat`'. To reverse a dimension, prefix its name with a negative sign in the dimension list, e.g., '`-a -lat`'. Re-ordering and reversal may be performed simultaneously, e.g., '`-a lon,-lat,time,-lev`'.

Users may specify any permutation of dimensions, including permutations which change the record dimension identity. The record dimension is re-ordered like any other dimension. This unique `ncpdq` capability makes it possible to concatenate files along any dimension. See Section 2.6.1 [Concatenation], page 20, for a detailed example. The record dimension is always the most slowly varying dimension in a record variable (see Section 3.14 [C and Fortran Index Conventions], page 61). The specified re-ordering fails if it requires creating more than one record dimension amongst all the output variables[1].

Two special cases of dimension re-ordering and reversal deserve special mention. First, it may be desirable to completely reverse the storage order of a variable. To do this, include all the variable's dimensions in the dimension re-order list in their original order, and prefix each dimension name with the negative sign. Second, it may useful to transpose a variable's storage order, e.g., from C to Fortran data storage order (see Section 3.14 [C and Fortran Index Conventions], page 61). To do this, include all the variable's dimensions in the dimension re-order list in reversed order. Explicit examples of these two techniques appear below.

NB: fxm ncpdq documentation will evolve through Fall 2004. I will upload updates to documentation linked to by the NCO homepage. ncpdq is a powerful operator, and I am unfamiliar with the terminology needed to describe what ncpdq does. Sequences, sets, sheesh! I just know that it does "The right thing" according to my gut feelings. Now do you feel more comfortable using it?

Let $\mathbf{D}(x)$ represent the dimensionality of the variable $x$. Dimensionality describes the order and sizes of dimensions. If $x$ has rank $N$, then we may write $\mathbf{D}(x)$ as the $N$-element vector

$$\mathbf{D}(x) = [D_1, D_2, D_3, \ldots, D_{n-1}, D_n, D_{n+1}, \ldots, D_{N-2}, D_{N-1}, D_N]$$

where $D_n$ is the size of the $n$'th dimension.

The dimension re-order list specified with '`-a`' is the $R$-element vector

$$\mathbf{R} = [R_1, R_2, R_3, \ldots, R_{r-1}, R_r, R_{r+1}, \ldots, R_{R-2}, R_{R-1}, R_R]$$

[1] This limitation, imposed by the netCDF storage layer, may be relaxed in the future with netCDF4.

There need be no relation between $N$ and $R$. Let the $S$-element vector $\mathbf{S}$ be the intersection (i.e., the ordered set of unique shared dimensions) of $\mathbf{D}$ and $\mathbf{R}$ Then

$$\begin{aligned}\mathbf{S} &= \mathbf{R} \cap \mathbf{D} \\ &= [S_1, S_2, S_3, \ldots, S_{s-1}, S_s, S_{s+1}, \ldots, S_{S-2}, S_{S-1}, S_S]\end{aligned}$$

$\mathbf{S}$ is empty if $\mathbf{R} \notin \mathbf{D}$.

Re-ordering (or re-shaping) a variable means mapping the input state with dimensionality $\mathbf{D}(x)$ to the output state with dimensionality $\mathbf{D}'(x')$. In practice, mapping occurs in three logically distinct steps. First, we tranlate the user input to a one-to-one mapping $\mathcal{M}$ between input and output dimensions, $\mathbf{D} \mapsto \mathbf{D}'$. This tentative map is final unless external constraints (typically netCDF restrictions) impose themselves. Second, we check and, if necessary, refine the tentative mapping so that the re-shaped variables will co-exist in the same file without violating netCDF-imposed storage restrictions. This refined map specifies the final (output) dimensionality. Third, we translate the output dimensionality into one-dimensional memory offsets for each datum according to the C language convention for multi-dimensional array storage. Dimension reversal changes the ordering of data, though not the rank or dimensionality, and so is part of the third step.

Dimensions $R$ disjoint from $\mathbf{D}$ play no role in re-ordering. The first step taken to re-order a variable is to determine $\mathbf{S}$. $\mathbf{R}$ is constant for all variables, whereas $\mathbf{D}$, and hence $\mathbf{S}$, is variable-specific. $\mathbf{S}$ is empty if $\mathbf{R} \notin \mathbf{D}$. This may be the case for some extracted variables. The user may explicitly specify the one-to-one mapping of input to output dimension order by supplying (with '`-a`') a re-order list $\mathbf{R}$ such that $S = N$. In this case $D'_n = S_n$. The degenerate case occurs when $\mathbf{D} = \mathbf{S}$. This produces the identity mapping $D'_n = D_n$.

The mapping of input to output dimension order is more complex when $S \neq N$. In this case $D'_n = D_n$ for the $N - S$ dimensions $D'_n \notin \mathbf{S}$. For the $S$ dimensions $D'_n \in \mathbf{S}$, $D'_n = S_s$.

EXAMPLES

Pack and unpack all variables in file `in.nc` and store the results in `out.nc`:

```
ncpdq in.nc out.nc # Same as ncpack in.nc out.nc
ncpdq -P all_new -M flt_sht in.nc out.nc # Defaults
ncpdq -P all_xst in.nc out.nc
ncpdq -P upk in.nc out.nc # Same as ncunpack in.nc out.nc
ncpdq -U in.nc out.nc # Same as ncunpack in.nc out.nc
```

The first two commands pack any unpacked variable in the input file. They also unpack and then re-pack every packed variable. The third command only packs unpacked variables in the input file. If a variable is already packed, the third command copies it unchanged to the output file. The fourth and fifth commands unpack any packed variables. If a variable is not packed, the third command copies it unchanged.

The previous examples all utilized the default packing map. Suppose you wish to archive all data that are currently unpacked into a form which only preserves 256 distinct values. Then you could specify the packing map *pck_map* as '`hgh_byt`' and the packing policy *pck_plc* as '`all_xst`':

```
ncpdq -P all_xst -M hgh_byt in.nc out.nc
```

Many different packing maps may be used to construct a given file by performing the packing on subsets of variables (e.g., with '-v') and using the append feature with '-A' (see Section 2.4 [Appending Variables], page 19).

Users may wish to unpack data packed with the HDF convention, and then re-pack it with the netCDF convention so that all their datasets use the same packing convention prior to intercomparison.

```
# One-step procedure: For NCO 4.4.0+, netCDF 4.3.1+
# 1. Convert, unpack, and repack HDF file into netCDF file
ncpdq --hdf_upk -P xst_new modis.hdf modis.nc # HDF4 files
ncpdq --hdf_upk -P xst_new modis.h5  modis.nc # HDF5 files

# One-step procedure: For NCO 4.3.7--4.3.9
# 1. Convert, unpack, and repack HDF file into netCDF file
ncpdq --hdf4 --hdf_upk -P xst_new modis.hdf modis.nc # HDF4
ncpdq        --hdf_upk -P xst_new modis.h5  modis.nc # HDF5

# Two-step procedure: For NCO 4.3.6 and earlier
# 1. Convert HDF file to netCDF file
ncl_convert2nc modis.hdf
# 2. Unpack using HDF convention and repack using netCDF convention
ncpdq --hdf_upk -P xst_new modis.nc modis.nc
```

NCO now[2] automatically detects HDF4 files. In this case it produces an output file `modis.nc` which preserves the HDF packing used in the input file. The `ncpdq` command first unpacks all packed variables using the HDF unpacking algorithm (as specified by '--hdf_upk'), and then repacks those same variables using the netCDF algorithm (because that is the only algorithm NCO packs with). As described above the '--P xst_new' packing policy only repacks variables that are already packed. Not-packed variables are copied directly without loss of precision[3].

Re-order file `in.nc` so that the dimension `lon` always precedes the dimension `lat` and store the results in `out.nc`:

```
ncpdq -a lon,lat in.nc out.nc
ncpdq -v three_dmn_var -a lon,lat in.nc out.nc
```

The first command re-orders every variable in the input file. The second command extracts and re-orders only the variable `three_dmn_var`.

---

[2] Prior to NCO 4.4.0 and netCDF 4.3.1 (January, 2014), NCO requires the '--hdf4' switch to correctly read HDF4 input files. For example, 'ncpdq --hdf4 --hdf_upk -P xst_new modis.hdf modis.nc'. That switch is now obsolete, though harmless for backwards compatibility. Prior to version 4.3.7 (October, 2013), NCO lacked the software necessary to workaround netCDF library flaws handling HDF4 files, and thus NCO failed to convert HDF4 files to netCDF files. In those cases, use the `ncl_convert2nc` command distributed with NCL to convert HDF4 files to netCDF.

[3] `ncpdq` does not support packing data using the HDF convention. Although it is now straightforward to support this, we think it might sow more confusion than it reaps. Let us know if you disagree and would like NCO to support packing data with HDF algorithm.

Suppose the dimension `lat` represents latitude and monotonically increases increases from south to north. Reversing the `lat` dimension means re-ordering the data so that latitude values decrease monotonically from north to south. Accomplish this with

```
% ncpdq -a -lat in.nc out.nc
% ncks -C -v lat in.nc
lat[0]=-90
lat[1]=90
% ncks -C -v lat out.nc
lat[0]=90
lat[1]=-90
```

This operation reversed the latitude dimension of all variables. Whitespace immediately preceding the negative sign that specifies dimension reversal may be dangerous. Quotes and long options can help protect negative signs that should indicate dimension reversal from being interpreted by the shell as dashes that indicate new command line switches.

```
ncpdq -a -lat in.nc out.nc # Dangerous? Whitespace before "-lat"
ncpdq -a '-lat' in.nc out.nc # OK. Quotes protect "-" in "-lat"
ncpdq -a lon,-lat in.nc out.nc # OK. No whitespace before "-"
ncpdq --rdr=-lat in.nc out.nc # Preferred. Uses "=" not whitespace
```

To create the mathematical transpose of a variable, place all its dimensions in the dimension re-order list in reversed order. This example creates the transpose of `three_dmn_var`:

```
% ncpdq -a lon,lev,lat -v three_dmn_var in.nc out.nc
% ncks -C -v three_dmn_var in.nc
lat[0]=-90 lev[0]=100 lon[0]=0 three_dmn_var[0]=0
lat[0]=-90 lev[0]=100 lon[1]=90 three_dmn_var[1]=1
lat[0]=-90 lev[0]=100 lon[2]=180 three_dmn_var[2]=2
...
lat[1]=90 lev[2]=1000 lon[1]=90 three_dmn_var[21]=21
lat[1]=90 lev[2]=1000 lon[2]=180 three_dmn_var[22]=22
lat[1]=90 lev[2]=1000 lon[3]=270 three_dmn_var[23]=23
% ncks -C -v three_dmn_var out.nc
lon[0]=0 lev[0]=100 lat[0]=-90 three_dmn_var[0]=0
lon[0]=0 lev[0]=100 lat[1]=90 three_dmn_var[1]=12
lon[0]=0 lev[1]=500 lat[0]=-90 three_dmn_var[2]=4
...
lon[3]=270 lev[1]=500 lat[1]=90 three_dmn_var[21]=19
lon[3]=270 lev[2]=1000 lat[0]=-90 three_dmn_var[22]=11
lon[3]=270 lev[2]=1000 lat[1]=90 three_dmn_var[23]=23
```

To completely reverse the storage order of a variable, include all its dimensions in the re-order list, each prefixed by a negative sign. This example reverses the storage order of `three_dmn_var`:

```
% ncpdq -a -lat,-lev,-lon -v three_dmn_var in.nc out.nc
% ncks -C -v three_dmn_var in.nc
lat[0]=-90 lev[0]=100 lon[0]=0 three_dmn_var[0]=0
```

```
lat[0]=-90 lev[0]=100 lon[1]=90 three_dmn_var[1]=1
lat[0]=-90 lev[0]=100 lon[2]=180 three_dmn_var[2]=2
...
lat[1]=90 lev[2]=1000 lon[1]=90 three_dmn_var[21]=21
lat[1]=90 lev[2]=1000 lon[2]=180 three_dmn_var[22]=22
lat[1]=90 lev[2]=1000 lon[3]=270 three_dmn_var[23]=23
% ncks -C -v three_dmn_var out.nc
lat[0]=90 lev[0]=1000 lon[0]=270 three_dmn_var[0]=23
lat[0]=90 lev[0]=1000 lon[1]=180 three_dmn_var[1]=22
lat[0]=90 lev[0]=1000 lon[2]=90 three_dmn_var[2]=21
...
lat[1]=-90 lev[2]=100 lon[1]=180 three_dmn_var[21]=2
lat[1]=-90 lev[2]=100 lon[2]=90 three_dmn_var[22]=1
lat[1]=-90 lev[2]=100 lon[3]=0 three_dmn_var[23]=0
```

Creating a record dimension named, e.g., `time`, in a file which has no existing record dimension is simple with `ncecat`:

```
ncecat -O -u time in.nc out.nc # Create degenerate record dimension named "time"
```

Now consider a file with all dimensions, including `time`, fixed (non-record). Suppose the user wishes to convert `time` from a fixed dimension to a record dimension. This may be useful, for example, when the user wishes to append additional time slices to the data. As of NCO version 4.0.1 (April, 2010) the preferred method for doing this is with `ncks`:

```
ncks -O --mk_rec_dmn time in.nc out.nc # Change "time" to record dimension
```

Prior to 4.0.1, the procedure to change an existing fixed dimension into a record dimension required three separate commands, `ncecat` followed by `ncpdq`, and then `ncwa`. The recommended method is now to use '`ncks --fix_rec_dmn`', yet it is still instructive to present the original procedure, as it shows how multiple operators can achieve the same ends by different means:

```
ncecat -O in.nc out.nc # Add degenerate record dimension named "record"
ncpdq -O -a time,record out.nc out.nc # Switch "record" and "time"
ncwa -O -a record out.nc out.nc # Remove (degenerate) "record"
```

The first step creates a degenerate (size equals one) record dimension named (by default) `record`. The second step swaps the ordering of the dimensions named `time` and `record`. Since `time` now occupies the position of the first (least rapidly varying) dimension, it becomes the record dimension. The dimension named `record` is no longer a record dimension. The third step averages over this degenerate `record` dimension. Averaging over a degenerate dimension does not alter the data. The ordering of other dimensions in the file (`lat`, `lon`, etc.) is immaterial to this procedure. See Section 4.5 [ncecat netCDF Ensemble Concatenator], page 228, and Section 4.8 [ncks netCDF Kitchen Sink], page 237, for other methods of changing variable dimensionality, including the record dimension.

## 4.10 ncra netCDF Record Averager

SYNTAX

```
ncra [-3] [-4] [-6] [-7] [-A] [-C] [-c] [--cb]
[--cnk_byt sz_byt] [--cnk_dmn nm,sz_lmn] [--cnk_map map]
[--cnk_min sz_byt] [--cnk_plc plc] [--cnk_scl sz_lmn]
[-D dbg] [-d dim,[min][,[max][,[stride][,[subcycle]]]] [-F]
[-G gpe_dsc] [-g grp[,...]] [--glb ...] [-h] [--hdf] [--hdr_pad nbr]
[-L dfl_lvl] [-l path] [--mro] [-N] [-n loop]
[--no_cll_msr] [--no_cll_mth] [--no_frm_trm] [--no_tmp_fl]
[-O] [-o output-
file] [-p path] [--ppc ...] [-R] [-r] [--ram_all] [--rec_apn] [--rth_dbl|flt]
[-t thr_nbr] [--unn] [-v var[,...]] [-w wgt] [-X ...] [-x] [-y op_typ]
[input-files] [output-file]
```

DESCRIPTION

`ncra` computes statistics (including, though not limited to, averages) of record variables across an arbitrary number of *input-files*. The record dimension is, by default, retained as a degenerate (size 1) dimension in the output variables. See Section 2.6 [Statistics vs. Concatenation], page 20, for a description of the distinctions between the various statistics tools and concatenators. As a multi-file operator, `ncra` will read the list of *input-files* from `stdin` if they are not specified as positional arguments on the command line (see Section 2.7 [Large Numbers of Files], page 21).

Input files may vary in size, but each must have a record dimension. The record coordinate, if any, should be monotonic (or else non-fatal warnings may be generated). Hyperslabs of the record dimension which include more than one file work correctly. `ncra` supports the *stride* argument to the '`-d`' hyperslab option (see Section 3.15 [Hyperslabs], page 62) for the record dimension only, *stride* is not supported for non-record dimensions. `ncra` *always averages* coordinate variables (e.g., `time`) regardless of the arithmetic operation type performed on non-coordinate variables (see Section 3.35 [Operation Types], page 114).

As of NCO version 4.4.9, released in May, 2015, `ncra` accepts user-specified weights with the '`-w`' (or long-option equivalent '`--wgt`', '`--wgt_var`', or '`--weight`') switch. When no weight is specified, `ncra` weights each record (e.g., time slice) in the *input-files* equally. `ncra` does not attempt to see if, say, the `time` coordinate is irregularly spaced and thus would require a weighted average in order to be a true time average.

Weights specified with '`-w wgt`' may take one of two forms. In the first form, the '`wgt`' argument is a comma-separated list of values by which to weight each *file*. Thus the number of values must equal the number of files specified in the input file list, or else the program will exit. In the second form, the '`wgt`' argument is the name of a weighting variable present in every input file. The variable may be a scalar or a one-dimensional record variable. Scalar weights are applied uniformly to the entire file (i.e., a per-file weight). One-dimensional weights apply to each corresponding record (i.e., per-record weights), and are suitable for dynamically changing timesteps.

By default, any weights specified (whether by value or by variable name) are normalized to unity by dividing each specified weight by the sum of all the weights. This means, for example, that, '-w 0.25,0.75' is equivalent to '-w 2.0,6.0' since both are equal when normalized. This behavior simplifies specifying weights based on countable items. For example, time-weighting monthly averages for March, April, and May to obtain a spring seasonal average can be done with '-w 31,30,31' instead of '-w 0.33695652173913043478,0.32608695652173913043,0.33695652173913043478'.

However, sometimes one wishes to use weights in "dot-product mode", i.e., multiply by the (non-normalized) weights. As of NCO version 4.5.2, released in July, 2015, `ncra` accepts the '-N' (or long-option equivalent '--no_nrm_by_wgt') switch that prevents automatic weight normalization. When this switch is used, the weights will not be normalized (unless the user provides them as normalized), and the numerator of the weighted average will not be divided by the sum of the weights (which is one for normalized weights).

Bear these two exceptions in mind when weighting input: First, `ncra` only applies weights if the arithmetic operation type is averaging (see Section 3.35 [Operation Types], page 114), i.e., for timeseries mean and for timeseries mean absolute value. Second, weights are never applied for minimization, square-roots, etc. `ncra` *never weights* coordinate variables (e.g., `time`) regardless of the weighting performed on non-coordinate variables.

As of NCO version 4.6.0 (May, 2016) `ncra` can honor the CF `climatology` and climatological statistics conventions described in Section 3.41 [CF Conventions], page 131. This functionality only works when each input file contains only a single record (timestep). Currently this is opt-in with the '--cb' flag (or long-option equivalent '--clm_bnd'), or with the '--c2b' flag (or its long-option equivalent '--clm2bnd') switches. Invoking '--cb' causes `ncra` to:

1. Add a `climatology` attribute with value "climatology_bounds" the time coordinate, if necessary
2. Remove the `bounds` attribute from the time coordinate, if necessary
3. Output a variable named `climatology_bounds` with values that are minima/maxima of the input time coordinate `bounds` variable.
4. Omit any input time coordinate `bounds` attribute and variable
5. Ensure the `cell_methods` attribute for all variables is appropriate for climatologies within and over years. Climatologies within days will have incorrect units (the switch is currently opt-in so that incorrect units are not inadvertently generated). Please contact the authors if this functionality is important to you (The omission of climatologies within days is mainly a matter of trying to keep the switches and interface clean).

Use the '--c2b' flag (instead of '--cb') to convert the input `climatology` bounds to a non-climatology `bounds` in the output. In other words, use '--c2b' when averaging sub-sampled climatologies together to produce a continuous (non-climatologically sub-sampled) mean.

```
# Use --cb to average months into a climatological month
ncra --cb 2014_01.nc 2015_01.nc 2016_01.nc clm_JAN.nc
# Use --cb to average climatological months into a climatological season
ncra --cb clm_DEC.nc clm_JAN.nc clm_FEB.nc clm_DJF.nc
# Four seasons make a complete year so use --c2b
ncra --c2b clm_DJF.nc clm_MAM.nc clm_JJA.nc clm_SON.nc clm_ANN.nc
```

Currently this functionality only works with climatologies within and over years (not within or over days).

EXAMPLES

Average files 85.nc, 86.nc, ... 89.nc along the record dimension, and store the results in 8589.nc:

```
ncra 85.nc 86.nc 87.nc 88.nc 89.nc 8589.nc
ncra 8[56789].nc 8589.nc
ncra -n 5,2,1 85.nc 8589.nc
```

These three methods produce identical answers. See Section 3.5 [Specifying Input Files], page 33, for an explanation of the distinctions between these methods.

Assume the files 85.nc, 86.nc, ... 89.nc each contain a record coordinate *time* of length 12 defined such that the third record in 86.nc contains data from March 1986, etc. NCO knows how to hyperslab the record dimension across files. Thus, to average data from December, 1985 through February, 1986:

```
ncra -d time,11,13 85.nc 86.nc 87.nc 8512_8602.nc
ncra -F -d time,12,14 85.nc 86.nc 87.nc 8512_8602.nc
```

The file 87.nc is superfluous, but does not cause an error. The '-F' turns on the Fortran (1-based) indexing convention. The following uses the *stride* option to average all the March temperature data from multiple input files into a single output file

```
ncra -F -d time,3,,12 -v temperature 85.nc 86.nc 87.nc 858687_03.nc
```

See Section 3.16 [Stride], page 64, for a description of the *stride* argument.

Assume the *time* coordinate is incrementally numbered such that January, 1985 = 1 and December, 1989 = 60. Assuming '??' only expands to the five desired files, the following averages June, 1985–June, 1989:

```
ncra -d time,6.,54. ??.nc 8506_8906.nc
ncra -y max -d time,6.,54. ??.nc 8506_8906.nc
```

The second example identifies the maximum instead of averaging. See Section 3.35 [Operation Types], page 114, for a description of all available statistical operations.

ncra includes the powerful subcycle and multi-record output features (see Section 3.18 [Subcycle], page 66). This example uses these features to compute and output winter (DJF) averages for all winter seasons beginning with year 1990 and continuing to the end of the input file:

```
ncra -O --mro -d time,"1990-12-01",,12,3 in.nc out.nc
```

The '-w wgt' option weights input data *per-file* or *per-timestep*:

```
ncra -w 31,31,28 dec.nc jan.nc feb.nc out.nc
ncra -w delta_t in1.nc in2.nc in3.nc out.nc
```

The first example weights the input differently per-file to produce correctly weighted winter seasonal mean statistics. The second example weights the input per-timestep to produce correctly weighted mean statistics. The last example

## 4.11 ncrcat netCDF Record Concatenator

SYNTAX

```
ncrcat [-3] [-4] [-6] [-7] [-A] [-C] [-c]
[--cnk_byt sz_byt] [--cnk_dmn nm,sz_lmn] [--cnk_map map]
[--cnk_min sz_byt] [--cnk_plc plc] [--cnk_scl sz_lmn]
[-D dbg] [-d dim,[min][,[max][,[stride][,[subcycle]]]] [-F]
[-G gpe_dsc] [-g grp[,...]] [--glb ...] [-h] [--hdr_pad nbr]
[-L dfl_lvl] [-l path] [--md5_digest] [-n loop]
[--no_tmp_fl] [--no_cll_msr] [--no_frm_trm] [--no_tmp_fl]
[-O] [-o output-
file] [-p path] [--ppc ...] [-R] [-r] [--ram_all] [--rec_apn]
[-t thr_nbr] [--unn] [-v var[,...]] [-X ...] [-x]
[input-files] [output-file]
```

DESCRIPTION

`ncrcat` concatenates record variables across an arbitrary number of *input-files*. The final record dimension is by default the sum of the lengths of the record dimensions in the input files. See Section 2.6 [Statistics vs. Concatenation], page 20, for a description of the distinctions between the various statistics tools and concatenators. As a multi-file operator, `ncrcat` will read the list of *input-files* from `stdin` if they are not specified as positional arguments on the command line (see Section 2.7 [Large Numbers of Files], page 21).

Input files may vary in size, but each must have a record dimension. The record coordinate, if any, should be monotonic (or else non-fatal warnings may be generated). Hyperslabs along the record dimension that span more than one file are handled correctly. `ncra` supports the *stride* argument to the '`-d`' hyperslab option for the record dimension only, *stride* is not supported for non-record dimensions.

Concatenating a variable packed with different scales multiple datasets is beyond the capabilities of `ncrcat` (and `ncecat`, the other concatenator (Section 2.6.1 [Concatenation], page 20). `ncrcat` does not unpack data, it simply *copies* the data from the *input-files*, and the metadata from the *first input-file*, to the *output-file*. This means that data compressed with a packing convention must use the identical packing parameters (e.g., `scale_factor` and `add_offset`) for a given variable across *all* input files. Otherwise the concatenated dataset will not unpack correctly. The workaround for cases where the packing parameters differ across *input-files* requires three steps: First, unpack the data using `ncpdq`. Second, concatenate the unpacked data using `ncrcat`, Third, re-pack the result with `ncpdq`.

`ncrcat` applies special rules to ARM convention time fields (e.g., `time_offset`). See Section 3.42 [ARM Conventions], page 135, for a complete description.

EXAMPLES

Concatenate files `85.nc`, `86.nc`, ... `89.nc` along the record dimension, and store the results in `8589.nc`:

```
ncrcat 85.nc 86.nc 87.nc 88.nc 89.nc 8589.nc
ncrcat 8[56789].nc 8589.nc
ncrcat -n 5,2,1 85.nc 8589.nc
```

These three methods produce identical answers. See Section 3.5 [Specifying Input Files], page 33, for an explanation of the distinctions between these methods.

Assume the files `85.nc`, `86.nc`, ... `89.nc` each contain a record coordinate *time* of length 12 defined such that the third record in `86.nc` contains data from March 1986, etc. NCO knows how to hyperslab the record dimension across files. Thus, to concatenate data from December, 1985–February, 1986:

```
ncrcat -d time,11,13 85.nc 86.nc 87.nc 8512_8602.nc
ncrcat -F -d time,12,14 85.nc 86.nc 87.nc 8512_8602.nc
```

The file `87.nc` is superfluous, but does not cause an error. When `ncra` and `ncrcat` encounter a file which does contain any records that meet the specified hyperslab criteria, they disregard the file and proceed to the next file without failing. The '`-F`' turns on the Fortran (1-based) indexing convention.

The following uses the *stride* option to concatenate all the March temperature data from multiple input files into a single output file

```
ncrcat -F -d time,3,,12 -v temperature 85.nc 86.nc 87.nc 858687_03.nc
```

See Section 3.16 [Stride], page 64, for a description of the *stride* argument.

Assume the *time* coordinate is incrementally numbered such that January, 1985 = 1 and December, 1989 = 60. Assuming `??` only expands to the five desired files, the following concatenates June, 1985–June, 1989:

```
ncrcat -d time,6.,54. ??.nc 8506_8906.nc
```

## 4.12 ncremap netCDF Remapper

SYNTAX

```
ncremap [-a alg_typ] [-D dbg_lvl] [-d dst_fl] [-E esmf_opt]
[-G grd_sng] [-g grd_dst] [-I drc_in] [-i input-file] [-j job_nbr]
[-M] [-m map_fl] [-n nco_opt] [-O drc_out] [-o output-file]
[-P pdq_typ] [-p par_typ] [-R rgr_opt] [-s grd_src]
[-T tempest_opt] [-t thr_nbr] [-U drc_tmp] [-u unq_sfx]
[-V rgr_var] [-v var_lst[,...]] [-w wgt_gnr] [-x xtn_lst[,...]]
```

DESCRIPTION

`ncremap` remaps the data file(s) in *input-file*, in *drc_in*, or piped through standard input, to the grid specified by (in descending order of precedence) *map_fl*, *grd_dst*, or *dst_fl* and stores the result in *output-file*(s). When no *input-file* is provided, `ncremap` operates in "map-only" mode where it exits after producing an annotated map-file. `ncremap` was introduced to NCO in version 4.5.4 (December, 2015). As a newer operator, its interface is evolving in response to user needs, feedback, and new features. `ncremap` orchestrates the regridding features of several different programs. Under the hood NCO applies pre-computed remapping weights or, when necessary, generates and infers grids, and calls external programs to generate the remapping weights that NCO then applies.

Unlike the rest of NCO, `ncremap` is a shell script, not a compiled binary. `ncremap` wraps the underlying regridder (`ncks`) and external executables to produce a friendly interface to regridding. Without any external dependencies, `ncremap` applies weights from a preexisiting mapfile to a source data file to produce a regridded dataset. Source and destination datasets may be on any Curvilinear, Rectangular, or Unstructured Data (CRUD) grid. `ncremap` will also, when necessary, use external programs ESMF's `ESMF_RegridWeightGen` (ERWG) or TempestRemap's `GenerateOverlapMesh/GenerateOfflineMap`) to generate weights and mapfiles. In order to use the weight-generation options, ensure that one or both of the weight-generation packages is installed and on your `$PATH`. The recommended way to obtain ERWG is as distributed in binary format. Many (most?) NCO users already have NCL on their system(s), and NCL usually comes with ERWG. Since about June, 2016, the Conda NCO package will also install ERWG[1]. Then be sure the directory containing the ERWG executable is on your `$PATH` before using `ncremap`. As a fallback, ERWG may also be installed from source: `https://earthsystemcog.org/projects/esmf/download_last_public`. `ncremap` can also generate and utilize mapfiles created by TempestRemap, `https://github.com/ClimateGlobalChange/tempestremap`. As far as we know TempestRemap must be built from source because there are no binary distributions of it. Please contact those projects for support on building and installing their software, which makes `ncremap` more functional and user-friendly. Please ensure you have the latest version of ERWG or TempestRemap before reporting any related problems to NCO.

As mentioned above, `ncremap` orchestrates the regridding features of several different programs. `ncremap` runs most quickly when it is supplied with a pre-computed mapfile. However, `ncremap` will also (call other programs to) compute mapfiles when necessary and when given sufficient grid information. Thus it is helpful to understand when `ncremap` will

[1] Install the Conda NCO package with '`conda install -c conda-forge nco`'.

and will not internally generate a mapfile. Supplying input data files and a pre-computed mapfile *without* any other grid information causes `ncremap` to regrid the data files without first pausing to internally generate a mapfile. On the other hand, supplying any grid information (i.e., using any of the '`-d`', '`-G`', '`-g`', or '`-s`' switches described below), causes `ncremap` to internally (re-)generate the mapfile by combining the supplied and inferred grid information. A generated mapfile is given a default name unless a user-specified name is supplied with '`-m map_fl`'.

## Options specific to `ncremap`

The following summarizes features unique to `ncremap`. Features common to many operators are described in Chapter 3 [Shared features], page 29.

'`-a alg_typ (--alg_typ, --algorithm, --regrid_algorithm)`'
: Specifies the interpolation algorithm for weight-generation for use by `ESMF_RegridWeightGen` (ERWG). `ncremap` unbundles this algorithm choice from the rest of the ERWG invocation syntax because interpolation algorithms are more frequently change by users than other ERWG options (that can be changed with '`-E esmf_opt`'). The *alg_typ* argument must be one of ERWG's five interpolation algorithms: `bilinear` (default, acceptable abbreviation is `bln`), `conserve` (or `conservative` or `cns`), `nearestdtos` (or `nds` or `dtos`), `neareststod` (or `nds` or `stod`), and `patch` (or `pch` or `ptc`). See ERWG documentation here (`http://www.earthsystemmodeling.org/esmf_releases/public/ESMF_6_3_0rp1/ESMF_refdoc/node3.html#SECTION03020000000000000000`) for detailed descriptions of each algorithm. This option currently has no effect on TempestRemap weight-generation.

'`-D dbg_lvl (--dbg_lvl, --dbg, --debug, --debug_level)`'
: Specifies a debugging level similar to the rest of NCO. If *dbg_lvl* = 1, `ncremap` prints more extensive diagnostics of its behavior. If *dbg_lvl* = 2, `ncremap` prints the commands it would execute at any higher or lower debugging level, but does not execute these commands. If *dbg_lvl* > 2, `ncremap` prints the diagnostic information, executes all commands, and passes-through the debugging level to the regridder (`ncks`) for additional diagnostics.

'`-d dst_fl (--dst_fl, --destination_file, --template_file, --template)`'
: Specifies a data file on the destination grid. Currently *dst_fl* must be a data file (not a gridfile, SCRIP or otherwise) from which NCO can infer the destination grid. The more coordinate and boundary information and metadata the better NCO will do at inferring the grid. If *dst_fl* has cell boundaries then NCO will use those. If *dst_fl* has only cell-center coordinates (and no edges), then NCO will guess-at (for rectangular grids) or interpolate (for curvilinear grids) the edges. Unstructured grids must supply cell boundary information, as it cannot be interpolated or guessed-at. NCO only reads coordinate and grid data and metadata from *dst_fl*. *dst_fl* is not modified, and may have read-only permissions.

'`-E esmf_opt (--esmf_opt, --esmf, --esmf_options)`'
: `ncremap` passes *esmf_opt* directly through to ERWG. The user-specified contents of *esmf_opt* supercede its default contents ('`--ignore_unmapped`'). Some-

times users may wish ERWG to assume regional grids, in which case *esmf_opt* could be '-r --ignore_upmapped'.

'-g *grd_dst* (--grd_dst, --grid_dest, --dest_grid, --destination_grid)'
: Specifies the destination gridfile in SCRIP format. NCO will use ERWG to combine *grd_dst* with a source gridfile (either inferred from *input-file*, supplied with '-s *grd_src*', or generated from '-G *grd_sng*') to produce the remapping weights. *grd_dst* is not modified, and may have read-only permissions.

'-G *grd_sng* (--grd_sng, --grid_generation, --grid_gen, --grid_string)'
: Specifies, with NCO options (see Section 3.22 [Grid Generation], page 73), a source gridfile to create. (Warning: NCO's syntax for gridfile generations is ugly and needs streamlining. It does, however, work well and produces finer rectangular grids than any other software we know of.) NCO creates the gridfile in SCRIP format, and then uses ERWG to combine that with the destination grid (either inferred from *input-file* or supplied with '-g *grd_dst*' and generate mapping weights. This option is seldom used since NCO can infer the input grid directly from *input-file*. However, there may be no easier way to visually tune the choice of destination grid than by rapidly generating candidates with this option and inspecting the results.

'-I *in_drc* (--in_drc, --drc_in, --dir_in, --in_dir, input)'
: Specifies the input directory, i.e., the directory which contains the input file(s). If *in_fl* is also specified, then the input filepath is constructed by appending a slash and the filename to the directory: '*in_drc*/*in_fl*'. Specifying *in_drc* without *in_fl* causes ncremap to attempt to remap every file in *in_drc* that ends with one of these suffixes: .nc, .nc3, .nc4, .cdf, .hdf, .he5, or .h5. When multiple files are regridded, each output file takes the name of the corresponding input file. There is no namespace conflict because the input and output files are in separate directories. Note that ncremap can instead accept the list of input files through standard input, e.g., 'ls *.nc | ncremap ...'.

'-i *in_fl* (--in_fl, --in_file, --input_file)'
: Specifies the file containing data on the source grid to be remapped to the destination grid. When provided with the optional *map_fl*, ncremap only reads data from *in_fl* in order to regrid it. Without the optional *map_fl* or *src_grd*, ncremap will try to infer the source grid from *in_fl*, and so must read coordinate and metatdata information from *in_fl*. In this case the more coordinate and boundary information and metadata, the better NCO will do at inferring the source grid. If *in_fl* has cell boundaries then NCO will use those. If *in_fl* has only cell-center coordinates (and no edges), then NCO will guess (for rectangular grids) or interpolate (for curvilinear grids) the edges. Unstructured grids must supply cell boundary information, as it cannot be interpolated or guessed-at. *in_fl* is not modified, and may have read-only permissions. Note that ncremap can instead accept the input file name through standard input, e.g., 'ls *.nc | ncremap ...'.

'-j *job_nbr* (--job_nbr, --job_number, --jobs)'
: Specifies the number of simultaneous regridding processes to spawn during parallel execution for both Background and MPI modes. In both parallel modes

`ncremap` spawns processes in batches of *job_nbr* jobs, then waits for those processes to complete. Once a batch finishes, `ncremap` spawns the next batch. In Background mode, all jobs are spawned to the local node. In MPI mode, all jobs are spawned in round-robin fashion to all available nodes until *job_nbr* jobs are running.

If regridding consumes so much RAM (e.g., because variables are large and/or the number of threads is large) that a single node can perform only one regridding job at a time, then a reasonable value for *job_nbr* is the number of nodes, *node_nbr*. Often, however, nodes can regrid multiple files simultaneously. It can be more efficient to spawn multiple jobs per node than to increase the threading per job because I/O contention for write access to a single file prevents threading from scaling indefinitely.

By default *job_nbr* = 2 in Background mode, and *job_nbr* = *node_nbr* in MPI mode. This helps prevent users from overloading nodes with too many jobs. Subject to the availability of adequate RAM, expand the number of jobs per node by increasing *job_nbr* until, ideally, each core on the node is used. Remember that processes and threading are multiplicative in core use. Four jobs each with four threads consumes sixteen cores.

As an example, consider regridding 100 files with a single map. Say you have a five-node cluster, and each node has 16 cores and can simultaneously regrid two files using eight threads each. (One needs to test a bit to determine these parameters.) Then an optimal (in terms of wallclock time) invocation would request five nodes with 10 simultaneous jobs of eight threads. On many batch systems this would involve a scheduler command like this '`qsub -l nodes=5 ...`' followed by '`ncremap -p mpi -j 10 -t 8 ...`'. This job will likely complete between five and ten-times faster than a serial invocation of `ncremap`. The uncertainty range is due to unforeseeable, system-dependent load and I/O charateristics. Nodes that can simultaneously write to more than one file fare better with multiple jobs per node. Nodes with only one I/O channel to disk may be better exploited by utilizing more threads per process.

'`-m` *map_fl* `(--map_fl, --map, --map_file, --rgr_map, --regrid_map)`'

Specifies a mapfile (i.e., weight-file) to remap the source to destination grid. If *map_fl* is specified in conjunction with any of the '`-d`', '`-G`', '`-g`', or '`-s`' switches, then `ncremap` will name the internally generated mapfile *map_fl*. Otherwise (i.e., if none of the source-grid switches are used), `ncremap` assumes that *map_fl* is a pre-computed mapfile. In that case, the *map_fl* must be in SCRIP format, although it may have been produced by any application (usually ERWG or TempestRemap). If *map_fl* has only cell-center coordinates (and no edges), then NCO will guess-at or interpolate the edges. If *map_fl* has cell boundaries then NCO will use those. A pre-computed *map_fl* is not modified, and may have read-only permissions. The user will be prompted to confirm if a newly generated map-file named *map_fl* would overwrite an existing file. `ncremap` adds provenance information to any newly generated map-file whose name was specified with '`-m map_fl`'. This provenance includes a `history` attribute that contains the command invoking `ncremap`, and the map-generating command invoked by `ncremap`.

'-M (--mlt_map, --multimap, --no_multimap, --nomultimap)'

ncremap assumes that every input file is on a unique grid unless a source grid-file is specified (with '-s *grd_src*') or multiple-mapfile generation is explicitly turned-off (with '-M'). The '-M' switch is toggled, it requires and accepts no argument. Toggling '-M' tells ncremap to generate at most one mapfile regardless of the number of input files. If '-M' is not toggled (and neither '-m *map_fl*' nor '-s *grd_src*' is invoked) then ncremap will use ERWG to generate a new mapfile for each input file. Generating new mapfiles for each input file is necessary for processing batches of data on different grids (e.g., swath-like data), and slow, tedious, and unnecessary when batch processing data on the same grids.

'-n *nco_opt* (--nco_opt, --nco_options, --nco)'

Specifies a string of options to pass-through unaltered to ncks. *nco_opt* defaults to '-O --no_tmp_fl'.

'-O *out_drc* (--out_drc, --drc_out, --dir_out, --out_dir, --output)'

Specifies the output directory, i.e., the directory name to contain the output file(s). If *out_fl* is also specified, then the output filepath is constructed by appending a slash and the filename to the directory: '*out_drc*/*out_fl*'. Specifying *out_drc* without *out_fl* causes ncremap to name each output file the same as the corresponding input file. There is no namespace conflict because the input and output files will be in separate directories.

'-o *out_fl* (--out_fl, --output_file, --out_file)'

Specifies the output filename, i.e., the name of the file to contain the data from *in_fl* remapped to the destination grid. If *out_fl* already exists it will be overwritten. Specifying *out_fl* when there are multiple input files (i.e., from using '-I *in_drc*' or standard input) generates an error (output files will be named the same as input files).

'-P *pdq_typ* (--pdq_typ, --prm_typ, --permutation, --permute)'

Specifies the permutation mode desired. As of January~15, 2016, one can tell ncremap to automatically tagpermute the dimensions in the data file prior to regridding for a limited (though growning) number of data-file types that suffer from the ncremap limitation concerning dimension ordering. Valid types are 'airs' (for NASA AIRS satellite data), 'mpas' (for MPAS ocean/ice model data), and 'nil' (for none). The default *pdq_typ* is 'nil', which means ncremap does not permute the dimension order prior to regridding. In AIRS-mode, ncremap calls ncpdq to permute dimensions from their order in the input file to this order: StdPressureLev,GeoTrack,GeoXTrack. In MPAS-mode the order is Time,nVertLevels,maxEdges,MaxEdges2,nEdges,nCells.

'-p *par_typ* (--, --, --, --)'

Specifies the parallelism mode desired. Parallelism accelerates throughput when regridding multiple files in one ncremap invocation. Valid types are 'bck' (for Background mode), 'mpi' (for MPI mode), and 'nil' (for none). The default *par_typ* is 'nil', which means ncremap will run in serial mode, and process one file at a time. Background and MPI parallelism modes both issue all regridding commands at one time. In Background mode these commands are spawned as UNIX background processes on the local node. Nodes with mutiple cores will take advantage of this and simultaneously execute regridding commands. In MPI mode these commands are issued round-robin fashion to all the compute nodes available to the job. Typically both parallel modes scale well with sufficent CPUs until I/O contention becomes the bottleneck. Furthermore, a naming conflict among intermediate files still exists (see Limitations, below) so parallel mode is currently only supported when all source files share the same grid.

'-R *rgr_opt* (--rgr_opt, --regrid_options)'
: `ncremap` passes *rgr_opt* directly through to the regridder. This is useful to customize output grids and metadata. The default value is '`--rgr lat_nm_out=lat --rgr lon_nm_out=lon`', i.e., by default `ncremap` always names latitude and longitude "lat" and "lon", respectively, regardless of their input names.

'-s *grd_src* (--grd_src, --grid_source, --source_grid, --src_grd)'
: Specifies the source gridfile in SCRIP format. NCO will use ERWG to combine this with a destination gridfile (either inferred from *dst_fl*, or generated by supplying a '`-G` ***grd_sng***' option) to generate remapping weights. *grd_src* is not modified, and may have read-only permissions. One appropriate circumstance to specify *grd_src* is when the *input-file*(s) do not contain sufficient information for NCO to infer an accurate or complete source grid. (Unfortunately many dataset producers do not record information like cell edges/vertices in their datasets. This is problematic for non-rectangular grids.) NCO assumes that *grd_src*, when supplied, applies to every *input-file*. Thus NCO will call ERWG only once, and will use that *map_fl* to regrid every *input-file*.

'-T *tempest_opt* (--tps_opt, --tempest_opt, --tempest, --tempest_options)'
: `ncremap` passes *tempest_opt* directly through to `GenerateOfflineMap` (not to `GenerateOverlapMesh`). The user-specified contents of *tempest_opt* supercede its default contents, which are currently empty. For example, to cause `GenerateOfflineMap` to use a `_FillValue` of −1, pass '`-T "--fillvalue -1.0"`' to `ncremap`. Other common options include enforcing monotonicity (which is not the default in TempestRemap) constraints. To guarantee monotonicity in regridding from Finite Volume FV to FV maps (e.g., MPAS-to-rectangular), pass '`-T "-in_np 1"`' to `ncremap`. To guarantee monotonicity in regridding from Finite Element FE to FV maps, pass '`-T "--mono"`'.

'-t *thr_nbr* (--thr_nbr, --thread_number, --threads)'
: Specifies the number of threads used per regridding process (see Section 3.3 [OpenMP Threading], page 29). The NCO regridder scales well up to 8–16 threads.

'-U *tmp_drc* (--tmp_drc, --drc_tmp, --tmp_dir, --dir_tmp, --tmp_drc)'
: Specifies the directory in which to place intermediate output files. Depending on how it is invoked, `ncremap` may generate a few or many intermediate files (grids and maps) that it will, by default, remove upon successful completion. These files can be large, so the option to set *tmp_drc* is offered to ensure their location is convenient to the system. If the user does not specify *tmp_drc*, then

ncremap uses the value of $TMPDIR, if any, or else /tmp if it exists, or else it uses the current working director ($PWD).

'-u *unq_sfx* (--unq_sfx, --unique_suffix, --suffix)'
: Specifies the suffix used to label intermediate (internal) files generated by the regridding workflow. Unique names are required to avoid interference among parallel invocations of ncremap. The default *unq_sfx* is '.pid*PID*.ncremap.tmp', where *PID* is the process ID. Applications that invoke ncremap can provide more or less informative suffixes. The suffix should be unique so that no two simultaneously executing instances of ncremap can generate the same file. For instance, a climatology script that issues a dozen ncremap commands may find it useful to encode the climatological month in the unique suffix. If *unq_sfx* is 'noclean' then ncremap retains (not removes) all intermediate files after completion.

'-v *var_lst* (--var_lst, --var, --vars, --variables, --variable_list)'
: The '-v' option causes ncremap to regrid only the variables in *var_lst*. It behaves like subsetting (see Section 3.11 [Subsetting Files], page 46) in the rest of NCO.

'-V *var_rgr* (--var_rgr, --rgr_var, --var_cf, --cf_var, cf_variable)'
: The '-V' option tells ncremap to use the same grid as *var_rgr* in the input file. If *var_rgr* adheres to the CF coordinates convention described here (http://cfconventions.org/1.6.html#coordinate-system), then ncclimo will infer the grid as represented by those coordinate variables. This option simplifies inferring grids when the grid coordinate names are unknown, since ncclimo will follow the CF convention to learn the identity of the grid coordinates.

Until NCO version 4.6.0 (May, 2016), ncremap would not follow CF conventions to identify coordinate variables. Instead, ncremap used an internal database of "usual suspects" to identify latitude and longitude coordinate variables. Now, if *var_rgr* is CF-compliant, then ncremap will automatically identify the horizontal spatial dimensions. If *var_rgr* is supplied but is not CF-compliant, then ncremap will use its internal database to identify horizontal spatial dimensions. If both these automated methods fail, manually supply ncremap with the names of the horizontal spatial dimensions

```
# Method used to obtain horizontal spatial coordinates:
ncremap -V var_rgr -i in.nc -d dst.nc -O ~/rgr # CF coordinates convention
ncremap -i in.nc -d dst.nc -O ~/rgr # Internal database
ncremap -R "--rgr lat_nm=xq --rgr lon_nm=zj" -i in.nc -d dst.nc -O ~/rgr # M
```

'-w *wgt_gnr* (--wgt_gnr, --weight_generator, --generator)'
: Specifies the weight-generator to use when a map-file is not provided. The *wgt_gnr* argument must be esmf for ESMF's ESMF_RegridWeightGen (ERWG), or tempest for TempestRemaps's GenerateOverlapMesh and GenerateOfflineMap. Specifying *wgt_gnr* and supplying (with '-m') a map-file is not permitted (since the weight-generator would not be used).

'-x *xtn_lst* (--xtn_lst, --xtn_var, --var_xtn, --extensive, --extensive_variables)'
: The '-x' option causes ncremap to treat the variables in *xtn_lst* as *extensive*, meaning that their value depends on the gridcell boundaries. Support for ex-

tensive variables during regridding is nascent. Currently variables marked as extensive are summed, not regridded.

## Limitations to ncremap

There are two significant limitations to **ncremap** that we hope to remove in the coming year. First, the fields to be regridded must have latitude and longitude as the final two dimension in *in_fl*. Fields with other dimension orders (e.g., '`lat,lev,lon`') will not regrid properly. To workaround this limitation for the time-being, please employ **ncpdq** (see Section 4.9 [ncpdq netCDF Permute Dimensions Quickly], page 254) to permute the dimensions before (and un-permute them after) regridding. For example

```
# AIRS Level2 vertical profiles
ncpdq -a StdPressureLev,GeoTrack,GeoXTrack AIRS_L2.hdf AIRS_L2_ncpdq.nc
ncremap -i AIRS_L2_ncpdq.nc -d dst_1x1.nc -O ~/rgr
# MPAS-O fields
ncpdq -a Time,nVertLevels,maxEdges,MaxEdges2,nEdges,nCells mpas.nc mpas_ncpdq.nc
ncremap -R "--rgr col_nm=nCells" -i mpas_ncpdq.nc -m mpas120_to_t62.nc -O ~/rgr
```

The previous two examples occur so frequently that **ncremap** has been specially equipped to handle AIRS and MPAS files. As of 20160115, the following **ncremap** commands with '`-P`' switches automagically perform all the required permutation and renaming necessary:

```
# AIRS Level2 vertical profiles
ncremap -P airs -i AIRS_L2.nc -d dst_1x1.nc -O ~/rgr
# MPAS-O/I fields
ncremap -P mpas -i mpas.nc -m mpas120_to_t62.nc -O ~/rgr
```

The machinery to handle permutations and special options for other datafiles is relatively easy to extend. If you work with common datasets that could benefit from their own `ncremap` '`-P`' options, contact us and we will try to implement them.

The second limitation is that **ncremap** currently must read weights from an on-disk mapfile, it cannot yet compute weights itself and use them directly from RAM. This makes **ncremap** an "offline regridder" and unnecessarily slow compared to an "integrated regridder" that computes weights and immediately applies them in RAM without any disk-access. In practice, the difference is most noticeable when the weights are easily computable "on the fly", e.g., rectangular-to-rectangular mappings. Otherwise the weight-generation takes much more time than the weight-application, at which **ncremap** is quite fast. To workaround this limitation, build **ESMF_RegridWeightGen** with parallel capabilities and ask me to enhance **ncremap** to call ERWG with the options to exploit those capabilities.

A side-effect of **ncremap** being an offline regridder is that, when necessary, it generates intermediate files to store grids and maps. These files are named, by default, `ncremap_tmp_grd_dst.nc`'`unq_sfx`', `ncremap_tmp_grd_src.nc`'`unq_sfx`', `ncremap_tmp_gnr_out.nc`'`unq_sfx`', `ncremap_tmp_map_*.nc`'`unq_sfx`', `ncremap_tmp_msh_ovr_*.nc`'`unq_sfx`', and `ncremap_tmp_pdq.nc`'`unq_sfx`'. They are placed in *drc_out* with the output file(s). In general, no intermediate grid or map files are generated when the mapfile is provided. Intermediate files are always generated when the '`-P` *`prm_typ`*' option is invoked. By default these files are automatically removed upon successful completion of the script. Early or unexpected termination of **ncremap** leaves these intermediate files behind.

Should intermediate files proliferate and/or annoy you, locate and/or remove all such files under the current directory with

```
find . -name 'ncremap_tmp*'
rm `find . -name 'ncremap_tmp*'`
```

EXAMPLES

Regrid input file `in.nc` to the spatial grid in file `dst.nc` and write the output to `out.nc`:

```
ncremap -i in.nc -d dst.nc -o out.nc
ncremap -i in.nc -d dst.nc -O regrid -o out.nc
ncremap -i in.nc -d dst.nc -o regrid/out.nc
ncremap -i in.nc -d dst.nc -O regrid # output named in.nc
```

NCO infers the destination spatial grid from `dst.nc` by reading its coordinate variables and CF attributes. In the first example, `ncremap` places the output in `out.nc`. In the second and third examples, the output file is `regrid/out.nc`. In the fourth example, `ncremap` places the output in the specified output directory. Since no output filename is provided, the output file will be named `regrid/in.nc`.

Generate a mapfile with `ncremap` and store it for later re-use. A pre-computed mapfile (supplied with '-m *map_fl*') eliminates time-consuming weight-generation, and thus considerably reduces wallclock time:

```
ncremap -i in.nc  -m map.nc -o out.nc
ncremap -I drc_in -m map.nc -O regrid
```

`ncremap` annotates the gridfiles and mapfiles that it creates with helpful metadata containing the full provenance of the command. Consequently, `ncremap` is a sensible tool for generating mapfiles for later use. To generate a mapfile with the specified (non-default) name `map.nc`, and then regrid a single file,

```
ncremap -i in.nc -d dst.nc -m map.nc -o out.nc
```

To test the remapping workflow, regrid only one or a few variables instead of the entire file:

```
ncremap -v T,Q,FSNT -i in.nc -m map.nc -o out.nc
```

Regridding generally scales linearly with the size of data to be regridded, so eliminating unnecessary variables produces a snappier response.

Regrid multiple input files with a single mapfile `map.nc` and write the output to the `regrid` directory:

```
ncremap -I drc_in -m map.nc -O regrid
ls drc_in/*.nc | ncremap -m map.nc -O regrid
```

The three ways NCO obtains the destination spatial grid are, in decreasing order of precedence, from *map_fl* (specified with '-m'), from *grd_dst* (specified with '-g'), and (inferred) from *dst_fl* (specified with '-d'). In the first example all likely data files from *drc_in* are regridded using the same specified mapfile, *map_fl* = `map.nc`. Each output file is written to *drc_out* = `regrid` with the same name as the corresponding input file. The second example obtains the input file list from standard input, and uses the mapfile and output directory as before.

If multiple input files are on the same grid, yet the mapfile does not exist in advance, one can still regrid all input files without incurring the time-penalty of generating multiple mapfiles. To do so, provide the (known-in-advance) source gridfile or toggle the '`-M`' switch:

```
ncremap -M -I drc_in -d dst.nc -O regrid
ls drc_in/*.nc | ncremap -M -d dst.nc -O regrid
ncremap -I drc_in -s grd_src.nc -d dst.nc -O regrid
ls drc_in/*.nc | ncremap -s grd_src.nc -d dst.nc -O regrid
ncremap -I drc_in -s grd_src.nc -g grd_dst.nc -O regrid
ls drc_in/*.nc | ncremap -s grd_src.nc -g grd_dst.nc -O regrid
```

The first two examples explicitly toggle the multi-map-generation switch (with '`-M`'), so that `ncremap` refrains from generating multiple mapfiles. In this case the source grid is inferred from the first input file, the destination grid is inferred from `dst.nc`, and `ncremap` uses ERWG to generate a single mapfile and uses that to regrid every input file. The next four examples are variants on this theme. In these cases, the user provides (with '`-s grd_src.nc`') the source gridfile, which will be used directly instead of being inferred. Any of these styles works well when each input file is known in advance to be on the same grid, e.g., model data for successive time periods in a simulation.

The most powerful, time-consuming (yet simultaneously time-saving!) feature of `ncremap` is its ability to regrid multiple input files on unique grids. Both input and output can be on any CRUD grid.

```
ncremap -I drc_in -d dst.nc -O regrid
ls drc_in/*.nc | ncremap -d dst.nc -O regrid
ncremap -I drc_in -g grd_dst.nc -O regrid
ls drc_in/*.nc | ncremap -g grd_dst.nc -O regrid
```

There is no pre-supplied *map_fl* or *grd_src* in these examples, so `ncremap` first infers the output grid from `dst.nc` (first two examples), or directly uses the supplied gridfile `grd_dst` (second two examples), and calls ERWG to generate a new mapfile for each input file, whose grid it infers. This is necessary when each input file is on a unique grid, e.g., swath-like data from satellite observations or models with time-varying grids. These examples require remarkably little input, since `ncremap` automates most of the work.

Finally, `ncremap` uses the parallelization options '`-p` *par_typ*' and '`-j` *job_nbr*' to help manage high-volume workflow. On a single node such as a local workstation, use Background mode to regrid multiple files in parallel

```
ls drc_in/*.nc | ncremap -p bck -d dst.nc -O regrid
ls drc_in/*.nc | ncremap -p bck -j 4 -d dst.nc -O regrid
```

Both examples will eventually regrid all input files. The first example regrids two at a time because two is the default batch size `ncremap` employs. The second example regrids files in batches of four at a time. Increasing *job_nbr* will increase throughput so long as the node is not I/O-limited.

Multi-node clusters can exploit inter-node parallelism in MPI-mode:

```
qsub -I -A CLI115 -V -l nodes=4 -l walltime=03:00:00 -N ncremap
ls drc_in/*.nc | ncremap -p mpi -j 4 -d dst.nc -O regrid
```

This example shows a typical request for four compute nodes. After receiving the login prompt from the interactive master node, execute the `ncremap` command with '`-p mpi`'. `ncremap` will send regridding jobs in round-robin fashion to all available compute nodes until all jobs finish. It does this by internally prepending an MPI execution command, like '`mpirun -H` *`node_name`* `-npernode 1 -n 1`', to the usual regridding command. MPI-mode typically has excellent scaling because most nodes have independent access to hard storage. This is the easiest way to speed your cumbersome job by factors of ten or more. As mentioned above under Limitations, parallelism is currently only supported when all regridding uses the same map-file.

## 4.13 ncrename netCDF Renamer

SYNTAX

```
ncrename [-a old_name,new_name] [-a ...] [-D dbg]
[-d old_name,new_name] [-d ...] [-g old_name,new_name] [-g ...]
[--glb ...] [-h] [--hdf] [--hdr_pad nbr] [-l path] [-O] [-o output-
file] [-p path] [-R] [-r]
[-v old_name,new_name] [-v ...]
input-file [[output-file]]
```

DESCRIPTION

`ncrename` renames netCDF dimensions, variables, attributes, and groups. Each object that has a name in the list of old names is renamed using the corresponding name in the list of new names. All the new names must be unique. Every old name must exist in the input file, unless the old name is preceded by the period (or "dot") character '`.`'. The validity of *old_name* is not checked prior to the renaming. Thus, if *old_name* is specified without the '`.`' prefix that indicates the presence of *old_name* is optional, and *old_name* is not present in *input-file*, then `ncrename` will abort. The *new_name* should never be prefixed by a '`.`' (or else the period will be included as part of the new name). As of NCO version 4.4.6 (released October, 2014), the *old_name* and *new_name* arguments may include (or be, for groups) partial or full group paths. The OPTIONS and EXAMPLES show how to select specific variables whose attributes are to be renamed.

> Caveat lector: Unforunately from 2007–present (July, 2016) the netCDF library (versions 4.0.0–4.4.1) contains bugs or limitations that sometimes prevent NCO from correctly renaming coordinate variables, dimensions, and groups in netCDF4 files. (To our knowledge the netCDF library calls for renaming always work well on netCDF3 files so one workaround to some netCDF4 issues is convert to netCDF3, rename, then convert back). To understand the renaming limitations associated with particular netCDF versions, read the `ncrename` documentation below in its entirety.

Although `ncrename` supports full pathnames for both *old_name* and *new_name*, this is really "window dressing". The full-path to *new_name* must be identical to the full-path to *old_name* in all classes of objects (attributes, variables, dimensions, or groups). In other words, `ncrename` can change only the local names of objects, it cannot change the location of the object in the group hierarchy within the file. Hence using a full-path in *new_name* is redundant. The object name is the terminal path component of *new_name* and this object must already exist in the group specified by the *old_name* path.

`ncrename` is an exception to the normal NCO rule that the user will be interactively prompted before an existing file is changed, and that a temporary copy of an output file is constructed during the operation. If only *input-file* is specified, then `ncrename` changes object names in the *input-file* in place without prompting and without creating a temporary copy of `input-file`. This is because the renaming operation is considered reversible if the user makes a mistake. The *new_name* can easily be changed back to *old_name* by using `ncrename` one more time.

Note that renaming a dimension to the name of a dependent variable can be used to invert the relationship between an independent coordinate variable and a dependent variable. In this case, the named dependent variable must be one-dimensional and should have no missing values. Such a variable will become a coordinate variable.

According to the *netCDF User Guide*, renaming objects in netCDF files does not incur the penalty of recopying the entire file when the *new_name* is shorter than the *old_name*. Thus `ncrename` may run much faster (at least on netCDF3 files) if judicious use of header padding (see Section 3.2 [Metadata Optimization], page 29) was made when producing the *input-file*. Similarly, using the '`--hdr_pad`' option with `ncrename` helps ensure that future metadata changes to *output-file* occur as swifly as possible.

OPTIONS

'`-a` *old_name,new_name*'
: Attribute renaming. The old and new names of the attribute are specified with '`-a`' (or '`--attribute`') by the associated *old_name* and *new_name* values. Global attributes are treated no differently than variable attributes. This option may be specified more than once. As mentioned above, all occurrences of the attribute of a given name will be renamed unless the '`.`' form is used, with one exception. To change the attribute name for a particular variable, specify the *old_name* in the format *old_var_name@old_att_name*. The '`@`' symbol delimits the variable from the attribute name. If the attribute is uniquely named (no other variables contain the attribute) then the *old_var_name@old_att_name* syntax is redundant. The *old_var_name* variable names `global` and `group` have special significance. They indicate that *old_att_nm* should only be renamed where it occurs as a global (i.e., root group) metadata attribute (for `global`), or (for `group`) as *any* group attribute, and not where it occurs as a variable attribute. The *var_name@att_name* syntax is accepted, though not required, for the *new_name*.

'`-d` *old_name,new_name*'
: Dimension renaming. The old and new names of the dimension are specified with '`-d`' (or '`--dmn`', '`--dimension`') by the associated *old_name* and *new_name* values. This option may be specified more than once.

'`-g` *old_name,new_name*'
: Group renaming. The old and new names of the group are specified with '`-g`' (or '`--grp`', '`--group`') by the associated *old_name* and *new_name* values. This option may be specified more than once. This functionality is only available in NCO version 4.3.7 (October, 2013) or later, and only when built on netCDF library version 4.3.1-rc1 (August, 2013) or later.

'`-v` *old_name,new_name*'
: Variable renaming. The old and new names of the variable are specified with '`-v`' (or '`--variable`') by the associated *old_name* and *new_name* values. This option may be specified more than once.

EXAMPLES

Rename the variable `p` to `pressure` and `t` to `temperature` in netCDF `in.nc`. In this case `p` must exist in the input file (or `ncrename` will abort), but the presence of `t` is optional:

```
ncrename -v p,pressure -v .t,temperature in.nc
```

Rename the attribute `long_name` to `largo_nombre` in the variable `u`, and no other variables in netCDF `in.nc`.

```
ncrename -a u@long_name,largo_nombre in.nc
```

Rename the group `g8` to `g20` in netCDF4 file `in_grp.nc`:

```
ncrename -g g8,g20 in_grp.nc
```

Rename the variable `/g1/lon` to `longitude` in netCDF4 `in_grp.nc`:

```
ncrename -v /g1/lon,longitude in_grp.nc
ncrename -v /g1/lon,/g1/longitude in_grp.nc # Alternate
```

`ncrename` does not automatically attach dimensions to variables of the same name. This is done to make renaming an easy way to change whether a variable is a coordinate. If you want to rename a coordinate variable so that it remains a coordinate variable, you must separately rename both the dimension and the variable:

```
ncrename -d lon,longitude -v lon,longitude in.nc
```

Unfortunately, the netCDF4 library had a longstanding bug (all versions until 4.3.1-rc5 released in December, 2013) that crashed NCO when performing this operation. Simultaneously renaming variables and dimensions in netCDF4 files with earlier versions of netCDF is impossible; it must instead be done in two separate `ncrename` invocations (e.g., first rename the variable, then rename the dimension) to avoid triggering the libary bug.

A related bug causes unintended side-effects with `ncrename` also built with all versions of the netCDF4 library until 4.3.1-rc5 released in December, 2013): This bug caused renaming *either* a dimension *or* its associated coordinate variable (not both, which would fail as above) in a netCDF4 file to inadvertently rename both:

```
# Demonstate bug in netCDF4/HDF5 library prior to netCDF-4.3.1-rc5
ncks -O -h -m -M -4 -v lat_T42 ~/nco/data/in.nc ~/foo.nc
ncrename -O -v lat_T42,lat ~/foo.nc ~/foo2.nc # Also renames dimension
ncrename -O -d lat_T42,lat ~/foo.nc ~/foo2.nc # Also renames variable
```

To avoid this faulty behavior, either build NCO with netCDF version 4.3.1-rc5 or later, or convert the file to netCDF3 first, then rename as intended, then convert back. Unforunately while this bug and the related coordinate renaming bug were fixed in 4.3.1-rc5 (released in December, 2013), a new and related bug was discovered in October 2014.

Another netCDF4 bug that causes unintended side-effects with `ncrename` affects (at least) versions 4.3.1–4.3.2 and all snapshots of the netCDF4 library until January, 2015. This bug (fixed in 4.3.3 in February, 2015) corrupts values or renamed netCDF4 coordinate variables (i.e., variables with underlying dimensions of the same name) and other (non-coordinate) variables that include an underlying dimension that was renamed. In other words, *renaming* coordinate variables and dimensions succeeds yet it corrupts the values contained by the affected array variables. This bug corrupts affected variables by replacing their values with the default `_FillValue` for that variable's type:

```
# Demonstate bug in netCDF4/HDF5 library prior to netCDF-4.3.3
ncks -O -4 -C -M -v lat ~/nco/data/in.nc ~/bug.nc
ncrename -O -v lat,tal ~/bug.nc ~/foo.nc # Broken until netCDF-4.3.3
ncrename -O -d lat,tal ~/bug.nc ~/foo.nc # Broken until netCDF-4.3.3
ncrename -O -d lat,tal -v lat,tal ~/bug.nc ~/foo.nc # Broken too
ncks --cdl ~/foo.nc
```

To avoid this faulty behavior, either build NCO with netCDF version 4.3.3 or later, or convert the file to netCDF3 first, then rename as intended, then convert back. This bug does not affect renaming of groups or of attributes.

Yet another netCDF4 bug that causes unintended side-effects with `ncrename` affects only snapshots from January–February, 2015, and released version 4.3.3 (February, 2015). It was fixed in (and was the reason for releasing) netCDF version 4.3.3.1 (March, 2015). This bug causes renamed attributes of coordinate variables in netCDF4 to files to disappear:

```
# Demonstate bug in netCDF4/HDF5 library netCDF-4.3.3
ncrename -O -h -a /g1/lon@units,new_units ~/nco/data/in_grp.nc ~/foo.nc
ncks -v /g1/lon ~/foo.nc # Shows units and new_units are both gone
```

Clearly, renaming dimensions in netCDF4 files is non-trivial. The latest chapter in this saga is a netCDF4 bug discovered in September, 2015, and present in versions 4.3.3.1 (and possibly earlier versions too) and later. As of this writing (July, 2016) the bug has not been fixed and is still present in netCDF4 version 4.4.1. This bug causes `ncrename` to create corrupted output files when attempting to rename two dimensions simultaneously. The workaround is to rename the dimensions sequentially, in two separate `ncrename` calls.

```
# Demonstate bug in netCDF4/HDF5 library netCDF-4.3.3.1
ncrename -d y,rlat -d x,rlon dayclim_withoutpr.nc dayclim2.nc
ncdump dayclim2.nc # File is unreadable
```

Create netCDF `out.nc` identical to `in.nc` except the attribute `_FillValue` is changed to `missing_value`, the attribute `units` is changed to `CGS_units` (but only in those variables which possess it), the attribute `hieght` is changed to `height` in the variable `tpt`, and in the variable `prs_sfc`, if it exists.

```
ncrename -a _FillValue,missing_value -a .units,CGS_units \
  -a tpt@hieght,height -a prs_sfc@.hieght,height in.nc out.nc
```

The presence and absence of the '`.`' and '`@`' features cause this command to execute successfully only if a number of conditions are met. All variables *must* have a `_FillValue` attribute *and* `_FillValue` must also be a global attribute. The `units` attribute, on the other hand, will be renamed to `CGS_units` wherever it is found but need not be present in the file at all (either as a global or a variable attribute). The variable `tpt` must contain the `hieght` attribute. The variable `prs_sfc` need not exist, and need not contain the `hieght` attribute.

Rename the global or group attribute `Convention` to `Conventions`

```
ncrename -a Convention,Conventions  in.nc # Variable and group atts.
```

```
ncrename -a .Convention,Conventions in.nc # Variable and group atts.
ncrename -a @Convention,Conventions  in.nc # Group atts. only
ncrename -a @.Convention,Conventions in.nc # Group atts. only
ncrename -a global@Convention,Conventions   in.nc # Group atts. only
ncrename -a .global@.Convention,Conventions in.nc # Group atts. only
ncrename -a global@Convention,Conventions   in.nc # Global atts. only
ncrename -a .global@.Convention,Conventions in.nc # Global atts. only
```

The examples without the `@` character attempt to change the attribute name in both Global or Group and variable attributes. The examples with the `@` character attempt to change only global and group `Convention` attributes, and leave unchanged any `Convention` attributes attached directly to variables. Attributes prefixed with a period (`.Convention`) need not be present. Attributes not prefixed with a period (`Convention`) must be present. Variables prefixed with a period (`.` or `.global`) need not be present. Variables not prefixed with a period (`global`) must be present.

## 4.14 ncwa netCDF Weighted Averager

SYNTAX

```
ncwa [-3] [-4] [-6] [-7] [-A] [-a dim[,...]] [-B mask_cond] [-b] [-C] [-c]
[--cnk_byt sz_byt] [--cnk_dmn nm,sz_lmn] [--cnk_map map]
[--cnk_min sz_byt] [--cnk_plc plc] [--cnk_scl sz_lmn]
[-D dbg] [-d dim,[min][,[max][,[stride]]] [-F]
[-G gpe_dsc] [-g grp[,...]] [--glb ...] [-h] [--hdr_pad nbr] [-I]
[-L dfl_lvl] [-l path] [-M mask_val] [-m mask_var] [-N]
[--no_cll_msr] [--no_cll_mth] [--no_frm_trm] [--no_tmp_fl]
[-O] [-o output-
file] [-p path] [--ppc ...] [-R] [-r] [--ram_all] [--rth_dbl|flt]
[-T mask_comp] [-t thr_nbr] [--unn] [-v var[,...]] [-w weight]
[-X ...] [-x] [-y op_typ]
input-file [output-file]
```

DESCRIPTION

`ncwa` performs statistics (including, but not limited to, averages) on variables in a single file over arbitrary dimensions, with options to specify weights, masks, and normalization. See Section 2.6 [Statistics vs. Concatenation], page 20, for a description of the distinctions between the various statistics tools and concatenators. The default behavior of `ncwa` is to arithmetically average every numerical variable over all dimensions and to produce a scalar result for each.

Averaged dimensions are, by default, eliminated as dimensions. Their corresponding coordinates, if any, are output as scalar variables. The '`-b`' switch (and its long option equivalents '`--rdd`' and '`--retain-degenerate-dimensions`') causes `ncwa` to retain averaged dimensions as degenerate (size 1) dimensions. This maintains the association between a dimension (or coordinate) and variables after averaging and simplifies, for instance, later concatenation along the degenerate dimension.

To average variables over only a subset of their dimensions, specify these dimensions in a comma-separated list following '`-a`', e.g., '`-a time,lat,lon`'. As with all arithmetic operators, the operation may be restricted to an arbitrary hyperslab by employing the '`-d`' option (see Section 3.15 [Hyperslabs], page 62). `ncwa` also handles values matching the variable's `_FillValue` attribute correctly. Moreover, `ncwa` understands how to manipulate user-specified weights, masks, and normalization options. With these options, `ncwa` can compute sophisticated averages (and integrals) from the command line.

*mask_var* and *weight*, if specified, are broadcast to conform to the variables being averaged. The rank of variables is reduced by the number of dimensions which they are averaged over. Thus arrays which are one dimensional in the *input-file* and are averaged by `ncwa` appear in the *output-file* as scalars. This allows the user to infer which dimensions may have been averaged. Note that that it is impossible for `ncwa` to make make a *weight* or *mask_var* of rank $W$ conform to a *var* of rank $V$ if $W > V$. This situation often arises when coordinate variables (which, by definition, are one dimensional) are weighted and averaged. `ncwa` assumes you know this is impossible and so `ncwa` does not attempt to broadcast *weight* or *mask_var* to conform to *var* in this case, nor does `ncwa` print a warning message telling you this, because it is so common. Specifying *dbg > 2* does cause `ncwa` to emit warnings in these situations, however.

Non-coordinate variables are always masked and weighted if specified. Coordinate variables, however, may be treated specially. By default, an averaged coordinate variable, e.g., `latitude`, appears in *output-file* averaged the same way as any other variable containing an averaged dimension. In other words, by default `ncwa` weights and masks coordinate variables like all other variables. This design decision was intended to be helpful but for some applications it may be preferable not to weight or mask coordinate variables just like all other variables. Consider the following arguments to `ncwa`: `-a latitude -w lat_wgt -d latitude,0.,90.` where `lat_wgt` is a weight in the `latitude` dimension. Since, by default `ncwa` weights coordinate variables, the value of `latitude` in the *output-file* depends on the weights in *lat_wgt* and is not likely to be 45.0, the midpoint latitude of the hyperslab. Option '`-I`' overrides this default behavior and causes `ncwa` not to weight or mask coordinate variables[1]. In the above case, this causes the value of `latitude` in the *output-file* to be 45.0, an appealing result. Thus, '`-I`' specifies simple arithmetic averages for the coordinate variables. In the case of latitude, '`-I`' specifies that you prefer to archive the arithmetic mean latitude of the averaged hyperslabs rather than the area-weighted mean latitude.[2].

As explained in See Section 3.35 [Operation Types], page 114, `ncwa` *always averages* coordinate variables regardless of the arithmetic operation type performed on the non-coordinate variables. This is independent of the setting of the '`-I`' option. The mathematical definition of operations involving rank reduction is given above (see Section 3.35 [Operation Types], page 114).

### 4.14.1 Mask condition

Each $x_i$ also has an associated masking weight $m_i$ whose value is 0 or 1 (false or true). The value of $m_i$ is always 1 unless a *mask_var* is specified (with '`-m`'). As noted above, *mask_var* is broadcast, if possible, to conform to the variable being averaged. In this case, the value of $m_i$ depends on the *mask condition* also known as the *truth condition*. As expected, $m_i = 1$ when the mask condition is *true* and $m_i = 0$ otherwise.

The mask condition has the syntax *mask_var mask_comp mask_val*. The preferred method to specify the mask condition is in one string with the '`-B`' or '`--mask_condition`' switches. The older method is to use the three switches '`-m`', '`-T`', and '`-M`' to specify the *mask_var*, *mask_comp*, and *mask_val*, respectively.[3]. The *mask_condition* string is automatically parsed into its three constituents *mask_var*, *mask_comp*, and *mask_val*.

Here *mask_var* is the name of the masking variable (specified with '`-m`', '`--mask-variable`', '`--mask_variable`', '`--msk_nm`', or '`--msk_var`'). The truth *mask_comp* argument (specified with '`-T`', '`--mask_comparator`', '`--msk_cmp_typ`', or '`--op_rlt`' may be any one of the six arithmetic comparators: *eq*, *ne*, *gt*, *lt*, *ge*, *le*. These are the Fortran-style character abbreviations for the logical comparisons $=$, $\neq$, $>$,

1 The default behavior of ('`-I`') changed on 19981201—before this date the default was not to weight or mask coordinate variables.

2 If `lat_wgt` contains Gaussian weights then the value of `latitude` in the *output-file* will be the area-weighted centroid of the hyperslab. For the example given, this is about 30 degrees.

3 The three switches '`-m`', '`-T`', and '`-M`' are maintained for backward compatibility and may be deprecated in the future. It is safest to write scripts using '`--mask_condition`'.

$<$, $\geq$, $\leq$. The mask comparator defaults to `eq` (equality). The *mask_val* argument to '`-M`' (or '`--mask-value`', or '`--msk_val`') is the right hand side of the *mask condition*. Thus for the $i$'th element of the hyperslab to be averaged, the mask condition is $mask_i$ *mask_comp* *mask_val*.

Each $x_i$ is also associated with an additional weight $w_i$ whose value may be user-specified. The value of $w_i$ is identically 1 unless the user specifies a weighting variable *weight* (with '`-w`', '`--weight`', or '`--wgt_var`'). In this case, the value of $w_i$ is determined by the *weight* variable in the *input-file*. As noted above, *weight* is broadcast, if possible, to conform to the variable being averaged.

$M$ is the number of input elements $x_i$ which actually contribute to output element $x_j$. $M$ is also known as the *tally* and is defined as

$$M = \sum_{i=1}^{i=N} \mu_i m_i$$

$M$ is identical to the denominator of the generic averaging expression except for the omission of the weight $w_i$. Thus $M = N$ whenever no input points are missing values or are masked. Whether an element contributes to the output, and thus increments $M$ by one, has more to do with the above two criteria (missing value and masking) than with the numeric value of the element per se. For example, $x_i = 0.0$ does contribute to $x_j$ (assuming the `_FillValue` attribute is not 0.0 and location $i$ is not masked). The value $x_i = 0.0$ will not change the numerator of the generic averaging expression, but it will change the denominator (unless its weight $w_i = 0.0$ as well).

### 4.14.2 Normalization and Integration

`ncwa` has one switch which controls the normalization of the averages appearing in the *output-file*. Short option '`-N`' (or long options '`--nmr`' or '`--numerator`') prevents `ncwa` from dividing the weighted sum of the variable (the numerator in the averaging expression) by the weighted sum of the weights (the denominator in the averaging expression). Thus '`-N`' tells `ncwa` to return just the numerator of the arithmetic expression defining the operation (see Section 3.35 [Operation Types], page 114).

With this normalization option, `ncwa` can integrate variables. Averages are first computed as sums, and then normalized to obtain the average. The original sum (i.e., the numerator of the expression in Section 3.35 [Operation Types], page 114) is output if default normalization is turned off (with '`-N`'). This sum is the integral (not the average) over the specified (with '`-a`', or all, if none are specified) dimensions. The weighting variable, if specified (with '`-w`'), plays the role of the differential increment and thus permits more sophisticated integrals (i.e., weighted sums) to be output. For example, consider the variable `lev` where $lev = [100, 500, 1000]$ weighted by the weight `lev_wgt` where $lev\_wgt = [10, 2, 1]$. The vertical integral of `lev`, weighted by `lev_wgt`, is the dot product of *lev* and *lev_wgt*. That this is is 3000.0 can be seen by inspection and verified with the integration command

```
ncwa -N -a lev -v lev -w lev_wgt in.nc foo.nc;ncks foo.nc
```

EXAMPLES

Given file `85_0112.nc`:

```
netcdf 85_0112 {
```

```
dimensions:
        lat = 64 ;
        lev = 18 ;
        lon = 128 ;
        time = UNLIMITED ; // (12 currently)
variables:
        float lat(lat) ;
        float lev(lev) ;
        float lon(lon) ;
        float time(time) ;
        float scalar_var ;
        float three_dmn_var(lat, lev, lon) ;
        float two_dmn_var(lat, lev) ;
        float mask(lat, lon) ;
        float gw(lat) ;
}
```

Average all variables in `in.nc` over all dimensions and store results in `out.nc`:

```
ncwa in.nc out.nc
```

All variables in `in.nc` are reduced to scalars in `out.nc` since `ncwa` averages over all dimensions unless otherwise specified (with '`-a`').

Store the zonal (longitudinal) mean of `in.nc` in `out.nc`:

```
ncwa -a lon in.nc out1.nc
ncwa -a lon -b in.nc out2.nc
```

The first command turns `lon` into a scalar and the second retains `lon` as a degenerate dimension in all variables.

```
% ncks -C -H -v lon out1.nc
lon = 135
% ncks -C -H -v lon out2.nc
lon[0] = 135
```

In either case the tally is simply the size of `lon`, i.e., 180 for the `85_0112.nc` file described by the sample header above.

Compute the meridional (latitudinal) mean, with values weighted by the corresponding element of *gw*[4]:

```
ncwa -w gw -a lat in.nc out.nc
```

Here the tally is simply the size of `lat`, or 64. The sum of the Gaussian weights is 2.0.

Compute the area mean over the tropical Pacific:

```
ncwa -w gw -a lat,lon -d lat,-20.,20. -d lon,120.,270. in.nc out.nc
```

Here the tally is $64 \times 128 = 8192$.

---

[4] `gw` stands for *Gaussian weight* in many climate models.

Compute the area-mean over the globe using only points for which $ORO < 0.5$[5]:

```
ncwa -B 'ORO < 0.5'       -w gw -a lat,lon in.nc out.nc
ncwa -m ORO -M 0.5 -T lt -w gw -a lat,lon in.nc out.nc
```

It is considerably simpler to specify the complete *mask_cond* with the single string argument to '-B' than with the three separate switches '-m', '-T', and '-M'[6]. If in doubt, enclose the *mask_cond* within quotes since some of the comparators have special meanings to the shell.

Assuming 70% of the gridpoints are maritime, then here the tally is $0.70 \times 8192 \approx 5734$.

Compute the global annual mean over the maritime tropical Pacific:

```
ncwa -B 'ORO < 0.5'       -w gw -a lat,lon,time \
  -d lat,-20.0,20.0 -d lon,120.0,270.0 in.nc out.nc
ncwa -m ORO -M 0.5 -T lt -w gw -a lat,lon,time \
  -d lat,-20.0,20.0 -d lon,120.0,270.0 in.nc out.nc
```

Further examples will use the one-switch specification of *mask_cond*.

Determine the total area of the maritime tropical Pacific, assuming the variable *area* contains the area of each gridcell

```
ncwa -N -v area -B 'ORO < 0.5' -a lat,lon \
  -d lat,-20.0,20.0 -d lon,120.0,270.0 in.nc out.nc
```

Weighting *area* (e.g., by *gw*) is not appropriate because *area* is *already* area-weighted by definition. Thus the '-N' switch, or, equivalently, the '-y ttl' switch, correctly integrate the cell areas into a total regional area.

Mask a file to contain *_FillValue* everywhere except where *thr_min* <= *msk_var* <= *thr_max*:

```
# Set masking variable and its scalar thresholds
export msk_var='three_dmn_var_dbl' # Masking variable
export thr_max='20' # Maximum allowed value
export thr_min='10' # Minimum allowed value
ncecat -O in.nc out.nc # Wrap out.nc in degenerate "record" dimension
ncwa -O -a record -B "${msk_var} <= ${thr_max}" out.nc out.nc
ncecat -O out.nc out.nc # Wrap out.nc in degenerate "record" dimension
ncwa -O -a record -B "${msk_var} >= ${thr_min}" out.nc out.nc
```

After the first use of `ncwa`, `out.nc` contains *_FillValue* where `${msk_var} >= ${thr_max}`. The process is then repeated on the remaining data to filter out points where `${msk_var} <= ${thr_min}`. The resulting `out.nc` contains valid data only where *thr_min* <= *msk_var* <= *thr_max*.

[5] `ORO` stands for *Orography* in some climate models and in those models $ORO < 0.5$ selects ocean gridpoints.

[6] Unfortunately the '-B' and '--mask_condition' options are unsupported on Windows (with the MVS compiler), which lacks a free, standard parser and lexer.

# 5 Contributing

We welcome contributions from anyone. The project homepage at `https://sf.net/projects/nco` contains more information on how to contribute.

Financial contributions to NCO development may be made through PayPal (`https://www.paypal.com/xclick/business=zender%40uci.edu&item_name=NCO+development&item_number=nco_dnt_dvl&no_note=1&tax=0¤cy_code=USD`). NCO has been shared for over 10 years yet only two users have contributed any money to the developers[1]. So you could be the third!

## 5.1 Contributors

NCO would not exist without the dedicated efforts of the remarkable software engineers who conceive, develop, and maintain netCDF, UDUnits, and OPeNDAP. Since 1995 NCO has received support from, I believe, the entire staff of all these projects, including Russ Rew, John Caron, Glenn Davis, Steve Emmerson, James Gallagher, Ed Hartnett, and Dennis Heimbigner. In addition to their roles in maintaining the software stack on which NCO perches, Yertl-like, some of these gentlemen have advised or contributed to NCO specifically. That support is acknowledged separately below.

The primary contributors to NCO development have been:

Charlie Zender
: All concept, design and implementation from 1995–2000. Since then autotools, bug-squashing, CDL, chunking, documentation, anchoring, recursion, GPE, packing, regridding, CDL/XML backends, compression, NCO library redesign, `ncap2` features, `ncbo`, `ncpdq`, SMP threading and MPI parallelization, netCDF4 integration, external funding, project management, science research, releases.

Henry Butowsky
: Non-linear operations and `min()`, `max()`, `total()` support in `ncra` and `ncwa`. Type conversion for arithmetic. Migration to netCDF3 API. `ncap2` parser, lexer, GSL-support, and I/O. Multislabbing algorithm. Variable wildcarding. JSON backend. Numerous hacks. `ncap2` language.

Rorik Peterson
: Original autotools build support. Long command-line options. Original UDUnits support. Debianization. Numerous bug-fixes.

Joe Hamman
: Python bindings (PyNCO).

Daniel Wang
: Script Workflow Analysis for MultiProcessing (SWAMP). RPM support.

---

[1] Happy users have sent me a few gifts, though. This includes a box of imported chocolate. Mmm. Appreciation and gifts are definitely better than money. Naturally, I'm too lazy to split and send gifts to the other developers. However, unlike some NCO developers, I have a steady "real job". My intent is to split monetary donations among the active developers and to send them their shares via PayPal.

Harry Mangalam
Benchmarking. OPeNDAP configuration.

Pedro Vicente
Windows Visual Studio support. netCDF4 groups.

Jerome Mao
Multi-argument parsing.

Russ Rew Advice on NCO structural algorithms

Brian Mays
Original packaging for Debian GNU/Linux, `nroff` man pages.

George Shapovalov
Packaging for Gentoo GNU/Linux.

Bill Kocik Memory management.

Len Makin
NEC SX architecture support.

Jim Edwards
AIX architecture support.

Juliana Rew
Compatibility with large PIDs.

Karen Schuchardt
Auxiliary coordinate support.

Gayathri Venkitachalam
MPI implementation.

Scott Capps
Large work-load testing

Peter Campbell, Martin Dix, Mark Flanner, Markus Liebig, Keith Lindsay, Mike Page, Martin Schmidt, Michael Schulz, Lori Sentman, Rich Signell, Gary Strand, George White Andrew Wittenberg, Remik Ziemlinski
Excellent bug reports and feature requests.

Filipe Fernandes, Rich Signell, Kyle Wilcox
Anaconda packaging

Daniel Baumann, Nick Bower, Luk Claebs, Bas Couwenberg, Barry deFreese, Aleksandar Jelenak, Francesco Lovergine, Matej Vela
Debian packaging

Patrice Dumas, Ed Hill, Orion Poplawski
RedHat packaging

George Shapavalov, Patrick Kursawe, Manfred Schwarb
Gentoo packaging

Filipe Fernandes
OpenSuse packaging

Takeshi Enomoto, Alexander Hansen, Ian Lancaster, Alejandro Soto
Mac OS packaging

Eric Blake Autoconf/M4 help

Gavin Burris, Kyle Wilcox
RHEL and CentOS build scripts and bug reports.

Andrea Cimatoribus
NCO Spiral Logo

Martin Otte, Etienne Tourigny
Single bug reports and fixes

Wenshan Wang
CMIP5 and MODIS processing documentation, reference card

Please let me know if your name was omitted!

## 5.2 Citation

The recommended citations for NCO software are

```
Zender, C. S. (2008), Analysis of Self-describing Gridded Geoscience
Data with netCDF Operators (NCO), Environ. Modell. Softw., 23(10),
1338-1342, doi:10.1016/j.envsoft.2008.03.004.

Zender, C. S. and H. J. Mangalam (2007), Scaling Properties of Common
Statistical Operators for Gridded Datasets, Int. J. High
Perform. Comput. Appl., 21(4), 485-498, doi:10.1177/1094342007083802.

Zender, C. S. (2016), Bit Grooming: Statistically accurate
precision-preserving quantization with compression, evaluated in the
netCDF Operators (NCO, v4.4.8+), Geosci. Model Dev., 9, 3199-3211,
doi:10.5194/gmd-9-3199-2016.

Zender, C. S. (Year), netCDF Operator (NCO) User Guide,
http://nco.sf.net/nco.pdf.
```

Use the first when referring to overall design, purpose, and optimization of NCO, the second for the speed and throughput of NCO, the third for compressions, and the fourth for specific features and/or the User Guide itself, or in a non-academic setting. A complete list of NCO publications and presentations is at `http://nco.sf.net#pub`. This list links to the full papers and seminars themselves.

## 5.3 Proposals for Institutional Funding

From 2004–2007, NSF funded a project (`http://nco.sf.net#prp_sei`) to improve Distributed Data Reduction & Analysis (DDRA) by evolving NCO parallelism (OpenMP, MPI) and Server-Side DDRA (SSDDRA) implemented through extensions to OPeNDAP and netCDF4. The SSDDRA features were implemented in SWAMP, the PhD Thesis of Daniel Wang. SWAMP dramatically reduced bandwidth usage for NCO between client and server.

With this first NCO proposal funded, the content of the next NCO proposal became clear. We had long been interested in obtaining NASA support for HDF-specific enhancements to NCO. From 2012–2015 the NASA ACCESS program funded us to implement support support netCDF4 group functionality. Thus NCO will grow and evade bit-rot for the foreseeable future.

We are considering other interesting ideas for still more proposals. Please contact us if you wish to be involved with any future NCO-related proposals. Comments on the proposals and letters of support are also very welcome.

# 6 Quick Start

Simple examples in Bash shell scripts showing how to average data with different file structures. Here we include monthly, seasonal and annual average with daily or monthly data in either one file or multiple files.

## 6.1 Daily data in one file

Suppose we have daily data from Jan 1st, 1990 to Dec. 31, 2005 in the file of `in.nc` with the record dimension as `time`.

**Monthly average:**

```
for yyyy in {1990..2005}; do      # Loop over years
  for moy in {1..12}; do          # Loop over months
    mm=$( printf "%02d" ${moy} )  # Change to 2-digit format

    # Average specific month yyyy-mm
    ncra -O -d time,"${yyyy}-${mm}-01","${yyyy}-${mm}-31" \
         in.nc in_${yyyy}${mm}.nc
  done
done

# Concatenate monthly files together
ncrcat -O in_??????.nc out.nc
```

**Annual average:**

```
for yyyy in {1990..2005}; do      # Loop over years
  ncra -O -d time,"${yyyy}-01-01","${yyyy}-12-31" in.nc in_${yyyy}.nc
done

# Concatenate annual files together
ncrcat -O in_????.nc out.nc
```

The `-O` switch means to overwrite the pre-existing files (see Section 3.37 [Batch Mode], page 128). The `-d` option is to specify the range of hyperslabs (see Section 3.15 [Hyperslabs], page 62). There are detailed instructions on `ncra` (see Section 4.10 [ncra netCDF Record Averager], page 262, and `ncrcat` (see Section 4.11 [ncrcat netCDF Record Concatenator], page 265). NCO supports UDUnits so that we can use readable dates as time dimension (see Section 3.24 [UDUnits Support], page 84).

## 6.2 Monthly data in one file

Inside the input file `in.nc`, the record dimension `time` is from Jan 1990 to Dec 2005.

**Seasonal average (e.g., DJF):**

```
ncra -O --mro -d time,"1990-12-01",,12,3 in.nc out.nc
```

**Annual average:**

```
ncra -O --mro -d time,,,12,12 in.nc out.nc
```

Here we use the subcycle feature (i.e., the number after the fourth comma: '3' in the seasonal example and the second '12' in the annual example) to retrieve groups of records separated by regular intervals (see Section 3.18 [Subcycle], page 66). The option `--mro` switches `ncra` to produce a Multi-Record Output instead of a single-record output. For example, assume *snd* is a 3D array with dimensions `time` * `latitude` * `longitude` and `time` includes every month from Jan. 1990 to Dec. 2005, 192 months as total, which are 16 years. Let's look at the following two command lines.

```
ncra --mro -v snd -d time,"1990-12-01",,12,3 in.nc out_mro.nc
ncra -v snd -d time,"1990-12-01",,12,3 in.nc out_sro.nc
```

In the first output file, `out_mro.nc`, *snd* is still a 3D array with dimensions `time` * `latitude` * `longitude`, but the length of `time` now is 16, meaning 16 winters. In the second output file, `out_sro.nc`, the length of `time` is only 1. It is now the average of all the 16 winters.

when using '`-d` ***dim***`,min[,max]`' to specify the hyperslabs, you can leave it blank if you want to include the minimum or the maximum of the data, like we did above.

## 6.3 One time point one file

This means if you have daily data of 30 days, there will be 30 data files. Or if you have monthly data of 12 months, there will be 12 data files. Dealing with this kind of files, you need to specify the file names in shell scripts and pass them to NCO operators. For example, your daily data files may look like `snd_19900101.nc`, `snd_19900102.nc`, `snd_19900103.nc` ... If you want to know the monthly average of Jan 1990, you can write like,

```
ncra -O snd_199001??.nc out.nc
```

You might want to use loop if you need the average of each month.

```
for moy in {1..12}; do           # Loop over months
  mm=$( printf "%02d" ${moy} )  # Change to 2-digit format

  ncra -O snd_????${mm}??.nc out_${mm}.nc
done
```

## 6.4 Multiple files with multiple time points

Similar as the last one, it's more about shell scripts. Suppose you have daily data with one month of them in one data file. The monthly average is simply to apply `ncra` on the specific data file. And for seasonal averages, you can specify the three months by shell scripts.

# 7 CMIP5 Example

The fifth phase of the Coupled Model Intercomparison Project (CMIP5 (http://cmip-pcmdi.llnl.gov/cmip5/index.html?submenuheader=0)) provides a multi-model framework for comparing the mechanisms and responses of climate models from around the world. However, it is a tremendous workload to retrieve a single climate statistic from all these models, each of which includes several ensemble members. Not only that, it is too often a tedious process that impedes new research and hypothesis testing. Our NASA ACCESS 2011 project simplified and accelerated this process.

Traditional geoscience data analysis requires users to work with numerous flat (data in one level or namespace) files. In that paradigm instruments or models produce, and then repositories archive and distribute, and then researchers request and analyze, collections of flat files. NCO works well with that paradigm, yet it also embodies the necessary algorithms to transition geoscience data analysis from relying solely on traditional (or "flat") datasets to allowing newer hierarchical (or "nested") datasets.

Hierarchical datasets support and enable combining all datastreams that meet user-specified criteria into a single or small number of files that hold *all* the science-relevant data. NCO (and no other software to our knowledge) exploits this capability now. Data and metadata may be aggregated into and analyzed in hierarchical structures. We call the resulting data storage, distribution, and analysis paradigm Group-Oriented Data Analysis and Distribution (GODAD). GODAD lets the scientific question organize the data, not the *ad hoc* granularity of all relevant datasets. This chapter illustrates GODAD techniques applied to analysis of the CMIP5 dataset.

To begin, we document below a prototypical example of CMIP5 analysis and evaluation using traditional NCO commands on netCDF3-format model and HDF-EOS format observational (NASA MODIS satellite instrument) datasets. These examples complement the NCO User Guide by detailing in-depth data analysis in a frequently encountered "real world" context. Graphical representations of the results (NCL scripts available upon request) are provided to illustrate physical meaning of the analysis. Since NCO can process hierarchical datasets, i.e., datasets stored with netCDF4 groups, we present sample scripts illustrating group-based processing as well.

## 7.1 Combine Files

Sometimes, the data of one ensemble member will be stored in several files to reduce single file size. It is more convenient to concatenate these files into a single timeseries, and the following script illustrates how. Key steps include:

1. Obtain number and names (or partial names) of files in a directory
2. Concatenate files along the record dimension (usually time) using `ncrcat` (see Section 4.11 [ncrcat netCDF Record Concatenator], page 265).

```
#!/bin/bash       # shell type
shopt -s extglob # enable extended globbing

#===========================================================================
```

```
# Some of the models cut one ensemble member into several files,
#  which include data of different time periods.
# We'd better concatenate them into one at the beginning so that
#  we won't have to think about which files we need if we want
#  to retrieve a specific time period later.
#
# Method:
#       - Make sure 'time' is the record dimension (i.e., left-most)
#       - ncrcat
#
# Input files like:
# /data/cmip5/snc_LImon_bcc-csm1-1_historical_r1i1p1_185001-190012.nc
# /data/cmip5/snc_LImon_bcc-csm1-1_historical_r1i1p1_190101-200512.nc
#
# Output files like:
# /data/cmip5/snc_LImon_bcc-csm1-1_historical_r1i1p1_185001-200512.nc
#
# Online:  http://nco.sourceforge.net/nco.html#Combine-Files
#
# Execute this script:  bash cmb_fl.sh
#============================================================================

drc_in='/home/wenshanw/data/cmip5/' # Directory of input files

var=( 'snc' 'snd' )                 # Variables
rlm='LImon'                         # Realm
xpt=( 'historical' )                # Experiment ( could be more )

for var_id in {0..1}; do            # Loop over two variables
  # Names of all the models (ls [get file names];
  #  cut [get model names];
  #  sort; uniq [remove duplicates]; awk [print])
  mdl_set=$( ls ${drc_in}${var[var_id]}_${rlm}_*_${xpt[0]}_*.nc | \
    cut -d '_' -f 3 | sort | uniq -c | awk '{print $2}' )
  # Number of models (echo [print contents]; wc [count])
  mdl_nbr=$( echo ${mdl_set} | wc -w )
  echo "=============================="
  echo "There are" ${mdl_nbr} "models for" ${var[var_id]}.

  for mdl in ${mdl_set}; do             # Loop over models
    # Names of all the ensemble members
    nsm_set=$( ls ${drc_in}${var[var_id]}_${rlm}_${mdl}_${xpt[0]}_*.nc | \
      cut -d '_' -f 5 | sort | uniq -c | awk '{print $2}' )
    # Number of ensemble members in each model
    nsm_nbr=$( echo ${nsm_set} | wc -w )
    echo "------------------------------"
    echo "Model" ${mdl} "includes" ${nsm_nbr} "ensemble member(s):"
```

```
    echo ${nsm_set}"."

    for nsm in ${nsm_set}; do         # Loop over ensemble members
      # Number of files in this ensemble member
      fl_nbr=$( ls ${drc_in}${var[var_id]}_${rlm}_${mdl}_${xpt[0]}_${nsm}_*.nc \
        | wc -w )

      # If there is only 1 file, continue to next loop
      if [ ${fl_nbr} -le 1 ]
      then
        echo "There is only 1 file in" ${nsm}.
        continue
      fi

      echo "There are" ${fl_nbr} "files in" ${nsm}.

      # Starting date of data
      #   (sed [the name of the first file includes the starting date])
      yyyymm_str=$( ls ${drc_in}${var[var_id]}_${rlm}_${mdl}_${xpt[0]}_${nsm}_*.nc\
        | sed -n '1p' | cut -d '_' -f 6 | cut -d '-' -f 1 )
      # Ending date of data
      #   (sed [the name of the last file includes the ending date])
      yyyymm_end=$( ls ${drc_in}${var[var_id]}_${rlm}_${mdl}_${xpt[0]}_${nsm}_*.nc\
        | sed -n "${fl_nbr}p" | cut -d '_' -f 6 | cut -d '-' -f 2 )

      # Concatenate one ensemble member files
      #   into one along the record dimension (now is time)
      ncrcat -O ${drc_in}${var[var_id]}_${rlm}_${mdl}_${xpt[0]}_${nsm}_*.nc \
        ${drc_in}${var[var_id]}_${rlm}_${mdl}_${xpt[0]}_\
        ${nsm}_${yyyymm_str}-${yyyymm_end}

      # Remove useless files
      rm ${drc_in}${var[var_id]}_${rlm}_${mdl}_${xpt[0]}_${nsm}_\
        !(${yyyymm_str}-${yyyymm_end})
    done
  done
done
```

CMIP5 model data downloaded from the Earth System Grid Federation (ESGF (`http://pcmdi9.llnl.gov/esgf-web-fe/`)) does not contain group features yet. Therefore users must aggregate flat files into hierarchical ones themselves. The following script shows how. Each dataset becomes a group in the output file. There can be several levels of groups. In this example, we employ two experiments ("scenarios") as the top-level. The second-level comprises different models (e.g., CCSM4, CESM1-BGC). Many models are run multiple times with slight perturbed initial conditions to produce an ensemble of realizations. These ensemble members comprise the third level of the hierarchy. The script selects two variables, *snc* and *snd* (snow cover and snow depth).

```
#!/bin/bash
#
#============================================================
# Aggregate models to one group file
#
# Method:
# - Create files with groups by ncecat --gag
# - Append groups level by level using ncks
#
# Input files like:
# snc_LImon_CCSM4_historical_r1i1p1_199001-200512.nc
# snd_LImon_CESM1-BGC_esmHistorical_r1i1p1_199001-200512.nc
#
# Output files like:
# sn_LImon_199001-200512.nc
#
# Online:  http://nco.sourceforge.net/nco.html#Combine-Files
#
# Execute this script:  bash cmb_fl_grp.sh
#============================================================

# Directories
drc_in='../data/'
drc_out='../data/grp/'

# Constants
rlm='LImon'          # Realm:  LandIce; Time frequency:  monthly
tms='200001-200512' # Timeseries
flt='nc'             # File Type

# Geographical weights
# Can be skipped when ncap2 works on group data
# Loop over all snc files
for fn in $( ls ${drc_in}snc_${rlm}_*_${tms}.${flt} ); do
  ncap2 -O -s \
    'gw = float(cos(lat*3.1416/180.)); gw@long_name="geographical weight";'\
    ${fn} ${fn}
done

var=( 'snc' 'snd' )
xpt=( 'esmHistorical' 'historical' )
mdl=( 'CCSM4' 'CESM1-BGC' 'CESM1-CAM5' )

for i in {0..1}; do     # Loop over variables
  for j in {0..1}; do   # Loop over experiments
    for k in {0..2}; do # Loop over models
      ncecat -O --glb_mtd_spp -G ${xpt[j]}/${mdl[k]}/${mdl[k]}_ \
```

```
        ${drc_in}${var[i]}_${rlm}_${mdl[k]}_${xpt[j]}_*_${tms}.${flt} \
        ${drc_out}${var[i]}_${rlm}_${mdl[k]}_${xpt[j]}_all-nsm_${tms}.${flt}
      ncks -A \
        ${drc_out}${var[i]}_${rlm}_${mdl[k]}_${xpt[j]}_all-nsm_${tms}.${flt} \
        ${drc_out}${var[i]}_${rlm}_${mdl[0]}_${xpt[j]}_all-nsm_${tms}.${flt}
    done                # Loop done: models
    ncks -A \
      ${drc_out}${var[i]}_${rlm}_${mdl[0]}_${xpt[j]}_all-nsm_${tms}.${flt} \
      ${drc_out}${var[i]}_${rlm}_${mdl[0]}_${xpt[0]}_all-nsm_${tms}.${flt}
  done                  # Loop done: experiments
  ncks -A \
    ${drc_out}${var[i]}_${rlm}_${mdl[0]}_${xpt[0]}_all-nsm_${tms}.${flt} \
    ${drc_out}${var[0]}_${rlm}_${mdl[0]}_${xpt[0]}_all-nsm_${tms}.${flt}
done                    # Loop done: variables

# Rename output file
mv ${drc_out}${var[0]}_${rlm}_${mdl[0]}_${xpt[0]}_all-nsm_${tms}.${flt} \
  ${drc_out}sn_${rlm}_all-mdl_all-xpt_all-nsm_${tms}.${flt}
# Remove temporary files
rm ${drc_out}sn?_${rlm}*.nc

#- Rename Group:
#   E.g., file snc_LImon_CESM1-CAM5_historical_r1i1p1_199001-200512.nc
#   is now group /historical/CESM1-CAM5/CESM1-CAM5_00.
#   You can rename it to /historical/CESM1-CAM5/r1i1p1 to make more sense.
#  Note: You don't need to write the full path of the new name.
ncrename -g ${xpt}/${mdl}/${mdl}_00,r1i1p1 \
  ${drc_out}${var}_${rlm}_${mdl}_all-nsm_${tms}.${flt}

#------------------------------------------------------------
# Output file structure
#------------------------------------------------------------
# esmHistorical
# {
#   CESM1-BGC
#   {
#     CESM1-BGC_00
#     {
#       snc(time, lat, lon)
#       snd(time, lat, lon)
#     }
#   }
# }
# historical
# {
#   CCSM4
#   {
```

```
#       CCSM4_00
#       {
#        snc(time, lat, lon)
#        snd(time, lat, lon)
#       }
#       CCSM4_01
#       {
#        snc(time, lat, lon)
#        snd(time, lat, lon)
#       }
#       CCSM4_02 { ... }
#       CCSM4_03 { ... }
#       CCSM4_04 { ... }
#     }
#     CESM1-BGC
#     {
#       CESM1-BGC_00 { ... }
#     }
#     CESM1-CAM5
#     {
#       r1i1p1 { ... }
#       CESM1-CAM5_01 { ... }
#       CESM1-CAM5_02 { ... }
#     }
# }
```

## 7.2 Global Distribution of Long-term Average

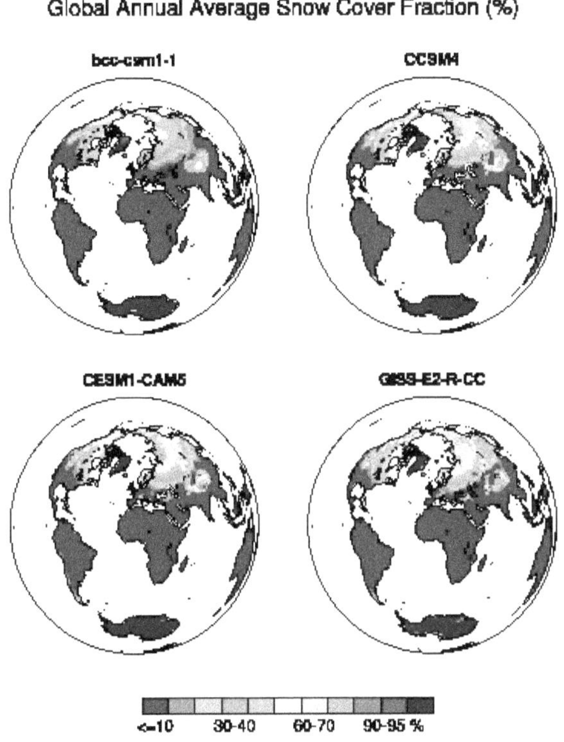


Figure 7.1: Global Distribution of Long-term Average.

This section illustrates how to calculate the global distribution of long-term average (see Figure 7.1) with either flat files or group file (`http://nco.sourceforge.net/nco.html#index-groups`). Key steps include:

1. Average ensemble members of each model using `nces` (see Section 4.6 [nces netCDF Ensemble Statistics], page 231)
2. Average the record dimension using `ncra` (see Section 4.10 [ncra netCDF Record Averager], page 262)
3. Store results of each model as a distinct group in a single output file using `ncecat` (see Section 4.11 [ncrcat netCDF Record Concatenator], page 265) with the `--gag` option

The first example shows how to process flat files.

```
#!/bin/bash

#===========================================================================
```

```
# After cmb_fl.sh
# Example:  Long-term average of each model globally
#
# Input files like:
# /data/cmip5/snc_LImon_bcc-csm1-1_historical_r1i1p1_185001-200512.nc
#
# Output files like:
# /data/cmip5/output/snc/snc_LImon_all-mdl_historical_all-nsm_clm.nc
#
# Online:
#  http://nco.sourceforge.net/nco.html#Global-Distribution-of-Long_002dterm-Avera
#
# Execute this script:  bash glb_avg.sh
#===========================================================================

#---------------------------------------------------------------------------
# Parameters
drc_in='/home/wenshanw/data/cmip5/'         # Directory of input files
drc_out='/home/wenshanw/data/cmip5/output/' # Directory of output files

var=( 'snc' 'snd' )                         # Variables
rlm='LImon'                                 # Realm
xpt=( 'historical' )                        # Experiment ( could be more )

fld_out=( 'snc/' 'snd/' )                   # Folders of output files
#---------------------------------------------------------------------------

for var_id in {0..1}; do                          # Loop over two variables
  # Names of all models
  #   (ls [get file names]; cut [get the part for model names];
  #   sort; uniq [remove duplicates]; awk [print])
  mdl_set=$( ls ${drc_in}${var[var_id]}_${rlm}_*_${xpt[0]}_*.nc | \
    cut -d '_' -f 3 | sort | uniq -c | awk '{print $2}' )
  # Number of models (echo [print contents]; wc [count])
  mdl_num=$( echo ${mdl_set} | wc -w )

  for mdl in ${mdl_set}; do                                       # Loop over mod
        # Average all the ensemble members of each model
    # Use nces file ensembles mode:  --nsm_fl
        nces --nsm_fl -O -4 -d time,"1956-01-01 00:00:0.0","2005-12-31 23:59:9.9"
      ${drc_in}${var[var_id]}_${rlm}_${mdl}_${xpt[0]}_*.nc \
      ${drc_out}${fld_out[var_id]}${var[var_id]}_${rlm}_${mdl}_${xpt[0]}\
      _all-nsm_195601-200512.nc

        # Average along time
        ncra -O ${drc_out}${fld_out[var_id]}${var[var_id]}_${rlm}_${mdl}_${xpt[0]
      _all-nsm_195601-200512.nc \
```

```
        ${drc_out}${fld_out[var_id]}${var[var_id]}_${mdl}.nc

        echo Model ${mdl} done!
  done

        # Remove temporary files
        rm ${drc_out}${fld_out[var_id]}${var[var_id]}*historical*.nc

  # Store models as groups in the output file
  ncecat -O --gag ${drc_out}${fld_out[var_id]}${var[var_id]}_*.nc \
    ${drc_out}${fld_out[var_id]}${var[var_id]}_${rlm}_\
    all-mdl_${xpt[0]}_all-nsm_clm.nc

        echo Var ${var[var_id]} done!
done
```

With the use of group, the above script will be shortened to ONE LINE.

```
# Data from cmb_fl_grp.sh
# ensemble averaging
nces -O --nsm_grp --nsm_sfx='_avg' \
sn_LImon_all-mdl_all-xpt_all-nsm_200001-200512.nc \
  sn_LImon_all-mdl_all-xpt_nsm-avg.nc
```

The input file, sn_LImon_all-mdl_all-xpt_all-nsm_200001-200512.nc, produced by cmb_fl_grp.sh, includes all the ensemble members as groups. The option '--nsm_grp' denotes that we are using group ensembles mode (http://nco.sf.net/nco.html#nsm_grp) of nces, instead of file ensembles mode (http://nco.sf.net/nco.html#nsm_fl), '--nsm_fl'. The option '--nsm_sfx='_avg'' instructs nces to store the output as a new child group /[model]/[model name]_avg/var; otherwise, the output will be stored directly in the parent group /[model]/var. In the final output file, sn_LImon_all-mdl_all-xpt_nsm-avg_tm-avg.nc, sub-groups with a suffix of 'avg' are the long-term averages of each model. One thing to notice is that for now, ensembles with only one ensemble member will be left untouched.

## 7.3 Annual Average over Regions

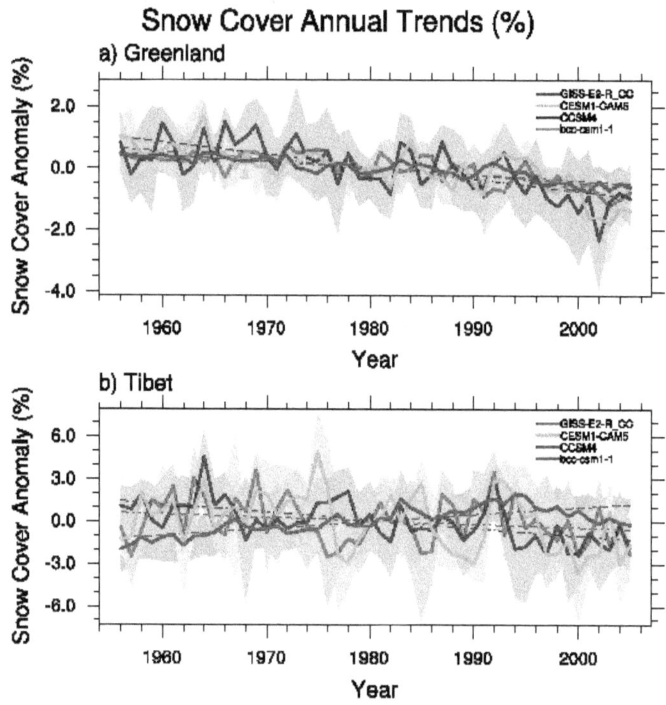


Figure 7.2: Annual Average over Regions.

This section illustrates how to calculate the annual average over specific regions (see Figure 7.2). Key steps include:

1. Spatial average using `ncap2` (see Section 4.1 [ncap2 netCDF Arithmetic Processor], page 138) and `ncwa` (see Section 4.14 [ncwa netCDF Weighted Averager], page 283);
2. Change dimension order using `ncpdq` (see Section 4.9 [ncpdq netCDF Permute Dimensions Quickly], page 254);
3. Annual average using `ncra` (see Section 4.10 [ncra netCDF Record Averager], page 262);
4. Anomaly from long-term average using `ncbo` (see Section 4.3 [ncbo netCDF Binary Operator], page 207);
5. Standard deviation using `ncbo` (see Section 4.3 [ncbo netCDF Binary Operator], page 207) and `nces` (see Section 4.6 [nces netCDF Ensemble Statistics], page 231);
6. Rename variables using `ncrename` (see Section 4.13 [ncrename netCDF Renamer], page 278);
7. Edit attributions using `ncatted` (see Section 4.2 [ncatted netCDF Attribute Editor], page 200);
8. Linear regression using `ncap2` (see Section 4.1 [ncap2 netCDF Arithmetic Processor], page 138);

9. Use ncap2 (see Section 4.1 [ncap2 netCDF Arithmetic Processor], page 138) with nco script file (i.e., .nco file);
10. Move variables around using ncks (see Section 4.8 [ncks netCDF Kitchen Sink], page 237).

### Flat files example

```
#!/bin/bash
# Includes gsl_rgr.nco

#===========================================================================
# After cmb_fl.sh
# Example:  Annual trend of each model over Greenland and Tibet
#   ( time- and spatial-average, standard deviation,
#   anomaly and linear regression)
#
# Input files:
# /data/cmip5/snc_LImon_bcc-csm1-1_historical_r1i1p1_185001-200512.nc
#
# Output files:
# /data/cmip5/outout/snc/snc_LImon_all-mdl_historical_all-nsm_annual.nc
#
# Online:  http://nco.sourceforge.net/nco.html#Annual-Average-over-Regions
#
# Execute this script:  bash ann_avg.sh
#===========================================================================

#---------------------------------------------------------------------------
# Parameters
drc_in='/home/wenshanw/data/cmip5/'         # Directory of input files
drc_out='/home/wenshanw/data/cmip5/output/' # Directory of output files

var=( 'snc' 'snd' )                         # Variables
rlm='LImon'                                 # Realm
xpt=( 'historical' )                        # Experiment ( could be more )

fld_out=( 'snc/' 'snd/' )                   # Folders of output files
# ------------------------------------------------------------

for var_id in {0..1}; do                    # Loop over two variables
  # Names of all models
  #   (ls [get file names]; cut [get the part for model names];
  #   sort; uniq [remove duplicates]; awk [print])
  mdl_set=$( ls ${drc_in}${var[var_id]}_${rlm}_*_${xpt[0]}_*.nc | \
    cut -d '_' -f 3 | sort | uniq -c | awk '{print $2}' )

  for mdl in ${mdl_set}; do                           # Loop over models
```

```
  # Loop over ensemble members
for fn in $( ls ${drc_in}${var[var_id]}_${rlm}_${mdl}_${xpt[0]}_*.nc ); do
  pfx=$( echo ${fn} | cut -d'/' -f6 | cut -d'_' -f1-5 )

  # Two regions
  # Geographical weight
  ncap2 -O -s 'gw = cos(lat*3.1415926/180.); gw@long_name="geographical weigh
    ;gw@units="ratio"' ${fn} ${drc_out}${fld_out[var_id]}${pfx}_gw.nc
  # Greenland
  ncwa -O -w gw -d lat,60.0,75.0 -d lon,300.0,340.0 -a lat,lon \
    ${drc_out}${fld_out[var_id]}${pfx}_gw.nc \
    ${drc_out}${fld_out[var_id]}${pfx}_gw_1.nc
  # Tibet
  ncwa -O -w gw -d lat,30.0,40.0 -d lon,80.0,100.0 -a lat,lon \
    ${drc_out}${fld_out[var_id]}${pfx}_gw.nc \
    ${drc_out}${fld_out[var_id]}${pfx}_gw_2.nc

  # Aggregate 2 regions together
  ncecat -O -u rgn ${drc_out}${fld_out[var_id]}${pfx}_gw_?.nc \
    ${drc_out}${fld_out[var_id]}${pfx}_gw_rgn4.nc

  # Change dimensions order
  ncpdq -O -a time,rgn ${drc_out}${fld_out[var_id]}${pfx}_gw_rgn4.nc \
    ${drc_out}${fld_out[var_id]}${pfx}_gw_rgn4.nc

  # Remove temporary files (optional)
  rm ${drc_out}${fld_out[var_id]}${pfx}_gw_?.nc \
    ${drc_out}${fld_out[var_id]}${pfx}_gw.nc

  # Annual average (use the feature of 'Duration')
  ncra -O --mro -d time,"1956-01-01 00:00:0.0","2005-12-31 23:59:9.9",12,12 \
    ${drc_out}${fld_out[var_id]}${pfx}_gw_rgn4.nc \
    ${drc_out}${fld_out[var_id]}${pfx}_yrly.nc

  # Anomaly
  # Long-term average
  ncwa -O -a time ${drc_out}${fld_out[var_id]}${pfx}_yrly.nc \
    ${drc_out}${fld_out[var_id]}${pfx}_clm.nc
  # Subtract long-term average
  ncbo -O --op_typ=- ${drc_out}${fld_out[var_id]}${pfx}_yrly.nc \
    ${drc_out}${fld_out[var_id]}${pfx}_clm.nc \
    ${drc_out}${fld_out[var_id]}${pfx}_anm.nc
done

rm ${drc_out}${fld_out[var_id]}${var[var_id]}_${rlm}_${mdl}_${xpt[0]}_*_yrly.

# Average over all the ensemble members
```

```
ncea -O -4 ${drc_out}${fld_out[var_id]}${var[var_id]}_\
  ${rlm}_${mdl}_${xpt[0]}_*_anm.nc ${drc_out}${fld_out[var_id]}\
  ${var[var_id]}_${rlm}_${mdl}_${xpt[0]}_all-nsm_anm.nc

# Standard deviation ------------------------------
for fn in $( ls ${drc_out}${fld_out[var_id]}${var[var_id]}_${rlm}_${mdl}_\
  ${xpt[0]}_*_anm.nc ); do
  pfx=$( echo ${fn} | cut -d'/' -f8 | cut -d'_' -f1-5 )

  # Difference between each ensemble member and the average of all members
  ncbo -O --op_typ=- ${fn} \
    ${drc_out}${fld_out[var_id]}${var[var_id]}_\
    ${rlm}_${mdl}_${xpt[0]}_all-nsm_anm.nc \
    ${drc_out}${fld_out[var_id]}${pfx}_dlt.nc
done

# RMS
ncea -O -y rmssdn ${drc_out}${fld_out[var_id]}${var[var_id]}_${rlm}_\
  ${mdl}_${xpt[0]}_*_dlt.nc \
  ${drc_out}${fld_out[var_id]}${var[var_id]}_${rlm}_\
  ${mdl}_${xpt[0]}_all-nsm_sdv.nc
# Rename variables
ncrename -v ${var[var_id]},sdv \
  ${drc_out}${fld_out[var_id]}${var[var_id]}_${rlm}_\
  ${mdl}_${xpt[0]}_all-nsm_sdv.nc
# Edit attributions
ncatted -a standard_name,sdv,a,c,"_standard_deviation_over_ensemble" \
  -a long_name,sdv,a,c," Standard Deviation over Ensemble" \
  -a original_name,sdv,a,c," sdv" \
  ${drc_out}${fld_out[var_id]}${var[var_id]}_${rlm}_\
  ${mdl}_${xpt[0]}_all-nsm_sdv.nc
#------------------------------------------------------------

# Linear regression -----------------------------------------
#!!!!!!!!!!!!!!!!!!!!!!!!!!!!!!!!!!!!!!!!!!!!!!!!!!!!!!!!!!!!!!!!!!!!!!!!!!!!
# Have to change the name of variable in the commands file
#   of gsl_rgr.nco manually (gsl_rgr.nco is listed below)
ncap2 -O -S gsl_rgr.nco \
  ${drc_out}${fld_out[var_id]}${var[var_id]}_${rlm}_\
  ${mdl}_${xpt[0]}_all-nsm_anm.nc ${drc_out}${fld_out[var_id]}${var[var_id]}\
  _${rlm}_${mdl}_${xpt[0]}_all-nsm_anm_rgr.nc
#!!!!!!!!!!!!!!!!!!!!!!!!!!!!!!!!!!!!!!!!!!!!!!!!!!!!!!!!!!!!!!!!!!!!!!!!!!!!

# Get rid of temporary variables
ncks -O -v c0,c1,pval,${var[var_id]},gw \
  ${drc_out}${fld_out[var_id]}${var[var_id]}_${rlm}_${mdl}_\
  ${xpt[0]}_all-nsm_anm_rgr.nc \
```

```
      ${drc_out}${fld_out[var_id]}${var[var_id]}_${mdl}.nc
    #------------------------------------------------------------

    # Move the variable 'sdv' into the anomaly files (i.e., *anm.nc files)
    ncks -A -v sdv \
      ${drc_out}${fld_out[var_id]}${var[var_id]}_${rlm}_\
      ${mdl}_${xpt[0]}_all-nsm_sdv.nc \
      ${drc_out}${fld_out[var_id]}${var[var_id]}_${mdl}.nc
    rm ${drc_out}${fld_out[var_id]}${var[var_id]}_*historical*

    echo Model ${mdl} done!
  done

  # Store models as groups in the output file
  ncecat -O --gag ${drc_out}${fld_out[var_id]}${var[var_id]}_*.nc
  ${drc_out}${fld_out[var_id]}${var[var_id]}_\
    ${rlm}_all-mdl_${xpt[0]}_all-nsm_annual.nc

  echo Var ${var[var_id]} done!
done
```

**gsl_rgr.nco**

```
// Linear Regression
// Called by ann_avg.sh
// Caution:  make sure the variable name is
//  in agreement with the main script (now is 'snd')
// Online:  http://nco.sourceforge.net/nco.html#Annual-Average-over-Regions

// Declare variables
*c0[$rgn]=0.;         // Intercept
*c1[$rgn]=0.;         // Slope
*sdv[$rgn]=0.;        // Standard deviation
*covxy[$rgn]=0.;      // Covariance
*x = double(time);

for (*rgn_id=0;rgn_id<$rgn.size;rgn_id++)   // Loop over regions
{
        gsl_fit_linear(time,1,snd(:,rgn_id),1,$time.size, \
    &tc0, &tc1, &cov00, &cov01,&cov11,&sumsq); // Linear regression function
        c0(rgn_id) = tc0;    // Output results
        c1(rgn_id) = tc1;
        covxy(rgn_id) = gsl_stats_covariance(time,1,\
    $time.size,double(snd(:,rgn_id)),1,$time.size); // Covariance function
        sdv(rgn_id) = gsl_stats_sd(snd(:,rgn_id), \
    1, $time.size);   // Standard deviation function
}
```

```
// P value-----------------------------------------------------------
*time_sdv = gsl_stats_sd(time, 1, $time.size);
*r_value = covxy/(time_sdv*sdv);
*t_value = r_value/sqrt((1-r_value^2)/($time.size-2));
pval = abs(gsl_cdf_tdist_P(t_value, $time.size-2) - \
  gsl_cdf_tdist_P(-t_value, $time.size-2));
//----------------------------------------------------------------

// Write RAM variables to disk
//------------------------------------------------------------
// Usually NCO writes the outputs directly to disk
// Using RAM variables, declared by *, will shorten running time
// Output the final results using ram_write()
//------------------------------------------------------------
ram_write(c0);
ram_write(c1);
```

With the group feature, all the loops over experiments, models and ensemble members can be omitted. As we are working on implementing group feature in all NCO operators, some functions (e.g., regression and standard deviation over ensemble members) may have to wait until the new versions.

```
#!/bin/bash
#
#============================================================
# Group data output by cmb_fl_grp.sh
# Annual trend of each model over Greenland and Tibet
# Time- and spatial-average, standard deviation and anomaly
# No regression yet (needs ncap2)
#
# Input files:
# sn_LImon_all-mdl_all-xpt_all-nsm_200001-200512.nc
#
# Online:  http://nco.sourceforge.net/nco.html#Annual-Average-over-Regions
#
# Execute this script:  bash ann_avg_grp.sh
#===========================================================================
# Input and output directory
drc='../data/grp/'

# Constants
pfx='sn_LImon_all-mdl_all-xpt_all-nsm'
tms='200001-200512'           # Time series

# Greenland
ncwa -O -w gw -d lat,60.0,75.0 -d lon,300.0,340.0 -a lat,lon \
  ${drc}${pfx}_${tms}.nc \
  ${drc}${pfx}_${tms}_grl.nc
```

```
# Tibet
ncwa -O -w gw -d lat,30.0,40.0 -d lon,80.0,100.0 -a lat,lon \
  ${drc}${pfx}_${tms}.nc \
  ${drc}${pfx}_${tms}_tbt.nc

# Aggregate 2 regions together
ncecat -O -u rgn ${drc}${pfx}_${tms}_???.nc \
  ${drc}${pfx}_${tms}_rgn2.nc

# Change dimensions order
ncpdq -O -a time,rgn ${drc}${pfx}_${tms}_rgn2.nc \
  ${drc}${pfx}_${tms}_rgn2.nc

# Remove temporary files (optional)
rm ${drc}${pfx}_${tms}_???.nc

#Annual average
ncra -O --mro -d time,,,12,12 ${drc}${pfx}_${tms}_rgn2.nc \
  ${drc}${pfx}_${tms}_rgn2_ann.nc

# Anomaly
#------------------------------------------------------------
# Long-term average
ncwa -O -a time ${drc}${pfx}_${tms}_rgn2_ann.nc \
  ${drc}${pfx}_${tms}_rgn2_clm.nc
# Subtract
ncbo -O --op_typ=- ${drc}${pfx}_${tms}_rgn2_ann.nc \
  ${drc}${pfx}_${tms}_rgn2_clm.nc \
  ${drc}${pfx}_${tms}_rgn2_anm.nc
#------------------------------------------------------------

# Standard Deviation:  inter-annual variability
# RMS of the above anomaly
ncra -O -y rmssdn ${drc}${pfx}_${tms}_rgn2_anm.nc \
  ${drc}${pfx}_${tms}_rgn2_stddev.nc
```

## 7.4 Monthly Cycle

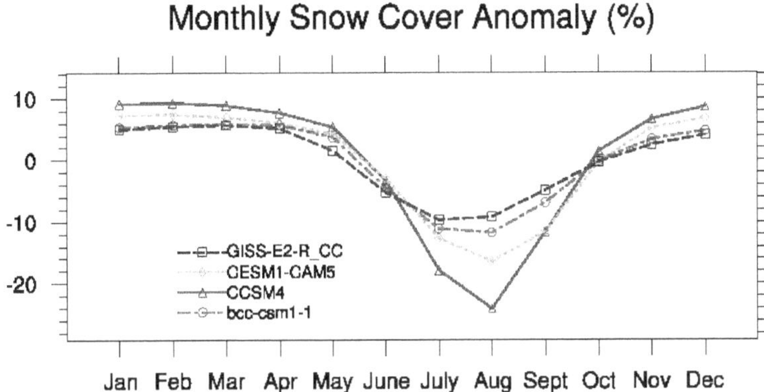


Figure 7.3: Monthly Cycle.

This script illustrates how to calculate the monthly anomaly from the annual average (see Figure 7.3). In order to keep only the monthly cycle, we will subtract the annual average of each year from the monthly data, instead of subtracting the long-term average. This is a little more complicated in coding since we need to loop over years.

**Flat files example**

```
#!/bin/bash

#===========================================================
# After cmb_fl.sh
# Example:  Monthly cycle of each model in Greenland
#
# Input files:
# /data/cmip5/snc_LImon_bcc-csm1-1_historical_r1i1p1_185001-200512.nc
#
# Output files:
# /data/cmip5/snc/snc_LImon__all-mdl_historical_all-nsm_GN_mthly-anm.nc
#
# Online:  http://nco.sourceforge.net/nco.html#Monthly-Cycle
#
# Execute this script:  bash mcc.sh
#===========================================================

#-----------------------------------------------------------
# Parameters
drc_in='/home/wenshanw/data/cmip5/'           # Directory of input files
drc_out='/home/wenshanw/data/cmip5/output/'   # Directory of output files

var=( 'snc' 'snd' )             # Variables
```

```
rlm='LImon'                        # Realm
xpt=( 'historical' )               # Experiment ( could be more )

fld_out=( 'snc/' 'snd/' )                  # Folders of output files
#-------------------------------------------------------------

for var_id in {0..1}; do                   # Loop over two variables
  # names of all models
  #  (ls [get file names]; cut [get the part for model names];
  #  sort; uniq [remove duplicates]; awk [print])
  mdl_set=$( ls ${drc_in}${var[var_id]}_${rlm}_*_${xpt[0]}_*.nc | \
    cut -d '_' -f 3 | sort | uniq -c | awk '{print $2}' )

  for mdl in ${mdl_set}; do                ## Loop over models
    # Average all the ensemble members of each model
    ncea -O -4 -d time,"1956-01-01 00:00:0.0","2005-12-31 23:59:9.9" \
      ${drc_in}${var[var_id]}_${rlm}_${mdl}_${xpt[0]}_*.nc \
      ${drc_out}${fld_out[var_id]}${var[var_id]}_${rlm}_${mdl}_${xpt[0]}_all-nsm.

    # Greenland
    # Geographical weight
    ncap2 -O -s \
      'gw = cos(lat*3.1415926/180.); \
      gw@long_name="geographical weight";gw@units="ratio"' \
      ${drc_out}${fld_out[var_id]}${var[var_id]}_${rlm}_${mdl}_${xpt[0]}_all-nsm.
      ${drc_out}${fld_out[var_id]}${var[var_id]}_${rlm}_${mdl}_${xpt[0]}_all-nsm.
    ncwa -O -w gw -d lat,60.0,75.0 -d lon,300.0,340.0 -a lat,lon \
      ${drc_out}${fld_out[var_id]}${var[var_id]}_${rlm}_${mdl}_${xpt[0]}_all-nsm.
      ${drc_out}${fld_out[var_id]}${var[var_id]}_${rlm}_${mdl}_${xpt[0]}_all-nsm_

    # Anomaly----------------------------------------
    for moy in {1..12}; do                 # Loop over months
      mm=$( printf "%02d" ${moy} )         # Change to 2-digit format

      for yr in {1956..2005}; do                # Loop over years
        # If January, calculate the annual average
        if [ ${moy} -eq 1 ]; then
                ncra -O -d time,"${yr}-01-01 00:00:0.0","${yr}-12-31 23:59:9.9" \
            ${drc_out}${fld_out[var_id]}${var[var_id]}_${rlm}_${mdl}_\
            ${xpt[0]}_all-nsm_GN.nc ${drc_out}${fld_out[var_id]}${var[var_id]}_\
            ${rlm}_${mdl}_${xpt[0]}_all-nsm_GN_${yr}.nc
        fi

        # The specific month
        ncks -O -d time,"${yr}-${mm}-01 00:00:0.0","${yr}-${mm}-31 23:59:9.9" \
          ${drc_out}${fld_out[var_id]}${var[var_id]}_\
          ${rlm}_${mdl}_${xpt[0]}_all-nsm_GN.nc \
```

```
        ${drc_out}${fld_out[var_id]}${var[var_id]}_${rlm}_${mdl}_${xpt[0]}_\
        all-nsm_GN_${yr}${mm}.nc
      # Subtract the annual average from the monthly data
      ncbo -O --op_typ=- ${drc_out}${fld_out[var_id]}${var[var_id]}_\
        ${rlm}_${mdl}_${xpt[0]}_all-nsm_GN_${yr}${mm}.nc \
        ${drc_out}${fld_out[var_id]}${var[var_id]}_${rlm}_${mdl}_${xpt[0]}_\
        all-nsm_GN_${yr}.nc ${drc_out}${fld_out[var_id]}${var[var_id]}_${rlm}_\
        ${mdl}_${xpt[0]}_all-nsm_GN_${yr}${mm}_anm.nc
    done

    # Average over years
    ncra -O ${drc_out}${fld_out[var_id]}${var[var_id]}_${rlm}_${mdl}_\
      ${xpt[0]}_all-nsm_GN_????${mm}_anm.nc \
      ${drc_out}${fld_out[var_id]}${var[var_id]}_${rlm}_${mdl}_\
      ${xpt[0]}_all-nsm_GN_${mm}_anm.nc
  done
  #--------------------------------------------------

  # Concatenate months together
  ncrcat -O ${drc_out}${fld_out[var_id]}${var[var_id]}_${rlm}_${mdl}_\
    ${xpt[0]}_all-nsm_GN_??_anm.nc \
    ${drc_out}${fld_out[var_id]}${var[var_id]}_${mdl}.nc

  echo Model ${mdl} done!
done

rm -f ${drc_out}${fld_out[var_id]}${var[var_id]}*historical*

# Store models as groups in the output file
ncecat -O --gag -v ${var[var_id]} \
  ${drc_out}${fld_out[var_id]}${var[var_id]}_*.nc \
  ${drc_out}${fld_out[var_id]}${var[var_id]}_${rlm}_all-mdl_\
  ${xpt[0]}_all-nsm_GN_mthly-anm.nc

echo Var ${var[var_id]} done!
done
```

Using group feature and hyperslabs (http://nco.sourceforge.net/nco.html#Hyperslabs) of ncbo, the script will be shortened.

```
#!/bin/bash

#===========================================================
# Monthly cycle of each ensemble member in Greenland
#
# Input file from cmb_fl_grpsh
#   sn_LImon_all-mdl_all-xpt_all-nsm_199001-200512.nc
# Online:  http://nco.sourceforge.net/nco.html#Monthly-Cycle
```

```
#
# Execute this script in command line:  bash mcc_grp.sh
#============================================================
# Input and output directory
drc='../data/grp/'

# Constants
pfx='sn_LImon_all-mdl_all-xpt_all-nsm_200001-200512'

# Greenland
ncwa -O -w gw -d lat,60.0,75.0 -d lon,300.0,340.0 -a lat,lon \
  ${drc}${pfx}.nc ${drc}${pfx}_grl.nc

# Anomaly from annual average of each year
for yyyy in {2000..2005}; do
  # Annual average
  ncwa -O -d time,"${yyyy}-01-01","${yyyy}-12-31" \
    ${drc}${pfx}_grl.nc ${drc}${pfx}_grl_${yyyy}.nc

  # Anomaly
  ncbo -O --op_typ=- -d time,"${yyyy}-01-01","${yyyy}-12-31" \
    ${drc}${pfx}_grl.nc ${drc}${pfx}_grl_${yyyy}.nc \
    ${drc}${pfx}_grl_${yyyy}_anm.nc
done

# Monthly cycle
for moy in {1..12}; do
  mm=$( printf "%02d" ${moy} )      # Change to 2-digit format
  ncra -O -d time,"2000-${mm}-01",,12 \
    ${drc}${pfx}_grl_????_anm.nc ${drc}${pfx}_grl_${mm}_anm.nc
done
# Concatenate 12 months together
ncrcat -O ${drc}${pfx}_grl_??_anm.nc \
  ${drc}${pfx}_grl_mth_anm.nc
```

## 7.5 Regrid MODIS Data

In order to compare the results between MODIS and CMIP5 models, one usually regrids one or both datasets so that the spatial resolutions match. Here, the script illustrates how to regrid MODIS data. Key steps include:

1. Regrid using bilinear interpolation (see Section 4.1.21 [Bilinear interpolation], page 175)
2. Rename variables, dimensions and attributions using `ncrename` (see Section 4.13 [ncrename netCDF Renamer], page 278).

**Main Script**

```
#!/bin/bash
```

```
# include bi_interp.nco

#===========================================================================
# Example for
#       - regrid (using bi_interp.nco):  the spatial resolution of MODIS data
#               is much finer than those of CMIP5 models.  In order to compare
#               the two, we can regrid MODIS data to comform to CMIP5.
#
# Input files (Note:  the .hdf files downloaded have to be converted to .nc at
# the present):
# /modis/mcd43c3/MCD43C3.A2000049.005.2006271205532.nc
#
# Output files:
# /modis/mcd43c3/cesm-grid/MCD43C3.2000049.regrid.nc
#
# Online:  http://nco.sourceforge.net/nco.html#Regrid-MODIS-Data
#
# Execute this script:  bash rgr.sh
#===========================================================================

var=( 'MCD43C3' )     # Variable
fld_in=( 'monthly/' )     # Folder of input files
fld_out=( 'cesm-grid/' )      # Folder of output files
drc_in='/media/grele_data/wenshan/modis/mcd43c3/'     # Directory of input files

for fn in $( ls ${drc_in}${fld_in}${var}.*.nc ); do             # Loop over files
  sfx=$( echo $fn | cut -d '/' -f 8 | cut -d '.'  -f 2 ) # Part of file names

  # Regrid
  ncap2 -O -S bi_interp.nco ${fn} ${drc_in}${fld_out}${var}.${sfx}.regrid.nc
  # Keep only the new variables
  ncks -O -v wsa_sw_less,bsa_sw_less ${drc_in}${fld_out}${var}.${sfx}.regrid.nc \
    ${drc_in}${fld_out}${var}.${sfx}.regrid.nc
  # Rename the new variables, dimensions and attributions
  ncrename -O -d latn,lat -d lonn,lon -v latn,lat -v lonn,lon \
    -v wsa_sw_less,wsa_sw -v bsa_sw_less,bsa_sw -a missing_value,_FillValue \
    ${drc_in}${fld_out}${var}.${sfx}.regrid.nc

  echo $sfx done.
done
```

**bi_interp.nco**

```
// Bilinear interpolation
// Included by rgr.sh
// Online:  http://nco.sourceforge.net/nco.html#Regrid-MODIS-Data

defdim("latn",192);              // Define new dimension:  latitude
```

```
defdim("lonn",288);             // Define new dimension: longitude
latn[$latn] = {90,89.0576 ,88.1152 ,87.1728 ,86.2304 ,85.288  ,\
  84.3456 ,83.4031 ,82.4607 ,81.5183 ,80.5759 ,79.6335 ,78.6911 ,\
  77.7487 ,76.8063 ,75.8639 ,74.9215 ,73.9791 ,73.0367 ,72.0942 ,\
  71.1518 ,70.2094 ,69.267  ,68.3246 ,67.3822 ,66.4398 ,65.4974 ,\
  64.555  ,63.6126 ,62.6702 ,61.7277 ,60.7853 ,59.8429 ,58.9005 ,\
  57.9581 ,57.0157 ,56.0733 ,55.1309 ,54.1885 ,53.2461 ,52.3037 ,\
  51.3613 ,50.4188 ,49.4764 ,48.534  ,47.5916 ,46.6492 ,45.7068 ,\
  44.7644 ,43.822  ,42.8796 ,41.9372 ,40.9948 ,40.0524 ,39.11   ,\
  38.1675 ,37.2251 ,36.2827 ,35.3403 ,34.3979 ,33.4555 ,32.5131 ,\
  31.5707 ,30.6283 ,29.6859 ,28.7435 ,27.8011 ,26.8586 ,25.9162 ,\
  24.9738 ,24.0314 ,23.089  ,22.1466 ,21.2042 ,20.2618 ,19.3194 ,\
  18.377  ,17.4346 ,16.4921 ,15.5497 ,14.6073 ,13.6649 ,12.7225 ,\
  11.7801 ,10.8377 ,9.89529 ,8.95288 ,8.01047 ,7.06806 ,6.12565 ,\
  5.18325 ,4.24084 ,3.29843 ,2.35602 ,1.41361 ,0.471204,-0.471204,\
  -1.41361,-2.35602,-3.29843,-4.24084,-5.18325,-6.12565,-7.06806,\
  -8.01047,-8.95288,-9.89529,-10.8377,-11.7801,-12.7225,-13.6649,\
  -14.6073,-15.5497,-16.4921,-17.4346,-18.377 ,-19.3194,-20.2618,\
  -21.2042,-22.1466,-23.089 ,-24.0314,-24.9738,-25.9162,-26.8586,\
  -27.8011,-28.7435,-29.6859,-30.6283,-31.5707,-32.5131,-33.4555,\
  -34.3979,-35.3403,-36.2827,-37.2251,-38.1675,-39.11  ,-40.0524,\
  -40.9948,-41.9372,-42.8796,-43.822 ,-44.7644,-45.7068,-46.6492,\
  -47.5916,-48.534 ,-49.4764,-50.4188,-51.3613,-52.3037,-53.2461,\
  -54.1885,-55.1309,-56.0733,-57.0157,-57.9581,-58.9005,-59.8429,\
  -60.7853,-61.7277,-62.6702,-63.6126,-64.555 ,-65.4974,-66.4398,\
  -67.3822,-68.3246,-69.267 ,-70.2094,-71.1518,-72.0942,-73.0367,\
  -73.9791,-74.9215,-75.8639,-76.8063,-77.7487,-78.6911,-79.6335,\
  -80.5759,-81.5183,-82.4607,-83.4031,-84.3456,-85.288,-86.2304,\
  -87.1728,-88.1152,-89.0576,-90};                // Copy of CCSM4 latitude
lonn[$lonn] = {-178.75,-177.5,-176.25,-175,-173.75,-172.5,-171.25,\
  -170,-168.75,-167.5,-166.25,-165,-163.75,-162.5,-161.25,-160,\
  -158.75,-157.5,-156.25,-155,-153.75,-152.5,-151.25,-150,-148.75,\
  -147.5,-146.25,-145,-143.75,-142.5,-141.25,-140,-138.75,-137.5,\
  -136.25,-135,-133.75,-132.5,-131.25,-130,-128.75,-127.5,-126.25,\
  -125,-123.75,-122.5,-121.25,-120,-118.75,-117.5,-116.25,-115,\
  -113.75,-112.5,-111.25,-110,-108.75,-107.5,-106.25,-105,-103.75,\
  -102.5,-101.25,-100,-98.75,-97.5,-96.25,-95,-93.75,-92.5,-91.25,\
  -90,-88.75,-87.5,-86.25,-85,-83.75,-82.5,-81.25,-80,-78.75,-77.5,\
  -76.25,-75,-73.75,-72.5,-71.25,-70,-68.75,-67.5,-66.25,-65,-63.75,\
  -62.5,-61.25,-60,-58.75,-57.5,-56.25,-55,-53.75,-52.5,-51.25,-50,\
  -48.75,-47.5,-46.25,-45,-43.75,-42.5,-41.25,-40,-38.75,-37.5,\
  -36.25,-35,-33.75,-32.5,-31.25,-30,-28.75,-27.5,-26.25,-25,-23.75,\
  -22.5,-21.25,-20,-18.75,-17.5,-16.25,-15,-13.75,-12.5,-11.25,-10,\
  -8.75,-7.5,-6.25,-5,-3.75,-2.5,-1.25,0,1.25,2.5,3.75,5,6.25,7.5,\
  8.75,10,11.25,12.5,13.75,15,16.25,17.5,18.75,20,21.25,22.5,23.75,\
  25,26.25,27.5,28.75,30,31.25,32.5,33.75,35,36.25,37.5,38.75,40,\
  41.25,42.5,43.75,45,46.25,47.5,48.75,50,51.25,52.5,53.75,55,56.25,\
```

```
  57.5,58.75,60,61.25,62.5,63.75,65,66.25,67.5,68.75,70,71.25,72.5,\
  73.75,75,76.25,77.5,78.75,80,81.25,82.5,83.75,85,86.25,87.5,88.75,\
  90,91.25,92.5,93.75,95,96.25,97.5,98.75,100,101.25,102.5,103.75,\
  105,106.25,107.5,108.75,110,111.25,112.5,113.75,115,116.25,117.5,\
  118.75,120,121.25,122.5,123.75,125,126.25,127.5,128.75,130,131.25,\
  132.5,133.75,135,136.25,137.5,138.75,140,141.25,142.5,143.75,145,\
  146.25,147.5,148.75,150,151.25,152.5,153.75,155,156.25,157.5,\
  158.75,160,161.25,162.5,163.75,165,166.25,167.5,168.75,170,171.25,\
  172.5,173.75,175,176.25,177.5,178.75,180};    // Copy of CCSM4 longitude

*out[$time,$latn,$lonn]=0.0;           // Output structure

// Bi-linear interpolation
bsa_sw_less=bilinear_interp_wrap(bsa_sw,out,latn,lonn,lat,lon);
wsa_sw_less=bilinear_interp_wrap(wsa_sw,out,latn,lonn,lat,lon);

// Add attributions
latn@units = "degree_north";
lonn@units = "degree_east";
latn@long_name = "latitude";
lonn@long_name = "longitude";
bsa_sw_less@hdf_name = "Albedo_BSA_shortwave";
bsa_sw_less@calibrated_nt = 5;
bsa_sw_less@missing_value = 32767.0;
bsa_sw_less@units = "albedo, no units";
bsa_sw_less@long_name = "Global_Albedo_BSA_shortwave";
wsa_sw_less@hdf_name = "Albedo_WSA_shortwave";
wsa_sw_less@calibrated_nt = 5;
wsa_sw_less@missing_value = 32767.0;
wsa_sw_less@units = "albedo, no units";
wsa_sw_less@long_name = "Global_Albedo_WSA_shortwave";
```

## 7.6 Add Coordinates to MODIS Data

**Main Script**

```
#!/bin/bash

#===========================================================
# Example for
#       - regrid (using bi_interp.nco): the spatial resolution of MODIS data
#               is much finer than those of CMIP5 models. In order to compare
#               the two, we can regrid MODIS data to comform to CMIP5.
#       - add coordinates (using coor.nco): there is no coordinate information
#               in MODIS data. We have to add it manually now.
#
# Input files:
# /modis/mcd43c3/cesm-grid/MCD43C3.2000049.regrid.nc
```

```
#
# Output files:
# /modis/mcd43c3/cesm-grid/MCD43C3.2000049.regrid.nc
#
# Online:  http://nco.sourceforge.net/nco.html#Add-Coordinates-to-MODIS-Data
#
# Execute this script:  bash add_crd.sh
#===================================================================

var=( 'MOD10CM' )     # Variable
fld_in=( 'snc/nc/' )  # Folder of input files
drc_in='/media/grele_data/wenshan/modis/' # directory of input files

for fn in $( ls ${drc_in}${fld_in}${var}*.nc ); do              # Loop over files
  sfx=$( echo ${fn} | cut -d '/' -f 8 | cut -d '.'  -f 2-4 )    # Part of file na

  echo ${sfx}

  # Rename dimension names
  ncrename -d YDim_MOD_CMG_Snow_5km,lat -d XDim_MOD_CMG_Snow_5km,lon -O \
    ${drc_in}${fld_in}${var}.${sfx}.nc ${drc_in}${fld_in}${var}.${sfx}.nc
  # Add coordinates
  ncap2 -O -S crd.nco ${drc_in}${fld_in}${var}.${sfx}.nc \
    ${drc_in}${fld_in}${var}.${sfx}.nc
done
```

**crd.nco**

```
// Add coordinates to MODIS HDF data
// Included by add_crd.sh
// Online:  http://nco.sourceforge.net/nco.html#Add-Coordinates-to-MODIS-Data

lon = array(0.f, 0.05, $lon) - 180;
lat = 90.f- array(0.f, 0.05, $lat);
```

## 7.7 Permute MODIS Coordinates

MODIS orders latitude data from 90°N to -90°N, and longitude from -180°E to 180°E. However, CMIP5 orders latitude from -90°N to 90°N, and longitude from 0°E to 360°E. This script changes the MODIS coordinates to follow the CMIP5 convention.

```
#!/bin/bash

##===========================================================================
## Example for
##      - permute coordinates:  the grid of MODIS is
##              from (-180 degE, 90 degN), the left-up corner, to
##              (180 degE, -90 degN), the right-low corner.  However, CMIP5 is
##              from (0 degE, -90 degN) to (360 degE, 90 degN). The script
##              here changes the MODIS grid to CMIP5 grid.
```

```
##
## Input files:
## /modis/mcd43c3/cesm-grid/MCD43C3.2000049.regrid.nc
##
## Output files:
## /modis/mcd43c3/cesm-grid/MCD43C3.2000049.regrid.nc
##
## Online:  http://nco.sourceforge.net/nco.html#Permute-MODIS-Coordinates
##
## Execute this script:  bash pmt_crd.sh
##============================================================================

##----------------------------------------------------------------------------
## Permute coordinates
##      - Inverse lat from (90,-90) to (-90,90)
##      - Permute lon from (-180,180) to (0,360)
for fn in $( ls MCD43C3.*.nc ); do      # Loop over files
  sfx=$( echo ${fn} | cut -d '.'  -f 1-3 )     # Part of file names
  echo ${sfx}

  ## Lat
  ncpdq -O -a -lat ${fn} ${fn}      # Inverse latitude (NB: there is '-' before 'lat')

  ## Lon
  ncks -O --msa -d lon,0.0,180.0 -d lon,-180.0,-1.25 ${fn} ${fn}

  ## Add new longitude coordinates
  ncap2 -O -s 'lon=array(0.0,1.25,$lon)' ${fn} ${fn}
done
```

# 8 Parallel

This section will describe NCO scripting strategies. Many techniques can be used to exploit script-level parallelism, including GNU Parallel and Swift.

```
ls *historical*.nc | parallel ncks -O -d time,"1950-01-01","2000-01-01" {} 50y/{}
```

# 9 CCSM Example

This chapter illustrates how to use NCO to process and analyze the results of a CCSM climate simulation.

```
************************************************************************
Task 0: Finding input files
x************************************************************************
The CCSM model outputs files to a local directory like:

/ptmp/zender/archive/T42x1_40

Each component model has its own subdirectory, e.g.,

/ptmp/zender/archive/T42x1_40/atm
/ptmp/zender/archive/T42x1_40/cpl
/ptmp/zender/archive/T42x1_40/ice
/ptmp/zender/archive/T42x1_40/lnd
/ptmp/zender/archive/T42x1_40/ocn

within which model output is tagged with the particular model name

/ptmp/zender/archive/T42x1_40/atm/T42x1_40.cam2.h0.0001-01.nc
/ptmp/zender/archive/T42x1_40/atm/T42x1_40.cam2.h0.0001-02.nc
/ptmp/zender/archive/T42x1_40/atm/T42x1_40.cam2.h0.0001-03.nc
...
/ptmp/zender/archive/T42x1_40/atm/T42x1_40.cam2.h0.0001-12.nc
/ptmp/zender/archive/T42x1_40/atm/T42x1_40.cam2.h0.0002-01.nc
/ptmp/zender/archive/T42x1_40/atm/T42x1_40.cam2.h0.0002-02.nc
...

or

/ptmp/zender/archive/T42x1_40/lnd/T42x1_40.clm2.h0.0001-01.nc
/ptmp/zender/archive/T42x1_40/lnd/T42x1_40.clm2.h0.0001-02.nc
/ptmp/zender/archive/T42x1_40/lnd/T42x1_40.clm2.h0.0001-03.nc
...

************************************************************************
Task 1: Regional processing
************************************************************************
The first task in data processing is often creating seasonal cycles.
Imagine a 100-year simulation with its 1200 monthly mean files.
Our goal is to create a single file containing 12 months of data.
Each month in the output file is the mean of 100 input files.

Normally, we store the "reduced" data in a smaller, local directory.
```

```
caseid='T42x1_40'
#drc_in="${DATA}/archive/${caseid}/atm"
drc_in="${DATA}/${caseid}"
drc_out="${DATA}/${caseid}"
mkdir -p ${drc_out}
cd ${drc_out}

Method 1: Assume all data in directory applies
for mth in {1..12}; do
  mm=`printf "%02d" $mth`
  ncra -O -D 1 -o ${drc_out}/${caseid}_clm${mm}.nc \
    ${drc_in}/${caseid}.cam2.h0.*-${mm}.nc
done # end loop over mth

Method 2: Use shell 'globbing' to construct input filenames
for mth in {1..12}; do
  mm=`printf "%02d" $mth`
  ncra -O -D 1 -o ${drc_out}/${caseid}_clm${mm}.nc \
    ${drc_in}/${caseid}.cam2.h0.00??-${mm}.nc \
    ${drc_in}/${caseid}.cam2.h0.0100-${mm}.nc
done # end loop over mth

Method 3: Construct input filename list explicitly
for mth in {1..12}; do
  mm=`printf "%02d" $mth`
  fl_lst_in=''
  for yr in {1..100}; do
    yyyy=`printf "%04d" $yr`
    fl_in=${caseid}.cam2.h0.${yyyy}-${mm}.nc
    fl_lst_in="${fl_lst_in} ${caseid}.cam2.h0.${yyyy}-${mm}.nc"
  done # end loop over yr
  ncra -O -D 1 -o ${drc_out}/${caseid}_clm${mm}.nc -p ${drc_in} \
    ${fl_lst_in}
done # end loop over mth

Make sure the output file averages correct input files!
ncks -M prints global metadata:

  ncks -M ${drc_out}/${caseid}_clm01.nc

The input files ncra used to create the climatological monthly mean
will appear in the global attribute named 'history'.

Use ncrcat to aggregate the climatological monthly means

  ncrcat -O -D 1 \
```

```
    ${drc_out}/${caseid}_clm??.nc ${drc_out}/${caseid}_clm_0112.nc

Finally, create climatological means for reference.
The climatological time-mean:

  ncra -O -D 1 \
    ${drc_out}/${caseid}_clm_0112.nc ${drc_out}/${caseid}_clm.nc

The climatological zonal-mean:

  ncwa -O -D 1 -a lon \
    ${drc_out}/${caseid}_clm.nc ${drc_out}/${caseid}_clm_x.nc

The climatological time- and spatial-mean:

  ncwa -O -D 1 -a lon,lat,time -w gw \
    ${drc_out}/${caseid}_clm.nc ${drc_out}/${caseid}_clm_xyt.nc

This file contains only scalars, e.g., "global mean temperature",
used for summarizing global results of a climate experiment.

Climatological monthly anomalies = Annual Cycle:
Subtract climatological mean from climatological monthly means.
Result is annual cycle, i.e., climate-mean has been removed.

  ncbo -O -D 1 -o ${drc_out}/${caseid}_clm_0112_anm.nc \
    ${drc_out}/${caseid}_clm_0112.nc ${drc_out}/${caseid}_clm_xyt.nc

************************************************************************
Task 2: Correcting monthly averages
************************************************************************
The previous step appoximates all months as being equal, so, e.g.,
February weighs slightly too much in the climatological mean.
This approximation can be removed by weighting months appropriately.
We must add the number of days per month to the monthly mean files.
First, create a shell variable dpm:

unset dpm # Days per month
declare -a dpm
dpm=(0 31 28.25 31 30 31 30 31 31 30 31 30 31) # Allows 1-based indexing

Method 1: Create dpm directly in climatological monthly means
for mth in {1..12}; do
  mm=`printf "%02d" ${mth}`
  ncap2 -O -s "dpm=0.0*date+${dpm[${mth}]}" \
    ${drc_out}/${caseid}_clm${mm}.nc ${drc_out}/${caseid}_clm${mm}.nc
done # end loop over mth
```

```
Method 2: Create dpm by aggregating small files
for mth in {1..12}; do
  mm=`printf "%02d" ${mth}`
  ncap2 -O -v -s "dpm=${dpm[${mth}]}" ~/nco/data/in.nc \
    ${drc_out}/foo_${mm}.nc
done # end loop over mth
ncecat -O -D 1 -p ${drc_out} -n 12,2,2 foo_${mm}.nc foo.nc
ncrename -O -D 1 -d record,time ${drc_out}/foo.nc
ncatted -O -h \
  -a long_name,dpm,o,c,"Days per month" \
  -a units,dpm,o,c,"days" \
  ${drc_out}/${caseid}_clm_0112.nc
ncks -A -v dpm ${drc_out}/foo.nc ${drc_out}/${caseid}_clm_0112.nc

Method 3: Create small netCDF file using ncgen
cat > foo.cdl << 'EOF'
netcdf foo {
dimensions:
        time=unlimited;
variables:
        float dpm(time);
        dpm:long_name="Days per month";
        dpm:units="days";
data:
        dpm=31,28.25,31,30,31,30,31,31,30,31,30,31;
}
EOF
ncgen -b -o foo.nc foo.cdl
ncks -A -v dpm ${drc_out}/foo.nc ${drc_out}/${caseid}_clm_0112.nc

Another way to get correct monthly weighting is to average daily
output files, if available.

************************************************************************
Task 3: Regional processing
************************************************************************
Let's say you are interested in examining the California region.
Hyperslab your dataset to isolate the appropriate latitude/longitudes.

ncks -O -D 1 -d lat,30.0,37.0 -d lon,240.0,270.0 \
    ${drc_out}/${caseid}_clm_0112.nc \
    ${drc_out}/${caseid}_clm_0112_Cal.nc

The dataset is now much smaller!
To examine particular metrics.
```

```
************************************************************************
Task 4: Accessing data stored remotely
************************************************************************
OPeNDAP server examples:

UCI DAP servers:
ncks -M -p http://dust.ess.uci.edu/cgi-bin/dods/nph-dods/dodsdata in.nc
ncrcat -O -C -D 3 \
  -p http://dust.ess.uci.edu/cgi-bin/dods/nph-dods/dodsdata \
  -l /tmp in.nc in.nc ~/foo.nc

Unidata DAP servers:
ncks -M -p http://thredds-test.ucar.edu/thredds/dodsC/testdods in.nc
ncrcat -O -C -D 3 \
  -p http://thredds-test.ucar.edu/thredds/dodsC/testdods \
  -l /tmp in.nc in.nc ~/foo.nc

NOAA DAP servers:
ncwa -O -C -a lat,lon,time -d lon,-10.,10. -d lat,-10.,10. -l /tmp -p \
http://www.esrl.noaa.gov/psd/thredds/dodsC/Datasets/ncep.reanalysis.dailyavgs/surface
pres.sfc.1969.nc ~/foo.nc

LLNL PCMDI IPCC OPeNDAP Data Portal:
ncks -M -p http://username:password@esgcet.llnl.gov/cgi-bin/dap-cgi.py/ipcc4/sresa1b/n

Earth System Grid (ESG): http://www.earthsystemgrid.org

caseid='b30.025.ES01'
CCSM3.0 1% increasing CO2 run, T42_gx1v3, 200 years starting in year 400
Atmospheric post-processed data, monthly averages, e.g.,
/data/zender/tmp/b30.025.ES01.cam2.h0.TREFHT.0400-01_cat_0449-12.nc
/data/zender/tmp/b30.025.ES01.cam2.h0.TREFHT.0400-01_cat_0599-12.nc

ESG supports password-protected FTP access by registered users
NCO uses the .netrc file, if present, for password-protected FTP access
Syntax for accessing single file is, e.g.,
ncks -O -D 3 \
  -p ftp://climate.llnl.gov/sresa1b/atm/mo/tas/ncar_ccsm3_0/run1 \
  -l /tmp tas_A1.SRESA1B_1.CCSM.atmm.2000-01_cat_2099-12.nc ~/foo.nc

# Average surface air temperature tas for SRESA1B scenario
# This loop is illustrative and will not work until NCO correctly
# translates '*' to FTP 'mget' all remote files
for var in 'tas'; do
for scn in 'sresa1b'; do
for mdl in 'cccma_cgcm3_1 cccma_cgcm3_1_t63 cnrm_cm3 csiro_mk3_0 \
gfdl_cm2_0 gfdl_cm2_1 giss_aom giss_model_e_h giss_model_e_r \
```

```
iap_fgoals1_0_g inmcm3_0 ipsl_cm4 miroc3_2_hires miroc3_2_medres \
miub_echo_g mpi_echam5 mri_cgcm2_3_2a ncar_ccsm3_0 ncar_pcm1 \
ukmo_hadcm3 ukmo_hadgem1'; do
for run in '1'; do
        ncks -R -O -D 3 -p ftp://climate.llnl.gov/${scn}/atm/mo/${var}/${mdl}/run$
done # end loop over run
done # end loop over mdl
done # end loop over scn
done # end loop over var

cd sresa1b/atm/mo/tas/ukmo_hadcm3/run1/
ncks -H -m -v lat,lon,lat_bnds,lon_bnds -M tas_A1.nc | m
bds -x 096 -y 073 -m 33 -o ${DATA}/data/dst_3.75x2.5.nc # ukmo_hadcm3
ncview ${DATA}/data/dst_3.75x2.5.nc

# msk_rgn is California mask on ukmo_hadcm3 grid
# area is correct area weight on ukmo_hadcm3 grid
ncks -A -v area,msk_rgn ${DATA}/data/dst_3.75x2.5.nc \
${DATA}/sresa1b/atm/mo/tas/ukmo_hadcm3/run1/area_msk_ukmo_hadcm3.nc

Template for standardized data:
${scn}_${mdl}_${run}_${var}_${yyyymm}_${yyyymm}.nc

e.g., raw data
${DATA}/sresa1b/atm/mo/tas/ukmo_hadcm3/run1/tas_A1.nc
becomes standardized data

Level 0: raw from IPCC site--no changes except for name
         Make symbolic link name match raw data
Template: ${scn}_${mdl}_${run}_${var}_${yyyymm}_${yyyymm}.nc

ln -s -f tas_A1.nc sresa1b_ukmo_hadcm3_run1_tas_200101_209911.nc
area_msk_ukmo_hadcm3.nc

Level I: Add all variables (not standardized in time)
         to file containing msk_rgn and area
Template: ${scn}_${mdl}_${run}_${yyyymm}_${yyyymm}.nc

/bin/cp area_msk_ukmo_hadcm3.nc sresa1b_ukmo_hadcm3_run1_200101_209911.nc
ncks -A -v tas sresa1b_ukmo_hadcm3_run1_tas_200101_209911.nc \
               sresa1b_ukmo_hadcm3_run1_200101_209911.nc
ncks -A -v pr  sresa1b_ukmo_hadcm3_run1_pr_200101_209911.nc \
               sresa1b_ukmo_hadcm3_run1_200101_209911.nc

If already have file then:
mv sresa1b_ukmo_hadcm3_run1_200101_209911.nc foo.nc
/bin/cp area_msk_ukmo_hadcm3.nc sresa1b_ukmo_hadcm3_run1_200101_209911.nc
```

```
ncks -A -v tas,pr foo.nc sresa1b_ukmo_hadcm3_run1_200101_209911.nc

Level II: Correct # years, months
Template: ${scn}_${mdl}_${run}_${var}_${yyyymm}_${yyyymm}.nc

ncks -d time,....... file1.nc file2.nc
ncrcat file2.nc file3.nc sresa1b_ukmo_hadcm3_run1_200001_209912.nc

Level III: Many derived products from level II, e.g.,

      A. Global mean timeseries
      ncwa -w area -a lat,lon \
           sresa1b_ukmo_hadcm3_run1_200001_209912.nc \
           sresa1b_ukmo_hadcm3_run1_200001_209912_xy.nc

      B. Califoria average timeseries
      ncwa -m msk_rgn -w area -a lat,lon \
           sresa1b_ukmo_hadcm3_run1_200001_209912.nc \
           sresa1b_ukmo_hadcm3_run1_200001_209912_xy_Cal.nc
```

# 10 References


- [ZeM07] Zender, C. S., and H. J. Mangalam (2007), Scaling Properties of Common Statistical Operators for Gridded Datasets, Int. J. High Perform. Comput. Appl., 21(4), 485-498, doi:10.1177/1094342007083802.
- [Zen08] Zender, C. S. (2008), Analysis of Self-describing Gridded Geoscience Data with netCDF Operators (NCO), Environ. Modell. Softw., 23(10), 1338-1342, doi:10.1016/j.envsoft.2008.03.004.
- [WZJ07] Wang, D. L., C. S. Zender, and S. F. Jenks (2007), DAP-enabled Server-side Data Reduction and Analysis, Proceedings of the 23rd AMS Conference on Interactive Information and Processing Systems (IIPS) for Meteorology, Oceanography, and Hydrology, Paper 3B.2, January 14-18, San Antonio, TX. American Meteorological Society, AMS Press, Boston, MA.
- [ZMW06] Zender, C. S., H. Mangalam, and D. L. Wang (2006), Improving Scaling Properties of Common Statistical Operators for Gridded Geoscience Datasets, Eos Trans. AGU, 87(52), Fall Meet. Suppl., Abstract IN53B-0827.
- [ZeW07] Zender, C. S., and D. L. Wang (2007), High performance distributed data reduction and analysis with the netCDF Operators (NCO), Proceedings of the 23rd AMS Conference on Interactive Information and Processing Systems (IIPS) for Meteorology, Oceanography, and Hydrology, Paper 3B.4, January 14-18, San Antonio, TX. American Meteorological Society, AMS Press, Boston, MA.
- [WZJ06] Wang, D. L., C. S. Zender, and S. F. Jenks (2006), Server-side netCDF Data Reduction and Analysis, Eos Trans. AGU, 87(52), Fall Meet. Suppl., Abstract IN53B-0826.
- [WZJ073] Wang, D. L., C. S. Zender, and S. F. Jenks (2007), Server-side parallel data reduction and analysis, in Advances in Grid and Pervasive Computing, Second International Conference, GPC 2007, Paris, France, May 2-4, 2007, Proceedings. IEEE Lecture Notes in Computer Science, vol. 4459, edited by C. Cerin and K.-C. Li, pp. 744-750, Springer-Verlag, Berlin/Heidelberg, doi:10.1007/978-3-540-72360-8_67.
- [WZJ074] Wang, D. L., C. S. Zender and S. F. Jenks (2007), A System for Scripted Data Analysis at Remote Data Centers, Eos Trans. AGU, 88(52), Fall Meet. Suppl., Abstract IN11B-0469.
- [WZJ081] Wang, D. L., C. S. Zender and S. F. Jenks (2008), Cluster Workflow Execution of Retargeted Data Analysis Scripts, Proceedings of the 8th IEEE Int'l Symposium on Cluster Computing and the Grid (IEEE CCGRID '08), pp. 449-458, Lyon, France, May 2008.
- [WZJ091] Wang, D. L., C. S. Zender, and S. F. Jenks (2009), Efficient Clustered Server-side Data Analysis Workflows using SWAMP, Earth Sci. Inform., 2(3), 141-155, doi:10.1007/s12145-009-0021-z.
- [PFT88] Press, Flannery, Teukolsky, and Vetterling (1988), Numerical Recipes in C, Cambridge Univ. Press, New York, NY.

# General Index

## .



## /



## :



## ;



## <

## ?



## @



## [



## ^



## _



## \



## |



## 0



## 3



## 6



## A

# B



# C

# D

## G



## H

## M

## O



## P

# T



# U

www.ingramcontent.com/pod-product-compliance
Lightning Source LLC
LaVergne TN
LVHW060135070326
832902LV00018B/2799
*9789888407026*